D1635846

The Beaten Track

The Big Walks of Great Britain

DAVID BATHURST

SUMMERSDALE

Summersdale Publishers Ltd
46 West Street
Chichester
West Sussex
PO19 1RP

www.summersdale.com

Printed and bound in Great Britain
by Creative Print & Design (Wales), Ebbw Vale

ISBN 1 84024 144 6

Illustrations: Terry Whitlock

About the author

David Bathurst has been a keen walker all his adult life. He has not only walked every route described in this book but has also conquered all the major Lakeland peaks as well as Ben Nevis and Snowdon. David is a solicitor by profession, and has written seven other books on a wide range of subjects. His chief claim to fame is the recitation of the four Gospels from memory in July 1998.

By the same author

The Selsey Tram, Phillimore, 1992
Six of the Best!, Romansmead, 1994
The Jennings Companion, Summersdale, 1995
Financial Penalties, Barry Rose, 1996
Around Chichester in Old Photographs, Sutton, 1997
Here's A Pretty Mess!, Romansmead, 1998
Magisterial Lore, Romansmead, 2000

I would like to thank Summersdale Publishers, especially Liz Kershaw and Rachael Osborne, for their assistance and advice in getting the book into print; Terry Whitlock, for his beautiful line drawings; and most of all, my wife Susan for her constant love, understanding and patience as I put this volume together.

Contents

About This Book

Despite the increasingly sophisticated range of leisure pursuits and interests available to us, walking still enjoys huge popularity as a form of recreation. At its most basic, it may consist of a stroll around the block to walk off an excessively large Sunday lunch. Real devotees, however, far from being satisfied with a short piece of post-prandial exercise once a week, will head for the hills or the mountains every weekend whatever the weather, clad in the most expensive equipment, only happy when they have completed their regulation twenty-five miles for the day, and regarding anyone content with less as a sad couch potato. Whatever their degree of devotion, most walking enthusiasts will agree that it is nice to have an objective to aim for. It may just be the windmill on the hilltop above the town which rewards its visitors with a beautiful view on a clear day. It could be a high mountain that requires several hours' toil and effort to reach the summit. Your objective need not be a particular place; it could for instance be the completion of a sponsored challenge walk, the desire to walk further in a single day than you have ever done before, or simply the desire to put as much distance as possible between yourself and your neighbours' Saturday afternoon barbecue party.

In recognition of the fact that walkers like to have an objective or purpose for their wanderings, a number of long-distance walking routes have been created across Great Britain. They all aim to incorporate places and features of particular historic or scenic interest, and the completion of a single route is itself a worthy objective for any hiker. The purpose of this book is to give an overview of the fourteen most popular and famous long-distance routes, with one chapter devoted to each walk. The fourteen routes I have chosen include the eleven routes in England and Wales that have been designated as national trails (meaning that responsibility for them rests with the Countryside Commission); the two most popular long-distance routes in Scotland; and Wainwright's Coast to Coast Walk which, although not properly waymarked or maintained to national trail standards, is still hugely popular nearly thirty years after its conception. The fourteen routes range in difficulty from the gentle 93-mile Peddars Way and Norfolk Coast Path, an easy walk through the attractive and undemanding Norfolk countryside, to the formidable 270-mile Pennine Way and the massive 613-mile South West Coast Path.

Every chapter begins with some basic details about the route described in it, brief information about its origin, and then a reasonably detailed but always informal and light-hearted description of the route itself, highlighting all the places of interest on or near it, and pointing out aspects of the walk that are of potential interest, challenge, difficulty or sometimes even amusement to the walker. I have indicated cumulative mileages in brackets at various stages on the walk rather than break the description into sections; not only would sectional description break the flow of the text but everyone likes to go at his own pace and should not feel obliged to conform to pattern.

Each chapter ends with a summary of places of interest on the route (an asterisk indicates a place of special interest) and also towns and villages on or close to the route where amenities, i.e. refreshment, supplies and accommodation, are available (L indicates limited range, asterisk denotes extensive range). I have tended not to mention establishments by name, because one cannot guarantee they will be open or will even still exist when you do the walk! Finally, in the course of each description, I have taken the opportunity to mention aspects of long-distance walking generally, drawn from my walking adventures over the years, that you might like to be aware of before planning your journey, from the peculiar delights of youth-hostelling to the peculiar horrors of dangerous dogs, tortuous thirsts and ballooning blisters.

Perhaps I should make three other things clear about the book. Firstly, it is not enough on its own; I would not and could not advise you to walk one of the described routes using this book alone, flattered though I would undoubtedly feel. By all means have the book with you on your travels if you have the room in your rucksack, but on its own it is not enough. You will need a proper guidebook dedicated to your chosen route, that includes the necessary mapping. The best are the Aurum Press *National Trail*

Guides for the national trails, their *Recreational Path Guides* for the two Scottish routes, and Wainwright's *Companion* for the Coast to Coast Walk. You will also need an up-to-date accommodation guide, and if you are planning to use public transport to get you to and from the route, you will have to check the latest timetables. All this information is easily obtainable from local tourist information centres.

Secondly, the book makes no assumptions about your level of experience and fitness; it is written just as much for the uninitiated and inexperienced walker as it is for the super-fit super-equipped traveller. You must draw your own conclusions, from having read about each route, as to whether or not you feel sufficiently fit and able to attempt it. I have included below a section for those who have no or limited experience of long-distance walking. You can skip that if you count yourself amongst the experienced.

Thirdly, I have made no assumptions about how each walk should be tackled logistically. There is certainly no rule which dictates that you must walk the whole route in one go, and in fact you may find it more rewarding to do bits at a time, taking each section slowly and making detours to places of interest that you might otherwise miss. Accommodation is also, of course, a matter of personal preference. We all like to be pampered a little from time to time, but hotels and guest houses are not always easy to come by, particularly on the more remote stretches of the route, and here campers have a distinct advantage. The freedom of erecting a tent on a remote hillside brings joys that others miss: escape from the hectic rat-race that modern society has sadly become, seeing at first-hand the glories of a perfect sunset, suddenly feeling blissfully, harmoniously at one with the mysteries of night . . . and scurrying for the nearest shelter when a violent thunderstorm blows your tent away at half past three in the morning.

A book of this nature can never be completely up to date. While I have made every effort to check information for accuracy at the time of writing, you may find things are different when you walk the routes described. Hotels or pubs may shut, visitor attractions may disappear or indeed spring up beside the route, and the routing of paths may change either temporarily or permanently, owing to erosion, bad weather, development or other unforeseen circumstances. The best advice is always to follow waymarked diversions carefully, and ring ahead to check the availability of food and accommodation. The more sadistic purveyors of torture equipment would be hard pressed to devise a nastier punishment than arriving at a little village after twenty miles of hard footslogging, only to find that the old inn advertised as offering a fine range of real ales and bar meals has now shut, its sign replaced by another which reads 'Prestigious Retirement Accommodation: More Sites Urgently Required.'

Happy walking.

Long-distance Walking For Beginners

In the pre-amble above, I wrote that this book is written just as much for those with little or no experience of long-distance walking as it is for those who have a lot. However, it seemed appropriate to add a few words of advice for 'wannabe' long-distance walkers whose walking experience is limited to exercising the dog on a Sunday visit to the in-laws or a sponsored twenty laps round the school playing field at the age of twelve to raise money for a new school minibus.

The most important advice I can give you is to be aware of your capabilities. It should not be difficult to test them should you wish to do so. When you next have a day free, and assuming the weather is kind, go for a long walk. Make up a picnic lunch, set off after a good breakfast, and keep walking. Stop for regular rests, enjoy your picnic, and make sure you are home well before dark with sufficient time to recuperate and have supper. Then ask yourself how much you think you did. Did you march confidently on to the hills and back, covering a good sixteen miles, and still have energy to spare? Or did you just manage to make it to the nearest town two miles away, and stagger home again afterwards, deciding that you may prefer the company of daytime TV on your next day off?

Bearing in mind that the *shortest* route described in this book is 79 miles, and many of the routes have stretches where even small settlements can lie more than ten miles apart with featureless countryside in between, you will quickly appreciate that if you are unable to manage more than six miles or so in one day, and even then cannot put one foot in front of the other for two days afterwards, long-distance walking is not *yet* for you. You will need to get fit. We all take our cars far too much for granted. Is it possible for you to walk from your home to work or college, or at least walk to the bus stop or the railway station rather than use the car? Are you prepared to tear yourself away from the television, DVD or Internet for thirty minutes or so each day? If you are prepared to make the commitment, you will soon find that you do get a lot fitter. Go to the library or your local bookshop and you will find pamphlets and books describing a multitude of walks in your home area, set out so carefully that even little Noddy could not get lost. Tea shop and pub walks, starting or ending with a nice meal or cuppa, have gained immeasurably in popularity in recent years for obvious reasons. Soon you may be devising your own walks into the countryside or the park and finding that *Trisha* or *Ricki Lake* really are worth missing after all.

While you are getting yourself fit, get properly equipped. Don't be conned by the owner of the town's outdoor-wear shop into thinking that for your modest rambling round the park you need an accumulation of gear that even Chris Bonington would regard as excessive for an assault on K2. By all means take expert advice, but don't go overboard or it will cost you a fortune. The most important thing to get right is footwear. Get yourself a decent pair of walking shoes or boots. Until you get into really serious walking, comfort is more important than durability, so don't get yourself anything too fancy to begin with. New boots are agony at first, so for goodness' sake don't set off on a major expedition in a pair of boots you only wore to try on round the shop, with the owner, desperate for his first sale of the day, saying what a wonderful fit they were.

Now you have trained yourself up and look the part, you can start thinking about your first adventure, and putting together a number of days' consecutive walking. If the idea of one of the walks described in this book is still daunting, there are an ever-increasing number of smaller long-distance routes available, in the 30–40 mile range, that can easily be broken into sections of say ten or twelve miles. Lonely Planet's excellent guide, entitled *Walking In Britain*, lists enough of these to keep you going for a lifetime. Other routes, such as the Dales Way or Cotswold Way, offer a rather longer walk (90–100 miles) and a bigger but still easily manageable expedition. In due course however, you may feel ready for the challenge offered by one of the fourteen major routes listed in this book. I would strongly recommend you start with the South Downs Way. It is very easy to get to, there are no route-finding problems, it is relatively short and can be completed comfortably in ten days by even the fairly inexperienced traveller, and the scenery is tremendous. Do not be tempted to go straight for the 'big one' and attempt the Pennine Way as your first major undertaking, or indeed any of the other routes described in this book as strenuous or severe. There will be plenty of time for those once you have experienced easier routes and the mental, physical and logistical demands that even they will entail. It really is not worth putting your life at risk by struggling in the pouring rain and biting winds through often treacherous, remote and uncompromising scenery just so that at the end you can boast about how David Bathurst got it all wrong in his stupid book.

Finally, a word about safety which is of course paramount. You do not go walking as a penance but to enjoy yourself. There may be certificates and other mementos for successful completion of some routes, but there are no Olympic medals and no mentions in *The Times* next day. Never attempt more than you feel you are capable of, particularly bearing in mind that the demands posed by many days' consecutive walking will be very great. In fact I would go so far as to suggest that you always aim to cover a little *less* than you think you can manage; if you finish walking earlier in the day, you will have no difficulty in filling any spare time by detouring to places of interest or refreshment. I would also respectfully suggest that it is pointless to put your life at risk by venturing outside in the worst weather. If you do decide to keep going no matter what, ensure you have a good breakfast inside you, that someone knows where you are, you have sufficient clothing and high-energy food to keep you warm and sustained, and ideally that you carry a mobile phone in case of an emergency. When walking through featureless terrain in bad light, low cloud or mist, you should carry a torch and a compass, which of course you should know how to use. But take it from me that it's better to stay indoors and come back another day. You need to have something to look forward to when you get home, besides the wondrous prospect of the monthly trip to Sainsbury's or grouting round the skirting board in the utility room.

The South Downs Way

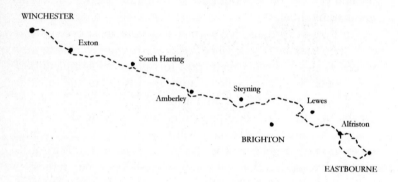

Length: 97 miles (main route) or 100 miles (via alternative bridleway).
Start: Winchester, Hampshire.
Finish: Eastbourne, East Sussex.
Nature: A well-defined route along the chalk ridges of the South Downs.
Difficulty rating: Moderate.
Average time of completion: 10–12 days.

The South Downs Way

It was some sixty million years ago that great chalk deposits on the sea bed bulged up into a great dome, the crest of which eroded over time to leave two chalk masses which form the North and South Downs. When the first settlers arrived on the Downs some six thousand years ago, they and their descendants preferred the drier, safer hills to the swampy Weald below. Thus originated the long, unerring tracks over the area now known as the South Downs, which were to be used by generations of settlers, including Bronze Age traders who used them for the transport of minerals such as jet and gold, and the Romans, who fully exploited the downland routes as a vital link between the rest of Britain and mainland Europe. Now, with the flat lands of the Weald somewhat more hospitable than they were, the Downs have become ideal for recreational use and a means of escaping from the rush of motorists heading for the Channel ports and the flesh pots of the Continent.

The South Downs Way is the ideal walk for those with little or no previous experience of long-distance walking. There is good access to all parts of the route by road and public transport, accommodation is plentiful throughout and although there are some strenuous climbs, it is reasonably easy to accomplish, with well-signposted and well-defined paths and tracks. On days of clear visibility the march across the chalk downlands of Hampshire and Sussex, described by Kipling as 'our blunt, bowheaded, whalebacked Downs,' brings massive rewards. From this platform of chalk you can gaze across the English Channel towards France, across the endless patchwork of fields, forests and villages of the Weald, or perhaps down to the great valleys of the South Downs, with their lovely rivers – the Arun, the Adur, the Ouse and the Cuckmere – that have cut through the soft downland chalk. You can enjoy the multitude of bird, insect and animal life on the Way, which may include skylark, linnet, yellowhammer, corn bunting, Adonis blue butterfly, rabbit, common shrew, harvest mouse, brown hare, badger, and of course the famous black-faced Southdown sheep.

You can gaze down at the chalk grassland, bedecked with squinancywort, knapweed, wild thyme, vetch, trefoil and speedwell. Whilst looking groundwards you may find a shallow depression of chalk or clay constituting a dew-pond, of which there are many on the South Downs, created to provide drinking water for sheep. You can descend to a multitude of delightful villages with their solid Norman churches, indicative of the commitment of the Normans to Christianity after their invasion, and the cottages of that vital local building material, downland flint. Indeed there is so much to see off route, including a wealth of fine churches and other historic buildings, that copious detours are to be recommended in order to get the best out of what the Way has to offer. A further advantage of a detour to a small town or village is that having gained a hearty appetite by the satisfying march along the roof of Hampshire and Sussex, you can enjoy a drink or a meal at one of the many pubs and tearooms that are available.

Most of the guidebooks describe the route from east to west. My opinion, however, is that the walk works far better in reverse. The prevailing wind will be on your back, and there is something rather special about ending at the seaside, in the delightful and hospitable town of Eastbourne. It has to be said that the final few miles of the main route, across the Seven Sisters chalk cliffs and past Beachy Head, are as thrilling a climax as can be imagined, whilst the walker approaching Winchester travelling westwards and tramping along anonymous paths and tracks in the middle of Hampshire might well feel like a diner whose gourmet chef, having served him an exquisite plate of *Anchoves aux Poivrons* followed by *Cromesquis a La Polonaise*, has gone home early leaving him with a tin of Happy Shopper fruit salad and a bottle of squirty cream.

Winchester to Queen Elizabeth Country Park

The walk starts at Winchester, the ancient capital of Saxon England, and worth a day of any walker's time. Anyone entering the city from the east cannot fail to miss the massive statue of King Alfred, who was largely responsible for Winchester's prominence in pre-Norman times. The city's chief glory however, is its cathedral, begun in 1079 and at 556ft, one of the longest in Europe. It is renowned for its magnificent chapels and medieval wall paintings. Nearby is a thirteenth-century deanery and a Pilgrim's Hall where pilgrims lodged in the Middle Ages on their way to Canterbury. You will not have been the first walker to set off from this city on a long journey eastwards! The Way uses metalled roads to head eastward out of the city and having crossed the M3, sets off into the countryside. Close by is Twyford Down, scene of bitter protests as the M3 was being built, and indeed traffic noise seems to dominate as the Way follows a field-edge path eastwards, then turns left on to a metalled road that enters Chilcomb, a pretty village with an early Saxon church.

After leaving Chilcomb you carry on along a metalled road, turning left to join a track, climbing all the time. Proceeding over Telegraph Hill, from which Winchester can be viewed, the Way crosses the busy A272 and reaches Cheesefoot Head (3.5), the first significant viewpoint of the walk, with fine vistas across Hampshire. It is the site of a great natural amphitheatre and it was here that General Eisenhower addressed the Allied troops in 1944 before the D-Day landings. From Cheesefoot Head the Way descends, heading north-east, then turns right on to a track and strikes south-eastwards across Gander Down, with views to the north-east across a pleasant but unremarkable patchwork of fields. The A272 is crossed again, and good firm tracks are followed southwards and uphill to reach Milbury's (8.1), one of only a handful of pubs that are on the South Downs Way itself. It is a popular pub, despite – or perhaps because of – its remote location. The pub name is presumably derived from the ancient burial mound known as Mill Barrows, lying immediately to the south of the hostelry. The Way turns left at the crossroads by the pub and follows a hilltop road, rounding Kilmeston Down. Good views are available from here towards Hinton Ampner House, a rebuilt eighteenth-century manor house close to Cheriton, the site of a major battlefield in the English Civil War.

For a couple of miles you lose the views as you turn right on to a track, heading south-eastwards towards Beacon Hill. The only highlight hereabouts is Lomer, the site of a lost medieval village, and its picturesque pond immediately adjacent to the path. Then suddenly, by Beacon Hill, the ground seems to fall away; the Way turns right then left along metalled roads and plunges off the plateau and steeply down to Exton, offering splendid views to Old Winchester Hill and the Meon valley as it goes. Exton (12), in this valley, is a beautiful village with an attractive church and pretty cottages, while the Meon is a lovely chalk stream, praised by Izaak Walton for its fishing. The river also adds a timeless charm to the nearby picture book villages of East Meon, West Meon, Warnford, Corhampton and Droxford before emerging into Southampton Water just west of Lee-on-the-Solent.

Having followed a road north-east out of Exton, the Way crosses the busy A32, crosses the Meon and follows a succession of narrow, stony tracks eastwards out of the valley, in the shade of trees and under the old Meon Valley Railway. Opened in June 1903 and closed in February 1955, this picturesque line linked Alton with Fareham. The hilly terrain meant that construction was not always straightforward and a number of navvies were killed or injured in the building work. Drunken fights were commonplace and it is reported that one very drunken navvy was stripped of his clothes and thrashed by his mates with stinging nettles. In mid 1933 the line was used to transport an entire farm, including animals; the only animal to 'miss' the train being the farm cat.

It is messy walking for a while after leaving the old railway, but becomes clearer and more open, if also steeper, as the Way turns south then east again and climbs up to reach Old Winchester Hill (14.7), at 648ft the most elevated ground so far. The summit is noteworthy for its Iron Age fort and associated defensive earthworks which date back to around 200 BC. However, you do not need to be a historian to enjoy the summit for its wonderful views, that on a half-decent day extend as far as the Isle of Wight, and also the nature trail and nature reserve that are situated here. Sadly, the airy hilltop grassland walking does not last; the Way reaches a road, turns left on to it, and then right on to a path that plunges downhill again to pass Whitewool Farm, just beyond which you turn right on to a metalled road, and shortly left on to a track leading to Henwood Down. There is then another right turn on to a track, crossing a minor road at Coombe Cross. By turning left, however, you may soon reach East Meon and its beautiful church, famous for its magnificent Tournai font of black marble, depicting the Creation. It has been described as 'a Bayeux Tapestry in stone'.

Returning to the route, further climbing leads to the good viewpoint of Salt Hill (well over 700ft), and, beyond Wether Down, the stark buildings comprising the former naval base of HMS *Mercury* (18.9). You reach a metalled road and turn left on to it to pass this less than lovely complex. At length you reach a road junction, cross straight over and head eastwards, beginning the final march on Butser Hill. You proceed initially on a track and then turn left to proceed beside a road. The rise of the ground towards Butser is almost imperceptible – the hard work has been done reaching the top of Salt Hill – and you can enjoy the lovely views to East Meon Church.

As the summit draws closer it is likely that you will not be alone and may indeed become one of a multitude enjoying the hilltop (20.4) that, at 888ft, represents one of the major summits of the South Downs Way. Only those walkers who are very pressed for time, or those urged on by inclement weather, will not stop here. The hilltop is a magnet for hang-gliding and kite-flying enthusiasts, its Bronze Age tumuli will interest the archaeologist, and its panoramic views across Hampshire and to the Isle of Wight will impress anybody fortunate enough to be there on a clear day.

The Way swings to the south-east and a glorious downhill plunge on springy grass takes you underneath the A3 London–Portsmouth road. Beyond the underpass you reach the information centre and café on the edge of the huge woodlands making up Queen Elizabeth Country Park (21.2). The Park not only has good facilities but also a huge range of very well-marked walks and paths amongst the woodland. The network of paths hereabouts, and the symbols attached to each, can be a little bewildering to the walker who may search in vain for the familiar acorn symbol or simply the words 'South Downs Way' amongst a menu of options which are liable to include everything from 'Cyclists May-Time Nature Trail' to 'Kiddies Forest Fun.'

Assuming the correct route is found, there is then a long climb through the forest, heading north-east on a good track, and on fine weekends there are certain to be other walkers and cyclists for company. At last, at Faggs Farm, things level out, the trees relent and there is then excellent well-signposted eastward walking on good paths and metalled tracks above the pretty village of Buriton with its fine Georgian manor house and rectangular pond. The views from the Way are improving all the time. At Sunwood Farm (25.3), you reach the border with West Sussex. Until the extension to Winchester was opened in 1989, this used to be the western end of the route, and although it is a pleasant enough spot, it seemed a lame start or end to a great walk.

At length you cross the B2146, where you can detour to the left to visit the pretty village of South Harting, which offers both accommodation and refreshment. Nearer at hand, and accessible by a detour to the right down the B2146, is Uppark. Built around 1685–1690, it has been described as a copybook example of the Wren-style country house. The author H. G. Wells spent part of his boyhood there. The house was very badly damaged by fire in 1989 but has been miraculously restored, and you may well wish to break off from your exertions to enjoy a tour of the house. It should be borne in mind, however, that shuffling slowly from room to room in a stately home or castle can feel as exhausting on the feet as actual path walking, and you may be forgiven for being one of the less appreciative students of the set of paintings in the Long Gallery or the detail on the ornamental vase which Lady Emprynghame-Beaumont brought back from Outer Mongolia in 1739.

Uppark to Upwaltham

Beyond the B2146 you enter thick woodland, climbing up in a south-easterly direction to reach the B2141 (the main Chichester–Petersfield road) then, having crossed this road, you go forward to reach Harting Hill (27.3), the first real highlight in West Sussex. Though at roughly 750ft it lacks the loftiness of Butser Hill, there are splendid views to the north of the escarpment, most notably to the village of South Harting, whilst looking back there are views which can extend as far as the Isle of Wight and Portsmouth. Harting Hill, like Butser Hill, is a popular haunt for day-trippers, perhaps because its superb views are obtainable within a few yards of the well-used car park. It is also the start of a magnificent seven miles of South Downs Way walking, on a succession of well-marked paths that are free from road tramping or traffic noise.

After following the top of the escarpment on excellent tracks, with more splendid views to the north, the Way turns sharp right and changes direction to go round the western side of Beacon Hill. You then turn abruptly from south/south-east to due north to contour the hill's eastern side. There seems no obvious reason why Beacon Hill, with its Iron Age summit fort, is bypassed by the route, although it has to be said that the traverse of it is very demanding and you may be glad to be spared its rigours. Having met the path coming down off Beacon Hill, you have a short descent followed by a swift climb to the summit of Pen Hill. Ahead you can make out the beautifully-shaped downland slopes, largely wooded, that comprise Treyford Hill and Didling Hill; moreover, on a clear day it is possible to identify Bognor Regis on the Channel coast.

There is a less interesting interlude as the Way descends to pass Buriton Farm, turning left then almost immediately right on to a good track, and there follows a climb through the woods of Philliswood Down, passing the memorial to Hauptmann Josef Oesterman who one assumes was a Luftwaffe pilot. A sharp left turn at a crossroads of paths brings some relief from the woodland theme, a clearing in the woods revealing five Bronze Age round barrows known as the Devil's Jumps (31.3). The woodland thickens for a while as you pass the grounds of Monkton House, once lived in by the art collector Edward James, and you may hear the shrill cries of the resident peacock. At length, the woodland relents and there is a sequence of magnificent open walking, heading just south of east, with breathtaking views to the Sussex countryside including some tremendous panoramas of Chichester harbour. Indeed, one of the most satisfying moments on your entire journey is to emerge from the trees and find yourself on the open ridge, high above the Weald, with the spire of Chichester Cathedral soaring proudly from the flatlands close to the harbour and, in the immediate foreground, the tree-clad slopes of Treyford Hill, Didling Hill, Linch Ball and Cocking Down.

A footpath leading off to the left soon after the woodland is cleared will take you to the so-called Shepherd's Church of Didling. Started by the Saxons, only the font remains from that time. The rest is early thirteenth-century. Its gnarled bench-ends are its most remarkable internal feature, but its field setting gives it a beauty and solitude that is timeless. When the field is not cultivated, another possible detour is to the trig. point at Linch Ball at just over 800ft. On a clear day not only can you see across the Solent to the Isle of Wight, but you can also identify Chanctonbury Ring to the east. Shortly after Linch Ball, the path drops to the A286 just above Cocking, and on the descent you may be accompanied by vanloads of marksmen travelling to or from shooting butts on the Downs. At the A286 (34.5) the bus company have kindly placed a stop right on the route, and there are regular buses to Cocking. It is fairly easy for the purist, who will insist even on off-route diversions being walked, to stick to his principles for the descent to the village for rest and refreshment. His principles will be more severely tested next morning on the realisation that after a steep climb *up* on a pavement-less main road, there is another climb to regain the height lost since Linch Ball, and twelve miles to the next pint of beer.

The Way continues in an easterly direction with a long climb from the A286 via Manorfarm Down on to Heyshott Down, with only very restricted views to the south. However, a short detour takes you to the trig. point at the summit of Heyshott Down, from which there are fine views to the north. Thereafter, you enter another thickly forested section. The going is very fast at most times of year, as the trees provide welcome shelter from summer heat and reasonable protection from the rain. You continue over Graffham Down, above the attractive village of Graffham which is hidden from view by the trees, although easy footpath access to the village is possible. As you reach Woolavington Down, the woodland begins to thin out and a slight incline upwards takes you to the summit of this section, the 830ft junction of paths known as Crown Tegleaze. There is an elegant signpost here but the views are still limited because of the thickness of the surrounding forests. However, beyond this point you leave the dense forest behind and suddenly the ground falls away, your route dropping steeply through fields to reach the A285 Chichester–Petworth road at Littleton Farm (39.8).

If there is time to spare, it is worth walking a short way down the main road to the right to view the little flint church of Upwaltham. Originally built in the twelfth century, the nave and apse have remained completely unchanged since. Visits to downland churches such as Didling and Upwaltham are an integral part of walking the South Downs Way, and you should try to include time to explore them in your itinerary. It has to be said, sadly, that access to churches on this or indeed any other national trail can be something of a hit-and-miss affair in these days of vandalism. At worst, the building may be locked with no information as to how to gain legitimate entry. Alternatively, it may be locked but information provided as to the availability of a key, and the keyholder may not only open the church up but offer an impromptu guided tour. Thankfully, there do remain many churches around which you are able to wander at will, with literature to assist and enlighten you. Again, however, it is uncertain whether the written material provided will consist of a glossy guidebook or a selection of ageing copies of the monthly church magazine with an intriguing list of services not only for that church but also neighbouring ones, suggesting that at any given time on a Sunday morning the vicar can be found in at least six places at once.

Upwaltham to Washington

After crossing straight over the A285 the route climbs again, following a wide track which passes the edge of woodlands on Burton Down, and emerges just south of two prominent masts signifying the advent of Bignor Hill from which there are superb views on a clear day. These will include the spire of Chichester Cathedral and the coastal settlements of Bognor Regis and Pagham, with the sea forming a rich blue backcloth. Nearer at hand, but worthy of a photograph or two, is Halnaker Windmill, sitting proudly on its hilltop; it dates back to 1750 although has been heavily restored since. Shortly, the Way meets Stane Street, a Roman road constructed to link Chichester with London. The area is steeped not only in history but pre-history; just south-east of the junction with Stane Street is the site of a neolithic camp, and there are numerous tumuli nearby.

The Way passes across a car park, with a very steep road running down to Bignor and its Roman villa which was discovered in 1811. Wooden buildings with thatched roofs have been built over the exposed foundations to give some idea of what the villa may have looked like, and there are also some fine mosaics to see. Back on the Way, an airy walk on a wide track just north of east takes one to Toby's Stone (42.5), a memorial to a well-known local huntsman. Here is one of the best views so far, encompassing the Arun valley and downland beyond, the Sussex coastal plain, and the sweep of countryside north of the Downs. It is at its most spectacular when the Arun has flooded and many parts of the valley are under water, but on any clear day the views to the coast and the sea are stunning.

Reluctantly, you have to drop down to the foot of Westburton Hill, then after a sharp right turn the Way gradually climbs once more on to Bury Hill, skirting the extensive woodlands of

Houghton Forest to the immediate south. Excellent views open up once more, the most enticing prospect being the Arun valley straight ahead. There is a slight descent to cross the very busy A29, then the Way plunges down to the flat valley bottom and having reached and crossed the Arun, follows alongside it for a short while before rising to meet the B2139 and turning right. A left turn here takes you to the village of Amberley which contains an imposing castle ruin dating back to 1380, thatched cottages and a Norman church.

The Way follows alongside the B2139 (46.4) briefly before branching left on a country lane, but by continuing straight on you arrive at the railway station and the refreshment facilities at Houghton. Adjacent to the station is the Chalkpits Museum, which contains a wealth of fascinating exhibits relating to the work of blacksmiths, wheelwrights and other manual workers, and there are examples of bygone forms of transport. The sight of a double-decker bus parked close to the route should not therefore encourage you into thinking that you have an easy ride back to base, for it may simply be the museum's latest exhibit, having been declared unroadworthy some forty years ago and not been driven at all since ferrying a troop of Girl Guides to Butlins in 1958.

The initial climb out of the Arun valley consists of a gentle incline up the lane, with the added bonus of a free glimpse at some of the exhibits of the Chalkpits Museum. Then, having turned right at a T-junction of roads, you leave the road by turning left, and make a long steep ascent on farm tracks to the top of Rackham Hill. You should watch out for cyclists coming down the hill towards you at enormous speed. It is a relief to reach the top of the escarpment, now proceeding more decisively eastwards again. The reward for the effort, apart from the satisfaction of reaching the halfway mark on the route, is a splendid view of the Arun valley and the hills that have been left behind, and a return to ridge walking, where views to the Weald and the sea are equally impressive. You can clearly make out the towns of Bognor Regis and Littlehampton, as well as the medieval ruins of Arundel Castle.

The whole of the 6-mile stretch from Amberley to Washington is South Downs Way walking at its very best, with no significant undulations and good open walking on wide tracks, virtually free from woodland. In fact woodland is much sparser on the second half of the walk. The Way passes close to Parham Park, and the beautiful Elizabethan mansion of Parham House, and then goes on past Springhead Hill and Chantry Post on Sullington Hill (50.3), where in each case the presence of a nearby car park and access road brings a brief spate of casual walkers.

In due course another break in the ridge signals another sharp descent, not to a river valley but the dangerously busy A24 London–Worthing road (52.4) which has to be crossed. (An alternative route, leaving the main route at Barnsfarm Hill, takes you down the north side of the escarpment on to a track, and in due course over a footbridge across the A24 into the picturesque village of Washington.) Having crossed straight over the A24, you briefly join a metalled road then turn right, but by continuing on the road downhill you reach Washington.

Though you may immediately think of the American city, 'Washington' actually means a Saxon settlement of the sons of Wassa. The church is largely uninteresting but the village is undeniably picturesque and there is a welcome pub. Admirers of Hilaire Belloc still gather at the pub to sing his West Sussex Drinking Song, ending with the words, 'The swipes they take in at Washington Inn is the very best beer I know.' Whether fortified with best bitter in best Belloc tradition, or content with a plateful of sausage and chips, the walker on either the main or the alternative route (which ends at Washington) will need his strength for the walk back up the road towards the A24 to rejoin the Way.

Washington to Devil's Dyke

There follows a short but steep climb to the Iron Age hill fort of Chanctonbury Ring (54), the path following a clearly defined but somewhat winding course to the summit. The Ring actually consists of a clump of beech trees, planted within the oval-shaped hill fort in 1760. It is still possible to make out parts of the low bank and ditch. Although many of the trees were lost in the great storm in October 1987, it remains a useful shelter on a wet day as well as a splendid viewpoint. There is another prominent Iron Age fort, Cissbury Ring, clearly visible nearby, and this is worth a detour if time permits. The Way proceeds in a south-easterly direction, and you will enjoy another splendid high-level promenade which soon passes the grand (but strictly private) buildings of the sixteenth-century stately home, Wiston House. The walk arcs in a crude semi-circle round Steyning Bowl which in turn borders the town of Steyning itself, and a metalled road just before the Bowl provides the best access to the town.

Steyning is a beautiful little place, its finest corner being Church Lane which shows off virtually every form of local building material – timber, flint, brick, tile, thatch, Horsham stone and slate – with some houses dating back to the fifteenth century. Arguably the finest building in the town is the part twelfth-century St Andrew's Church, which contains fine Norman carvings. The original building was founded in the eighth century by St Cuthman; legend says he arrived and settled in Steyning having pushed his invalid mother in a wheelbarrow from Devon, and residents should not be too surprised to be confronted with weary but waggish walkers asking where the wheelbarrow is parked as they themselves may have some use for it.

From Steyning Bowl the Way changes direction from south-east to north-east to go over Annington Hill and then descend gradually, by means of a track and along a minor road, to the next big valley, the Adur (pronounced 'Ada'), just below Upper Beeding. You enjoy a short riverside stroll before crossing the river by means of a footbridge (59.3), immediately beyond which is a most useful tap, provided by the Society of Sussex Downsmen; it is one of a number of useful water points on the South Downs Way. Most walkers will agree that the Adur valley, rather disfigured hereabouts with industrial workings, lacks the appeal of the Arun valley. Fortunately, perhaps, you do not linger here long, but after proceeding quickly to the busy A283 and crossing it, you immediately climb back on to the escarpment. Your reward for this brisk ascent will be the good views to Chanctonbury Ring as well as Lancing College Chapel. This Gothic-style building dates back to 1848 and in this country is beaten for height by only three other ecclesiastical buildings, namely Westminster Abbey, York Minster and Liverpool Cathedral.

As you near the top of the hill, you reach Truleigh Hill with its rather untidy assembly of buildings, but among them is a most useful youth hostel (60.9). Once past the buildings, fine eastward ridge walking returns with the crossing of Edburton Hill and the Fulking escarpment. The best views lie northwards to the Weald, a vast area of woodland, farmland, small villages and towns which separate the South Downs from the North Downs. Immediately below you are the villages of Edburton and Fulking. Edburton boasts an excellent fresh fishery, and Fulking is a beautiful village with a very popular pub. Both villages have given their names to hills which form part of this section of the route. These pleasant hills, however, serve merely as appetisers for Devil's Dyke (63.5), the undoubted highlight of this section of the Downs. Just before you reach the Dyke, you will clearly see the huge conurbation of Brighton from the Dyke Hotel, and indeed the Dyke area remains a splendid playground for the Brighton populace.

The Way passes along a splendid grassy promenade where a fine day will bring out hosts of hang-gliders, then begins the dramatic descent alongside the Dyke itself. This is a deep dry valley with Ice Age origins, and remains a remarkable natural feature, with an array of interesting vegetation. Legend has it that the Devil created it in a bid to flood the Weald where Christianity had taken hold, but when he saw a candle being held by a watching woman, he fled, leaving the job unfinished, believing the candle to be the rising sun. Since Sunday is one of the most popular days for visitors to this spot, local church leaders may ruefully reflect that in inadvertently leaving such a remarkable feature in the state he did, the Devil did not do too badly after all in wooing would-be churchgoers away from their weekly observance.

Devil's Dyke to Lewes

The combination of the Dyke itself and the considerable panorama to its north certainly makes for fine walking, and it is with reluctance that you will drop down to the road at Saddlescombe, only to climb up again almost immediately on to Newtimber Hill. A detour along the road to the left will take you to Poynings. With its fine fourteenth-century flint church, cosy pub, and picturesque assembly of buildings in the shadow of the Downs, it is almost the definitive downland village. Newtimber Hill commands fine views in all directions, and it is followed by a brisk descent to the A23, the busiest road crossing so far. Unlike the A24, this road, which links Brighton with the M25, Gatwick Airport and London, is fortunately crossed by means of a bridge.

Immediately after the crossing comes the pretty village of Pyecombe (66.2), and for once you find yourself passing through a village actually on the route rather than having to detour to reach it. Downland flint is the dominant motif of the village, and as well as many attractive flint cottages there is a lovely twelfth-century church of flint and pebbledash. The village was well known as a centre from which shepherds' crooks were supplied.

The Way reaches the busy A273 and turns left alongside it, but you soon cross over it to join a path which heads eastwards away from the road and climbs again, this time alongside a golf course. You then turn sharp left to come within sight of the Clayton Windmills (67.5), better known as Jack and Jill. Jack is a brick tower-mill of 1876, and Jill, a much older lady, is a wooden post-mill of 1821. She came from Dyke Road, Brighton, in about 1850. Near the windmills, from which there is easy path access to Hassocks and its convenient station, the Way swings again to the east and for several miles enjoys a glorious high-level promenade, with superb Wealden views to the north.

Around this point, you cross into East Sussex. The path maintains a good height, rising slightly to reach Ditchling Beacon (69.3), at 813ft one of the highest spots on the Way, with wonderful panoramic views not only to the Weald but also to the sea. The sprawl of Brighton is still visible, as are the coastal settlements to its east. The car park at the Beacon is a very popular spot, but the consolation for the thirsty walker is that ice creams will often be available. There is road access here to the village of Ditchling, which boasts a largely thirteenth-century church and a wide range of facilities. However, if you decide to make the detour you will have a very long climb back up afterwards. The splendid high-level walk continues, passing Streat Hill with evidence of Bronze Age habitation, and reaching Plumpton Plain above the village of Plumpton, famed for its picturesque racecourse. Then at Blackcap, amidst an abundance of tumuli, the Way turns away from the scarp edge and seems to turn half back on itself, heading initially in a south-westerly direction before swinging south-eastwards over Balmer Down. This is undoubtedly an anticlimax after what has gone before, with restricted views and the path losing height all the time.

The next section is bitty and you should follow the signposting carefully, for in recent years the Way has been re-routed to take advantage of a footbridge over the monstrously busy A27 road (74.6). In order to meet up with the original route, which crossed the A27 at Newmarket Inn, a tedious stretch beside the dual carriageway follows and it is only when you reach the garage at Newmarket Inn that you turn away from the A27 and things quieten down. However, having got to Newmarket Inn, you could choose to walk on alongside the A27 into Lewes, the ancient county town of East Sussex. The town, which suffered extremely badly from flooding in the autumn of 2000, contains Norman castle remains and a jumble of medieval streets with a variety of buildings, mostly Georgian and made of local materials. Lewes comes to life on 5 November with one of the most elaborate and impressive bonfire processions in the country, while the wealth of antique shops and both ancient and modern bookdealers provide constant delight for the connoisseur and bibliophile. A bookworm could quite easily come here and spend £25 on a dusty first-edition of a children's comic book with two pages missing and six other badly torn ones, and then pick up a pristine new hardback 800-page *Illustrated History Of the World* for £3.75.

Lewes to Firle Beacon

The route moves away from the A27 and begins a climb back on to the escarpment, which now faces north-east rather than north. Soon you reach Juggs Road, an ancient route that was used to carry fish to the market at Lewes. As the route proceeds south-eastwards, there are good views all along this stretch to the buildings of the town, as well as Newhaven and out towards Seaford. The contrast with, say, Heyshott Down and Graffham Down could not be starker, for this area of downland is almost totally exposed with a virtual absence of trees throughout this section. Well-defined tracks take you over Swanborough Hill, Iford Hill, Front Hill and Mill Hill above the Ouse valley and its villages of Kingston-near-Lewes, Itford and Rodmell; in due course you descend to this valley, dropping down to a track then turning left along it to reach the unclassified Lewes–Newhaven road. You turn right on to the road and shortly left, and it is then a short stroll to the pretty village of Southease. Undoubtedly its most interesting feature is its flint church (80.6) complete with round Saxon tower – one of only three in the whole of Sussex. The church, which contains box pews and some thirteenth-century paintings depicting scenes from the life of Christ, is right on the route and its shady churchyard is a lovely place for a rest on a hot day.

A short road walk eastwards takes you across the River Ouse and then over the railway line. There is a useful railway halt here, with trains to Lewes and Newhaven, although train times should be checked carefully in advance to avoid a long wait. Immediately beyond the railway is a useful water tap; those wondering whether to partake of the waters would be well advised to do so, for after crossing the busy A26, the main road linking the port of Newhaven with the A27 trunk road, you have an immediate steep ascent on to Itford Hill. Once the lost height is regained there follows another splendid high-level eastward march on excellent paths, the escarpment now more north-facing again. The ridge walking is easy and satisfying, as the Way passes Beddingham Hill and Firle Plantation, with views out towards Glyndebourne, well known for its festival of opera. The nearby village of Glynde will forever be associated with John Ellman, whose claim to fame is as a first-class sheep breeder. Esther Meynell goes so far as to say that Ellman almost *invented* the black-faced Southdown sheep, which can be found grazing along parts of the route.

The ridge walk culminates in another of the great summits of the South Downs Way, the 713ft Firle Beacon, bestrewn with tumuli, and the sight, unusual on this part of the walk, of a large clump of trees making up Firle Plantation. As with Ditchling Beacon, the best views are to the north, with Charleston farmhouse immediately ahead. Charleston farmhouse has no dancing connections but was in fact the headquarters of the Bloomsbury Group, a set of influential English writers and philosophers which included Virginia Woolf and Lytton Strachey. H. J. Massingham once wrote, 'On the dullest day, the wonderful form of the Downs, curving out from Firle Beacon, and the way their spurs and bays and bosses shape into a kind of intricate pattern against the chequered floor of the Weald, are a sight whereof the resurrected dead in the barrows, watching through forty centuries, could never tire.' I cannot pass Firle Beacon without being reminded of the occasion when, resting there one afternoon some twenty years ago, I was approached by two walkers who offered me a tot of gin in exchange for some of my orange squash!

Firle Beacon to Seven Sisters (via main route)
From Firle Beacon the Way continues over Bostal Hill and past the quaintly-named Bopeep Bostal; the curious walker will be reassured to know that 'bostal' in this instance, a term peculiar to the South Downs, means a path up a steep hill and should not be confused with a penal institution. From here it is almost all downhill, the Way passing further tumuli as it drops down to the Cuckmere valley, the last great valley on the South Downs Way. In due course the buildings of Alfriston come into view, and you descend between two patches of woodland and on to a metalled road that leads into the village (88.2). This is one of the biggest settlements actually on the route itself. The resultant wide range of facilities alone would make it worthwhile to stop here, but it is a fascinating place in its own right, with numerous timber-framed, tile-hung and weatherboarded houses, particularly round the square. Several of them house attractive shops and eating places which are sure to entice you. There are a number of ancient inns in the village; the thirsty traveller who stops at the Star Inn might note that its timbers are ornamented with carvings of beasts, and at one corner of the inn stands what is arguably Alfriston's most celebrated landmark; a large red lion which was once the figurehead of a seventeenth-

century Dutch ship. Two other treasures in the village are the fourteenth-century Clergy House, the National Trust's very first acquisition, and the fourteenth-century flint church of St Andrew, known as the Cathedral of the Downs. The green in front of the church is an especially picturesque sight. The Way leaves Alfriston by crossing the footbridge; the main route then turns right while an alternative bridleway route proceeds straight on (a description of this section follows).

Having taken the right turn, the *main* route of the Way enjoys a delightful stroll southwards alongside the Cuckmere River, which serves as a very pleasant contrast to the high-level walking that characterises so much of the route. The riverside walking ends at Litlington, a pretty village of flint cottages. During my visit here I discovered a tea garden complete with puppet show! You cross straight over the road here and proceed away from Litlington on a track, rising all the while and passing Charleston Manor, part of which dates back to 1200. Amongst the manor's attractions are a walled garden, a medieval dovecot and one of the biggest tithe barns in the county. Having passed the manor, the Way climbs steeply and enters a substantial area of beech woodland known as Friston Forest. For a while the South Downs Way is on the route of another long-distance path. This is the Vanguard Way which links Croydon with Seaford, crossing a large section of the Weald and encompassing parts of the North and South Downs Way.

Soon the Way enters the beautiful village of Westdean (91), which, lying at the end of a cul-de-sac, is a peaceful and secluded place. This is another village of houses and barns dominated by flint, its flint-built rectory dating back to the thirteenth century. The part-Norman church of All Saints contains a memorial to Lord Waverley who, as Sir John Anderson, was Home Secretary during the Second World War and introduced the air-raid shelter bearing his name. It is believed that Alfred the Great had a palace here, probably on the site in the village centre where the ruins of the medieval manor and a nearby dovecot are preserved as ancient monuments. Some walkers may be reminded that Alfred is commemorated elsewhere on the route, but since the king's statue is right back at the start of the walk, a brisk 90 miles away, those who think they remember seeing him at some point in their travels but cannot remember precisely where, would do better to remain in blissful ignorance than attempt to retrace their steps to find out.

There follows a steep descent south-westwards to the Cuckmere at Exceat Bridge, and any sense of seclusion should quickly evaporate as you are confronted by the extremely busy A259, the main coast road of Sussex which runs all the way from Emsworth in Hampshire to Folkestone in Kent. It is at Exceat Bridge that the A259 crosses the Cuckmere. It is a major tourist honeypot, boasting a wildlife exhibition and complex, and numerous signposted walks beside the Cuckmere Estuary and back into Friston Forest. Amidst the wealth of signposting, it is quite easy to lose the route of the South Downs Way. It has changed in recent years and now follows the east side of the estuary, with its splendid array of wildlife, to reach the sea. It is a most exciting moment, signifying that the journey is almost at an end. First, however, you must negotiate the final significant range of hills of the South Downs: the Seven Sisters.

The Seven Sisters consist of a series of dramatic chalk clifftops rising to over 500ft. The depressions separating each clifftop, or Sister, are the valleys of ancient rivers, formed when the chalk extended further seawards, but later cut off when the sea pounded the chalk away. Even after nearly a hundred weary miles, you will not fail to be thrilled by this magnificent sequence of chalk cliffs, providing superb views both to the sea and inland, and serving as a fitting and splendid culmination to so much hard but satisfying downland walking.

Each Sister has a name; from west to east they are Haven Brow, Short Brow, Rough Brow, Bran Point, Flagstaff Point, Baily's Hill and Hill Brow. The names of the individual Sisters are obviously fertile ground for the setter of trivia quizzes about the topography of Sussex (*'first prize a case of genuine Sussex elderberry wine'*) but the walker tramping laboriously over each cliff at the end of a long walking holiday is unlikely to bother to commit the names to memory even at the risk of missing out on lucrative rewards when the question comes up on *Who Wants To Be A Millionaire*.

Seven Sisters to Eastbourne (main route)

Having negotiated the final Sister, you descend to a freak cleft in the South Downs known as Birling Gap (95), near to which is a flight of steep steps that saw use by eighteenth-century smugglers. This is another popular spot for visitors – refreshments may be available – but it can be a frightening place in stormy weather, and coastal erosion has made the houses here particularly vulnerable. The ground rises again, passing the Belle Tout lighthouse, which was operational between 1834 and 1901 and was subsequently turned into a private house. Coastal erosion recently led to the building being moved, piece by piece, from its original position! Using one of a plethora of available paths, you climb to the last but arguably most famous summit of the South Downs Way, namely Beachy Head, which at 534ft is one of the highest cliffs on the South Coast, and on a clear day it is possible to see the Isle of Wight and Dungeness in Kent. At the base of the cliff is the distinctive red and white lighthouse, built in 1902 to replace the Belle Tout lighthouse, and capable of sending a beam sixteen miles across the English Channel. In 1999 a portion of cliff fell down hereabouts, and you should take care on the cliff edges as erosion makes further cliff slips very possible.

Beachy Head is an immensely popular spot, and on most days you will not be alone as you stride over the turf and – again with a fair number of paths to choose from – begin the steady descent to the final objective: the town of Eastbourne (98.8). At the foot of the hill the South Downs Way officially ends, and you may then follow the promenade to reach the town centre and its impressive range of amenities. Eastbourne, with its 3-mile esplanade and fine array of shops, parks and theatres, is a most pleasant place to linger at the end of a long walk, if time is available.

Two features of particular interest are the Wish Tower, formerly a Martello tower (coastal defensive fort) and now a coastal defence museum, and the bandstand which contains seats for 3,000 and offers frequent band concerts to delight audiences and passers-by. As you proceed into the town after your long pilgrimage from Winchester, you might like to think that the band's robust rendition of the *Battle Hymn Of The Republic* or *When The Saints Go Marching*

In is really for you, even though at that precise moment you may feel a more appropriate tune to be *Leavin' On A Jet Plane* or *Show Me The Way To Go Home*.

Alfriston to Eastbourne (bridleway)

The *alternative* route from Alfriston is just over three miles shorter. After crossing the Cuckmere footbridge just beyond the village, the route continues eastwards along the track then turns left and enjoys a stroll through the water meadows by the Cuckmere. Soon you reach and cross a metalled road, then join a track that heads south-eastwards, shortly crossing another road. A right turn along this road takes you to the tiny church at Lullington, just 16ft square with room for over twenty people, while a left turn along the road provides easy access to Wilmington (see below). Beyond the road the Way, still following a track, proceeds eastwards then south-eastwards, climbing on to Windover Hill.

As well as commanding splendid views to the Cuckmere Valley, the Way is within easy reach of that most extraordinary Sussex Downs landmark, the 226ft high Long Man of Wilmington. Restored in 1874, nobody knows for certain how, or why, it came into existence, but one expert suggests that the figure, holding a staff in each of his outstretched hands, was a 'dodman' holding posts for surveying and establishing ley lines. Another theory is that he represented King Harold of the Saxons, with a spear in each hand. Others claim it represents a pagan god, a medieval pilgrim or even to have Roman origins. The South Downs Way passes directly above the Long Man so he cannot be properly appreciated from the path itself. If you wish to get a better view, you would be well advised to detour towards the village of Wilmington itself, which is also worth a visit, with its fourteenth-century Benedictine priory remains and a part Norman church with an enormous yew tree in the churchyard.

Windover Hill is of interest to the historian, for it contains a group of Neolithic flint mines on its south face, and further south of the mines is a well-preserved long barrow, 180ft long and stretching to 50ft wide. From the summit of Windover Hill there is then some fine high-level walking before the Way drops down through the Lullington Heath Nature Reserve and along the north-east fringe of Friston Forest to reach the village of Jevington (92). There is a most attractive flint church with a Saxon tower, and there are a number of pretty flint and tiled cottages and a picturesque pub, the Six Bells. From Jevington, the Way rises for the last time and the town of Eastbourne unfolds ahead. The route is joined by that of another long-distance path, the Wealdway, an 80-mile route linking Gravesend with Eastbourne. Passing Willingdon Hill, the route runs beside a golf course and drops down to Paradise Drive where, for walkers taking this alternative route, the South Downs Way ends (95.6). The ending is as anticlimactical as it is sudden, and, with some unexciting walking required to reach the seafront, the shops and perhaps most importantly the train home, the walker cannot be blamed for feeling like a party guest whose cab driver has dropped him by the bins in the back yard.

SUMMARY OF PLACES OF INTEREST
Winchester★, Cheesefoot Head, Exton, Old Winchester Hill, East Meon, Butser Hill, Uppark, Harting Hill★, Linch Ball, Didling, Bignor Hill, Toby's Stone, Amberley, Washington, Chanctonbury Ring★, Steyning★, Devil's Dyke★, Jack and Jill, Ditchling Hill★, Lewes, Southease, Firle Beacon, Alfriston★, Exceat, Seven Sisters★, Beachy Head★, Long Man★, Eastbourne.

AMENITIES ON OR NEAR THE ROUTE
Winchester★, Exton (L), East Meon (L), Queen Elizabeth Country Park (L), South Harting, Cocking, Graffham (L), Bignor (L), Amberley, Houghton (L), Washington, Steyning, Fulking (L), Poynings (L), Pyecombe (L), Hassocks, Ditchling, Lewes★, Alfriston, Jevington (L), Eastbourne★.

The North Downs Way

Length: 123 miles (main route) or 129 miles (loop route).
Start: Farnham, Surrey.
Finish: Dover, Kent.
Nature: A walk along the escarpment of the North Downs through Surrey and Kent.
Difficulty rating: Moderate.
Average time of completion: 10–12 days.

The North Downs Way

The North Downs Way, opened in 1978, may not be the oldest national trail but its roots lie in pre-history. The ridge of the North Downs (the formation of which I explained in the section describing the South Downs Way) is believed to have formed part of a trading link between the peoples of Surrey and Kent and the Isle of Portland after the retreat of the ice approximately 10,000 years ago. It is even claimed that paths along the North Downs were used by pre-Ice Age hunters some 250,000 years ago. Until England was separated from the rest of Europe about 5,000 years ago, people from what is now France and Germany may have gained access to central England by these routes. Since then, it is likely that the routes have been used for cattle-droving and long-distance travel on foot or on horseback – routes which the creation of newer roads has rendered obsolete.

There is a popular misconception that the North Downs Way follows the same course as the Pilgrims' Way, a route taken from England's former secular capital, Winchester, to what could be regarded as its spiritual capital, Canterbury. Although recognition has been given to the proximity of Canterbury with a loop route which leaves the principal route near Wye and continues to Dover right through the cathedral city, there are considerable differences between them. In any case, the Pilgrims' Way does not have quite the same scenic beauty or historic significance as one might hope or expect. Not only is it not a properly marked route, but it tends to remain beneath the chalk escarpment rather than climbing on to it as the North Downs Way does, it has probably only been called the Pilgrims' Way since the mid-nineteenth century, and some historians now doubt whether medieval pilgrims actually used it at all!

Logistically and technically the North Downs Way is not difficult. Access to amenities is never a problem, as there are so many towns and villages close to the route. There is a fair amount of up-and-down work, with the path rising to nearly 900ft in places but, save one or two steep climbs, there is nothing that is too arduous. There are ample rewards for modest effort in terms of some superb viewpoints and many attractive stretches of airy downland and beautiful beech-woods. Originally the North Downs were covered with dense woodlands of ash, hornbeam, beech and yew. Much of this has been cleared to expose grazing land, but several pockets of woodland remain, with many lovely flowers including violet, primrose, stitchwort, hazel, honeysuckle and lady orchid; the North Downs is the only area in Britain where the lady orchid is to be found. On the thin chalky soils of the Downs the walker can also find yellow trefoil, rock-rose, hawkbit, pinks and blues of the scabious and knapweed families, and autumn gentian.

Birds include the skylark, yellowhammer, woodpigeon, woodpecker, kestrel, chaffinch and grey partridge, and on the ground, you should look out for voles, rabbits, foxes and badgers. In August you may see the beautiful chalkhill blue butterfly on the more exposed grassland, but marbled white butterflies may be seen earlier in the year, especially on the first half of the journey.

However, despite the wealth of plant life and wildlife, the nearness of London to the chalk escarpment does undoubtedly have an adverse effect on the character of the route. In contrast to the South Downs Way there are few long uninterrupted stretches of path walking, and it can be fiddly and disjointed. Busy roads and railways run parallel to, and across the route in many places, creating a constant barrage of noise. Development is so intense that camping is difficult, if not impossible; even the smaller, prettier villages situated on or near the route have expanded through insensitive post-war building so there is little sense of isolation or tranquillity. Virtually the whole route is green belt commuter country, and a study of the path, and the places near or on it, may well instantly conjure images not so much of broad vistas of rolling pastures and unspoilt woodland as bowler-hatted *FT* readers scrambling for the last portion of standing-room on the 7.42.

Farnham to Puttenham

Farnham is a very agreeable place to start the journey; best known as the home of the writer William Cobbett, author of *Rural Rides*. Its loveliest street is the elegant Castle Street with its Georgian buildings and almshouses, overshadowed by its splendid red brick Norman castle. It dates from the twelfth century and was the palace of the bishops of Winchester until 1925. The North Downs Way starts rather unceremoniously by a busy road junction of the A31 with the road coming down from the station. It follows eastwards alongside the A31 but then thankfully leaves it by turning right, passing a fine timbered house and underneath the railway, and follows a track into a pleasant meadow, joining a peaceful country road. Detouring along this road for a mile or so brings you to Waverley Abbey, the first Cistercian house in England, dating back to 1128.

However, the route turns left off this road on to Compton Way, and crossing the River Wey, passes Moor Park College, then climbs steeply away from the valley. Near the top of the hill, the Way leaves the road, turns left, proceeds across fields and then passes through an area of woodland, broken up only by Crooksbury Road near the end. Emerging from the woods, you turn right on to Sands Road and drop down to Farnham Golf Club where there is a left turn into Blighton Lane. After passing the golf course turn right on to a pleasant path which climbs steadily alongside the golf course and, after crossing Binton Lane, proceed along a field edge. There are good views on the right to the wooded Crooksbury Hill and its distinctive mast.

The Way passes round the edge of the village of Seale; a detour down the road will bring you to Seale Church, almost entirely rebuilt in the nineteenth century but with some medieval fragments and a glorious view from the nearby war memorial. You continue through an area of woodland and then emerge on to pastures with fine views east towards Puttenham Common. The route descends gently to Totford Lane, then having crossed the lane enters Puttenham Common and begins climbing up again, soon reaching the village of Puttenham (6.6) and proceeding by road down its attractive street. Its church has features dating from the twelfth century and south of the church is Puttenham Priory, a Palladian building dating from 1762.

The village lies right below the very busy A31 Farnham–Guildford road, which runs along a narrow 500ft chalk ridge. As you proceed from Seale to Puttenham it is a constant and attractive feature to your left, and although you may be disappointed that the Way itself does not proceed along it, you would have to concede that the traffic noise would spoil the walk to some extent. The ridge is known as the Hog's Back, and one wonders how many local residents are dying to be asked by walkers or other visitors, 'Do you know the Hog's Back?' so they can reply, 'I didn't know he'd been away!'

Puttenham to St Martha's

From Puttenham the Way crosses the B3000 Compton–Hog's Back road and proceeds along a path past Puttenham golf course and through woodland. You pass underneath the busy and noisy A3 London–Portsmouth road, and soon reach a minor road. The route turns left on to the road and then shortly right on to a sandy lane, but a little further up the road is the Watts Gallery, exhibiting a collection of paintings by the nineteenth-century artist George Frederick Watts, best known for his allegorical works such as *Hope* and *Mammon* but also well known for his portraits of biblical and classical subjects. By detouring down the road in the opposite direction, you will pass by the ornate Watts memorial chapel and into the village of Compton. The church is worth visiting because it contains the only double-deck sanctuary to survive in England. The purpose of the second, 'upstairs' sanctuary is a mystery. The Norman railing, carved from a single piece of wood, is reputedly the oldest architectural wood carving in an English church.

Back on the Way, the route proceeds resolutely eastwards towards Guildford and round the edge of the Loseley Estate and its nature reserve, although views to Loseley House, built in 1562 with stone from Waverley Abbey, are restricted by woodland. The Way proceeds along the northern fringes of the woods, then into more open country past Piccard's Farm and on to the A3100 (11). A detour left along this road takes you into Guildford, a most attractive town with a steep cobbled high street containing many historic buildings, notably the seventeenth-century almshouses and the Angel Hotel which has an old wooden gallery and coaching yard. There is a castle, built by Henry II, of which only the keep survives, and a modern cathedral. The Way however goes more or less straight over the A3100, once again crosses the River Wey, and then after crossing the A281 and flirting briefly with the outskirts of the city, it begins the climb to St Martha's Hill.

The ascent, initially on the fringes of woodland known as Chantries, continues through woodland to reach the beautiful hilltop church of St Martha, rebuilt in the nineteenth century from a ruin, the original church dating back to 1200. During the climb there are glorious panoramic views of the Surrey countryside. From the church you begin to descend, soon meeting the Downs Link path. This route runs from Shoreham-by-Sea to Guildford and, as the name implies, forms a link between the escarpments of the North and South Downs. Where long-distance paths overlap, there is always the possibility of overlapping waymarking as well, and thereby the possibility of confusion; a tired walker late in the day following a sequence of beautifully formed arrows may receive an unpleasant surprise when, expecting to arrive in a village that has promised him dinner and a much-needed night's sleep, he is confronted with a signpost indicating that the village is now further away than when he started that morning.

St Martha's to Mole Crossing

The North Downs Way drops down to a road, turns left on to it and then bears right on to a path, climbing again to Newlands Corner (14.4). This provides another good viewpoint and, because it is on the A25 Guildford–Dorking road, is a popular stopping-place and picnic area for motorists. The A25, which you cross here, used to be a major arterial road, but with the completion of the M25 is rather quieter and if you have time you may wish to detour alongside it to visit the pretty villages of Albury and Shere. Albury has an attractive park with fine cedar and yew trees, and in the park is a church with a remarkably ornate chapel built by Pugin as a mortuary chapel for Henry Drummond, the owner of the park.

The Way, after crossing the A25, enters woodland, initially going eastwards as far as the Shere–East Clandon road. After crossing this road and emerging from the woods to pass Hollister Farm, the Way re-enters woodland and follows a broad forest track across Netley Heath and the edge of Hackhurst Downs, then leaves the track and descends steeply in a south-easterly direction to meet a minor road linking the A25 with Effingham. You turn left on to this road, and proceeding north-eastwards, begin climbing again. After briefly following the road, the Way turns right and continues across White Downs through a further area of woodland, although breaks in the woods do allow good views to Dorking and Leith Hill, which at 965ft is the highest point in Surrey.

Eventually the Way reaches a minor road at Ranmore Common (21.7), within sight of an attractively-situated church which, like St Martha's Church, is right on the path. Known as the Church on the North Downs Way, it is faced entirely with cobbles. The Way leaves Ranmore Common by means of a minor road and passes through the Denbies estate, joining a track to begin the descent to the valley. There was a large Italianate house here but it was demolished in 1954, and the estate is now better known for its vineyard beside which you pass during you descent. The valley – used by the Romans to take Stane Street to London – was created by the River Mole which has here cut a spectacular gap through the North Downs; Box Hill rises steeply on the other side, and the enjoyment you may feel as you drop downhill will be tempered with dread at the thought of a stiff climb almost immediately afterwards. The descent takes longer than somehow one feels it should, and its beauty is not enhanced by the noise of the busy A24, which runs through the valley.

On reaching the valley floor, you meet railway, road and river in close succession, crossing the railway to reach the A24 road. By detouring up the A24 northwards you will reach a station from which trains are available to the pleasant town of Dorking nearby. It will also be possible to view the Burford Bridge Hotel, where Lord Nelson finally separated from Lady Nelson in 1800 and Keats completed *Endymion* in 1818. Thankfully you are spared having to walk across the A24, an underpass having been created instead, and you can proceed safely to the crossing of the Mole.

The river crossing may be undertaken by a clearly signposted footbridge, but the more direct and romantic crossing is by means of a set of stepping stones. At times when the river level is higher than normal this crossing may not be feasible and the footbridge will have to be used. Even when the stones are usable, you would be well-advised, particularly in wet weather when the stones are already slippery, to check the soles of your boots for accumulations of mud or other alluvial deposit before making the crossing. Few things will be more harmful to the dignity of the intrepid traveller, equipped with all the latest hi-tech gear, than being involuntarily propelled into the murky depths of a Surrey river, particularly if the victim's performance is witnessed by a herd of tittering juveniles on the opposite bank.

Mole Crossing to Merstham

Assuming the stepping stones have been successfully negotiated, there is then a punishing climb from roughly 160ft to 560ft in less than half a mile, on to the chalk plateau of Box Hill (23.9), but at length the path levels out and the famous viewpoint is reached. With its sweeping views across the Weald, it is an immensely popular spot, particularly at weekends and holiday times. Thirsty walkers will be well catered for, with ice cream vans sure to be in attendance in summer, and the Boxhills pub, claiming to be the highest pub in Surrey, situated nearby. A stone on the hill marks the spot where one Peter Labellieres was buried upside down. Because he thought the 'world is turned topsy-turvy' he believed his body would eventually be righted! The hillside contains lovely woodland, including whitebeam, juniper, yew, oak, birch and the box trees on its flank which gave the hill its name. Box is in fact the densest English wood, and Thomas Bewick, a famous engraver of birds and animals, claimed that one of his blocks, made of the wood, was sound after being used 900,000 times.

The Way proceeds eastwards, passing through the woodland of Brockham Hills and losing height all the time, although the views remain good. You pass along the south edge of Betchworth Quarries and go forward to the B2032, just north of Betchworth which has a useful station on the Guildford–Redhill–Tonbridge line. You turn left on to the B2032, and follow this road round a right-hand and then left-hand bend. When it finally straightens out, the Way turns right off the road through a narrow strip of woodland, left again, uphill and then right once more to follow the side of the Buckland Hills and Juniper Hill. There is thick woodland along the steep slopes to the left, and more open country to the right. Just beyond Juniper Hill there is a sharp left turn, and you rise steeply upwards to the summit of Colley Hill. There then follows an exhilarating high-level walk, first on Colley Hill and then Reigate Hill (31.8), on a good track towards the A217 just north of Reigate. There are superb views both to the north and to the south; the south brings more excellent Wealden panoramas, while to the north you have views right into the heart of London. The great vistas prompted a senior Army officer to build an ornate viewing pavilion here in 1909.

Fast, largely level walking takes you past a motley collection of edifices including a watertower, Reigate Fort and a cat's home, and forward to the A217 which you cross by means of a footbridge. Beyond the crossing is a car park and a refreshment hut, but do not expect to drink your beaker of tea in peace, for you are just a stone's throw from its junction with the M25, and the traffic noise is considerable. By detouring southwards along the A217, you will reach the town of Reigate. Primarily a commuter town, it contains an eighteenth-century gatehouse marking the site of a twelfth-century castle; man-made tunnels associated with the castle were used as air-raid shelters and for storage in the Second World War. There is also an eighteenth-century town hall, and St Mary Magdalene church has a twelfth-century nave.

Back on the Way, beyond the car park, you proceed through attractive National Trust-owned woodland, then turn right on to a driveway through Gatton Park. The early nineteenth-century house is now a school, while St Andrew's Church, within its grounds, is of Gothic composition and has what Pevsner describes as one of the best private chapels in the country. Until 1832, despite having just 23 houses, Gatton returned two members to Parliament, making it the most rotten borough but three in the country. It is no wonder that Pevsner describes the Town Hall, built in 1765 and in which elections for the borough were solemnly held, as a 'very English political joke!'

The Way leaves Gatton Park and proceeds gently downhill through fields into Merstham (34). Merstham is a very pretty place; particularly noteworthy is the church of St Katharine, the tower of which dates back to 1220, and a road called Quality Street with attractive old buildings including examples of firestone, brick, half-timbering and tile-hanging. Merstham has the misfortune to have the M25 run right through its middle, and the walker lodging here overnight and kept awake by the traffic noise may not be the first to crack that Quality Street is not the only thing that gives the village a hard centre.

Merstham to Tatsfield

You cross the M25 and leave Merstham by way of a right turn into Rockshaw Road. The road runs parallel with the M25 which is on the right, and, with the M23 coming in from the left, you could be forgiven for feeling like the jam in a motorway sandwich. Immediately ahead is the interchange of these motorways, and the lover of motorway engineering can obtain a grandstand view of it from the bridge just ahead. The North Downs Way, however, leaves Rockshaw Road just short of the bridge, turns left and passes under the M23, climbing to a triangulation point some 660ft above sea level, higher than Box Hill. You continue eastwards, crossing a minor road and proceeding to Willey Park Farm where you turn right and follow a track heading south-east. You cross another minor road to join a road that proceeds over White Hill, where there is a good viewpoint, while just south of the path on White Hill is the Iron Age hill fort of War Coppice. Two roads head off to the left, leading into the commuter town of Caterham, and just after the second turning you leave the road, taking a right turn on a footpath to contour the partially-wooded Gravelly Hill. There are excellent southward views from the hillside before you enter the woods and head in a more north-easterly direction to pick up the crossing of the A22 London–Eastbourne road.

Almost immediately after crossing the A22, the Way forks right along a track which proceeds eastwards past Quarry Farm, and after crossing a wide track that leads on to Winders Hill, drops down south-eastwards to meet a minor road. You cross the road, following a track steeply uphill north-eastwards on to the wooded Tandridge Hill and the beautiful National Trust-owned South Hawke, providing splendid views. You then drop down the steep chalk cliffs through the woods, using steps. This is one of the finest moments of the walk so far, if a little unnerving for those with a fear of heights, for you are now crossing over a railway tunnel and, looking straight down, can see the railway emerging from the tunnel far below as it heads towards Oxted. It is a fine combination of natural beauty and man's ingenuity.

Once over the tunnel, the Way continues to lose height, proceeding through the woods and into open country, then having passed some limeworks, soon reaches a minor road (42). The Way crosses more or less straight over but by following the road to the right you will reach Oxted, where direct trains to London are available. Oxted is a commuter town with little to see; although the old town contains some old timber-framed cottages, even this area is described by Pevsner as 'narrow, battered and traffic ridden.' Prettier is the next-door village of Limpsfield where, among the yews of the churchyard, the composer Frederick Delius is buried. Beyond the Oxted road the North Downs Way proceeds eastwards, initially in open country and then alongside the thickly wooded slopes of the Titsey Plantation to the left. You reach a T-junction of paths on the edge of Titsey Park; Titsey Place, within the park, dates back to 1775. At the T-junction you turn left and climb steeply up Pitchfont Lane to the road junction at Botley Hill; at 882ft the highest point of the North Downs. At the junction you turn hard right on to the B269, then shortly turn left off it and cut through woodland and open country to the B2024, immediately below Tatsfield.

There are some fine views on the Botley–Tatsfield section; indeed local housebuilders tried to draw Londoners to developments around Tatsfield by saying 'Come to the London Alps!' It has to be said that there are occasions, particularly when rain and mist sweep over the North Downs, on which it is hard to visualise any similarity between these murky heights and sun-drenched snow-capped peaks of Switzerland and France. Indeed, I remember my first walk on the North Downs Way around Tatsfield where inclement weather caused me to lose my bearings, and my sufferings were compounded when, in attempting to regain my route, my borrowed plastic mackintosh and part of my trousers got spectacularly caught in a barbed wire fence. Perhaps my morale would have improved had I had the option, unavailable at that time, of making a brief detour southwards for refreshments at the handily-placed Clacket Lane service station on the nearby M25.

Tatsfield to Dunton Green

Joining the B2024 briefly, you proceed straight ahead at a three-way junction on to a lane beside the golf course, and a right turn at the next fork takes you on to a drive which goes forward to the A233 Westerham–Biggin Hill road. You have now crossed the border into Kent. Detouring to the right along the A233 brings you to Westerham. Referred to by Daniel Defoe as a 'handsome, well-built market town,' it is indeed an attractive place, and although rather spoilt with modern development, retains some pleasant features including a green, market square, the part-thirteenth-century church of St Mary, and two fine seventeenth-century buildings; namely Grosvenor House and Quebec House. After crossing the A233 the Way, having lost some height from Botley Hill, climbs up again, through woodland initially and then on to the more open country of Hogtrough Hill. You continue in a generally north-eastward direction, following firstly a minor road, then field edges, to the 760ft triangulation point on Sundridge Hill. You then skirt the northern fringes of the beech woodlands at the northern end of Chevening Park, briefly entering the woods themselves at one point, and then begin to veer to the south-east. As you do so, you pass close to the village of Knockholt that lies to your left.

The Way continues south-eastwards, dropping steeply downhill into the wide Darent valley, with magnificent views across Chevening Park, its tree-fringed lake, and its red brick house, thought to have been built for Lord Dacre who died in 1630. At length you reach the B2211 and follow it briefly to the left to reach the A224, turning right on to this road and crossing over the M25. Just to the south-west is the M25 interchange with the M26. The route soon leaves the A224 just short of Dunton Green to turn left on to a minor road and then immediately right, heading north-eastwards across fields and over the main London–Tonbridge railway line. It may make a pleasant change to observe rushing trains rather than rushing vehicles.

A glance at the map reveals that this particular stretch of line lies between two of the longest railway tunnels in southern England: the Knockholt and Sevenoaks tunnels (the former running underneath the escarpment of the North Downs). Weary walkers may wish to content themselves with this knowledge alone, rather than having to wait for the next train to rush past so that the railway buff in the party can, from its markings, identify everything from the London terminus from which it has started and the destination it is hoping to reach, to the year of manufacture of its bogies.

Dunton Green to Wrotham

From the railway the route continues on a well-defined track towards Otford, turning right on to a road and then proceeding eastwards over the Darent into the village centre (53.7). Otford is a most picturesque place, where even the roundabout comes with pond and weeping willow. Some parts of the church date back to the eleventh century, and the Bull Inn contains a sixteenth-century fireplace. There are also remains of an Archbishop's Palace, the work of Archbishop Warham and in use from the early sixteenth century. Refreshments should be available in the village, and if so it may be wise to take advantage of them; after a brief walk on the A225 the Way, continuing in the same easterly direction, leaves the road and heads very steeply uphill to Otford Mount, from where there are superb views across the Darent valley and beyond. The route stays at a good height, crossing a minor road and proceeding round the north edge of woodland within sight of Otford Manor, and above the village of Kemsing. Its church of St Mary is of Norman origin, but contains a remarkable decorated rood screen, Pre-Raphaelite reredos and gold altar canopy. All this was created in the twentieth century by the Gothic revivalist Comper, and described by Simon Jenkins as 'an uncommonly harmonious work of twentieth-century art.'

Back on the Way, you cross another minor road, after which there is a mixture of open and woodland walking, the route still proceeding roughly in an easterly direction, on the top fringes of the escarpment. Then, in Chalk Pit Wood, a more extensive patch of woodland, the Way swings in a southward direction and, crossing a minor road, drops down steeply through cornfields to reach a wide track; the course of the old Pilgrims' Way. Turning left on to the track, it is a straightforward walk eastwards below the escarpment to reach Wrotham (60.4). Once again, you are close to the convergence of two motorways, this time the M26 and M20.

The Way passes round the northern edge of Wrotham, but it is worth detouring to view the charming village centre with its outstanding medieval church which is particularly rich in brasses and has a remarkable portrait gallery with about fifty figures of five families, ranging in date from 1498 to 1615. A brass-rubbing is a most personal and rewarding souvenir of a visit to a church on a national trail, but the hiker, having completed it, would be well advised to post it home. It would be such a pity if rainwater, seeping through his rucksack, soaked his lovingly-finished reproduction of Lionel, Duke of Clarence (d.1368), Roger Mortimer, Earl of March (d.1398) or other such worthy, resulting in an indelible imprint both on the white carrier bag, bearing the rather less intricately fashioned Superdrug logo, and his only dry T-shirt that was nestling inside it.

Wrotham to Cuxton

Leaving Wrotham, the Way crosses the A227 and the M20, and proceeds north-eastwards on a minor road past Hognore Farm then, when the road executes a hairpin bend and starts to descend, it continues on up the hill and into the woods, gaining the upper fringes of the escarpment once more. The Way meets the A227 again but immediately turns right on to a minor road and soon left on to a footpath, staying in the woods as it continues eastwards through Trosley country park, immediately south of the sprawling Vigo Village. A detour down the escarpment brings you to the peaceful and isolated Norman church of Trottiscliffe, and half a mile or so to the east are the Coldrum Stones, a megalithic long barrow thought to date back to 2000 BC. Back on the Way, having gained all the height, you promptly lose it again, descending through woodland on the southern fringes of Whitehorse Wood, then climb back up to the top of the escarpment. The views hereabouts are truly magnificent, and this area is justifiably popular with visitors.

The Way crosses a minor road where you could, if you wished, detour to the right to visit the inelegantly-named village of Snodland. The national trail however proceeds northwards up a lane past the 643ft Holly Hill triangulation point, then when the lane ends it continues north through Greatpark Wood before turning eastwards and then north-eastwards. The going is still predominantly through woodland, broken up by just two patches of open land, but immediately to the east now is the less congenial Medway valley. You will be relieved to note that although the valley is heavily built-up with a number of industrial villages and towns, the woodland of beech, hornbeam and yew hides it from view.

In due course, you reach a crossroads of paths; while a right turn leads shortly down to North Halling in the valley, the Way turns left and follows a course slightly west of north, proceeding downhill through North Wood and on to the hamlet of Upper Bush. Swinging north-eastwards again on a track and then footpath, you arrive at the Cobham–Cuxton road just west of the village of

Cuxton. Instead of proceeding into the village, the Way appears to shy away from it, turning left and climbing steeply to cross the railway. The route then executes a rather crude semi-circle round Cuxton, heading north-eastwards initially, dropping steeply and then rising to a thin area of woodland. Superb views now open out across the Medway valley, with your eyes being irresistibly drawn to the Medway bridge, for which you are now heading. Before reaching it, however, you have to drop south-eastwards between two further areas of woodland to complete the circuit of Cuxton, then turn left and proceed beside the busy A228 to reach the junction with the M2 and the all-important Medway crossing.

Cuxton, despite being brutally shunned by the path planners, does have some redeeming features, including a hillside church with a Norman nave, and a sixteenth-century gateway which is the only surviving feature of a late fifteenth-century house called Whorne's Place. It also has a useful rail link with Maidstone, although with the promise of intermediate stations with such unpromising names as Snodland and New Hythe, it would be an unlikely contender for Great Railway Journeys Of The World. Indeed, nobody could blame the homeward bound walker for eschewing a gaze at the view out of the window in favour of hungrily rifling through his rucksack in search of the individual apricot pie that somehow became detached from his picnic lunch.

Cuxton to Kit's Coty
The exciting crossing of the Medway comes next, but may be delayed if you wish to visit nearby Rochester, reached by continuing north-eastwards along the A228. The city contains a twelfth-century 128ft high Norman castle keep (the largest in England), several timbered houses, Benedictine priory ruins, traces of the walls of the old Roman settlement of Durobrivae, a seventeenth-century guildhall, and a cathedral, built between the twelfth and fifteenth century, which has a magnificent west doorway with highly decorative carving. The cathedral contains the tomb of St William of Perth, who was murdered near Rochester in 1201 during a pilgrimage; after he was buried, a number of miracles were reported to have taken place at his tomb. The city has strong associations

with Charles Dickens who spent much of his life in the area, and parts of Rochester appear in his novels *Pickwick Papers*, *Great Expectations* and *The Mystery of Edwin Drood*.

Returning down the A228 to rejoin the Way, your next task will be to cross the Medway, using the right-hand side of the splendid M2 motorway bridge high above the river (71). It is an undeniably exhilarating experience, albeit somewhat alarming for the vertigo-sufferer. Coming off the bridge, you continue on a track running parallel with the M2, turning right just past Nashenden Farm and climbing on to Wouldham Downs with good views to the Medway valley and the woodlands beyond. The Way then veers south-eastwards over Burham Common to meet the A229 just below Chatham at Blue Bell Hill, the footpath graduating to a narrow metalled road and, soon after Burham Hill Farm, passing the Robin Hood, an isolated but most welcome pub.

At Blue Bell Hill the Way, rather than crossing the A229, turns southwards and proceeds along a path parallel with it, swinging west of south to reach Kit's Coty House, a Neolithic burial chamber consisting of three upright stones, 7–8ft high, surmounted by a capstone nearly 13ft long. Although their survival over several thousand years is remarkable, their preservation has not been assisted by the graffiti which has been carved on them. Some of the graffiti is in fact well over 100 years old and could therefore be said to have acquired historical interest of its own. However, the iron cage in which the stones are enclosed denies contemporary North Downs Way walkers the opportunity to fascinate future generations of pilgrims with their own suitably apposite inscriptions such as, 'My feet are killing me OK?' or 'Lord Lucan is alive and well and walking in circles round the M2/A229 interchange trying to get back on the North Downs Way.'

Kit's Coty to Hollingbourne

Beyond Kit's Coty House the Way goes on to meet and cross a road junction, then proceeds eastwards, going under the A229. You pass more prehistoric stones, consisting of a single megalith known as the White Horse Stone, and a whole group of fallen sarsen stones – actually the ruined burial chamber of a prehistoric long barrow –

known as as the Countless Stones but marked on the map as Little Kit's Coty. These lie on the west side of the A229 underpass, with the White Horse Stone on the east side. Immediately beyond the White Horse Stone you briefly follow a track then turn left and proceed extremely steeply up the escarpment, through beech-woods. Turning right at the top, you go south-eastwards along a path which hugs the border between the woods to the right and open fields to the left. The path takes you virtually all the way to Detling which lies immediately beyond the crossing of the A249 Sittingbourne–Maidstone road.

By detouring right at the one minor road crossing on this section, you may descend to reach Boxley, an unspoilt village with a green, pond, and ruins of a twelfth-century Cistercian abbey. The A249 crossing, reached by a sharp right turn and steep descent, is the closest you get to Maidstone. This bustling Medway town, badly affected by flooding in the autumn of 2000, boasts the largest church in Kent (All Saints) as well as a fourteenth-century Archbishops' Palace. After the introduction of hops from the Continent in the sixteenth century, the town became the centre of the Kentish brewery industry. As you walk through Kent you will see many fine examples of oast houses or kilns which were formerly used for drying newly picked hops.

The Way turns left at the A249 (81) and proceeds briefly alongside it in order to negotiate a safer crossing point of this very busy road. (Walkers wishing to visit Detling need to turn right on to the A249 and then cross at the next junction.) From the A249, you follow a rather disjointed course south-eastwards along footpaths to Hollingbourne. Although it keeps well above the old Pilgrims' Way, which follows a metalled road through Thurnham and Broad Street to Hollingbourne, there are a number of small ascents and descents. You pass through a mixture of woodland and open downland, from which there are excellent views.

Soon after the A249 crossing you reach the ruins of Thurnham Castle, described as a typical Norman defensive work, and known to have been occupied by Robert de Thurnham in the latter half of the twelfth century during the reign of Henry II. The only other obvious landmarks are three minor road crossings, leading respectively to Thurnham with its fine brick-and-timber Friars Place, Bearsted on the outskirts of Maidstone, and Broad Street. When you reach a fourth road, you turn right along it and descend to Hollingbourne (86.3), turning left at the first crossroads to continue. I have walked parts of the Detling–Hollingbourne section in glorious autumn sunshine, with splendid views across the Garden of England, but I once walked the whole of it under sullen overcast skies, with continuous mud underfoot; the descents were particularly unpleasant, since it was quite impossible to put one foot in front of another without at least one foot slithering out of control.

Muddy footpaths can of course occur on even the simplest stretch of a national trail. Sometimes the mud will cover only part of the path, leaving the walker ample room to pass by without soiling his footwear or his trousers. At other times, however, the mixture of mud and water can be so widespread that the walker is left with an unpalatable choice. He may attempt to chart a parallel course through an uncompromising army of spiteful pathside vegetation which seizes every opportunity it can to wrap itself round him, or deposit stings, thorns or other sharp objects on or through his person; alternatively, he may try to wade through the quagmire, each step into the treacle-like depths accompanied by the very real fear that the leg might emerge from it without a boot or shoe on the other end.

Hollingbourne to Boughton Lees

Hollingbourne is a very pleasant village of old timber-framed houses, and its church contains a number of fine features including a chapel with 124 shields round its walls, and a life-size marble effigy of one Lady Elizabeth who died in 1638. The good news is that it also marks the start of a fast, easy stretch of the Way along excellent tracks and paths that follow the line of the old Pilgrims' Way, continuing right up to the commencement of the loop section near Boughton Lees. Although your route stays some way down the escarpment, with no real scenic highlights, the views across Kent are still excellent and despite the presence of two major roads nearby, there is a pleasantly rural feel, and a sense of relief that

London suburbia and the industrial Medway valley have been left behind. Ironically the route does have to pass the big Marley factory complex about three miles beyond Hollingbourne. This stretch runs parallel with three important lines of communication, namely the M20 (motorways are never far away on the North Downs Way), the Maidstone–Ashford railway with several useful stations, and the A20.

Three pretty villages lie on the A20 close to the route of the Way along this stretch, and they are all easily reachable from the path using the numerous crossing tracks and roads available. First is Harrietsham, which contains charming seventeenth-century cottages and almshouses, and a church with a beautiful fifteenth-century west tower. Next is Lenham, with its fine square surrounded by medieval houses, a tithe barn, a church with excellent wood carvings, wall paintings, another splendid tower dating back to the fourteenth century, and a floor memorial dedicated to one Mary Honywood who died in 1620 leaving 16 children, 114 grandchildren and 228 great-grandchildren! Another interesting feature in Lenham is a building named Saxon Warriors, so called because of the discovery of a fifteenth-century house inside with foundations that contained three skeletons with swords, daggers and spearheads dating back to the sixth century.

Some four miles beyond Lenham is Charing. This again contains several attractive cottages of brick and timber; the sixteenth-century Peirce House in the High Street has fine overhanging gables and close timbers. There is a thirteenth-century church with yet another magnificent tower dating back to about 1500, and the remains of an Archbishop's Palace that was built here around 1300, and in which Henry VIII stayed in 1520 on his way to Calais.

The Way crosses the A252 at Charing (94.4) – from which it is a short walk to the right, down to the village – then continues along the edge of woodland, still following the Pilgrims' Way, to the hamlet of Dunn Street just above the village of Westwell. It is worth making a detour to visit the village to look at the lovely thirteenth-century flint church, which has a magnificent Gothic stone chancel screen. You enter Eastwell Park, passing right by the lake and also a church which was hit by a bomb during the Second World War, and is now a ruin; Eastwell House, though Tudor in appearance, is of twentieth-century origin. The Way reaches the A251 just beyond Eastwell Park at Boughton Lees (99.1) and goes over the main road. This marks the end of an almost continuous south-eastward progression which has persisted since leaving Hollingbourne.

Over the road, you follow a minor metalled road north-eastwards towards Boughton Aluph. It is along this road that you must choose whether to follow the direct route to Dover via Wye, or the longer loop route via Chilham and Canterbury. You may choose to proceed more directly towards your goal along the escarpment, picking your way along a disjointed sequence of often muddy lanes and tracks, the view eventually becoming dominated by the sprawl of Folkestone. Or there is the other route, where after taking cream teas by the old village square in Chilham, you can proceed to Canterbury, with its historic cathedral, its fine range of shops, its theatres, live music, medieval pubs, wine and jazz bars, restaurants offering choice foods from China, Italy, Spain, Mexico and Thailand . . . but you can take it or leave it.

Boughton Lees to Postling (direct route)

The *more direct* route leaves the Boughton Lees–Boughton Aluph road fractionally after the loop route does. It bears right, following a path that goes round an orchard and soon reaches the A28 Ashford–Canterbury road where it turns left. You briefly follow alongside this busy road, then cross it and proceed through more orchards and fields, crossing the Great Stour to reach Wye (101.4). The orchards, which have existed in Kent since Roman times, serve as a reminder of Kent's reputation as the Garden of England; the county's traditionally mild climate has allowed many types of fruit, especially apples, to flourish, and in late summer the trees hereabouts will be groaning with Cox's Orange Pippin, Bramley, Golden Delicious and Worcester Pearmain. Wye is a large and interesting village, with a college that dates back to the mid-fifteenth century, a mostly eighteenth-century church with a massive tower and magnificent Queen Anne chancel, some fine town houses including the early seventeenth-century Old Vicarage House and the timber-framed Yew Trees, and several Georgian buildings. At a crossroads in the village centre you turn left, then right on to a track that climbs back on to the escarpment, past another orchard then through open land and woodland. An unusual feature on the hillside is the Crown Memorial, a large chalk cross cut into the Downs.

Having gained the top of the escarpment, the Way turns right and some pleasant high-level walking follows in a south-easterly direction through the Wye and Crundale Nature Reserve. You may be fortunate enough to see badgers or fallow deer hereabouts, whilst plant life includes orchids, wild thyme and cowslips. The Way crosses the minor road connecting Wye with Hastingleigh and continues south-eastwards, then at the Brabourne–Waltham road, you turn right on to it and shortly left, following a metalled lane and then a good track below Hastingleigh. You turn right on to a minor road, and pass a triangulation point, from which there is a tremendous view on a good day.

As the road begins to drop steeply, the route turns left on to a track which contours the hillside for a while, then seems to give up the struggle and plunges down to a minor road. You turn left and follow this road through Stowting (108.1), avoiding the road bearing left to the church, and arrive at a T-junction of roads. You proceed straight over it, joining a footpath and climbing steeply up Cobbs Hill to reach the B2068 road. The Way turns right just before the road and proceeds parallel with it on a field edge, passing two junctions but staying on the right of it. Just past the second junction you cross, turn left on to a path, and continue in the same south-easterly direction passing to the north of the village of Postling and following a dry valley.

It is easy to detour to Postling, with its church bearing the unusual dedication of St Mary and St Radegund; it has a thirteenth-century tower, some twelfth-century wall painting, and a perfectly preserved dedication stone. The area has associations with the novelist Joseph Conrad, who wrote *Typhoon* and *Lord Jim* here. You reach another minor road and cross it, but by turning right and following this road it is possible to reach Sandling station on the Ashford–Folkestone railway line.

Small country stations like this may be of little interest to inner-city travellers, but they are invaluable for tired walkers with insufficient means for a taxi journey to centres offering accommodation and other amenities. It would, however, be a mistake to overestimate the number of trains serving them. I recall dropping down the aforementioned B2068 to reach Westenhanger station, a couple of miles west of Sandling, at ten to five on a cold Saturday evening in January, missing a train by no more than 30 seconds, and having to wait an hour on an unlit platform for the next. It is certainly a challenge to devise suitable means of passing that sort of time, and it will be very much down to the individual walker and his state of mind as to whether it is best spent exploring the innermost recesses of his consciousness and meditating upon his ultimate eternal destiny amidst the unfolding story of the universe, or popping down the road in search of a one-stop shop that will sell him a couple of bags of crisps.

Postling to Dover (direct route)

Having crossed the Sandling road, you then rise to and pass the giant masts of Swingfield radio station, still heading south-east, and enjoying excellent views from the hilltop. You arrive at the edge of a wood, where you turn left and drop down to the B2065 just south-east of the village of Etchinghill (112.7). The whole of the rest of the walk beyond Etchinghill overlaps with the Saxon Shore Way, a walk of just over 150 miles between Gravesend and Hastings, round the coasts of Kent and part of East Sussex. Crossing the B2065 by Etchinghill, the North Downs Way passes under the disused Canterbury–Lyminge–Folkestone railway and climbs steeply on to the escarpment, heading east then south to meet a minor road just south of the hamlet of Arpinge. You cross the road but stay roughly parallel with it, proceeding alongside first the left and then the right of minor roads heading eastwards, all the time remaining above the steep escarpment. The sprawl of Folkestone, and the sea behind, are now clearly visible below, signifying that journey's end is near, whilst dominating the foreground is the huge terminal for private and haulage traffic for the Eurotunnel. Still close to the road, but following a more winding course, the Way negotiates Castle Hill (also known as Caesar's Hill), passing Iron Age earthworks.

You veer north-east to meet the A260 Canterbury–Folkestone road (117.3), then cross it and proceed immediately alongside a minor road heading just south of east along Creteway Down. You pass a triangulation point at 557ft, and soon afterwards the road and path meet the B2011 (the old A20 Folkestone–Dover road), and the Valiant Sailor pub. From here you have reasonably convenient access to the town of Folkestone. Folkestone, a busy Channel port and seaside resort, is the birthplace of the physician William Harvey and the site of the first nunnery in England, established in AD 630. Although there are some quaint old buildings around the harbour, many of the town's buildings date from the nineteenth century, the resort having developed following the arrival of the railway.

It should be pointed out that although the Valiant Sailor is as near to the heart of Folkestone as the route gets, it is still quite a long walk from the pub into the town, with a long uphill trudge back to the Way afterwards. At this late stage in the journey, with progress severely hampered by aching feet and limbs, it is understandable that you may opt to forgo the attractions of the town, particularly if your previous experiences of it are confined to an interminable wait in a queue of stationary traffic for a place on a Eurotunnel crossing to the Continent, or standing on the quay as a school pupil with a hundred other gum-chewing, gobstopper-sucking 12-year-olds about to embark on the dreaded Day Trip To Boulogne.

Having crossed the A20, the Way takes a path immediately to the right of the pub, then turns left and for much of the remaining five miles or so to Dover, continues along the cliffs, high above the Channel. Initially you look down on the Warren, a chalk landslip basin rich in fossil remains, tree and scrub growth, and wild flowers. It has been described as one of the great classical landslip areas of the country. You then proceed along the cliffs all the way to Shakespeare Cliff, passing Abbot's Cliff and the old firing ranges at Lydden Spout. These clifftops mark the eastern end of the North Downs escarpment. Down below the cliffs is Samphire Hoe, created by the spoil from the Channel Tunnel construction, on which rye grass and other vegetation has been encouraged to grow. The cliff walking is a fine climax to the North Downs Way, with views out to sea which may on a clear day extend to the French coast, although the enjoyment of the walk is undoubtedly marred by the noise on the nearby A20.

The Way descends from Shakespeare Cliff to follow an underpass beneath the A20, and emerges in the village of Aycliff. The route turns right on to a metalled road, then shortly left through a housing estate. You climb some steps to reach an area of rough pasture, then follow a narrow but clear path north-eastwards across this pasture, with excellent views to Shakespeare Cliff and out to sea. You keep to the right of the buildings of Dover Young Offender Institution, passing the remains of a twelfth-century Knight's Templar church, with its distinctive circular nave. You then turn right into Citadel Road and follow it to a T-junction with the North Military Road. The Way turns left, but by detouring right you reach a viewpoint and car park from which there is a magnificent panoramic view of Dover Harbour. The viewpoint car park provides easy access to the Western Heights; these are earthworks which were enlarged to create a complex network of fortifications to protect the country against threats from France in the nineteenth century.

You follow the North Military Road, ignoring a metalled road signposted for the Drop Redoubt, but soon afterwards you turn right up some steps and head south-eastwards round the edge of part of the old fortifications, with wonderful views to the town and harbour of Dover. The route then swings north-eastwards, dropping steeply down two flights of steep steps, the second of which is the 64 St Martin's Steps. At the bottom you bear right and then left into Adrian Street, turn left up York Street, cross it and proceed via Queen Street and King Street into Market Square, where the North Downs Way ends (123.3).

Dover is Britain's nearest point to mainland Europe, and as Roman Dubris, was an important naval base and the starting point of Watling Street. There is a vast amount to see and do in the town; its most interesting feature is the Norman castle. The castle has a twelfth-century keep, a Roman beacon dating from AD 50 (one of the oldest Roman buildings in the country), the Saxon church of St Mary in Castro, and an underground network of secret wartime tunnels. These were dug during the Napoleonic war and used as a headquarters to plan the Dunkirk evacuation. Other attractions include the Roman Painted House which includes some Roman wall paintings, and the White Cliffs Experience which provides a history of Dover from the Roman times to the Second World War. Despite the construction of the Channel Tunnel there are still plenty of sea connections to the Continent, and in 1999 Dover was still the world's busiest passenger port.

The walk does not have to end in Dover. You may wish to head northwards to Canterbury using the loop route; or, your appetite whetted by the Saxon Shore Way signposts, you may feel tempted to take that route onwards to Deal, Sandwich, Herne Bay and Gravesend; or, you may hop on a ferry and begin a trek across Europe, linking the Channel coast with the Mediterranean coast, via the Massif Central, the French Alps or the Dolomites . . . or you can stagger back to Dover Priory station and hope to be home in time for *Emmerdale*.

Boughton Lees to Canterbury (loop route)

The *loop* route leaves the Boughton Lees–Boughton Aluph road by turning left, and follows a footpath across fields to reach Boughton Aluph with its flint church containing a thirteenth-century chancel and fourteenth-century nave and transepts. Continuing north-eastwards, the route crosses a minor road and passes the buildings of Soakham Farm, then climbs up into woodland. To the right, in the Stour valley, is Godmersham Park with its Georgian mansion which Jane Austen, who was often a guest here, is reputed to have used as the basis for her novel *Mansfield Park*. The Way stays on the fringe of the woodland then drops downhill away from it, heading initially south-east but turning north and joining a track which passes through the hamlet of Mountain Street and into Chilham (105 from Farnham via loop).

Chilham is a lovely village, dominated by its castle with a Norman keep and seventeenth-century Jacobean mansion built for Sir Dudley Digges, a high official of James I. There are some magnificent memorials to members of the Digges family in the church, which has a fine fifteenth-century tower with a chequerwork of flint and stone. There are many excellent old half-timbered houses in the village square. The Way proceeds northwards out of Chilham, crossing the A252 Maidstone–Canterbury road and following a metalled road to the village of Old Wives Lees, which is not as quaint or picturesque as it sounds. However, it does have one fine feature, namely North Court Oast, one of a number of old oast houses that have been converted into private dwellings.

You turn right in the village to join a wider metalled road, then when the road bends to the right you continue in a generally north-easterly direction, with a fair bit of up-and-down work. You pass firstly across an orchard, then through a small strip of woodland, emerging into further orchards and going under the railway, before joining a track that takes you to Chartham Hatch. This stretch is particularly attractive at apple blossom time, and with hopfields and more old oast houses also in evidence, you do feel very much in the Garden of England.

Chartham Hatch is unexciting but Chartham itself, reached by turning right at a minor road junction and detouring southwards, has a lovely thirteenth-century church. The church contains a splendid early fourteenth-century brass dedicated to Sir Robert Septvans, but is best known for its beautiful tracery in the upper parts of the windows. From Chartham Hatch the Way goes through pleasant woodland, still heading north-east, to reach the A2, passing the Iron Age settlement at Bigbury. It joins a minor road to cross over the A2, then turns right (south-east) and briefly runs parallel with it before resuming the north-easterly progression, dropping to cross a stream and rising to skirt the National Trust viewpoint of Golden Hill. Once over Golden Hill, you pick up a road leading into Harbledown, from which it is a short walk into the centre of Canterbury (112). The Way is not waymarked in Canterbury itself.

Canterbury is a lively university city, and though many of its historic buildings were destroyed in the Second World War, its magnificent cathedral survives. The first cathedral was built in AD 597, but this has disappeared, and the present cathedral was initiated by Archbishop Lanfranc in 1067. Its finest features are its Norman crypt with exceptionally fine carvings, its twelfth-century choirstalls, and its huge fourteenth-century nave. You will surely want to enjoy these for yourself, particularly if you have travelled from Farnham and like to think that, where the route of the North Downs Way coincides with the Pilgrims' Way, you have been travelling in the steps of the Canterbury pilgrims of long ago. It is unlikely, however, that your desire to identify yourself with your travel-weary forebears will assist in gaining you exemption from the now compulsory and not insubstantial admission charge.

Canturbury to Shepherdswell (loop route)

If you are continuing to Dover on the loop route you need to head for St Martin's Church on the A257 Canterbury–Sandwich road, just east of the city centre. By the church, built in AD 560 and one of the oldest in the country, the Way proceeds away from the A257 on a good, wide track in a south-easterly direction, passing through orchards to reach Patrixbourne (115.4). This is a very pretty village with a picturesque group of nineteenth-century cottages built for the tenants of a now vanished estate, and ornately designed in Tudor style. The late Norman flint church contains some exquisite carvings around its south door. Close by is the chalk stream called Nail Bourne, which dries up during periods of low rainfall: the flowing of the stream is traditionally regarded as an omen of disaster!

Having joined a minor road to pass through the village centre, the Way turns right on to another minor road by the church and then left, climbing past a patch of woodland on to Barham Downs – once a favourite gathering place of Roman legions – and continuing south-eastwards, roughly parallel with the A2. Shortly before reaching the B2046, the Way forks left, crosses that road and passes through two small settlements; Womenswold and Woolage. Womenswold has a pretty flint church on a grassy mound, surrounded on three sides by eighteenth-century red brick cottages. Still heading south-east, you pass over Three Barrows Down and through a narrow strip of woodland to cross the Canterbury–Dover railway. By turning sharp left right on the railway crossing you may detour to Barfrestone and its beautiful eleventh-century Norman church of flint and Caen stone. The church boasts some amazingly intricate and perfectly preserved late twelfth-century carvings.

The Way picks up a track, still heading south-east, then just beyond Long Lane Farm turns right to proceed in a southerly direction along a path towards Shepherdswell, also known as Sibbertswold. You soon cross a road (122.5) and the immediately adjacent East Kent Light Railway. This is actually a preserved fragment of the old East Kent Railway which was one of the least successful ventures of the remarkable railway entrepreneur, Colonel Stephens. Designed to serve what are now disused collieries between Shepherdswell and Richborough (just north of Sandwich), it certainly has its share of tales, some tall, some true. It is reported in that in 1945 a farmer on his way to market to sell his produce, incensed by the failure of a train to stop in response to his hand signal, lay in wait for the train as it returned two and a half hours later, and pelted it with rotten eggs, tomatoes, apples and other items from his compost heap.

Shepherdswell to Dover (loop route)
From the railway, the Way carries on southwards to meet another road (both these roads lead immediately to Shepherdswell village centre and its railway station on the Canterbury–Dover line) and heads out into the countryside again, apparently aiming straight towards Dover. Unexpectedly, however, you have to swing to the east and then north-east, *away* from your ultimate objective! You cross a minor road just above Coldred at its tiny church of St Pancras, with flint walls and some Saxon features. Soon afterwards you enter the grounds of Waldershare. The park, which contains many fine species of beech, lime and chestnut as well as a huge eighteenth-century Palladian belvedere, is dominated by a Queen Anne brick mansion. The route joins a driveway then, on leaving the park, forks left to pass the church which contains some splendid monuments.

Once past the A256 Dover–Margate road, you pass round the edge of Minacre Farm, crossing two tracks and turning left on to a third to reach a T-junction at the village of Ashley, where you turn right, head downhill and once again proceed south-eastwards on course for Dover. You reach another track by Maydensole Farm, turning right on to the track then bearing left to skirt an area of trees. Once round the woodland, you head in a more southerly direction towards Dover, now on an old Roman road which was built to link Dover with Richborough, where the Romans under Claudius landed in AD 43. The Way overlaps with the White Cliffs Country Trail, which links Dover with Sandwich Bay. You pass through the hamlet of Pineham, now enjoying straightforward walking on a well-defined track, before going under the A2. Soon the track becomes a metalled road which drops down steeply, crossing the Dover–Deal railway. At a T-junction, the Way goes straight over to pass the edge of Connaught Park, and carries on in a straight line to a street that emerges in the town centre of Dover (129.8).

The smug walker who has accomplished the loop route could of course head purposefully for Shakespeare Cliff and claim that in enjoying the flesh pots of Canterbury and the exhilarating sea views, he has had the best of both worlds. This, of course, presupposes that an excess of exotic cuisine has not severely disabled him and thereby left him benighted well short of his destination, thus reducing him, rather like the hapless farmer on the East Kent railway, to seeking out the nearest spot on the Canterbury–Dover railway line and hoping that a kindly train driver will respond somewhat more positively to his own desperate hand signals.

SUMMARY OF PLACES OF INTEREST

Farnham, Compton, Guildford, St Martha's★, Box Hill, Colley Hill★, Merstham, Tandridge Hill, Westerham, Chevening, Otford, Otford Mount, Wrotham, Holly Hill, Rochester★, M2 crossing★, Kit's Coty, Lenham, Charing★, Wye, Shakespeare Cliff, Chilham, Canterbury★, Dover★.

AMENITIES ON OR NEAR THE ROUTE

Farnham★, Puttenham (L), Guildford★, Albury (L), Westhumble, Betchworth, Reigate★, Merstham, Caterham, Oxted, Westerham, Dunton Green, Otford, Kemsing (L), Wrotham, Borough Green, Snodland (L), Halling (L), Cuxton (L), Rochester★, Detling (L), Hollingbourne (L), Lenham, Charing, Wye, Etchinghill (L), Folkestone★, Chilham, Chartham, Canterbury★, Patrixbourne (L), Dover★.

The Ridgeway Path

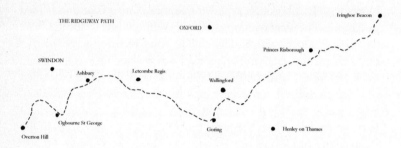

Length: 85 miles.
Start: Overton Hill, Wiltshire.
Finish: Ivinghoe Beacon, Buckinghamshire.
Nature: The first half of the walk consists of a journey along ancient downland tracks through the heart of Wiltshire and Oxfordshire. The second half, whilst following further old tracks, incorporates a wider variety of paths and landscapes of the Chiltern Hills.
Difficulty rating: Easy.
Average time of completion: 7 days.

The Ridgeway Path

A walk along the Ridgeway Path is also a walk back to pre-history. The Ridgeway Path as we know it today formed part of an old road with Bronze Age origins known as the Great Ridgeway which linked Lyme Regis in Dorset with Hunstanton in Norfolk, the route serving as a drove road, a trading route, and a convenient track for invaders. Parts of the Great Ridgeway were absorbed into routes such as the Wessex Ridgeway, the Ridgeway, the Icknield Way and the Peddars Way, created for a variety of reasons and uses by subsequent generations of travellers. It seems likely that the road already existed when the great religious monuments of unhewn stone were set up at Avebury, near to the start of the national trail. The light soils of the chalk proved to be workable by primitive implements, which in turn could be created and developed by the availability of flints. This encouraged settlers and traders, and explains the large number of burials and fortifications on the route.

The idea of a long-distance path which incorporated sections of the Great Ridgeway, offering the walker a combination of well-defined upland tracks, fine scenery, and many historic sites and monuments, was first suggested in 1947 and the official route opened in 1973. As has been stated above, it is a path of two halves. The western half, following the old Ridgeway, passes along seemingly endless broad tracks, often deeply rutted and used by riders as well as walkers, through open, rolling countryside with few habitations close at hand. The eastern half, using parts of the Icknield Way and passing through the Chiltern Hills, does have some stretches of a similar nature but these are punctuated by areas of woodland and housing, with a feeling of being rather closer to civilisation, and many of the paths are narrow and suitable only for walkers. However, the Chilterns offer some extremely pleasant scenery and a rich variety of trees and plants. Although the beech is prominent, there is also much oak and ash amongst the woodland, and the area is also noted for its wealth of orchids and rare gentians. If you are particularly fortunate you may also spot an edible dormouse, a species that is more common to the Chilterns than anywhere else in the country.

Technically, the Ridgeway Path poses no special demands for the walker; climbs and descents are always fairly gentle and the most gruelling ascent is literally within 100 yards of the finish. However, one should not be complacent, for the exposed sections on the first half of the walk could render the ill-equipped walker quite vulnerable in wet weather, and heavy rain may also turn many sections into mudbaths. I made the mistake of thinking that trainers would be adequate footwear for a traverse of the Ridgeway at the end of a particularly soggy May, and limped home sporting a pair of feet that looked as if they had been processed through the office shredder.

Avebury to Liddington Hill
Most walkers arriving by public transport to tackle the Ridgeway will get off the bus at Avebury, and indeed this village is deserving of inspection by all eastbound walkers before the pilgrimage begins. Its stone circle is the largest monument of its kind in the country,

and goes back 4,000 years, certainly earlier than the main phase in the building of Stonehenge. It consists of a circular bank and adjacent ditch, and on the inside of the ditch is a collection of over 100 standing sarsen stones (sarsen meaning Saracen, or foreign to the indigenous chalk), some weighing up to 50 tons. It is believed that the circle represented a religious or social centre for the primitive farming communities drawn to the downs of Wessex. The village also boasts a large thatched barn and a part-Saxon church, containing Norman aisles and a fine Norman tub-font. The walk from Avebury to the start of the route goes past the site of a 50ft wide avenue of megaliths, and then through West Kennett. This village is most famous for its long barrow which dates back to 2500 BC it is notable for its exceptional size (350ft long and up to 80ft wide), and contains several burial chambers where large numbers of skeletons have been discovered.

An unpleasant walk eastwards alongside the busy A4 brings you to Overton Hill – the site of further stone circles – and the official start of the route. Immediately, as you join a wide track that strikes out northwards into open downland, the scene is set for the next 42 miles. Overton Down and nearby Fyfield Down bring more sarsen stones, once believed to be old pagan monuments but subsequently realised to be the weathered-down remains of a layer of rock which once covered the chalk. In fact the stone has been a useful source of building material in the area. Having proceeded a fraction east of north to pass Avebury Down (walkers coming from Avebury can cheat slightly by joining the Ridgeway here instead of Overton Hill) and Monkton Down, the track then swings in a more north-easterly direction over Hackpen Hill. The views are extensive and totally unspoilt.

You cross the Broad Hinton–Marlborough road, and after passing three tidy pockets of woodland you reach Uffcott Down and drop slightly to reach another road crossing. Immediately beyond is the first highlight of the walk itself, Barbury Castle, a huge Iron Age circular hill fort commanding spectacular views. The route continues through the large car park and past useful refreshment and toilet facilities, serving visitors not only to the fort but the country park which has also been created around this important prehistoric site. In 1985 workmen digging a new pipeline hereabouts uncovered a body dating back to AD 300 which tests showed came from a Romano-British farming community. They christened the body Eric (Early Remains In Chalk) but later the body had to be re-christened Erica when it was found to be that of a female . . .

Beyond the car park the track continues, but very soon there is a turn to the left off a much less well defined track. You should avoid the temptation to continue along the broader one, on pain of going severely off course. The reward for leaving this better-defined track is a splendid march along Smeathe's Ridge, a true ridge route with the ground falling steeply away on either side. This is an ancient route which was used when the lower path across the plain was too wet. You avoid the apparently laborious climb to Coombe Down but turn left on to another comparatively thin track through the pasture, dropping down to join a wider track and then a metalled road. You turn right on to it but when the road shortly bends left, the route goes straight on along an unmetalled lane.

By detouring along the road you arrive at the pretty village of Ogbourne St George (9), which contains a seventeenth-century manor house built on the site of a twelfth-century Benedictine priory. The lane bypasses the village, heading south, but in due course the route takes a left turn off it, descending to cross the pretty River Og and then passing through the extremely picturesque hamlet of Southend with its red brick half-timbered and thatched cottages.

Having scurried straight over the busy A345, the attractive town of Marlborough lying just a few miles to the south, you then follow a lane uphill, passing beneath the abutments of an old railway bridge. You turn left on to another lane, still climbing out of the Og valley, until you reach a crossroads of paths where you turn left and proceed on to Round Hill Downs, having now regained the height lost since Smeathe's Ridge. Soon the track reaches a metalled road, turning left on to it and following it to a crossroads, going straight over; beyond the crossroads, the track becomes unmetalled again and heads resolutely northwards, still climbing. The walking on this section is quite exposed and the only real shelter is to be found in a clump of trees lying immediately to the right of the path. In just that spot one abormally wet Friday in late spring, I found solace in an umbrella of thickly-leaved trees and a twin pack of Sainsbury's scotch eggs.

Liddington Hill to Scutchamer Knob

You should watch for an important left turn off the main track which initially descends and then climbs to pass over Liddington Hill, just to the right of Liddington Castle. The castle dates from the Iron Age but seems also to have been used until the Anglo-Saxon period, while Liddington Hill is one of the highest points on the national trail. The walking is exhilarating and it is a shame when the track begins to descend quite steeply to reach a metalled road. The route turns left on to this road and shortly right on to another, and there follows a desperately tedious tramp along this busy highway, which passes over the M4 and continues to the hamlet of Fox Hill (16.5). Here, at least, is the comforting sight of a pub right on the route.

Shortly after passing the pub, you turn right off the road on to a track. This is the start of an almost unbroken 23 miles or so in which the national trail proceeds along broad upland tracks in a first north-easterly and then south-easterly direction, the route well signposted and carrying no possibilities of going astray. Having left the metalled road just beyond Fox Hill, the track climbs gently and then continues pleasantly above the pretty villages of Bishopstone, Idstone and Ashbury, moving into Oxfordshire as it does so. Ashbury boasts pretty chalk-built cottages – the church of St Mary is built of chalk and brown stone – and Idstone is a hamlet of chalk, sarsen and brick with two fine old farmhouses.

Just beyond the road leading down to Ashbury (20), and only a short stroll away from the route, is Wayland's Smithy, a chambered Neolithic tomb or long barrow, built in about 2800 BC. Excavations in 1919 and 1920 revealed eight Stone Age skeletons and one possibly Iron Age or Romano-British burial, but subsequently an earlier Stone Age barrow was found within the larger one, with fourteen further graves. The tomb is named after Wayland the Smith who actually figures in Scandinavian mythology as a manufacturer of invincible weapons; legend says he lived in the cave on the site and re-shod overnight the horses of those who left money in payment.

Soon after Wayland's Smithy the route crosses a metalled road leading to Compton Beauchamp. In this village is Compton House, a Georgian mansion, and a church which contains many twentieth-century additions, including reredos, font cover and chapel screens, all designed by Martin Travers. Beyond the Compton Beauchamp turning, you rise quite steeply to pass White Horse Hill above Uffington. It is worth pausing at this Iron Age site; although the earthworks are unimpressive, the view from the escarpment, which requires a short detour, is magnificent. The White Horse itself is generally thought to have been cut into the chalk scarp in the first century AD, although other possibilities are that King Alfred cut it to celebrate his victory over the Danes in the ninth century or that it was cut as a tribute to Hengist, the Saxon leader, who had a white horse on his standard.

Slight anticlimax follows as the track drops down again, although the views remain excellent. The problem for walkers along much of the section from Fox Hill to Streatley is the excessive use of the track by wheeled transport which, although much resurfacing has been done, has created several badly rutted sections. You will often be forced to choose between walking a grassy tightrope or preferring to chart a course through one of the channels, the latter becoming impracticable in very wet or muddy conditions. The only real payoff is a certain smug satisfaction at seeing an immaculate four-wheel drive vehicle heading confidently towards a section which you know, having just sploshed through it, to hold as much likelihood for successful motor negotiation as the legendary Wayland producing a magical formula that would enable Norway to achieve invincibility in the Eurovision Song Contest.

As you now head south-east, the unmistakeable sight of Didcot Power Station looms large in the distance. This will rarely be out of sight for the next few hours, although the sight of this is more than made up for by the lovely views across huge areas of unspoilt Oxfordshire countryside which can be enjoyed from numerous viewpoints over the ensuing miles. Soon a road is signposted that leads off to Kingston Lisle with its Georgian mansion and Blowing Stone, which legend states was used by King Alfred to summon his troops. The next significant road crossing is close to the attractive woodland of Sparsholt Firs, and there then follows a stretch of lovely open walking past the summit of Hackpen Hill. From here you get good views to the thatched village of Letcombe Bassett, whose church of St Michael contains a Norman chancel, while also near the route hereabouts are the impressive earthworks of the Iron Age fort of Segsbury. The route continues over the A338 (28) where a detour to the left brings you to the Ridgeway Centre, offering accommodation, and Wantage a couple of miles beyond.

Wantage is the birthplace of King Alfred and contains a statue in his honour, cobbled streets with many seventeenth and eighteenth-century houses, and a part-thirteenth-century church containing tombs of some of the Fitzwarren family into which Dick Whittington married. The next crossing, also with the possibility of a detour to Wantage, is the B4494, and after this is one of the more distinctive landmarks on this section, the tall monument to the soldier and some time Baron of Wantage, Robert Loyd-Lindsay. Beyond the monument the track is almost absurdly wide, although you will be thankful for the extra room when you are passed – as I was along this section one fine Bank Holiday weekend morning – by motorcyclists, motorists, cyclists, joggers and horseriders. This is definitely horse country, with numerous gallops marked on the map close to and sometimes adjoining the route.

The walking remains easy, airy and almost too well-defined as you pass Ridgeway Down, Ardington Down and East Ginge Down. Just beyond East Ginge Down is the triangulation point of Cuckhamsley Hill, nearby to which, to the right of the track, is the green mound known as Scutchamer Knob, a Saxon long barrow or burial mound. It is not one of the most magnetic sights on the route, although its name is certainly one of the most colourful. It is believed to have been derived from the Saxon king Cwicchelm who died in AD 593, but the uninitiated walker who has yet to venture on to Cuckhamsley Hill may be forgiven for supposing Scutchamer Knob to be either a locally-baked bread roll or a particularly painful affliction affecting male long-distance hikers whose breeches have been pulled on too tightly.

Scutchamer Knob to Nuffield

Very shortly you cross another metalled road due south of East Hendred, and the track continues over East Hendred Down and onwards to Bury Down. You are now walking through Berkshire. The sprawls of Harwell, with its atomic energy station, and Didcot, with its power station, are clearly visible to the left, and another eyesore comes into view, namely the A34 dual carriageway. The Ridgeway negotiates this by means of an underpass, but if the prevailing westerly wind is blowing, the traffic noise will continue to be heard for a good mile or two beyond. The route heads resolutely south-east over Several Down and Compton Downs; a right turn off the route on Several Down provides a detour to East Ilsley. This pretty village has a Georgian hall, a pond, the seventeenth-century Kennet House, an early thirteenth-century church, and numerous stables, providing a reminder that East Ilsley has traditionally been an important base for racehorse training.

Continuing along the route on to Compton Downs, you join a concrete drive, but soon turn left off it and head temporarily north-eastwards before continuing due east and then returning to a south-easterly course. As you continue over Blewbury Down and Roden Downs, the going can be very muddy. Beyond Roden Downs you begin to descend, and you find yourself looking down to the lush green valley of Streatley Warren immediately to the right, with the Thames valley to be seen just a short way ahead. The straight, comfortable descent to the valley is a paradise for mountain bikers, and walkers should be aware that they may approach from behind at speed with only a few seconds warning.

At length you reach a metalled road, then follow it eastwards for just over a mile past Thurle Grange to the A417; at the end of a hard day's walk, it can seem a very long and tedious stretch. The route turns right on to the A417 and right again on to the A329, which leads into Streatley (42) with its Georgian houses and nineteenth-century malt-house. To continue the Ridgeway Path, you need to turn left in the village on to the B4009, and proceed over the Thames into Goring. You may feel a touch of the London bus syndrome here, reflecting it to be somewhat ironic that you should have to walk 42 miles without passing through a single settlement of any size to reach two almost adjacent to each other, each offering a wide range of amenities including (at the time of writing) a youth hostel in Streatley.

The original ethos of youth hostels – to provide reasonable but low-budget accommodation to young people who might otherwise be unable to afford to get out and enjoy the countryside – has been somewhat eroded by the extension of facilities with consequent price increases, and their availability to motorists and others who have not arrived 'by their own steam,' although it is fair to say that many hostels, particularly the remoter ones, have striven to retain their character and special atmosphere.

Whatever the future for youth hostelling in this country, it is a fair bet that all walkers, even those who can now afford to sleep in luxury hotels during their walking holidays, will treasure their memories of youth hostel life. They might nostalgically recall the surly warden standing balefully by the locked door, only deigning to open it at 5 p.m. precisely to admit the queue of thirty that for the last 35 minutes had been standing in the pouring rain outside; the all-pervading smell of dirty, sweaty feet in every corner of the building; the competition for worksurface space and utensils in the members' kitchen with a party of eight non-English speaking teenagers attempting to make a beef stroganoff with rice for 16 people; the loudmouth monopolising the commonroom conversation with his intrepid boasts about the mountains, rapids, jungles and seas he had successfully and contemptuously mastered; the night's sleep in the dormitory punctuated by nine distinctive types of snoring that proceeded on a rota basis throughout the hours of darkness; and, before escape was allowed next morning, the traditional (now apparently obsolete) hosteller's duty, consisting of sweeping a passageway with a broom that was so full of dust, dirt and fluff that after 20 minutes' feverish activity the floor was three times as dirty as it had been at the beginning.

Soon after crossing the Thames you turn left, just bypassing the centre of Goring, a pleasant town with more amenities than

Streatley and containing a twelfth-century church, and the attractive old Miller of Mansfield Hotel. The route, now back in Oxfordshire, passes along a mixture of suburban roads and paths which proceed gently northwards to the pretty village of South Stoke with a partly thirteenth-century church. A left turn in the village takes you to the riverside, and there follows a delightful stretch of two miles or so along the east bank of the Thames, providing some contrast to the quite remote downland walking that has gone before. The riverside path passes under the main London–Bristol railway line, Brunel's fine bridge carrying the railway not only over your route but over the Thames at this point. The route then joins a path that is set a little way back from the river, and proceeds to North Stoke. It goes right past the extraordinarily attractive church, which contains fourteenth-century wall paintings and a Jacobean pulpit, and follows along the main street, the route continuing in the same (northerly) direction to enter Mongewell Park and pass a Jewish public school named Carmel College. Just before reaching a busy road and bridleway underpass, you turn right to follow a path that runs roughly parallel with the road.

You cross over the road and immediately join the course of an old earthwork known as Grim's Ditch, parts of which reach a height of six feet from the top of the dyke to the bottom of the ditch. Its purpose is unclear but it may have been a tribal boundary or, like Offa's Dyke, a boundary line between kingdoms. Although the latter explanation would be consistent with Saxon or Danish origins, there is also a possibility that the earthworks formed a sort of prehistoric network associated with the Ridgeway hill forts. Grim, incidentally, is another word for the Nordic god Odin.

From Mongewell Park to Nuffield, a distance of four miles, the path proceeds in an almost straight easterly line alongside the tree-lined remains of the ditch. To begin with it is like going through a narrow tunnel of woodland with open fields on each side, although the strip of woodland widens as progress is made. It is lovely relaxing walking, and it is almost a shame to bear left and climb up away from the ditch to reach a metalled road and the village of Nuffield (52). The route turns right on to the road and then left opposite the partly Norman church, in the churchyard of which the car magnate and philanthropist William Morris is buried. Having taken the left turn, you are soon following a perilous path across a golf course; numbered posts mark the way but do little to indicate from which direction the danger of low-flying golf balls lurks. One would suppose that golfers themselves would be equally wary of passing hikers, particularly as there is nothing in the laws of the game that specifically tells a player what to do when his ball lodges itself in a walker's cagoule hood or strikes a rucksack and ricochets into a bush.

Nuffield to Princes Risborough

If you have survived the golf course you must then cross the busy A423, and there follows a short very pleasant woodland walk and a confident march across open fields, bisected by a narrow strip of woodland. Beyond lie the buildings of Ewelme Park, a mock-Elizabethan house. The route passes just to the right of these, then bears right, passing round a field edge and then dipping quite steeply downhill through beautiful woodland, with the lovely Swyncombe Park on the right. This is indeed a most refreshing interlude between the bouts of pounding wide tracks. At the foot of the hill the route emerges from the woods, turning right on to a lane which passes the nineteenth-century Swyncombe House and its pretty Norman church of St Botolph, built partially of flint.

The lane meets the Ewelme–Cookley Green road and you cross over it, joining a very attractive path, that heads downhill with fine views to the woodland of Swyncombe Downs up ahead. Having dipped down, the path rises to enter the woods and then gradually drops through patchier woodland to reach a much wider track at the foot of the slope. You turn right on to this track and follow it eastwards. This is part of the Icknield Way; thought to be named after the Iceni tribe, it is probably pre-Roman, having been a trading route from Norfolk to the South West, and tending to follow a line at a slight distance from the Chiltern Hills rather than along the top of the escarpment. You must follow it north-eastwards for several miles, with the wooded slopes of the Chilterns as a constant companion to your right, and good views across more open countryside to your left.

The track is broken up by a number of road crossings, all providing the opportunity of a detour to visit a village or small town to the left, most of which are well signposted from the route. You could branch off at each one and thus visit Britwell Salome, Watlington, Shirburn, Lewknor, Aston Rowant, Kingston Blount, Crowell and Chinnor. Of all of them, Watlington (57) offers the widest range of amenities, and is worth visiting for its handsome Georgian houses and thatched cottages, and a fine seventeenth-century town hall.

There is a somewhat unwelcome intrusion just past the Lewknor crossing, namely the M40, but in due course peace reigns again and you can continue to enjoy lovely views to the Chiltern escarpment. Many of the villages beyond Watlington are worth detouring to visit: Shirburn has a castle dating back to the late fourteenth century, Lewknor boasts a part-thirteenth-century church with many fine memorials, the church of Aston Rowant has a Norman nave, Crowell boasts the fine seventeenth-century Elwood House, and the church in Chinnor contains a truncated effigy of a knight in chain-mail, although the landscape round Chinnor is somewhat disfigured by a cement works. After wet weather you may indeed prefer to stick to the roads linking these places, for the route itself hereabouts can get intolerably muddy and as you flounder along waterlogged sections, desperately trying (and often failing) to find alternatives, you may well have to remain philosophical and keep your spirits high either by a brisk refrain of the song of the bold hippopotamus with his call to 'let us wallow in glorious mud,' or the hope that your passage will be halted by cheque-book waving researchers seeking volunteers for a TV ad for the latest brand of biological washing powder.

Beyond Chinnor, at the hamlet of Hempton Wainhill, you should watch carefully for a right turn beside a house, but by detouring straight ahead you can reach the pretty village of Bledlow which has many attractive herringbone brick cottages, the seventeenth-century Red Lion Inn, and a remarkable church. It contains a twelfth-century font, fragments of medieval wall paintings, and much thirteenth-century work. Restoration appears minimal; as Simon Jenkins writes, 'Everything needs attention, but has mercifully failed to get it.' Having turned right at Hempton Wainhill, you climb into the woods above Bledlow, passing close to the seventeenth-century Bledlow Cross, a well-known local landmark which lies to the right on Wain Hill. As the route continues as a good path through the woods, care should be taken to branch off right rather than follow the Upper Icknield Way downhill again; the correct route, now in Buckinghamshire, heads south-east through open country, maintaining the height gained. After crossing a road, you proceed through fields, heading south-eastwards on to Lodge Hill, a most satisfying viewpoint. Following an all too brief walk across the hilltop, the route, now swinging to the north-east, drops down to a metalled road, crosses it and proceeds through open country past a cottage and alongside a golf course.

You cross a railway line and after a brief climb pass over a railway tunnel, these lines being respectively the down and the up lines of the Marylebone–Princes Risborough rail link. Shortly after the second line is crossed, the route reaches a metalled road, turns right on to it and then left to follow the busy A4010 northwards. Just as you reach the houses of Princes Risborough, you turn right into a lane, returning to the Upper Icknield Way, and there follows a somewhat tedious trudge north-eastwards round the edge of the town. At length the metalled Brimmers Road is reached, giving quick access to the amenities of Princes Risborough (68).

The town is not unattractive, with many timbered and thatched cottages, a seventeenth-century manor house, and a brick market house with arcades and crowned with a wooden cupola. There is a useful railway station here, and indeed this will be your first contact with the railway since Goring. Earlier in the century there were trains available from Princes Risborough to Oxford and also to Watlington, but if you decided to miss a section or two of the Ridgeway and go from Goring to Princes Risborough by train, you would have to travel to London Paddington, cross to Marylebone via the underground, and then take another train from Marylebone. Alternatively you could travel to Oxford, there joining a train to Banbury in the Midlands, and could then take a train south again to Princes Risborough via Aylesbury. Or you could attempt to find the bus station in Oxford and hope for a bus going to Aylesbury, enabling you to board the Princes Risborough train there. Or of course you could opt for a much quicker alternative, namely to stick to the Ridgeway after all . . .

Princes Risborough to Langton Wood

The route goes straight across Brimmers Road and continues along a lane, shortly turning right on to a path which climbs steeply up on to Whiteleaf Hill. It heads directly for a metalled road, but at the last minute swings left and proceeds into woodland to meet another road. You turn right on to it, then shortly left, proceeding northwards and passing close to Whiteleaf Cross which, like Bledlow Cross, is believed to date back to the seventeenth century. You bear right into the very attractive Giles Wood, and drop steeply downhill to reach a road at the hamlet of Lower Cadsden, the charms of which are infinitely enhanced by a route-side pub. You turn left on to the road and pass the pub, then soon turn right and climb again up on to Pulpit Hill. In good weather this is lovely open walking, and it is hard to believe London is so close.

The route avoids the thick woodland further up the slopes of Pulpit Hill but swings gently north-east and then south-east, keeping the woods to the right and heading towards the Chequers estate. Dropping slightly, along a path which can be extremely heavy-going owing to the clay soil underfoot, the route crosses the driveway leading to Chequers. Looking to the left as you cross, you will observe the sixteenth-century mansion for which Lord Lee of Fareham created a trust in 1917 enabling it to be used by British Prime Ministers. It remains the PM's country residence to this day. Michael Marriott remarks, 'There can be few countries in the world where foot-travellers may approach so close to the residence of the national leader.'

After crossing the driveway, you soon reach a metalled road which you go over, entering woodland almost immediately on the opposite side. Clearly defined, albeit often muddy, tracks take you northwards and uphill to reach a metalled road – confusingly, this area is described on maps as another Lodge Hill – on to which you turn right and soon left, still heading north. You pass through another patch of woodland, but soon the route emerges on to the upper slopes of Coombe Hill, the highest and one of the best viewpoints in the Chilterns and indeed on the Ridgeway Path, with good views to the nearby town of Wendover and a magnificent panorama of the Vale of Aylesbury. The route passes a distinctive monument, dedicated to the men of Buckinghamshire who died in the Boer War, then swings to the north-east and begins a lovely descent by means of an excellent path which proceeds unerringly towards Wendover along the wooded slopes of Bacombe Hill.

At the foot of the hill, you turn right on to the B4010 then proceed over the bypass and the railway and enter the little town (74), which boasts an excellent range of amenities. Besides the early fourteenth-century church of St Mary, there are a number of attractive old buildings, some of which are timber-framed. One of the most impressive is the Red Lion; Oliver Cromwell stayed here in 1642 and the room where he slept is kept much as it was in his time. The walker nearing the end of his Ridgeway Path pilgrimage and perhaps tiring after all his exertions may wonder what future generations would think if his own lodgings in the town were left for posterity in this way, but might after all decide that the imagination is the best place to keep the mark he left on them, to wit the bagful of banana skin and orange peel from his previous day's packed lunch, his discarded leaky water bottle, half a dozen used pieces of sticking plaster, and a pair of socks with more holes and a riper smell than a pound of Swiss cheese.

You proceed confidently down Wendover's main street, then shortly before the street curves to the left, you turn right on to an attractive metalled path which continues beside a stream and arrives at a road near the church. You turn left on to the road and continue along it to a crossroads, going straight over on to the somewhat inelegantly named Hogtrough Lane. You head steadily uphill along the lane going south-east, but in due course you reach an area of woodland and bear left, initially heading just south of east and then swinging resolutely north-east through Hale Wood on Cock's Hill. This is quite delightful woodland walking along a comparatively narrow path, serving as a real contrast to the wide open tracks through Wiltshire, Oxfordshire and Berkshire, although it can become extraordinarily muddy.

At length the surface becomes rather wider and firmer, providing quick walking as far as a metalled road. Crossing straight over, the route continues as a narrow path through the woods, but soon meets a deep gully into which it is necessary to descend before turning right and proceeding along its stony floor, climbing quite steeply. This is tough walking, but the gradient eases and you soon reach another metalled road, near the hamlet of Chivery. The route crosses the road and heads north-east across fields to pass a prominent mast, arriving at a metalled road, turning left on to it and then almost immediately bearing right into Pavis Wood.

There follows another pretty woodland walk along a well-defined track, heading north-east. Reaching a road as it negotiates a sharp bend, the route joins the road, heading just north of east and, effectively, going straight ahead. The walk from here to Wigginton is tedious, one has to say. The road walk continues through the unremarkable village of Hastoe, then just after a road leads off to the left, heading for Tring, the Ridgeway Path turns left and proceeds north-eastwards along a track, heading for Wigginton. A little way to the south, and running roughly parallel with the route, is the line of Grim's Ditch. You may sense some anticlimax along this section, which is in no way relieved as, just before Wigginton (80), the route bears left off the track and follows a narrow path which keeps a field and woodland to the left, and the houses of Wigginton to the right. The path, as in Hale Wood, can be insufferably muddy. The Wigginton–Tring road is reached and crossed, and more mud may be encountered as the route heads eastwards to round the south edge of Langton Wood.

On the way, a triangulation point is passed, but the walker who sees it on the map when planning his journey and expects to enjoy a great panoramic view from it will be disappointed. The view is not unpleasant, and Ivinghoe Beacon – journey's end – is visible hereabouts, but it has not the charisma of White Horse Hill or Coombe Hill. Moreover, the triangulation point itself, positioned anonymously halfway down the side of the field, looks no more comfortable or majestic than the goddess Aphrodite would if forced to drop down from the heavens and spend a wet Monday night propping up the saloon bar of the Railway Tavern in Scunthorpe.

Langton Wood to Ivinghoe

The route, now passing briefly through Hertfordshire before returning to Buckinghamshire, turns north-eastwards and heads downhill to cross the A41(M) by means of a bridge. Shortly after this bridge crossing you arrive at the old A41, turning right to follow it briefly, then leaving it by turning left on to a well-defined track that heads north-eastwards in a virtually straight line, proceeding downhill and keeping the grounds of Pendley Manor to the left. Arriving at a metalled road, you turn left on to it and reach a T-junction where you turn right. By detouring left here, you can follow the road to the pleasant small town of Tring, which boasts a park that was formerly the home of the Rothschild family, and a zoological museum which is part of the British Museum's natural history section. Having turned right at the T-junction, the route crosses over the Grand Union Canal and goes forward to Tring Station. Tempting though it may be to stop here and pick up a train homewards, there are still a few miles to go! Soon after the station a metalled road leads off to the left, and soon after this the route itself makes a left turn on to a track, but by detouring straight ahead along the road you reach the charming village of Aldbury with its triangular green, duckpond, part-thirteenth-century church and timber-framed cottages.

Having turned left on to the track, the route turns left again almost at once, proceeding along a well-defined track that heads north-westwards. Soon turning right, the route climbs up into attractive woodland, emerging on to the grassy slopes of Pitstone Hill, although the views are undoubtedly marred by the quarries and works to the left. The ultimate objective, Ivinghoe Beacon, can now be seen clearly ahead. Lovely, airy walking follows, as you head north-eastwards and dip down to cross the Ivinghoe–Aldbury road, from which you proceed on a good path up on to Steps Hill, entering an area of patchy woodland. Swinging in a more northerly direction, the route now drops, quite steeply in places, to meet another road, and after crossing this, you have a choice of paths which lead unerringly northwards to the 756ft summit of Ivinghoe Beacon (85.5).

The final climb is the steepest on the whole of the national trail, but the reward is a magnificent view in all directions, not least to the village of Ivinghoe and the splendidly-restored seventeenth-century windmill near Pitstone. The hilltop is not without historic interest; it is one of several beacon points that were established in the area during the reign of Elizabeth I to summon men in case of invasion from Spain, and there are barrows nearby dating back to the Bronze Age and beyond. It is however, a long and anticlimactical walk back to civilisation, unless of course you have prudently arranged a car to be waiting for you at the nearest road crossing. The nearest village with reasonable amenities is Ivinghoe; this is worth visiting in any event, with its part-fourteenth-century church, the Old Brewery House which dates back 200 years, and the King's Head, an inn dating back nearly half a century. Reaching it, however, will still involve a mile-long road walk beside a busy road, preceded by a very steep and possibly slippery descent from the Beacon itself, which will be a trying experience for all travel-weary hikers, not least those afflicted with the dreaded Scutchamer Knob.

PLACES OF INTEREST
Avebury★, West Kennett Long Barrow★, Barbury Castle, Smeathes Ridge, Liddington Castle, Wayland's Smithy★, White Horse Hill, Blowing Stone, Segsbury, Wantage, Scutchamer Knob, Goring, North Stoke, Grim's Ditch★, Swyncombe House, Watlington, Bledlow, Princes Risborough, Chequers, Coombe Hill★, Wendover, Tring, Pitstone Hill, Ivinghoe Beacon★.

AMENITIES ON OR NEAR THE ROUTE
Avebury, Ogbourne St George (L), Fox Hill (L), Ashbury (L), Uffington (L), Wantage★, Streatley (L), Goring, Nuffield (L), Watlington, Chinnor (L), Bledlow (L), Princes Risborough, Wendover, Wigginton (L), Tring, Ivinghoe (L).

The Thames Path

Length: 183.5 miles via the right bank route, 185.5 miles via the left bank route.
Start: The source of the Thames, near Cirencester, Gloucestershire.
Finish: The Thames Flood Barrier in south-east London.
Nature: A walk beside the river Thames from source to estuary.
Difficulty rating: Easy.
Average time of completion: 2 weeks.

The Thames Path

The Thames Path is the baby of the national trails of England and Wales, being officially opened in July 1996. Walking it has two principal attractions. Firstly, it is a very charming walk which progresses through some of England's loveliest and gentlest countryside and then proceeds through the fascinating heart of its capital. Secondly, the completion of the walk will allow the traveller to boast that he has followed England's longest and best-known river from source to estuary – from a few dribbles in a Gloucestershire field, to a wide band of water of immense historical, industrial and economic importance. Its bends and loops, its tributary streams, its weirs and locks combine to provide endless interest for the walker. The waters are cleaner than they have been for at least a century, and provide a home to many species of bird and fish including salmon, which once again successfully navigate what used to be one of the prime salmon rivers in Europe. The walker may also appreciate the rich variety of wildlife and plant life by the water, including water meadows resplendent with buttercups, meadowsweet and clover, and woodlands that are rich with oak, ash and beech.

There are many other things for the walker to enjoy. There is the tremendous range of rivercraft, from rowing boats to luxury cruisers. There are the beautiful towns and villages close to or right by the river, many of which repay a full day's exploration. Finally, there are the contrasts, from swathes of unspoilt countryside of Oxfordshire to the huge monoliths of central London. Your watering-hole may one day consist of a tranquil rural hotel formerly beloved of ladies and gentlemen of leisure wishing to take some rarefied country air, and on another could be a dockland pub such as the Prospect of Whitby at Wapping, where our aristocratic forebears would surely blench at the sight of bare-knuckle and cockfighting.

In an age of intensive urban development, it may surprise the walker to learn that the river can be followed along most of its length. The reason can perhaps be traced to the creation of a towpath alongside the river between Lechlade (about 20 miles downstream) and south-west London. Historically the canal system played a crucial role in the transportation of goods and materials around the country, and towpaths were required alongside the canals to enable men and horses to tow the barges prior to the advent of motor transport. It was in the late eighteenth century that the increasing importance of the Thames in the context of the growing canal network caused the Thames Commissioners to establish a Thames-side towpath. There were of course obstacles, but where these arose the towpath simply switched to the opposite bank, with navigation ferries being used to facilitate the switch. It was the closure of these ferries, following the decline of water transport, which provided the biggest difficulties for the powers-that-be in establishing a continuous riverside recreational path.

Other difficulties have arisen where (surprisingly rarely) access to the towpath has had to be suspended for development or security reasons, or where no towpath has ever existed – as is the case between the source and Lechlade, and from Putney onwards. At the time of opening in 1996 it had not been possible to fill every gap, but much work has been done before and since to create the necessary new rights of way to ensure appropriate continuity. Interestingly, in London the vast redevelopment of many riverside areas has fortuitously allowed new paths to emerge without assistance from the path planners.

Notwithstanding the difficulties, the route is an extremely satisfying one. Indeed one is amazed by the continuing availability of so much of the towpath despite the excesses of property developers. The continual switching from one bank to the other in order to adhere to the towpath where possible adds to the variety and helps to provide fresh perspectives of riverside scenes. In London one is given the choice, even before the towpath ends, of following either riverbank. It has to be said that the second half of the walk, with many places of scenic and historic interest, is more interesting than the first, where, especially in wet or muddy conditions, the incessant tramping through featureless water meadows could become monotonous. However, the remoter sections do offer peace and solitude, well away from centres of population, busy roads and tourist traps.

The path is well signposted and route finding is never a problem. Planning to walk the path is easy as well; public transport links are so good that the walk can easily be tackled in day trips and weekend breaks, and weather conditions will rarely be so bad as to preclude walking on it, whatever the time of year. No specialist walking equipment is needed; in fact, given the potential for blisters inherent in incessant pounding along flat paths in heavy footwear, it may actually benefit the walker to discard his Gore-Tex boots in favour of the trainers astutely snapped up at the local Sunday market for the princely sum of £1.99.

Source to Hannington Bridge

The start of the route is, fittingly enough, at the source of the Thames. The source, marked by an inscibed stone, is a short distance from the village of Kemble where there is a convenient railway station. The walk south-eastwards from the source stone to the A429, forming the first mile of the route, is a most peculiar one. Unless the weather conditions are exceptional, you will see no water at all on this section; it will simply be a tramp through a couple of fields indistinguishable from any other that you have seen from the window of your train, coach or car en route to the start. Near the A429, however, a shallow channel to your left suggests something more encouraging, and closer inspection may reveal a few token dribbles of water. Once over the A429 and heading south-eastwards towards Parker's Bridge, you may see the channel beginning to fill as a result of underground springs pushing water to above ground level. The channel is lost as the route turns left on to the road at Parker's Bridge and enters the small Cotswold village of Ewen, turning right in the village down a lane heading for Poole Keynes. Soon, however, the route turns left on to a track heading south-eastwards towards Upper Mill Farm, and you are reunited with the infant Thames, in the form of a moderate flow of water. From here to Neigh Bridge, past Upper Mill Farm and Old Mill Farm, the route continues alongside this modest stream, keeping it to the right.

At Old Mill Farm it is possible to detour to the left to visit the village of Somerford Keynes, where All Saints Church has an Anglo-Saxon doorway on the north side. The building is thought to be the remains of a church built around AD 685. At Neigh Bridge the Cotswold Water Park is reached; the route turns left on to a metalled road and shortly right into a lane which proceeds south-eastwards and then eastwards towards Ashton Keynes. The course of the Thames is lost once more, this time amongst a profusion of lakes which are the result of flooded gravel workings. Continuing eastwards, the route enters Ashton Keynes (7) where the infant river does become visible again and makes for a picturesque sight at the bottom of Church Walk by Brook House and Ashton Mill. The route passes right through the village, heading eastwards towards Kentend Farm. The village contains a seventeenth-century pub, some ancient crosses, a number of fine Cotswold houses, a manor house also dating from the seventeenth century, and Holy Cross Church which has a Norman chancel arch. Students of Pevsner's *Buildings of England* series will wish to make a masochistic beeline for the Gothic-style school of 1870, which Pevsner describes as 'truly horrible.'

Having left Ashton Keynes behind, the route heads resolutely south-eastwards to a point just north of Waterhay Bridge, then follows a serpentine course heading vaguely north-eastwards past a further grouping of flooded gravel workings that are now lakes. At length the route, having lost the Thames once more, meets it again and proceeds briefly beside it; near Hailstone Hill you forsake the river again, striking out north-westwards to join the course of an old railway. Turning right on to it, the route follows it and then, on reaching the river, turns left to resume its Thames-side course. The Thames is now noticeably wider than it was round Ewen and Somerford Keynes. There follows a pleasant, if sometimes rather muddy, walk through water meadows to the edge of Cricklade where you cross the river and proceed through fields to a road which is in fact the top end of Cricklade's main street (12.3).

Cricklade, the first town on the route and the only town in Wiltshire that lies on the Thames, is a useful stopping point for refreshment and accommodation. There is evidence that this was once a Roman town, lying as it does within a square earthwork enclosure near to the point where the Roman road from Silchester to Cirencester crossed the Thames. The town has two fine churches, the Norman church of St Mary and, better still, St Sampson. This has a splendid turreted tower built by the Duke of Northumberland around the Reformation, and some excellent carved heraldic work inside. Cricklade's wide main street has several good seventeenth and eighteenth-century houses, one of the best of which is Robert Jenner's School, founded in 1651. The national trail, having reached the top end of the main street, turns right along it briefly and then leaves it, following a lane that leads back to the Thames and joining an excellent riverside path.

Soon you pass underneath the horribly busy A419 road, but the traffic noise soon subsides as progress is made and the route switches to the opposite bank. In due course you reach a footbridge; at the time of writing it is necessary to cross this and proceed south-eastwards to a road, which you then follow north-eastwards to Castle Eaton. The expectation is that the river will be followed all the way to the village when necessary rights of way are established. Castle Eaton (16.5) is a lovely spot; thirsty walkers will doubtless appreciate the Georgian red brick Red Lion Inn, and the church is worth visiting too, with an idyllic riverside setting and a sumptuous Jacobean pulpit inside. The route leaves the village on the Hannington road, soon turning left on to a metalled road to Blackford Farm, then turns sharp left to pick up the river again and follow a riverside path as far as Hannington Bridge. Here it is worth making a detour to the left to visit Kempsford, a charming village of seventeenth and eighteenth-century cottages, some thatched, and the delightful church of St Mary with a preserved Norman ashlar nave dating back to 1120; four of the original windows have been retained. Those deciding not to make the detour can still enjoy a captivating view across the river and adjacent meadows to the church tower.

Back on the route, you then have to forsake the river again for a good part of the walk to Inglesham, turning right on to the road at Hannington Bridge and soon left on to a track that runs parallel to the Thames eastwards as far as Sterts Farm but some distance from it. There are good views to the attractive town of Highworth on its hill to the right, but the going can be unexciting and often extremely muddy, with a tendency for the local soil to stick to one's boots. You may reflect grimly, as you wade through the mud, that there is no real need to take any photographs of the countryside hereabouts as you will be bringing most of it home with you!

Hannington Bridge to Tadpole Bridge

At Sterts Farm it is anticipated that a right of way will shortly be available that returns you to the Thames and follows the river direct to Inglesham. At the time of writing, however, you must continue eastwards to Upper Inglesham, turning left on to the A361 and then first left down to the tiny village of Inglesham. The route passes right beside the tiny thirteenth-century church which, with its Jacobean box pews and wall paintings, is well worth a visit. The Thames is then followed all the way from Inglesham to Lechlade along the right bank (from now on, the expressions 'right bank' and 'left bank' will be used to denote, respectively, the right-hand side and left-hand side of the river facing downstream). Just beyond Inglesham there is a roundhouse to be seen on the opposite bank;

this was one of a number of lock-keepers' quarters on the now disused Thames and Severn Canal, which met the Thames here. By now the Thames, though still not the broad sweep of water which will in due course accommodate rowing crews and luxury cruisers, is beginning to look more recognisable as a major waterway.

Lechlade, reached by a most pleasant walk from Inglesham with the ever-maturing river to the left and broad meadows to the right, is a key point on the route. It is the highest navigable point on the Thames for cabin cruisers but, more crucially for the walker, it is here that the towpath starts, and continues all the way to Putney Bridge, one hundred and fifty miles downstream. The advent of the towpath heralds an end to the rather 'bitty' walking that has been experienced so far, and from now on the going is generally better defined and more comfortable.

Lechlade (23.2) is an obvious place to stop for rest and refreshment. Access to the town is over the river by means of Halfpenny Bridge, so called because of the amount of the toll at one time. This most attractive town, containing a number of Georgian houses, takes its name from the river Leach, one of the Thames' tributaries. It has a fine church, St Lawrence, notable firstly for its carving on the tower exterior, depicting a magnificent monster holding a sword, and secondly the roof bosses forming what has been described as a 'gallery of domestic and religious activity.' Many of Lechlade's buildings have become antique shops, and any guidebook writer should hesitate before recommending a particular eating place or store to replenish his rucksack for fear that, before the ink is dry on the page, that establishment will be similarly converted, and its proprietor, instead of offering chocolate bars and filled rolls to the hungry walker, can provide him with little more to sustain him on his journey than fading pine bookcases, vulgar porcelain figurines and mangy tiger-skin rugs.

Leaving Lechlade, it is a fairly short walk along the right bank to St John's Bridge. At nearby St John's Lock, the first of 47 locks on the Thames, there is a nineteenth-century statue of Old Father Thames. This was formerly placed at the source of the river but certainly enjoys more admirers in its present position. The path uses St John's Bridge to switch to the left bank and stays there for the next six miles, passing into Oxfordshire. A number of features are worthy of note along this stretch besides the river itself. These include some concrete pillboxes which were part of a Second World War defensive system, two locks, and the small riverside communities of Buscot, Eaton Hastings and Kelmscot.

Kelmscot boasts an impressive gabled Elizabethan manor house backing on to the river. The poet William Morris lived here; he came here in 1871 and when he started his private printing works in Hammersmith in 1891 he called it the Kelmscott (sic) Press. At the far end of the village is St George's Church, which contains a thirteenth-century gabled bell-cote and a Norman nave, and in a corner of the churchyard is the lichen-covered tomb of the Morris family. The manor house is now a Morris museum, with several rooms decorated, appropriately enough, in Morris wallpaper.

Buscot and Eaton Hastings are over the river but there is a charming view to the old church at Eaton Hastings, nestling in a small clump of trees. The path arrives at Radcot Bridge (29.8) and switches back to the right bank. The triple-arched Radcot Bridge, believed to have been completed by the fourteenth century, is the oldest bridge on the Thames. It was the site of a battle in 1387 and again in the English Civil War when its capture by Parliament forced the Royalists to abandon Oxford. The four miles beyond Radcot Bridge feel very remote, with no settlements of any significance and just tiny pockets of sturdy woodland to offset the starkness of the surrounding fields. You pass Rushey Lock and soon reach Tadpole Bridge, beside which is the Trout Inn. The Trout is one of the very few places of refreshment on this section of the path, and walkers who have been tramping without a break since Lechlade will welcome it warmly.

Pubs will always be something of a lottery for the long-distance walker. Although many route-side pubs are aware of the number of walkers likely to wish to use them, and cater sympathetically and welcomingly for them, there are always exceptions. At one extreme will be the 'spit and sawdust' establishment where one is fortunate to obtain as much as a packet of crisps with one's pint, never mind a cheese roll or a ham sandwich. At the other extreme will be the more exclusive establishments where cagoule-clad hikers are welcomed with less than open arms, the proprietors fearful that their arrival can only serve to diminish the tidiness and decorum of its smart carpeted lounge, or indeed its restaurant where even at lunchtime the cheapest available starter will swallow up two whole days' food budget.

Tadpole Bridge to Oxford

The route uses Tadpole Bridge to switch to the left bank and then enters Chimney Meadow Nature Reserve, an area of lovely riverside woodland. This makes an undeniably pleasant change from the open meadows, although appearances are perhaps deceptive; the woodland is but a long narrow strip, extending only a short distance from the river. The route crosses the river again at Tenfoot Bridge, from which it is anticipated that the definitive route will continue along the river to meet the Shifford lock cut. However, at the time of writing, it is necessary to leave the river and follow paths towards Lower Newton Farm before turning left and heading north-eastwards along a track to the tiny village of Duxford, picking up the river just beyond the village at Duxford Ford and following the right bank on to meet the eastern end of the lock cut. Lock cuts are short straight channels of water which have arisen at pronounced bends in the river, providing an apparent short cut for river craft. Beyond Shifford lock cut it is straightforward, albeit featureless walking, along the right bank to Newbridge (40.3).

Newbridge is situated on the busy A415 Witney–Abingdon road, and has a useful pub, the Rose Revived. Despite the name Newbridge, the fine four-arched bridge which carries the A415 over the Thames here is certainly not new, but is thought to have been completed by the fourteenth century. You must cross it and return to the left bank, continuing through pleasant but unremarkable water meadows. You pass Northmoor Lock and reach the pretty hamlet of Bablock Hythe with its little church and attractive pub. The village is mentioned by the nineteenth-century poet Matthew Arnold in his elegy *The Scholar-Gipsy*. Arnold's poetry was noted for being frequently informed by alienation, stoicism, despair and spiritual emptiness, and one suspects that if he were still alive now Bablock Hythe would provide ample scope for poetic works of this description, borne not of the area's want of natural beauty but the rather ugly proliferation of chalets that have grown up in the immediate vicinity.

At Bablock Hythe the towpath switches to the right bank, but the Thames Path is unable to do likewise, there being no permanent crossing point nearby. With no right of way available on the left bank, the route is forced to forsake the river for a spell, turning left to follow a road and then right along unexciting farm tracks through fields. It duly meets the river again shortly before Pinkhill Lock. There are good views eastwards to the high ground of wooded Wytham Hill, and a detour to the left before the path turns riverwards takes you to the fine village of Stanton Harcourt. The village is famous for Wesley's Cottage north of the church, so named because John and Charles Wesley together with their sister used to visit the vicar there. The other noteworthy feature of the village is Pope's Tower, one of the few remaining parts of a once impressive manor, and the original home of the Harcourt family. It was here that in 1718 Alexander Pope completed the fifth volume of his translation of *The Iliad*.

At Pinkhill Lock there is a weir bridge which allows for a return to the right bank and an uneventful 2-mile walk through the meadows to Swinford (48.1) with its eighteenth-century toll bridge carrying the B4044. There is a good opportunity to replenish supplies at Eynsham, a short walk up the road to the left; the town is an attractive one with a 20ft high fourteenth-century cross, and an arcaded hall in its square. From now on civilisation will never be far away and the sense of remoteness rather disappears. Oxford is now approaching, and not only its suburbs but its busy approach roads will be a constant feature until you reach the city in another six miles.

Beyond Swinford the route stays on the right bank, hugging the base of Wytham Hill and the woodland which clothes it. Once past Wytham Hill, water meadows again take over, and the only feature of note until the A34 bridge is King's Weir. There are one or two pronounced bends in the river on this section, and it will not take the brain of an Einstein to deduce that time lost by earlier stops and detours can be made up by taking short cuts across the open meadows without fear of losing the route. Such a strategy, though having much to recommend it, may backfire on the more thin-skinned walkers who, sitting in the pub that evening recounting their adventures to others, may be roundly accused of cheating. It will then depend on the degree to which their consciences gnaw away at them during the restless night that follows as to whether they feel constrained to return to the relevant section and do it all over again.

The Thames Path passes beneath the very busy and noisy A34 and continues towards Oxford. Walkers studying their maps will note that the Thames has an alternative name around the city, the rather more poetical Isis. Just after the A34 bridge are the ruins of the twelfth-century Godstow Abbey; Rosamund, the mistress of Henry II, was educated here. A bridge over the river just before the ruins takes you to the popular and picturesque Trout Inn, originally a hospice, and the attractive scene is further enhanced by the presence of a delightful weir. By turning right rather than left over the bridge to the Trout, you can detour to the outstandingly attractive village of Wytham which contains a turreted sixteenth-century abbey and fine thatched grey stone houses. The Thames Path continues along the right bank from Godstow; despite the A34 to the right and the suburbs of Oxford to the left, the immediate surroundings at least initially remain free from habitation and noise.

The huge green expanse of Port Meadow opens up on the opposite bank with the Summertown district of Oxford visible beyond, and as further progress is made, Oxford's housing seems to become more and more intrusive. The route switches to the left bank at Medley Bridge, just past the hamlet and pub at Binsey, and it is a short walk from here to Osney Bridge (54.3). This is the closest the Thames Path gets to the centre of Oxford, and the best place to leave the route and enjoy the city.

Whole books have been written about its treasures, but any visitor's itinerary should include the twelfth-century Christ Church cathedral, the smallest cathedral in England; Wren's Sheldonian Theatre; the seventeenth-century Bodleian Library; the eighteenth-century Radcliffe Camera, reckoned to be one of the finest examples of English Baroque architecture; and of course the university and its colleges. A university is reckoned to have existed in Oxford since the twelfth century, and many of the colleges for which Oxford is famous, including Corpus Christi, Magdalen, Christ Church, Trinity and St John's, date back to the fifteenth and sixteenth centuries. Walkers fortunate enough to be in the city at the right time of year may well get the chance to enter the quadrangles and sometimes even the buildings of the colleges. At other times the areas accessible to the public will be a good deal less easy, with the rucksack anchored to the walker's back, the camera, binoculars and map cover slung clumsily round his neck, and his sweaty, dishevelled appearance, somewhat hindering any chance of his being able to successfully masquerade as a college student, still less a lecturer or emeritus professor of microbiology.

Oxford to Wittenham Clumps

The route switches again to the right bank and proceeds tantalisingly round the edge of the city, not quite close enough to witness its treasures at first hand. Beyond the heavily built-up Osney and Grandpoint districts, things open out a little. Christ Church meadows can be viewed across the water, as can St Mary's Church at Iffley a little further downstream, reckoned to be one of the best preserved twelfth-century village churches in England with magnificent exterior carving. It is certainly worth making a detour over the nearby weir to see it, and what Simon Jenkins describes as 'the chunky, barbaric richness of door and window surrounds [. . .] mostly carved with zigzag and beakhead over roll-moulding, creating a jazzy effect of monsters with huge beaks biting into long rolls of bread.'

Continuing on the right bank, the Thames Path goes under another very busy highway, the A423, and on to Sandford-on-Thames. The lock here has the greatest fall of water on the Thames, and there is a charming lockside pub called the King's Arms. Once out of Sandford, the route moves into more open country and swings to the south-west, thereby becoming significantly exposed to the prevailing wind for the first time. A lane leads to Radley, famous for its public school, but there is also a useful railway station here. Meanwhile the Thames Path, continuing on the right bank, proceeds pleasantly but uneventfully towards Abingdon (64.2). You should however look out for the splendid eighteenth-century Nuneham House across the river. There is a switch to the left bank by means of a crossing of the foamy waters of Abingdon Weir, and after a pleasant walk through the meadows, the town of Abingdon itself is reached.

There is much of interest here, including the remains of a Benedictine abbey founded in 675, the Long Alley almshouses built in 1446, and the seventeenth-century County Hall, reckoned to be one of the finest in the country. It was built when Abingdon, now in Oxfordshire, was the county town of Berkshire. Walkers may be dismayed to note that the Thames at Abingdon, prior to its confluence with the Ock just south of the town centre, flows for a while in a westerly direction, seemingly *away* from the sea and their final destination. Even more to their consternation may they note that they are only nine miles or so by road from Newbridge, which was passed on the Thames Path some *twenty-five* miles back. Whilst stoicism and patience are necessary parts of the long-distance walker's make-up, he would not be human if he did not for a moment question the wisdom of perhaps two days' hard foot-slogging to make a journey which a motorist could accomplish in the space of less than three tracks of the Diana Ross cassette on the car stereo.

On leaving Abingdon the Thames swings southwards, with the route still on the left bank. The massive funnels of Didcot power station now come into view and will rarely be out of sight for the next few miles. The river swings eastwards, passing Culham to the left. Culham (66.4) is a delightful village with a manor house, parts of which date back to the fifteenth century, and gabled dovecote. Its setting, slightly back from the river, is enchanting. There is a railway station but this is some way beyond the village on a busy main road. If time allows, Sutton Courtenay, on the opposite bank but easily reachable from Culham, is another attractive village to visit, with medieval houses, a Norman church and a seventeenth-century manor. The novelist George Orwell is buried here.

The Thames Path runs in a south-easterly direction for a while, the walking enlivened only by the imposing spire of Appleford church on the opposite bank. There follows a large loop, the route swinging north-east to Clifton Hampden. Clifton Hampden, with its half-timbered and thatched cottages is a real joy; Pevsner describes the church, perched on a cliff, as having a theatrical quality both in position and manner of restoration. The restorer, Gilbert Scott, was also responsible for rebuilding the bridge in Gothic style in 1864. The Thames Path uses Scott's bridge, a fine arched brick-built structure, to switch to the right bank, then begins to loop south-eastwards and continues in that direction to Little Wittenham. There are views over the river to the sumptuous houses and manicured lawns of Burcot.

Immediately ahead are the twin Sinodun Hills, site of a Celtic camp and hill fort dating back to 1500 BC, and Wittenham Clumps, a wooded hill with fine views from the summit which stretch to the Vale of the White Horse, although before these hills are reached the Thames Path switches to the left bank at Day's Lock. Nonetheless, a detour to climb the hills may be a welcome antidote for the walker tiring of tramping along the flat and having to admit that the steepest climb of each of the last six days has been to the second-floor bedroom of his bed and breakfast.

Wittenham Clumps to Goring

The route continues along the left bank with good views to the attractive Little Wittenham Wood on the opposite bank. Close by to your left is Dorchester, a village which used to be a city; the cobbled street contains many timber-framed and brick-built houses, and there is a seventeenth-century coaching inn, the White Hart. Undoubtedly the finest treasure in the village, however, is the abbey. It is 200ft long and boasts a twelfth-century lead font and three magnificent fourteenth-century chancel windows, one of which, in its lights and carved mullions, represents Christ's descent from Jesse.

The towpath soon switches again to the right bank but in the absence of a crossing point the Thames Path walker has to abandon the river for a short while and endure a rather unpleasant piece of roadwalking along the A423. It is with relief that you soon turn right at a crossroads and come down to the pretty village of Shillingford. Its most interesting feature is a thatched boathouse, but there is a fine bridge beside a plush riverside hotel. Rejoining the Thames and remaining on the left bank, the route continues past a large marina at Benson. It then crosses the rushing waters of the weir by Benson Lock to switch to the right bank, and follows a straight course slightly west of south through the meadows to reach the market town of Wallingford (77.7). Wallingford was an important Royalist stronghold in the English Civil War. It has fine Georgian houses, and its seventeenth-century town hall, standing on stone pillars, contains several portraits by Gainsborough. Of just as much interest to the tired traveller is the fact that the town has ample facilities for refreshment and accommodation.

The route continues on the right bank beyond Wallingford, offering very pleasant walking through meadows dotted with pockets of woodland. There are views over the river to the lovely Mongewell Park and its college, and the romantic ruin of the small Norman church of St John the Baptist; its riverside setting is described by Pevsner as perfect. Three miles downstream from Wallingford, you come to Cholsey (80.9) where there is a railway station, although it is a long way from the river. At Cholsey, the towpath temporarily switches to the left bank but you cannot do likewise; it is anticipated that a right of way will become available on the right bank, but at the time of writing it is necessary to leave the river and join the A329 as far as the pretty village of Moulsford, with its picturesquely-named Beetle and Wedge pub. Near the pub the towpath returns, the route descends to the river, and it is then straightforward walking to Streatley, the meadows giving way to pleasant woodland just beyond Cleeve Lock. Streatley is a tidy village with Georgian houses, nineteenth-century malt-house, and fine view of the Thames valley from nearby Streatley Hill.

From here the Thames Path leads over the river to its twin village, Goring (84.8); as you cross, you can enjoy a fine view back to the riverside Swan Hotel. There is a brief overlap here with the Ridgeway Path, a rare instance of where two national trails follow the same route. Goring, the site of a twelfth-century Augustinian priory, contains some fine buildings including a church which contains much Norman work. The area around Goring Lock, and its associated weirs, is particularly attractive, and there is a profusion of luxurious rivercraft. The sight of boat-owners relaxing in their vessels or putting out on to the serene sunlit water must sow at least momentary regret in the mind of the passing walker that ten years ago he passed up the opportunity for traineeship in investment banking in favour of three months pub work on the Costa Brava, and must cause any passing hiker to reconsider his hitherto unshakeable opposition to the purchase of National Lottery scratchcards.

Goring to Reading

From Goring to Pangbourne the Thames Path initially follows the towpath along the left bank, passing underneath a fine Brunel railway bridge of robust red brick. The main London to Bristol railway line runs close to the route for several miles hereabouts, and the noise of trains will be a constant feature on this section. Shortly after the bridge, the towpath switches to the right bank but the Thames Path remains on the left bank, and climbs into Hartslock Wood. There follows a fine high-level promenade above the river, before the route turns away from the Thames and flirts briefly with the edges of the Chiltern Hills. The steep descent and uphill climb which follows is something of a culture shock after so much strolling on the flat. The route continues along a driveway through the woods before descending to the lovely village of Whitchurch, turning right on to the B471 and briefly following this road as far as the toll bridge, where there is a lock and weir with an impressive cascade. From the bridge there is a lovely view back to Whitchurch with its church and mill, while literary enthusiasts may care to note that the riverside Swan Hotel features in Jerome K. Jerome's *Three Men In A Boat*.

Immediately across the bridge you join the towpath on the right bank, but continuing straight on takes you to Pangbourne (89) which deserves a visit. Kenneth Grahame, author of *The Wind In The Willows*, lived here, and there are many fine seventeenth and eighteenth-century houses in the village. The route strikes out into the meadows again, with good views over the water to the Tudor splendour of Hardwick House. It was on this section that I observed a dog on a lead; its master was not walking but was propelling a boat. I reflected that notwithstanding the apparent peculiarity of the arrangement, and (one would have thought) its potential hazards, there had to be immense potential value as a conversational gambit at a social function to be able to inform fellow guests that one had just been out *rowing* the dog.

Between here and Reading the Thames Path sticks to the right bank, the river here forming a border between Berkshire and Oxfordshire. On the opposite bank is the beautiful secluded hamlet of Mapledurham, almost hidden amongst woodland, with seventeenth-century almshouses, a fourteenth-century church and a great sixteenth-century mansion where Elizabeth I was a guest. The towpath does in fact follow the left bank past the village, but there is nowhere for you to cross and no easy means of access nearby; instead you are forced to continue through a trim but characterless housing estate before gratefully descending to the river again at Tilehurst (92.5) and picking up the towpath once more. Despite the presence of housing nearby, there is still a rural feel to the walking, particularly across the river, but as Caversham Bridge comes within sight the residential and industrial buildings of Reading become more concentrated, and soon the towpath converts itself into an urban leisure facility for townsfolk. The importance of the river to the town's leisure industry is further emphasised at Caversham Bridge where there is a big rowing clubhouse, plush hotel and smart riverside pub. A short walk across a working quayside brings you to Reading Bridge (95.9), with the town's multifarious facilities just minutes away.

Reading, which was badly bombed during the Second World War, is hardly a beautiful place; it is a busy industrial and university town noted for the manufacture of biscuits, as well as brewing, engineering, printing and electronics. For obvious reasons, boats and boating also play an important part in the town's economy. Henry I lies buried in the remains of the town's twelfth-century Benedictine abbey, and Oscar Wilde spent two years in the town's jail in the 1890s. Reading is also a key railway junction and its very busy railway station provides direct trains to all parts of the country. Its platforms, especially in winter or at night, are not noted for their warmth and, unless there are no other waiting facilities available, will find favour only amongst walkers who are either shortly going into polar expedition training or who have applied for employment as testers of the efficiency of fridge-freezers.

Reading to Medmenham

As the Thames Path proceeds Londonwards from Reading Bridge along the right bank, the scene is hardly enticing, and is only partially mitigated by the green of King's Meadow to your immediate right. The huge gas-holders, the modern Tesco supermarket and the roar of the high-speed trains on the Reading to London line do little to enhance the beauty of the Thames at this point. The highlight of the walk out of Reading's urban sprawl is the crossing of the Kennet, one of the principal tributaries of the Thames. The route stays on the right bank and, having left Reading behind, proceeds through pleasanter meadows to reach Sonning and its immaculately kept lock. Sonning, where once a bishop's palace existed, is a very pretty place, boasting three inns and a beautiful eleven-arched red brick bridge over the river. There follows a switch to the left bank and some quite delectable walking on the border between Oxfordshire and Berkshire, the Chilterns providing a fine backcloth to the combination of lush meadows and woodland adjoining the river.

After passing Shiplake College and its extensive grounds, the route continues to a lock and associated weirs; you must leave the river at the lock and follow a path that leads to a road heading northwards into Lower Shiplake (102.6), a pretty village with a useful station on a single track line. It is anticipated that a right of way will become available which will avoid the road-walking into Lower Shiplake. A lane is then followed out of Lower Shiplake, coming down to the riverside beyond Bolney Court, and a broad stretch of meadow takes you forward to Marsh Lock, negotiated by means of a wooden causeway. On each side of the bank there are huge luxurious dwellings, whose back gardens lead directly down to the homeowners' boats on the river itself.

Having passed Marsh Lock there is then a straightforward walk into Henley-on-Thames (104.8). The town has many good timbered houses, including the fourteenth-century Chantry House, and many elegant Georgian houses on its main street. Henley is of course most famous for its June/July Royal Regatta, a rowing festival that has been held here since 1839, although only since 1998 have professionals been allowed to compete. There is a fine five-arched bridge across the river here, built in 1786, which the Thames Path crosses to switch to the right bank before continuing on through the meadows. The river is wide and straight here, and with the absence of locks and weirs is very popular boating country. One most interesting feature on this section is Temple Island, a fishing lodge topped by an Italianate cupola on an island in the river. Just beyond Temple Island on the opposite bank is the gleaming white mansion of Greenlands, built for Viscount Hambleden, better known as W. H. Smith.

The river curls from a north-easterly to a south-easterly direction, passing Hambleden lock and weir by Mill End, where there is a white weatherboarded mill whose records go back to Domesday. The turbulent waters of the weir claimed the life of a bargeman in 1753. Shortly beyond the mill there is a brief towpath switch; in the absence of a crossing the Thames Path temporarily leaves the river, now separating Berkshire from Buckinghamshire, turning right along a road into Aston to pass the conveniently-sited Flowerpot Inn. It then turns left along a path and proceeds slightly above the river past the magnificent red brick Culham Court, before descending to rejoin the river and towpath, and passing Medmenham Abbey on the opposite bank.

This was formerly a Cistercian house but the present Gothic building is largely late nineteenth-century. As river travellers proceed peacefully upstream, the timeless scene causing them to nostalgically recall a more civilised and quieter age, they may conveniently care to forget that the Abbey was leased to Sir Francis Dashwood in the eighteenth century, who used it to hold meetings of a club reputedly known as the Hellfire Club. Members met once or twice a week to devote their time to black magic rites and other dubious pursuits, and many statues with pornographic inscriptions found their way into the Abbey. Meetings of the Club were held in a chapel decorated with an indecent ceiling painting, and there was a temple with an entrance formed to resemble a vagina! The prurient walker will doubtless be heartbroken to discover that not only is there no easy way across to it, but the pornographic detail has all gone, and he will have to look elsewhere to satisfy such temptations of the flesh as may have assailed him that day, besides the six rashers of bacon offered him at breakfast.

Medmenham to Maidenhead

The Thames Path continues along the right bank past Hurley, an attractive village with two tithe barns and a twelfth-century inn, and passes over the lock island. It is always a delight to view the locks with their immaculately-kept gardens, as well as their nameboards, which give each an identity and character of their own. It is also fascinating – if one has the time – to watch a boat negotiate a lock before proceeding on its way. Shortly after Hurley the route uses a splendid bridge, built in 1989, to switch to the left bank; until 1953 the switch was accomplished with the aid of a ferry. From here you continue past Temple Lock through the meadows. Over the river there are the magnificent buildings of Bisham Abbey, used for training by the England international football squad, and the riverside Bisham Church. Despite it being inaccessible across the river, you can still enjoy viewing its restored Norman round-headed windows, steep gables and embattled tower.

Soon afterwards the route reaches Marlow (113.5), a picture-postcard town with elegant Georgian houses, a huge riverside church with a soaring spire, Marlow Place, thought to have been built in 1720 for the Prince of Wales, and the exclusive Compleat Angler hotel. Also there is William Tierney Clark's remarkable iron suspension bridge, completed in September 1832. Clark is better known for his bridge linking Buda and Pest in Hungary! It was in Marlow that Mary Shelley wrote the famous Gothic novel *Frankenstein*.

Beyond Marlow the route initially remains on the left bank and having passed the Marlow lock and weir, proceeds pleasantly through meadows to Bourne End, which hosts a chandlery and a vast profusion of rivercraft. There are so many idyllic spots on the river all the way from Sonning to Marlow and beyond, that one can understand its popularity with holidaymakers. Indeed at some stage on his journey the more mature walker is sure to be reminded of those Sunday teatimes when Cliff Michelmore, John Carter and their like were to be heard on the BBC *Holiday* programme extolling the virtues of a boating week on the Thames, with some suitably evocative background music, perhaps the second movement of Mozart's 39th Symphony in E flat as performed by the Berlin Philharmonic Orchestra directed by Herbert von Karajan, or failing that, *Messing About On The River* as performed by Tony Hatch.

The route crosses with the towpath to the right bank and passes the village of Cookham, which boasts a splendid nineteenth-century bridge as well as pretty red brick cottages round a green. The painter Stanley Spencer (1891–1959) lived here and his painting of the Last Supper hangs in the part-twelfth-century church. Below the bridge there are a number of boathouses, one of which is the office of the Keeper of the Royal Swans. Also, just downstream of Cookham, is Formosa Island, the largest island in the Thames; it contains the remains of an eighteenth-century house surrounded by 50 acres of green woodland.

The Thames Path regrettably has to leave the riverside just before Cookham Bridge, passing through the village itself, crossing the A4155 and then following a minor road back to the right bank. Patience, however, is rewarded, for the return to the river brings views to the Cliveden Estate and its glorious beech-woods which drop right down to the water. As you continue beside the river again, you can look back to Cliveden House. Built in 1851, this was once owned by the Astors and was a meeting-place of politicians and international celebrities known as the Cliveden Set before the Second World War. In 1942 the Second Viscount Astor gave Cliveden to the National Trust and its grounds are open to the public although the detour for the Thames Path walker will be considerable.

It is now only a short stroll downstream to Maidenhead (121.1), past the picturesque and popular Boulter's Lock. Maidenhead is not as charming as many towns on the Thames, but you will note two fine bridges: the seven-arched road bridge completed in 1777, and a railway bridge designed by Brunel, containing the flattest and widest brick arches in the world. From the railway station there are main-line trains to Reading and London. If you are returning to Reading by train, having hiked to Maidenhead from there in one or more days, you may feel that you have covered a considerable distance and that Reading is some way away. In fact, although it is 25 miles by the serpentine river, it is much shorter as the crow flies and just 15 minutes away by train, and you would do well not to get too absorbed in your slumbers or your newspaper for fear you will find that you have missed Reading altogether and will not be stopping again until Bristol Parkway.

Maidenhead to Walton-on-Thames
The Thames Path uses the road bridge to switch to the left bank from Berkshire into Buckinghamshire and then passes under Brunel's bridge. It is then a pleasant walk along the left bank through the meadows all the way to Windsor, with the open expanse of Thames Field to the left. Just before passing underneath the M4, you pass Bray lock and can see the village of Bray over the river to the right; the village has a large church and is famous for its sixteenth-century turncoat vicar, Simon Alleyn, who lived through four reigns and adjusted his religious attitude to suit each of them. Half a mile downstream from Bray is Monkey Island, on which is a hotel that incorporates part of an eighteenth-century fishing lodge built for the Third Duke of Marlborough.

For a while the peace of the river is somewhat shattered by the noise of the nearby M4, but tranquillity is restored by the time Boveney is reached. As you approach Boveney the route passes the fine lawns of private riverside houses that were built in Edwardian times for the earliest 'commuters'. There are also fine views of the Victorian Gothic splendour of Oakley Court across the river. Boveney is a beguiling spot with its lock and tiny riverside chapel, which was actually built from rubble and contains some Norman work. Just beyond Boveney the path returns to Berkshire, leaving Buckinghamshire for the last time, and Windsor Castle can now be seen across the meadows.

Soon after passing underneath the A332, you climb away from the riverbank and up to Eton High Street (127.8). The route bears right across the bridge which links Eton with Windsor, and then switches to the right bank to continue on its way. However, few walkers will resist the temptation to explore these two towns: Eton with its quaint old High Street and college, founded in 1440 by Henry VI, and Windsor with its magnificent royal castle founded by William the Conqueror and including the stunning Perpendicular Gothic St George's Chapel.

The route continues on the right bank to Victoria Bridge, following the towpath, then has to leave it and switch to the left bank to bypass a private area of castle grounds. After a short riverside walk it is then necessary to join a road through Datchet. Although its green lawns and gracious houses provide a pleasant interlude, it is hoped to re-route the Thames Path away from the road as far as Albert Bridge. At Albert Bridge the road arrives at the river, and you cross the bridge here to return to the towpath and continue along the right bank. There is then lovely walking past Ham Bridge and Old Windsor Lock; to pass Ham Island the Thames Path follows a lock cut rather than an extravagant loop made by the river. Then, after passing round the back of Old Windsor and its popular Bells of Ouseley pub, you reach the meadows of Runnymede and proceed past the Magna Carta memorial, a domed classical temple built by the American Bar Association.

Behind the memorial, and guarded by Lutyens' gatehouses, stands a splendid expanse of inclined parkland dotted with trees. In the park there are further memorials, one of which commemorates 20,000 airmen who died in the Second World War. An island in the river at this point is appropriately enough named Magna Carta Island. This of course is a magnet for visitors from home and abroad; even the walker with little historical knowledge will here recall the date 1215 and King John (who sealed the first draft of the Magna Carta at this spot), and permit himself a superior smile at the hopefully apocryphal story of the touring couple who reached it at lunchtime and when seeing a sign indicating 'Magna Carta signed 1215' the wife turned to the husband and remarked, 'What a pity. We must have just missed it!'

Beyond Runnymede you pass underneath the vast M25 bridges, thus getting a tangible indication of your progress towards the capital, and then proceed beside an ugly industrial estate, while close by to the left is a vast profusion of reservoirs and lakes. Soon you enter Surrey and arrive at Staines, where the route switches to the left bank. Staines (136) has little to interest the walker or tourist, although the nineteenth-century town hall has been converted into an impressive arts centre and may be worth a quick visit.

The route progresses out of Staines along a path interspersed with a section of road, but all the way to Laleham the journey is distinctly urban in character with houses and flats immediately beside you throughout. Unusually for a national trail, many of the waymarks along the route contain mileage signs. There is little along this section to capture your attention, with the exception of Penton Hook lock. Penton Hook is in fact a huge loop of the river, and the land round which the loop threads has become an island; hence the Thames Path does not attempt to follow the loop, but cuts round the top of it. To the south-west there are more lakes, the popular Thorpe Park being situated in an island in the middle of one of them. Just beyond Penton Hook the village of Laleham appears to your left, and at last the housing thins out as the path continues through Laleham Park. However the stillness is again shattered, this time by the M3.

Soon after passing under the motorway bridge, the route reaches Chertsey Bridge, a graceful seven-arched structure, and by detouring right across the bridge you can visit the town of Chertsey itself. It is an unremarkable commuter town but does have one interesting feature, namely the curfew bell in the church. This commemorates Blanche Herriot, who at the time of the Wars of the Roses, knowing her lover was to be executed at curfew, climbed the church tower and hung on to the clapper until he was reprieved. Walkers in the legal profession will reflect wryly that with the speed at which British justice moves today, a lover trying the same thing now would need either to be excessively devoted or to have a particular liking for the uppermost reaches of ecclesiastical buildings.

The section beyond Chertsey Bridge through Chertsey Meads provides the last stretch of open meadow walking on the whole route. Continuing along the left bank, it twists and turns with the river and passes through a further built up area on the north-western fringe of Weybridge, and goes on to Shepperton. The river Wey meets the Thames at this point. There are houses on both sides of the river and in the absence of bridges or ferries, the only way from one house to another across the water is by private boat. The variety of rivercraft on this section of the Thames is huge, ranging from small motorboats and rowing boats to pleasure cruisers; houseboats gaily decorated with lines of clean washing, to rather sad-looking barges sitting, dolefully and uselessly, in bankside decay and neglect.

At the confluence of the Wey and the Thames just south of Shepperton (141.5), an area dotted with small channels and islands, the Thames Path makes use of a ferry for the only time on the route; assistance needs to be summoned by means of a bell. Any delay in engaging the service of the ferryman, who is likely to be found in the nearby boating accessory shop, is compensated for by a lovely crossing over a breathtakingly beautiful piece of water, with trees all around. When the ferry is not operational, there is an alternative route away from the river and through the old village of Shepperton with its fine church of St Nicholas dominating a little square of red brick houses off the village street.

This route then returns to the main Path at Walton Bridge by means of field-edge and roadside walking. If the ferry is available, the ferry crossing will take you to Desborough Cut, a channel which is followed by the Thames Path along its right bank in preference to the serpentine course taken by the old Thames channel round the so-called Shepperton Loops. Appropriately enough, the land separating Desborough Cut from the Loops is known as Desborough Island. The Cut, completed in 1935, has a pleasantly rural feel with fields to the right, but at Walton Bridge beside Walton-on-Thames, where the Cut effectively ends, the urban theme returns. Incidentally, one of the islands passed near the ferry crossing is known as D'Oyly Carte Island; hikers who are amateur opera buffs will immediately think of Richard D'Oyly Carte who effectively masterminded the immortal Gilbert and Sullivan partnership. However, those who visit it hoping to see a festival of open-air Gilbert and Sullivan opera here are likely to be no more successful than those hoping to hear *Crown Imperial* and *Belshazzar's Feast* being performed on Walton Bridge.

Walton-on-Thames to Teddington

Walton-on-Thames is an unexciting commuter town, and the five miles from here to Hampton Court on the right bank provide but few highlights. That notwithstanding, this section of route is extremely popular with walkers and fishermen; hikers are also likely to be passed by cyclists, ranging from the casual in their baggy T-shirt and shorts, to the committed with their skintight black Lycra and designer helmets. Early on there are the picturesque Sunbury and Molesey locks and a view over the river to Sunbury and its church which has a tower and cupola. Beyond Sunbury, the Molesey Reservoirs are situated to the right, and there is a large waterworks across the river. It is not thrilling stuff.

However, things improve with the advent of Hurst Park where there is a designated swan-feeding area; sadly on my visit I found no budding Mary Poppins offering tuppeny bags of scraps for the purpose. Across the river there are views to Bushy Park and the church at Hampton, close to which is the actor David Garrick's domed temple, built to house a statue of Shakespeare. Soon the magnificent Hampton Court Palace comes into view. There is a timely switch to the left bank, using the bridge (designed by Lutyens in 1933) carrying the A308, and the entrance to the palace (147.6) is just over that bridge.

Unless you are in a tearing hurry, a visit to the palace, created by Cardinal Wolsey in 1514 and beloved of Henry VIII, must not be missed. It contains some of the finest examples of Tudor architecture and of Christopher Wren's work. Of particular interest is Anne Boleyn's Gateway, surmounted by a splendid astronomical clock made for Henry VIII, the Great Hall with its hammer-beam roof, and of course the Maze, where the blister-clad walker can aggravate his condition still further by potentially endless futile wandering.

Assuming he escapes, the Thames Path continues with a delightful walk along the left bank to Kingston-upon-Thames, with the open expanse of Hampton Park to the left and, by contrast, the built-up areas of Thames Ditton and Surbiton to the right. Kingston, a Royal Borough, is a huge sprawling place and has for centuries been a key river crossing; although the present bridge was opened in 1828, a bridge did exist here in the thirteenth century. Seven Saxon kings were crowned at Kingston and their coronation stone is preserved here. The route uses the bridge to switch to the right bank and proceeds downstream to Teddington Lock (152.4), the last lock on the Thames. The weir here marks the beginning – or end – of the tidal section of the Thames. Of note on this section are the massive weeping willow trees on the opposite bank.

From the bridge over the Thames at Teddington Lock to Greenwich, three miles from the end of the trail, a waymarked Thames Path route exists along the full length of both the right and left banks. You may choose to switch from one to another at will, or stick to one and avoid crossing the river at any time. Of course you may opt to walk *to* Greenwich on one bank, and then return *from* Greenwich using the other, a laudable objective indeed for the walker who wishes to maximise his knowledge of the river using both right and left bank perspectives, but if motivated solely by the belief that 185 miles' pounding on the flat is somehow insufficient, then surely deserving of urgent counselling and therapy, if not expert psychoanalytical investigation.

Teddington to Putney (right bank)
The *right* bank route stays by the river and there is a positively rural feel about the immediate surroundings as Richmond is approached; there are good views ahead to the natural platform of Richmond Hill, on which Joshua Reynolds once lived. The route passes seventeenth-century Ham House, close to Petersham, a charming village with fine seventeenth and eighteenth-century houses and a splendid old church with high box pews and galleries. Soon you reach Richmond itself (155.8), another Royal borough and containing much fine Palladian architecture. Particularly

noteworthy is Maids of Honour Row that was built to house the ladies of the court during the reign of George I.

Staying right beside the river, the route continues through the Old Deer Park, past a golf course and on to the 368-acre Royal Botanic Gardens, known popularly as Kew Gardens. These were founded in 1759 and contain a collection of over 25,000 living plant species and many noble buildings including the nineteenth-century Palm House and the eighteenth-century Chinese Pagoda. A recent addition is the Princess of Wales Conservatory, a futuristic building for plants from ten different climatic zones.

Beyond Kew Gardens is Kew Bridge, and beyond that is rather nondescript urban walking as far as Chiswick Bridge. There is now a definite sense of being in London surburbia. Beyond Chiswick Bridge you can marvel at the architectural contrast between a fine blue-washed Georgian house and, almost adjacent, the vast grey pile that was once Mortlake brewery. From here it is a short walk to Barnes, with impressive Regency riverside terraces, and the home of composer Gustav Holst for a time. Beyond Barnes are the playing-fields of St Paul's public school and then the blatant Victorian extravagance of Hammersmith Suspension Bridge with its remarkable turrets of gilt and green, designed by Sir Joseph Bazalgette and built in 1887. Just beyond the bridge you pass the Harrods Furniture Depository with its twin cupolas – a useful landmark for Boat Race commentators – then proceed past a cluster of lakes and on to the busy London suburb of Putney.

Putney Bridge (164) is the starting point for the Oxford v Cambridge boat race, and although boating eights can be seen at many places on the Thames and at any time of year, they are particularly noticeable downstream of Teddington, with no locks or weirs to interrupt their progress. Walkers may be entertained by the stentorian tones of their coaches, yelling encouragement at the crews from the banks. Putney is a very popular place for crews to begin and end their activity, and on busy days, when more competitive boating is in progress, the towpath hereabouts will be alive with wet-suited oarsmen, ambulancemen, refreshment vans, and signs indicating that anyone daring to park their car in a reserved area will meet dire retribution, ranging from an on-the-spot fine to forcible removal of vital parts of the anatomy.

Teddington to Putney (left bank)

The *left* bank route, having obviously crossed the bridge at Teddington Lock, has to follow the A310 road through Teddington itself to Strawberry Hill, notable for a Gothic Revival villa, built between 1750 and 1776 for the author Horace Walpole. After the briefest flirtation with the river, the route proceeds through the centre of Twickenham and then down to the Thames again where the true riverside walking recommences. Twickenham contains some impressive seventeenth and eighteenth-century houses, a pub delightfully named the Barmy Arms, and views to an island with another lovely name, Eel Pie Island – so called because it was a popular spot for Victorians who enjoyed their *ale* and pies there! More open country is reached and the route passes Marble Hill, a lovely eighteenth-century white villa. Having passed St Margarets to the left and Richmond (156.3) over the bridge, you reach Isleworth. The highlight here is the superb eighteenth-century London Apprentice inn, although there are many other fine houses in the old village area close to the river.

The Thames Path leaves the river and enters Syon Park, with a good view to Syon House, a remodelled Tudor building topped by a stone lion, with grounds laid out in the eighteenth century by Capability Brown. Catherine Howard was a prisoner at Syon House before her execution, and the park is also the site of an English Civil War battle in 1642. Between Syon Park and Kew Bridge the walking is fiddly, as Brentford, a market town and former county town of Middlesex, is negotiated, the only real highlight being a brief brush with the Grand Union Canal, which meets the Thames here. The walking improves once you have passed Kew Bridge and reach Strand on the Green, a marvellously preserved row of old riverside houses and pubs.

The walk on past Grove Park to Chiswick Bridge is unremarkable, but beyond Chiswick Bridge you reach the open fields of Duke's Meadows and there are good views across to the river to the cheerful waterside scene at Barnes. The route negotiates a new riverside development then enjoys a very pleasant road walk through the older villagey parts of Chiswick and its neighbour Hammersmith, with fine seventeenth and eighteenth-century houses and impressive Georgian architecture. The riverside Chiswick Mall includes Kelmscott House, built around 1780, and once the home of William Morris; you may recall Kelmscot village near Lechlade earlier in the walk and its strong associations with Morris. Also in Chiswick is the seventeenth-century Hogarth's House, for fifteen years the summer home of the artist William Hogarth.

Many of Hammersmith's finest riverside houses are to be found on Hammersmith Terrace, with a number of eighteenth-century houses, inns and boathouses. Beyond Hammersmith Terrace the Thames Path itself returns to the riverside and after passing Bazalgette's remarkable bridge it is a straightforward riverside walk to Putney Bridge (166.5). To the left lies Fulham Palace, described as one of the best medieval sites in London, with buildings dating from the fifteenth century. It was the residence of the Bishops of London from the twelfth century until as recently as 1973. The only slight deviation of the Thames Path from the river is at Craven Cottage, home of Fulham Football Club. The Thames Path is the only national trail that goes directly past a Football League ground, and therefore the only occasion on which you may find yourself mingling, not with fellow hikers or casual strollers, but football supporters. Walkers with a dislike of large crowds may indeed prefer to avoid this section of the walk at a time when supporters are arriving or leaving a game, particularly if they have inadvertently attired themselves in the club colours of the away side.

Putney to Hungerford Bridge (right bank)

There is no towpath downstream of Putney, so the walking becomes more fiddly on both banks. From Putney Bridge the *right* bank route leaves the Thames almost immediately and follows along streets before returning to the river with Wandsworth Park to the right. Soon, though, the route loses the river again and proceeds through Wandsworth. This part of London was made famous for hats in the eighteenth century by the influx of Huguenot refugees who were skilled hatters, and the brewing industry has been important here since the sixteenth century. Wandsworth also has a prison, built in 1857.

Any thought of picturesque rurality has now gone; this is an uncompromising urban landscape of sprawling concrete, relieved only by parks and gardens. The route returns to the river briefly and passes Wandsworth Bridge, then leaves the river and follows roads including a section of the A3205 towards Battersea. There is then a more sustained section of riverside walking which includes a fine riverside housing development and an eighteenth-century church. Battersea Bridge is passed, and, shortly afterwards, Albert Bridge. Built in 1873 it is a riot of gold, green and pink, but it is also weak; a notice warns marching troops to break step before crossing!

Beyond Albert Bridge there is pleasant riverside walking past Battersea Park, which houses an impressive 100ft high 'peace pagoda'. At Chelsea Bridge you leave the river and follow a road beside the park, passing a smart athletics track, then endure a messy walk back to the river beside traffic-choked roads, including another section of the A3205, and passing underneath the main railway lines into Victoria. There are two features of interest on this otherwise rather grim section: firstly Battersea power station, designed by Giles Gilbert Scott and built in the 1930s, closed in 1983 and redeveloped with a view to reuse as a leisure complex, and secondly the Dogs' Home, which was opened in 1860. The Path goes right past the home, and the sound of the dogs can easily be heard from the pavement. It is a relief to get back to the river at Nine Elms, close to the new Covent Garden market, for it is now straightforward riverside walking via the Albert Embankment all the way to Hungerford Bridge.

You pass two bridges, Vauxhall Bridge and Lambeth Bridge, but the undoubted highlight of this section is Lambeth Palace, home of the Archbishops of Canterbury for the past 750 years. It was begun in the thirteenth century and has been added to many times, its best building being the Great Hall of 1660. The march to Westminster Bridge (172) and on past the former Greater London Council buildings, through Jubilee Gardens to Hungerford Bridge, is particularly satisfying. In Jubilee Gardens is the magnificent Millennium Wheel, its rotating capsules giving superb views across London and up and down the river. With the Houses of Parliament and Big Ben to be seen across the river, there is a definite feeling, after so much messy walking from Putney, of having arrived in the heart of the capital. All human life is to be seen accompanying the walker along these walkways, from the sad tramps and beggars surveying the ground for discarded portions of takeaway meals, to wealthy men-about-town, striding confidently ahead, their glances pavementwards confined to checks for scuff marks on their new Gucci shoes.

Putney to Hungerford Bridge (left bank)

The *left* bank route also leaves the river immediately at Putney Bridge and makes an extravagant arc round Hurlingham Park which includes the Hurlingham Club and associated multifarious sports facilities. You stay with the river past Wandsworth Bridge, alongside wharves which may well remind you of former days when the Thames was of considerably greater commercial importance, and then pass a big retail park which in its way is another indicator of our changing world. After leaving the riverside and following roads to Sands End, you reach Chelsea Harbour, a most impressive marina with plush vessels surrounded by magnificent new buildings. During the rest of the journey you will see many more exciting modern waterside complexes, sitting cheek by jowl with rundown, often derelict areas that cry out for redevelopment. Indeed, just beyond Chelsea Harbour you reach Lots Road, with rows of older terraced houses that are considerably less aesthetically pleasing than the marina. Things do improve quickly, however; at the end of Lots Road you reach Cheyne Walk and from here the route follows the river all the way to the Houses of Parliament. The fine embankments on both sides of the river were the work of Joseph Bazalgette, chief engineer of the Board of Works and creator of Hammersmith Bridge (see above). Cheyne Walk contains many fine early eighteenth-century houses; their inhabitants have included the novelists George Eliot and Henry James, and the poet and painter Dante Gabriel Rossetti.

The route follows the Chelsea Embankment past the magnificent Albert Bridge and then the Royal Hospital and its grounds, where the annual Chelsea Flower Show is held. The Hospital, built by Wren and founded in 1682 by Charles II for invalid and veteran soldiers, is lodged in by several hundred Army pensioners today; they are a distinctive sight with their scarlet frock coats. Also of interest nearby is the Chelsea Physic Garden for botanical research, established in the seventeenth century.

After proceeding past Chelsea Bridge, you continue alongside Grosvenor Road and Millbank, passing the tiny Pimlico Gardens and the colourful and ornate Vauxhall Bridge. Between Vauxhall Bridge and Lambeth Bridge is the Tate Gallery; opened in 1897, it contains unique collections of the work of J. M. W. Turner and William Blake. Beyond Lambeth Bridge the route passes through gardens to reach the Houses of Parliament. Parts of the present Gothic-style building, designed by Sir Charles Barry and A. W. Pugin, go back to the mid-nineteenth-century, but the House of Commons was destroyed in an air-raid in 1941 and has been rebuilt to its old character. Big Ben, which many erroneously believe to be the clock towering above the Houses of Parliament (it is in fact the bell which chimes every 15 minutes) was named after Sir Benjamin Hall, First Commissioner of Works at the time the bell was cast at Whitechapel Bell Foundry in 1858. Westminster Bridge (173.5) lies immediately beyond; the bridge was the work of Thomas Page in the nineteenth-century, and the large statue on the bank here, completed in 1902, is of Boudicca, Queen of the Iceni.

The route continues to Hungerford Bridge along the Victoria Embankment, past Westminster Pier where, as at many other spots nearby, river trips are available. Hungerford Bridge on the left bank is the closest that you get on the Thames Path to the West End and its unrivalled eating and shopping facilities. With several miles still to walk, and only limited rucksack space, it might be seen as a little unwise for the hiker to embark on a spending spree in Piccadilly or Oxford Street, but if he is beginning to feel the effects of his walk from rural Gloucestershire, has a few pounds to spare, and wishes to impress present or prospective hiking partners, he could not be blamed for making a detour to Fortnum and Mason in search of their own-brand English Breakfast Tea and Foot Embrocation Cream.

Hungerford Bridge to Greenwich (right bank)

From Hungerford Bridge – an undoubted eyesore for which at the time of writing there are major refurbishment plans – the *right* bank walk stays with the river virtually all the way to Tower Bridge. It continues past the Royal Festival Hall and Waterloo Bridge, beyond which is the National Theatre, built in 1976. Next comes the exuberant Gabriel's Wharf plaza, the so-called Oxo tower, which houses modern shops, eateries and offices, and the ornate Blackfriars Bridge, which opened in 1869. Between here and Southwark Bridge there are three features of particular interest. The most notable is the thatched timber-framed reconstruction of the Globe Theatre; built by Shakespeare and others in 1599, it burned down in 1613 and was rebuilt in 1995. The other very exciting features of note hereabouts are the former Bankside Power Station, which has been converted into the Tate Gallery of Modern Art, and the new Millennium Bridge. Designed to provide easy pedestrian access to St Paul's Cathedral, this suffered major teething problems after opening in spring 2000 and had to be shut again almost immediately!

The route moves slightly away from the river to pass along the narrow Clink Street, site of the medieval Winchester Palace of which but a few traces remain. From the airy riverside walking it is quite a shock to be walking along this narrow lane with forbidding old stone buildings rising up on each side, one of which is a former jail that is now a museum. Before returning to the waterside, the route passes within sight of Southwark Cathedral; dating back to 1220, it is the earliest Gothic church in London. Nearby is London Bridge and its station of the same name. Beyond London Bridge the route returns to the riverside, passing a large new office and shopping complex, and then the warship HMS *Belfast*, which saw service in the Second World War and the Korean War and is now open to the public. Just beyond HMS *Belfast* is Tower Bridge (174.5). Built between 1886 and 1894, with bascules that weigh

1200 tons each, it is the last bridge over the Thames that walkers will see on the Thames Path.

After Tower Bridge the character of the route along the right bank changes. The busy tourist areas are now left behind and you see a different, albeit equally fascinating, side of London, and tangible reminders of its immense importance as a busy port. But although the warehouses and wharves still remain, they are now unused and empty, with bigger ships demanding deeper water and better facilities. From the ashes of a dead industry has a risen a phoenix in the form of massive development. The following stretch through Bermondsey and Rotherhithe, where the Thames swings southwards, sees you following long-established riverside walks, roads set slightly back from the river with closely-packed housing on either side, or new walkways which have been incorporated into the modern complexes. One moment you will pass a brand new block of luxury flats, and the next you will meet reminders of an earlier age, in the form of cobbled streets, cosy pubs and, at one point, a pumphouse which was built in 1930 to control Surrey Docks' water level. Efforts have been made to create some rurality amidst the concrete; there is now a nature park at Rotherhithe with pond and trees, and nearby there is a working city farm with a good variety of animals. The route runs right through the farm when it is open.

Soon after Surrey Docks, the right bank path moves well away from the river, and there is an uninspiring trudge through Deptford, with traffic noise, largely absent for many miles, returning with a vengeance. Francis Drake was knighted at Deptford and Peter the Great of Russia studied shipbuilding here, but apart from the old church of St Nicholas there is little to fire the imagination, and it is a relief to return to the river at Greenwich (180.3). Greenwich is at the bottom of a distinctive loop of the Thames, and it may be seen as a sad reflection on the popular culture of the age that the loop owes its familiarity not so much to the field trips organised so painstakingly by geography teachers but the designers of the opening titles of *EastEnders*.

Hungerford Bridge to Greenwich (left bank)

From Hungerford Bridge, the *left* bank walk proceeds alongside the river past Cleopatra's Needle, an ancient Egyptian granite obelisk that was moved to England in 1878. After Waterloo Bridge the route continues past the eighteenth-century Somerset House, once the general register office for births, marriages and deaths. You remain by the river past the impressive HMS *President* and Blackfriars Bridge as far as the new Millennium Bridge. However, from then on as far as Tower Bridge, past Southwark Bridge and London Bridge, the route is often forced away from the riverbank along parallel roads and walkways from which the river is obscured from view. Apart from St Paul's Cathedral, well signposted and easily reached from the Thames Path, and the fine old church of St Magnus the Martyr, which is right on the route, there is not the variety of attractions that exist on the right bank, although the new high-rise office buildings and luxury flats may be of interest to students of modern architecture. There are, however, good views to the multifarious attractions on the right bank.

At length you reach the Tower of London, home of the Crown Jewels and site of the imprisonment and execution of Thomas More, the Duke of Monmouth, two wives of Henry VIII, and many others. Tower Bridge (176.8) lies immediately beyond, and after that comes St Katherine's Dock, one of many rejuvenated areas of London dockland. This is particularly rewarding for the visitor, with Thomas Telford's huge warehouses being converted to shops, restaurants, and pubs; the waterside theme is maintained through the presence of ships of both ancient and modern design, with traditional sailing ships sitting alongside massive luxury cruisers. The character of the route changes now, and the tourists are largely left behind as you proceed along Wapping High Street. As on the right bank, modern development sits alongside often rundown and derelict old building, although along cobbled streets there are many pretty old houses and pubs, notably the Prospect of Whitby. Wapping, like the Tower, also saw executions, being the site of the execution docks; Captain Kidd was one of those executed here for crimes on the High Seas.

The route passes into Shadwell, where the northern end of the Rotherhithe Tunnel is situated, and follows a road named Narrow Street. There is more modern development here, including luxury flats with balconies looking down on the carefully redeveloped and refurbished waterfronts, and more new property is being built all the time. I was struck by the contrast between plush new property adjoining unappealing mudflats and shells of yet more prospective dwellings. Security is understandably tight, but many short stretches of riverside walkway are available, and as in Wapping, there are many houses of character including some fine Georgian red brick buildings.

Beyond Shadwell, the river begins its loop down to Greenwich. The area of land within the loop is known as the Isle of Dogs, formerly notable for its shipbuilding. You begin right by the river but soon are forced on to Westferry Road, which takes you round the edge of Millwall towards Greenwich. At length you reach the Greenwich foot tunnel (182.3) and use it to cross the river and be reunited with the right bank route for the first time since Teddington Lock. On the way to the tunnel, you leave Westferry Road twice, firstly for a pleasant foray into John McDougall Gardens, and secondly to visit Burrell's Wharf. This is a splendid, one might say Italianate, development; nearby is the Great Eastern Pier, a reminder that Brunel's famous *Great Eastern* ship was launched from the Isle of Dogs in 1858.

If you scan the river itself, with its backcloth of high-rise concrete on the other side, you will see nothing to rival Brunel's masterpiece today. There are a few container vessels but they do seem to be outnumbered by passenger craft. Westferry Road, apart from a splendid Victorian Presbyterian chapel, contains nothing of interest, with unattractive suburban housing plus the occasional dingy convenience store dominating the scene. It is all so different from the serene world of Lechlade or Clifton Hampden, where proposals to construct a single new block of luxury flats one fifth of the size of some seen in this section would provoke wrath from every conservationist within fifty miles, and delight desperate local newspaper editors by providing enough copy to fill their letters pages for six months.

Greenwich to Thames Barrier

There is lots to see in Greenwich, most notably the National Maritime Museum, designed by Wren in 1694 as a naval hospital and later housing the Royal Naval College. Also of interest is Queen's House, designed by Inigo Jones in 1637 and the first Palladian-style building in England, and, in Greenwich Park, the building which formerly housed the Royal Observatory, founded in 1675 by Charles II. The zero line of longitude, local time on which is known as Greenwich Mean Time, passes right through it, although the observatory itself has since moved to Cambridge. For lovers of old ships the focal point of Greenwich will be the *Cutty Sark*; built in 1869 and one of the great tea-clippers, it is now preserved as a museum. *Gipsy Moth*, in which Francis Chichester circumnavigated the world in 1966–7, is also here. The Thames Path follows the right bank out of Greenwich beside the river, past some working river wharves, but rather than following the riverbank right round the next bend, leaves it and takes a short cut, rejoining the river downstream of the bend, and staying with it until the end of the route.

The short cut takes you over the A102 just before that road plunges into the Blackwall Tunnel, and past the Millennium Dome on the left. Designed by the Richard Rogers Partnership, it opened on 31 December 1999 and in its opening months housed a variety of exhibitions combining education and leisure, although it was constantly plagued by well-publicised financial troubles. Covering an area of nearly 20 acres, and 164ft high, the Dome is certainly well worth a detour for a closer look, whatever its planned use may be. In November 2000, police at the Dome foiled what would have been one of the biggest robberies in history, when an audacious attempt was made to remove the priceless Millennium jewels from the building.

Returning to the Thames Path, there is just a mile or so of riverside walking to go, with the Barrier – the end of the route – in sight. To reach it involves a rather dismal trudge through a bleak landscape, with big industrial estates and works dominating the scene. The 1,706ft long Barrier, completed in 1982 is, however, a most impressive climax to the walk. While its stainless steel hoods shoot from the water like sea monsters from a sci-fi movie, the flood gates remain submerged and are rotated into position when exceptionally high tides are expected. Up until 1996 this had happened over two hundred times. You pass underneath the control centre to arrive at the magnificent mural on the wall of the subway depicting the river from source to finish (183.5 via right bank route, 185.5 via left bank route). Nearby I also found a spotlessly clean and friendly café, with a very good information centre, from which I needed only a short walk to Charlton station to commence the homeward journey.

The river itself carries on for some 25–30 miles and you may express some sadness that the route does not in fact extend all the way to the mouth of the river, thereby giving you a complete overview of the Thames from start to finish. However a closer look at the map, and the knowledge that a continuation to the river mouth would entail journeying through or by Erith, Greenhithe, Northfleet, Gravesend, Grays, Tilbury, Canvey Island and many more places of equally doubtful interest to the visitor, may quickly persuade you that the Countryside Commission were wise not to trouble your blistered feet any further.

SUMMARY OF PLACES OF INTEREST
Source stone, Ashton Keynes, Cricklade, Inglesham, Lechlade★, St John's Lock, Radcot Bridge, Newbridge, Godstow, Oxford★, Iffley, Abingdon, Culham, Clifton Hampden, Wittenham Clumps, Wallingford, Goring, Pangbourne, Mapledurham, Sonning, Shiplake, Henley★, Medmenham, Marlow★, Cliveden, Boveney, Windsor, Runnymede, Hampton Court★, Richmond★.

NB: Beyond Richmond you effectively enter the heart of London where every Thames-side district could be said to be a place of interest.

AMENITIES ON OR NEAR THE ROUTE
Ashton Keynes (L), Cricklade, Lechlade, Eynsham (L), Oxford★, Abingdon, Benson (L), Wallingford, Cholsey (L), Goring on Thames, Tilehurst, Reading★, Sonning (L), Shiplake, Henley, Marlow, Bourne End (L), Maidenhead, Windsor★.

NB: Beyond Windsor amenities of most descriptions are easily available within a few minutes of just about every available exit from the route!

The Peddars Way and Norfolk Coast Path

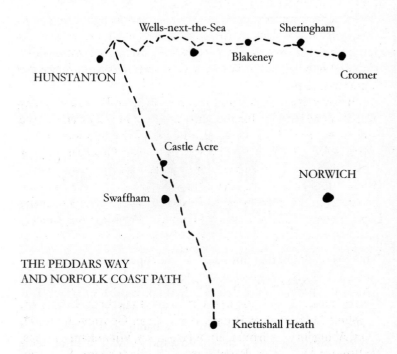

Length: 93 miles.
Start: Knettishall Heath, Suffolk.
Finish: Cromer, Norfolk.
Nature: A largely level walk along a stretch of old Roman road, and then a section of Norfolk Coast Path. The Peddars Way section makes up the first half of the walk, the Norfolk Coast Path the second. The two sections join at Holme-next-the-Sea, just outside Hunstanton.
Difficulty rating: Easy.
Average time of completion: 7 days.

The Peddars Way and Norfolk Coast Path

There is no doubt that this national trail, opened by the Prince of Wales in 1986, is a very undemanding route, and arguably the easiest national trail to complete, especially if taken in short stages. Any hills are very gentle – the path rarely climbs more than 300ft above sea level – and there are no technical demands on the walker. This is one of the driest parts of the country, and you will be unfortunate to meet bad weather, especially in summer. However, whilst on the face of it the journey represents an ideal introduction to national trail walking, it may still not rank as a great experience even for the first-time long-distance hiker. The attraction of the Norfolk Coast Path section of the walk, which starts at Hunstanton, is beyond doubt. The Norfolk coast is one of the richest areas in Britain for viewing seabirds at all times of year, and its salt marshes provide a great diversity of plant life. There are also many attractive coastal villages and towns with fine old buildings and some particularly interesting churches. The going, along the flat for most of the way, is largely very easy, although there is one tough stretch of walking on soft sand dunes, and another on shingle.

The Peddars Way section is, however, rather less satisfying. The Peddars Way was a Roman road which was built following the extensive Romanisation of Norfolk in the aftermath of the unsuccessful revolt inspired by Boudicca in AD 61, and it is thought that the Way was initially used to police the remnants of the tribes of the Iceni that remained following the revolt. The complete route linked the Roman garrison in Colchester to anchorages or a ferry on the north Norfolk coast, and the Way has since enjoyed extensive use by peasants, pilgrims and many others. The section that has been incorporated into the national trail faithfully follows the northern half of the original route for much of its course, passing through pleasant Norfolk countryside including the fascinating Breckland area, and close to a number of villages and small towns which repay a brief detour or stop. However there is not the endless interest and scenic variety which other national trails provide. Moreover, you may be disappointed not to be able to follow the whole Way from Colchester, which would near enough have created a coast to coast route. As it is, you are left, for the Peddars Way section at any rate, with a path which it has been suggested rather unkindly, 'starts in the middle of nowhere, ends in the middle of nowhere, and goes nowhere in between!'

The route begins at Knettishall Heath in Suffolk, and for its first section, as far as Little Cressingham, it passes right through Breckland. Brecks are defined as 'patches of exhausted land.' The shallow soil of this area was nutrient-poor as long ago as the Middle Ages, due to overgrazing, and farmers moved to richer pastures, leaving a waste of exposed sandy heathland on which conifer forests were planted to stabilise the soil and act as windbreaks. The area has now become a haven for wildlife and plant life. The heaths are now home in summer to 90 per cent of Britain's stone curlews; other feathered inhabitants of Breckland at various times of year include the ringed plover, tree pipit and woodlark.

A great range of butterflies populate the area, red deer can be seen in the forest, and you may also spot a brown hare. Breckland was the last mainland stronghold of the red squirrel, but the species is now almost extinct in this area and it will be a fortunate walker indeed who finds one. There are many species of wild flowers and plants which are very rare elsewhere, such as the Spanish catchfly, spring speedwell and grape hyacinth.

The start of the route, by a minor road at Knettishall Heath, is right in the heart of Breckland, some distance from Thetford, the nearest town, and quite a way from any railway station or regular bus route. Whilst this ensures that you are spared a gloomy hike through an area of suburban housing, it presents a certain amount of logistical difficulty for which the only practicable solution may be a taxi ride from Thetford. Taxi drivers ferrying long-distance walkers will react in different ways to hearing the purpose of their customers' ride. Some drivers, perhaps walkers themselves, will express great interest in the walk being undertaken, and may suggest detours to off-route sights as well as good eateries and pubs. Others, however, will remark, 'Rather you than me' and refer smugly to the fact that this is their last job before their shift ends and they will shortly be heading home for a hearty breakfast and a few hours well-earned kip. On a cold, wet, windy day it will indeed be a hardy walker who is not tempted not only to abandon his planned 20-mile hike but to ask the driver if he might join him at the breakfast table.

Knettishall Heath to the A47

You begin by heading north through pretty woodland, but almost immediately turn north-east to cross the Little Ouse and enter Norfolk, then proceed resolutely in a north-westerly direction across classic Breckland countryside. Soon the Way crosses the A1066 Thetford–Diss road, but by turning left down the road you reach Brettenham Church, lying on the edge of the picturesque Shadwell Park. This was an important crossing point of the River Thet, and a Roman village existed here between the first and fourth century AD. The Peddars Way crosses the Thet further east and continues north-west along good paths, with forestry dominating the views to your right, and the wide expanse of Brettenham Heath visible to your left. You then cross two important thoroughfares, namely the very busy A11 London–Norwich road, and then the Thetford–Norwich railway. The route proceeds through the forest of Roudham Heath and then continues through more open country to Stonebridge, on the A1075 Thetford–Watton road. Stonebridge itself (6.5) is uninteresting, though the enthusiast of old railways will doubtless appreciate the robust brickwork of an old bridge on the now disused Thetford–Watton line.

Just to the west of Stonebridge is East Wretham, beyond which is Wretham Park. This contains some fine reed-fringed lakes, which vary in levels as the water rises from the underlying chalk; dry one season, dark and deep the next. Beyond Stonebridge, forestry becomes even more dominant as the route heads north-westwards towards Little Cressingham. Initially you follow a metalled road, then proceed on a stony track through extensive woodland, with much of the surrounding countryside owned by the Ministry of Defence. At length you reach another attractive lake, Thompson Water, which was created by damming a tributary of the delightfully-named River Wissey nearby. On a dry warm morning you may see roe deer from the nearby woodlands taking a drink here.

By turning right just beyond Thompson Water it is possible to reach the village of Thompson, which has a pretty church of knapped flint, dating back to the early fourteenth century but sadly no guarantee of anything to assuage the sweaty hiker's thirst. Although there are many pleasant villages close to the route, you would be naïve to assume, whatever the local guide or map may say, that refreshments will be available at any of them, and although the thought of lugging a bumper pack of ten-for-the-price-of-six fruit drinks seems unpalatable when loading an already crammed rucksack, it becomes positively enchanting when compared with the thought of badgering the occupiers of The Old Tea House, The Old Post Office or The Old Village Stores with a request to refill an already empty water bottle.

Beyond Thompson Water the route passes through a lovely pine wood known as Shakers' Furze, then skirts Merton Wood and Merton Park. The park, populated by horses and geese, contains an interesting church including a Jacobean two-decker pulpit and a splendid font with angel wings. The little town of Watton lies beyond to the north-east. The national trail, however, moves away to the north-west and out of Breckland into more open farmland.

You join a farm track to reach the B1108 and then turn left to follow a path running parallel with that road as far as Little Cressingham.

It is worth taking a short detour to the right off this path to inspect the round-towered Threxton Church, which has a fine porch and excellent thirteenth-century north arcade. There is a useful pub at Little Cressingham (14.5), but its most noteworthy historical feature is a set of four bowl barrows over 200ft in diameter, one of which was found to contain an early Bronze Age Wessex burial. Great Cressingham, two miles to the north-west and off the route, has a church with a particularly good roof and chancel, and nearby there is an old priory and a fragment of a sumptuous sixteenth-century brick house.

The eleven miles of the Peddars Way from Little Cressingham to Castle Acre, still heading north-west, sees an almost exclusive reliance on metalled roads which, whilst allowing fast and easy progress, can be tiring on the feet. You climb gently to Caundle Common and then maintain a parallel course with the River Wissey, passing close to the neo-Georgian Pickenham Hall which lies immediately to your left as you cross the B1077 at South Pickenham. Soon afterwards the route turns left on to another minor road that crosses the Wissey and passes through North Pickenham. The winding course of this road from Little Cressingham contrasts with the dead-straight walking that has characterised much of what you have done so far, but when the metalled road out of North Pickenham reaches a crossroads you go straight on over, and the walking becomes straight and true once more.

This is known as Procession Lane, the name derived from the ancient custom of beating the bounds. Historically, beating the bounds meant marking parish boundaries by walking round them and striking certain points with rods. However, any illusions of having been transported to a more leisurely age are shattered when you reach the A47 Kings Lynn–Norwich trunk road, with a Drive-Thru MacDonalds clearly visible to the left. The nature-loving walker may in normal circumstances be quick to condemn such places as a crass and insensitive intrusion into a rural unspoilt landscape, although it could perhaps become less easy for him to do so when he finds his supplies are short and he, too, is making the brief detour to join the queue for an Egg MacMuffin and regular fries.

The A47 to Hunstanton

By turning left on to the A47 you will shortly reach the town of Swaffham, a useful place for the replenishment of supplies. Features of note in the town include the church of St Peter and St Paul with its squadron of 88 flying angels in its roof, a huge marketplace with an eighteenth-century market cross, and a rotunda built by Horace Walpole. One of Swaffham's most famous residents was John Chapman, known as the Pedlar of Swaffham; it is said he went to London in search of treasure, and on his way met a man who spoke of having dreamt of treasure in the Pedlar's garden. Chapman returned, found the treasure there, and used the money to build part of the church.

Returning to the national trail, the route uses a combination of winding track and metalled road to head on towards Castle Acre. The only real highlight of this walk is Palgrave Hall, situated close to the site of the medieval village of Great Palgrave of which there is now no trace. Easy walking beyond Palgrave Hall takes you to Castle Acre itself (26.4). The village, enclosed by earthworks of a castle built by the son-in-law of William the Conqueror, has a good range of amenities and a number of interesting features. Arguably the most notable is the ruin of Cluniac Priory, in a lovely setting amongst well-kept lawns. The west front of the priory church contains one of Britain's finest surviving tiers of Norman arcading, and one of the prior's rooms is still intact and contains a small museum.

The village contains several other attractive old buildings, many of flint; particularly noteworthy is the Ostrich Inn, with its huge fireplaces and beamed ceilings. The church of St James has a superb font cover and an ornate pulpit which incorporates painted panels of saints in deep blues, reds and golds, with texts emanating from their mouths. It has an early Gothic door, the opening of which may have been high enough for a knight in full armour to ride into the sanctuary for a blessing before a battle, without having to go to the trouble of dismounting. Since it is situated just a few miles north-west of the Drive-Thru MacDonalds, it seems wonderfully appropriate that Simon Jenkins, writing in *England's Thousand Best Churches*, should describe it as the world's first drive-in church!

For the 18 miles or so from Castle Acre to Ringstead (which lies just a couple of miles from the end of the Peddars Way section) the route continues north-westwards through unspectacular but pleasant rolling countryside, tending to bypass places of habitation. As it sticks faithfully to the old Roman road virtually throughout, the walking is straightforward and easy. Immediately after leaving Castle Acre there is a stretch of walking of some three miles either on, or beside, a metalled road. At a triangulation point signifying one of the highest points of the route – still only 302ft! – the metalled section ends and from here right up to Ringstead the walking is on good farm tracks, the only contact with motorised traffic occurring at the infrequent road crossings. Soon after forsaking tarmac for the farm track, the route crosses three roads in close succession, beginning with the B1145 Kings Lynn–Aylsham road, while detouring right down the second or third one brings you to Great Massingham. This is a very pretty village with a large pond, an attractive church with a fine porch and fourteenth-century font, and further facilities for rest and refreshment.

Back on the route, the next major crossing is at Harpley Dams (33.7) on the A148 Kings Lynn–Fakenham road just west of Harpley. It is worth following the busy road to this village to inspect its magnificent church, described as a superb work of decorated Gothic craftsmanship, with some splendid bench-end carvings depicting bears, monkeys, mythical beasts and bishops. The gentlest of inclines takes you on to Harpley Common, dotted with tumuli.

At the next road crossing, a detour along the road to the left will take you to Anmer, which as well as a fourteenth-century church contains a hall with a late Georgian brick façade, while east of the village there is a fine bell barrow. You then cross the B1153 Gayton–Brancaster road, enjoying fine views to the beautiful woods of the Houghton Hall estate. There is a splendidly remote feel to the walking hereabouts, with colour being provided in the summer by the profusion of poppies and rosebay willowherb. One other feature to look out for, over to the right, is the restored brick tower mill near the village of Great Bircham, which sounds as though it ought to be the setting for a 1940s comedy about an eccentric boarding-school headmaster.

You pass close by the village of Fring (40.4), which has a pretty woodland setting and an imposing church tower, but beyond Fring the feeling of remoteness begins to disappear, with more houses and hamlets dotted around the countryside. You cross the B1454 just east of the village of Sedgeford, and pass right by the Sedgeford Magazine, which looks rather like an old chapel but is in fact thought to have been built as an armoury or powder store shortly before the English Civil War. The route crosses a stretch of dismantled railway, which once linked Hunstanton with Wells-next-the-Sea, and continues on to Ringstead.

The village, the first community of any size actually on the route since Castle Acre, has one or two interesting features, including the tower of the ruined church of St Peter within the garden of a Georgian house, and a brick tower mill. The village also has a good range of facilities and you may be fortunate enough to find a cup of tea, a much-needed reward for pounding the tracks. For walkers doing the whole national trail, Ringstead is a major watershed in the route, marking the end of the 'lonely' part of the walk and the entry into an area that is immensely popular with both casual day visitors and holidaymakers, and from now until Cromer, other people will never be far away.

After a moderate climb out of the village on a metalled road, there is the exciting sight of the sea for the first time. The route leaves the metalled road just beyond the mill to follow a path down to the busy A149 north Norfolk coast road, then after crossing that, a metalled road is followed to Seagate (46.4), just to the west of Holme-next-the-Sea. Here the Peddars Way part of the walk ends, and you meet the Norfolk Coast Path.

However, to turn *right* along the Coast Path eastwards towards Cromer – the ultimate objective – would mean missing the initial stretch of the Norfolk Coast Path, which has actually started at Hunstanton, two miles to the *left*! A solution which may appeal to you will be to use a bus or taxi from here to Hunstanton, and then begin the Norfolk Coast Path from there. However, neither form of motorised transport can be guaranteed to be available when required, unless you have been particularly well-organised with planning and scheduling. The chances are that in the time taken and the money spent in procuring the services of GetUThere Cab Hire (*'comfy cabs and relaxing rides'*), you could have proceeded to Hunstanton under your own steam and enjoyed a relaxing three-course meal on a verandah overlooking the sea, followed by a session at Giovanni's Foot Masseur (*'blisters our speciality'*) next door.

Hunstanton to Stiffkey

Hunstanton is a pleasant seaside town with an essentially Victorian atmosphere and wide sandy beaches, and in the summer it becomes packed with holidaymakers. Centuries of erosion have undermined the cliffs near the town, revealing multicoloured layers of rock in stripes of red and white chalk and a form of brown sandstone known as carr stone. The town is unusual in being the only East Anglian coastal town to face west, looking out to the Wash. The Wash itself is interesting, being the second largest area of intertidal mudflats in Great Britain and home to rich communities of starfish and molluscs as well as a breeding colony of common seals. The area attracts a great number of birds, including brent geese, curlew, dunlin and knot, of which huge numbers congregate in winter. Indeed, much of the Norfolk coast is a birdwatcher's paradise. The start of the Norfolk Coast Path is indicated by a helpful national trail information board close to some ornamental gardens on the seafront.

The journey begins with a pleasant walk along a wide greensward, then after passing the coastguard lookout and St Edmund's Point you have a punishing tramp over the dunes behind the beach huts at Old Hunstanton, before an easier walk along the golf course approach road and then a section of narrow dirt track between the golf course and the river Hun. In due course you reach the join with the Peddars Way (2.7 from Hunstanton; all mileages hereafter are from Hunstanton) and the route then continues through the Gore Point nature reserve to the north of Holme, by means of a boardwalk laid across the dunes. Between the dunes are pools, known as slacks, which host many marsh-loving plants, most notably the marsh helleborine. Natterjack toads can be found in the marram tussocks and, on the edge of the woodland on the reserve, you can observe flycatchers and redstarts whilst the early summer brings green hairstreak butterflies on the gorse and brambles. You leave the boardwalk to follow the sea defence bank into Thornham (6.2).

Progress may well be slow along this stretch in summer, not because of the difficulty of the terrain, but the constant need to give way to other walkers. The sweaty national trail hiker hauling his heavy rucksack through the mid-afternoon heat with many miles to go will still hopefully forge a reasonably expeditious path past flip-flop-clad families who, out for their post-Sunday lunch stroll, will regard him with a mixture of sympathy, admiration and pity as they let him pass. Some parents may in fact feel a twinge of envy and nostalgia if they recall undertaking similar exploits themselves before their turn came to attempt to coax screaming offspring to undergo a walk taking them any more than two hundred yards from the family car.

Thornham is a fine village, with a busy harbour, three pubs, a Georgian hall, a large Iron Age earthwork and a partially thirteenth-century church with a very wide high nave. There is no coastal path available between Thornham and Brancaster, so rather than following the main A149 road through Titchwell the route heads inland, climbing south-eastwards away from Thornham on a metalled road, using farm tracks to progress east, and turning left to drop to Brancaster on another metalled road. The sea is clearly visible but it is a shame to miss out on the RSPB reserve at Titchwell, which contains a wide range of species including bearded tits, marsh harriers, godwits and avocets. A detour to the reserve is recommended when the A149 is reached at Brancaster (10.2), a pleasant village with a fourteenth-century church.

There is then a straightforward boardwalked route beside Brancaster Marsh to Brancaster Staithe, where refreshments should be available. The route then follows a path parallel with the A149 between the buildings of Brancaster Staithe and the marshes as far as Burnham Deepdale. From Burnham Deepdale you follow the sea bank all the way to Burnham Overy Staithe, with creeks, marshes and dunes all around. This is superb bird-watching country. To your left is Scolt Head Island, a National Trust-owned nature reserve which is home to thousands of nesting Sandwich terns, as well as gannets, skuas and oystercatchers; it may be possible to join a boat trip to the island from Brancaster Staithe. Even from the Coast Path itself, you should look out for red-throated divers, wigeons, teals, grey plovers, sanderlings and snipes.

The route reaches the A149 again by a windmill, and it is then a short walk north-eastwards alongside the A149 to Burnham Overy Staithe (16.2). This is a large village, popular with holidaymakers, and the closest you get to Burnham Thorpe, where Lord Nelson was born in 1758. Beyond Burnham Overy Staithe the route heads out again to the marshes between the A149 and the sea, initially following a good boardwalk but this gives out and there follows a weary trudge over the sand dunes across part of the extensive Holkham Nature Reserve, with woodland to the right and Holkham Bay to the left. The Reserve contains salt marshes which include a rich diversity of special plants, including sea lavender, sea pea and sea heath. No doubt to your relief, at Holkham Gap you leave the dry sands and enter the woodland.

There is a road hereabouts leading to Holkham village and the eighteenth-century Palladian Holkham Hall, which contains an impressive art collection. The road to Holkham Gap is often busy with holidaymakers heading for the wetter, firmer sands beyond the dunes (you may have resorted to these anyway!). You pick up a firmer path on the south side of the woods, and at Abram's Bosom Lake you join a road which proceeds south in a straight line to reach the seaside town of Wells-next-the-Sea (22.9). Famous for its sprat and whelk trade, Wells is the only port on the north Norfolk coast to have a usable harbour, and from the cheerful quayside, you can observe a variety of sea-going vessels. The route leaves Wells and follows a good path just inland of the Wells and Warham salt marshes; in the winter it is worth looking across the marshes for wintering wild pink-footed and brent geese.

Soon to your right you will see the village of Stiffkey, with its sixteenth-century flint-built hall, while on nearby Warborough Hill there is an Iron Age barrow. One of the vicars of Stiffkey, Harold Davidson, was known as the 'prostitutes' parson' because of his frequent forays to Soho. The village is also well-known for Stewkey Blues, which are in fact cockles; this may come as something of a disappointment to the overnight visitor who, having seen their availability advertised in the village, might have believed them to be the local football team or a band providing a night's entertainment at the village pub.

Stiffkey to Gramborough Hill

You proceed beside the marshes, passing the village of Morston with a church that boasts a thirteenth-century west tower, and continue on to Blakeney (30.4). This is a beautiful brick and flint village with some fine buildings, including the Georgian Red House on the quay, and the old Guildhall, which has a fourteenth-century undercroft. Its waterfront is crowded with yachts and cruisers; now the estuary has silted up, the village is no longer viable as a commercial port and only small pleasure boats can sail up the channel. It has a fine church with two towers, one of which is over 100ft high and is a prominent landmark for miles around. Between the village and the sea lies Blakeney Point, another National Trust-owned nature reserve and reachable only by boat from Blakeney, but accessible on foot from Cley next the Sea beyond the river Glaven. The Point is a breeding-ground for oystercatchers, terns and gulls, and in the summer you can see flowering sea-holly and the yellow-horned poppy.

The route continues by the area of marshes and creeks known as Blakeney Eye – with a similar area known as Cley Eye across the Glaven – then follows alongside the Glaven to reach Cley (33.3). The whole walk from Blakeney to Cley is fascinating at any time of year. The winter brings the twite, snow bunting and shore lark, the summer may see ringed plovers and marsh harriers, and in the autumn you may get sightings of rare migrants such as bluethroat, wryneck and warbler.

Cley, like Blakeney, is a most attractive village with flint-built houses and an early eighteenth-century windmill. There is a fine church, largely rebuilt in the fourteenth century, containing many interesting nave arch carvings including a musician, a lion chewing on a bone, and St George fighting what Simon Jenkins says looks like a 'domesticated village dragon!' The village, despite being called Cley next the Sea, is locally pronounced 'Cly' and has not been 'next the Sea' since the seventeenth century, when land reclamation left it one mile inland.

Beyond Cley, an easy walk along the sea bank across the marsh takes you to Cley Eye, from which you can get to Blakeney Point on foot via a path along a narrow strip of marshland called the Marrams. The Coast Path, however, turns right at Cley Eye and proceeds along a shingle path on the inland side of shingle bank sea defences. The trudge through the shingle is even harder work than the sand dunes at Holkham, and if you have just enjoyed Cley church you may wryly reflect that St George's resolve and commitment might well have been tested far more had the devil thrown a shingle bank across his path to saintly glory in preference to a domesticated village dragon.

Gramborough Hill to Cromer

At Gramborough Hill, just beyond Salthouse, the going gets marginally better. A brief climb on to the hill gives excellent views back to Cley and Blakeney, and also to the sea, of which there have been precious few uninterrupted views since leaving Hunstanton. Shingle then alternates with welcome sections of springy turf until the Coast Path reaches the car park at Weybourne Hope (38.5). In the last war the coastline here saw an extensive military presence because of its easy accessibility for large ships and thereby the possibility of invasion.

The nearby village of Weybourne contains the ruins of a thirteenth-century Augustinian priory, of which a remarkably large central tower remains. There follows some cliffwalking, culminating in Skelding Hill, alongside Sheringham golf course. The hill provides the most arduous climb of the walk so far, but you are well rewarded with good views to the sea, the nearby town of Sheringham and perhaps steam locomotives on the Sheringham–Weybourne–Holt preserved railway. Walking the cliffs is a rare treat after the low-level coastal walking that has characterised the Norfolk

Coast Path so far, but erosion is a serious problem and diversions round cracks in the cliff are likely. The Coast Path descends to reach the cheerful resort of Sheringham (41.6). Famous for its seafood, the town is a popular resort with a good sandy beach and promenade, while All Saints church has a west tower built around 1300.

Beyond Sheringham, you must move inland for the final section to Cromer. Having emerged from the town you take a right turn directly away from the sea, crossing the railway and A149. You then pass the ruins of the thirteenth-century Beeston Priory, bear left and then head right, just east of Beeston Regis, making for an area of woodland. There is then a climb through the woods to Beacon Hill, the highest point in Norfolk . . . all of 328ft above sea level! Beacon Hill is the site of a Roman encampment, and indeed reminders of the country's Roman occupation might revive memories of the tramp up the Peddars Way which may already seem a long way back. Campers of more modern origin are to be seen nearby, as there are two large caravan sites in the woodland. After crossing Sandy Lane which leads down to West Runton and the sea, the route heads north-eastwards and then eastwards towards Cromer, initially through woodland and then into more open country below East Runton. The national trail passes under the Norwich–Cromer railway by means of a fine arched brick bridge, and then continues along a good track to reach the A148. You turn left to reach Cromer and the end of the national trail (46.6; 93 for whole national trail).

Cromer is a lively coastal town with a pier, lifeboat station and good sandy beaches, and is famed for its fishing, especially for crabs. Its narrow streets of old houses twist round the church of St Peter and St Paul which boasts the highest church tower in Norfolk at 160ft. What it lacks is an obvious finishing point for the national trail. Whilst it might be churlish for the hiker to expect the local council to erect a board with a message of congratulation at a strategic spot in or around the town, it may be less unreasonable for the walker to know whether the completion of his march from Knettishall is rendered official only upon dipping his toes in the icy North Sea waters, or whether it will suffice simply to present himself at the first available licensed premises, be it a cosy oak-beamed pub beloved of mariners and smugglers for centuries, or the rather less intimate aisles of the town's supermarket.

SUMMARY OF PLACES OF INTEREST
Brettenham Heath, Wretham Park, Thompson Water, Shakers' Furze, Merton Park, Little Cressingham, Pickenham Hall, Swaffham, Castle Acre★, Harpley, Ringstead, Hunstanton, Holme next the Sea, Thornham, Titchwell, Brancaster, Scolt Head Island★, Burnham Overy Staithe, Holkham, Wells-next-the-Sea, Morston, Blakeney Eye, Blakeney★, Cley next the Sea★, Sheringham, Cromer.

AMENITIES ON OR NEAR THE ROUTE
Thetford★, Little Cressingham (L), Swaffham★, Castle Acre, Great Massingham (L), Ringstead, Hunstanton★, Holme next the Sea (L), Thornham (L), Brancaster (L), Burnham Overy Staithe, Wells-next-the-Sea★, Morston (L), Blakeney, Cley next the Sea, Weybourne, Sheringham★, Cromer★.

The Wolds Way

Length: 79 miles.
Start: Hessle, on the banks of the Humber near Hull.
Finish: Near Filey Brigg, on the North Sea coast just south of Scarborough.
Nature: An undulating walk through the chalk uplands known as the Yorkshire Wolds in the East Riding of Yorkshire.
Difficulty rating: Moderate.
Average time of completion: 7 days.

The Wolds Way

The Wolds Way, the shortest national trail, is of comparatively recent origin. The idea for such a route was first mooted in 1968 and the trail officially opened in October 1982 following extensive negotiations with landowners. However, walkers tramping the Yorkshire Wolds are in fact following in prehistoric footsteps; a Gallic tribe known as the Parisii is known to have settled here, and a number of prehistoric routes crossed the Wolds. Later, the Romans built a road from Brough to Malton which passed through the Wolds in preference to the gentler lowlands. For a long time the Wolds have been associated with sheep-rearing, though in more recent times large parts of the Wolds have become intensively farmed, and much farmland will be crossed along the Way. You may notice some of the dew-ponds which were dug by farmers to provide a supply of water to their animals. But although others have been here before, you will find a refreshing sense of stillness and solitude on this national trail.

Although there are a few stiff climbs, the terrain poses no technical demands for the walker, and the waymarking is excellent throughout. The Way avoids large centres of population, but villages and small towns are never too far away, and with a little forethought it should not be difficult to plan. The scenery, while unspectacular, is still delightful, with the uneven contours of the rolling hills producing a constantly changing landscape. The most distinctive and endearing feature of the Wolds are its dry valleys, created by erosion of the chalk hills. The trail passes through several of these valleys on the route, many clothed with attractive tree plantations.

The chalk grassland contains many colourful wild plants and flowers including scabious, hawkbit, salad burnet, crosswort and harebell. I had the good fortune to walk the Way on a succession of golden autumn days, where the lush green pasture coating steep slopes rising above me complemented the blaze of colour from the pockets of deciduous woodland. It was ample compensation indeed for having to stand or sit on the floor for the whole of the train journey from London to Doncaster en route for the path, and a night at a Hull hotel with a breakfast so meagre that it had to be supplemented by two bananas from the station buffet.

Hessle to North Newbald

Many walkers will opt to stay in Hull (more properly Kingston upon Hull) before starting the walk. Although it is hardly a place of great beauty, there is a huge amount to see there, including the thirteenth-century Holy Trinity Church, the Town Docks museum, the Ferens art gallery, the sixteenth-century Old Grammar School, and the Wilberforce Museum, named in honour of the anti-slavery campaigner who was born here in 1759. It is a short train ride to the start of the walk at Hessle, the official start being situated opposite the Ferryboat Inn on the west side of Hessle Haven. Hessle itself is an attractive place, with several Georgian houses.

The first few miles of the trail consist of a walk alongside the estuary of the Humber, formed by the meeting of the Ouse and Trent rivers, and flowing into the sea below Spurn Head east of Hull. Almost immediately you pass beneath the magnificent Humber road bridge; opened in July 1981, it is the world's longest single-span suspension bridge with a span of 4628ft and twin towers that are 535ft high. The Way continues beside the Humber, following an awkward course along a shingle beach, then immediately beyond North Ferriby turns right and proceeds, just west of north, through a strip of woodland called Long Plantation and over the busy A63 which links the M62 with Hull. The strip of woodland extends north-westwards beyond the A63 to Welton, the route following through the middle of the woods and climbing away from the Humber.

You cross a minor road then drop to the lovely village of Welton (6.6) which contains a pond, a stream running beside the main street, an early nineteenth-century stone pump, and several attractive houses including the eighteenth-century Welton Hall and Welton Grange. Perhaps Welton's chief claim to fame, however, is that its Green Dragon Inn saw the final capture of the highwayman Dick Turpin.

The Way turns right in the village and proceeds north-eastwards along Welton Dale, the first of the many lovely dry valleys on the route, with steep wooded slopes rising on either side. Close by is the Raikes Mausoleum, dating back to 1818. You rise out of the Dale and emerge in more open country, passing the splendid ivied grey-brick Wauldby Manor which contains a chapel in its garden, then turn more sharply north-east to reach a wider track. The route turns left on to this track and soon passes straight over the Welton–North Newbald road on to a narrower metalled road which goes south-westwards and drops down to Brantingham. Just before reaching the village centre, the Way turns right on to a footpath which descends to the village church, the valley setting of which amongst the fir trees is quite exquisite. Instead of taking the footpath, you may prefer to continue down into Brantingham; to the south-east of the village is the Victorian Brantinghamthorpe Hall in a parkland setting, and in the village itself, as well as the red brick eighteenth-century Brantingham Hall, is a Gothic memorial composed from fragments of the 1862 Hull Town Hall. Pevsner describes it as 'one of the most lovably awful things in East Riding.'

The walk from Brantingham to the next village of South Cave is fiddly but most rewarding. Turning right on to a metalled road to pass the church, the Way proceeds through the lovely wooded Brantingham Dale, bears left on to the track, then at Woodale Farm turns right. There is another stiff climb to Mount Airy Farm along the left-hand edge of the lovely Woodale Plantation, then by Mount Airy Farm you join a track, turning left on to it then quickly right, dropping down the open hillside to reach a road at the north-eastern extreme of South Cave (12.9). This is the largest habitation reached since leaving Hessle; among its attractive houses are Cave Castle (converted into a hotel) of 1802, and a market hall dating back to 1796. There used to be seven pubs in the village, although most of these have now closed.

The Way turns left on to the road, then shortly right off it following a footpath, then turning right on to a track which goes uphill past Little Wold Plantation to the left. The views from here to the Humber are spectacular. You are now beginning to pull more decisively away from the great estuary and its nearby communities, and the next section is quite delectable. The track reaches a T-junction with a wider track at the hilltop, and here you turn right. You then begin to descend, turning left on to a path which passes into Comber Dale with a glorious prospect of rolling hills and woodland, all quite unspoilt; this is Wolds Way walking at its very best.

You drop down to proceed briefly on to the course of the now defunct Barnsley–Hull railway, through that most traditional of Wolds Way landscapes, with steep banks rising on both sides. At first only the bank to the left is wooded, but soon the Way turns left off the old railway to head north-westwards through East Dale, with thick woods covering the banks on either side. You climb out of the woodland into more open country, passing a triangulation point at just over 530ft, the panoramic views only marginally spoilt by the sight of the cooling towers of Drax power station in the distance. Soon you reach the B1230 Howden–Beverley road, crossing over and immediately swinging right and shortly left. You emerge at a minor road, turn right on to it and just past a crossroads take a footpath which heads initially north then north-west through the unwooded dry valley of Swin Dale. You then drop down to emerge at a minor road linking North Newbald with Beverley.

North Newbold to Huggate

Although the Way bears right, North Newbold is quickly reached by turning left here and is well worth a visit. It contains a delightful cluster of greystone and whitewashed cottages on streets with such quaint names as The Mires and Rattan Row, a stream running between banks bright with flowers, a mid-twelfth-century church which has been called the most complete Norman church in the Riding, and the intriguingly-named Gnu Inn. It is not immediately obvious how it got its name (could it have been intended to be called the Gun, but the signwriter misspelt it?) but walkers who are lovers of English popular song will at once recall the Gnu of Michael Flanders and Donald Swann, and as they return to the Way after a pint or three at the pub may find themselves singing those immortal words, 'I'm a G-nu, I'm a G-nu, the g-nicest work of g-nature in the zoo!' A low-spirited walker anywhere may endeavour to revive himself, as he trudges towards journey's end, with a few well-chosen melodies, but may care to temporarily cease his renditions at the approach of other walkers who will not, unlike the singer, have the benefit of the imaginary backing of the London Symphony Orchestra or the Metropolitan Opera Chorus.

Soon after turning right on to the minor road, the Way turns left and climbs to meet another road, turning right and then again left to follow track, path and road in a northerly direction to meet the A1079 York–Hull trunk road. On this section you pass the excellent viewpoint of Newbald Wold, just under 475ft high. The Way goes straight over the A1079 then immediately branches left off the minor road on to a track to pass the hamlet of Arras. Immediately to the south-west, on either side of the A1079 crossing, is an Iron Age barrow cemetery with over 100 small round barrows, and nearby is the site of a Roman amphitheatre. Beyond Arras the Way follows a footpath heading north-westwards across rough grassland, then descends. The going can be quite slow and not hugely rewarding, but improves as you arrive at another delightful dry valley and meet the Hudson Way. Named after the nineteenth-century railway magnate George Hudson, this is a footpath linking Market Weighton with Beverley, using a substantial section of the old York–Pocklington–Market Weighton–Beverley railway, which shut in 1965.

You now have a choice. You may follow a road to Goodmanham, this being the more direct route, or you can may turn left on to the

Hudson Way to reach Market Weighton via an alternative *loop* route. The latter route is the obvious choice if you are seeking overnight accommodation in this pleasant unspoilt town. Of its many fine buildings, of which several date back to the eighteenth century, the red brick Londesborough Arms is arguably the best. To leave Market Weighton via the loop route you must take the road leading north-westwards from the church towards the A1079, then as the built-up area ends, you turn right across fields to reach the A163 Selby–Driffield road. You go straight over on to a track past the site of Towthorpe village, on alongside Towthorpe Beck, and then over a minor road on to a drive through Londesborough Park to reach the direct route at a junction of drives in the park (extra mileage for detour: 1.2 miles).

The *direct* route, meanwhile, proceeds easily along the road from the Hudson Way crossing to Goodmanham (23.9). Goodmanham is regarded as one of the earliest sites of Christianity in Britain; a window in the squat little Norman church – not the first Christian building on this site – commemorates the conversion to Christianity in AD 627 of Coifi, the pagan High Priest of Goodmanham, and his destruction of the pagan temple of Woden which is believed to have stood where the church stands now. The Way turns sharp right by the church and follows a track north-westwards to reach the A163, crossing straight over and then turning left off the track into Londesborough Park, eventually being met by the alternative route.

You now proceed straight through the village which contains a pretty church, some fine eighteenth-century red brick houses and a seventeenth-century almshouse. Londesborough Hall, historically the village's grandest building, has been pulled down, but there remains a pleasing red brick Victorian mansion in Londesborough Park. The estate was purchased by George Hudson in 1845; at that time he was planning the York–Market Weighton railway and went as far as to plan it with a private station for himself at the edge of the estate at Shiptonthorpe, a few miles to the south-west.

The railway has long since gone, and Londesborough and its surroundings have taken on a new air of beauty and timelessness, suggestive perhaps to today's visitor of a likely setting for a Sunday teatime television adaptation of a Jane Austen or George Eliot novel.

As you pass, you can be grateful for being able to appreciate it first-hand rather than on your TV screen at home, with no danger of insensitive interruptions by trailers for future programmes you have no wish to watch, and endless sequences of advertisements for cut-price furniture superstores and anti-dandruff shampoo.

The Way leaves Londesborough by following a metalled road that heads north-westwards to Partridge Hall, turning right briefly on to a minor road east of Burnby, then shortly bearing left on to a footpath to Nunburnholme (28.8), still reluctant to leave the lower ground. Nunburnholme, which derives its name from the twelfth-century Benedictine nunnery that once stood here, is a pretty place in a tranquil valley setting; it has an attractive stream running beside it, and a church with an Anglo-Saxon cross shaft that is at least 1,000 years old. The church minister from 1854 to 1895 was Francis Morris, who also found time to write *The Natural History of British Birds*.

The Way turns left on to the village street then right at the church to continue north-westwards, first along a path, then on a road, and then a track through Bratt Wood and across an open hillside to reach the B1246. You cross straight over this road. However, a left turn will take you to the town of Pocklington, with excellent connections for the city of York, whilst a right turn leads to the pretty village of Warter, which contains thatched cottages, a pond and a large park, and is the site of a twelfth-century Augustinian priory. It also marks the finishing post of the Kiplingcotes Derby, a horse race which supposedly started in 1519 and is claimed to be the oldest horse race in the world. Beyond the B1246 you continue north-westwards on the hillside, passing Jenny Firkin Wood and Kilnwick Percy Hall, superbly situated in a park which also contains large lakes and a Norman church.

Beyond Jenny Firkin Wood the Way turns right and climbs steeply uphill to begin the walk above the dry valley of Millington Dale, which I regard as the loveliest section of the route. At the hilltop you turn left and head north-eastwards, enjoying tremendous views across Yorkshire which on a good day might include York Minster. Soon after gaining the hilltop you could detour to Millington with its enchanting part-Norman church, but at the cost of losing all the height already gained. On two occasions it is necessary to drop steeply to the dale bottom and then rise equally precipitously up again, but the surroundings are so lovely that it is worth the effort. Although the valley walls are not as thickly wooded as some already seen, there are plenty of trees and bushes to decorate the steep slopes, and at one point near to the route hereabouts there is a small lake where, unusually, one of the many underground Wolds chalk streams has broken to the surface.

Eventually you reach the head of the dale and turn left on to a road, then at a T-junction you go straight over on to a path heading north, reaching nearly 650ft. Not only is this the highest point reached so far, but there is a real sense of remoteness. The route turns north-east and then south-east, crossing a minor road, joining a track and passing Glebe Farm to reach a T-junction of tracks. The Way turns left here, but by turning right you immediately reach the village of Huggate (37.4). Huggate contains some fine buildings including the former rectory, Kirkdale House, and a part-sixteenth-century Manor House. Its church contains a fourteenth-century west tower; a board in the church dated 9 October 1826 lists the names of a jury empowered to impose fines for such misdemeanours as harbouring vagrants, or 'suffering swine or geese to be in the streets between Old May Day and Old Lammas.'

Huggate to Duggleby

Having turned left at the T-junction above Huggate, the Way heads north-east along a track, then turns left on to a path and heads north-westwards into the next dry valley, Holm Dale. There is a steep drop into the valley, then a climb up to the head of the dale where you join a track and follow it northwards to reach Fridaythorpe, the halfway point of the national trail. It is necessary to turn right on to the A166 York–Bridlington road then left along the village street past the church. Fridaythorpe (39.9) is a pretty village with a green, two large ponds and St Mary's Church with a twelfth-century south doorway described by Pevsner as 'utterly barbaric . . . with three orders of columns, chip-carving, a rope motif, rosettes, decorated scallops, zigzag – any old thing that was going.'

Beyond the church, you turn left on to a track, which descends steeply to the dry valley of West Dale and then, passing Ings Plantation, climbs on a footpath to the head of the dale at Gill's Farm. Crossing straight over a minor road, there is then a very steep descent into Thixen Dale. The Way negotiates a hairpin bend, swinging southwards then, on reaching the valley floor, turns right on to a footpath heading northwards through what is a quite delightful dale. The flat dry valley bottom provides comfortable walking whilst hills decorated with mini-plantations rise up on each side. You reach a road and turn right on to it, still in the valley, then go forward into Thixendale village (44).

This lovely village, claimed by some to be the prettiest in Yorkshire, stands at a junction of a series of impressive dry valleys. Although the church, school and vicarage were all built around 1870, some houses in the village, notably Raisthorpe Manor and Round The Bend, date back to the eighteenth century. It has a delightfully tranquil atmosphere and, like Londesborough, enjoys a timeless quality. At the time of my visit, however, it was not without some amenities, which included a shop that also served as a tearoom and a filling station with a single petrol pump standing smartly on the forecourt outside it.

The harsh commercial realities of modern life have forced village shops to become more and more versatile in the range of services offered to the customer; in the twenty-first century you may expect to find the village store providing not only bars of chocolate and cartons of fruit juice, but dry-cleaning, photocopying, faxing and maybe even e-mailing facilities. In years to come the delighted hiker may, in even the remotest village community, be able to sit down and provide an instant electronic update of his walk for his sister and brother-in-law in Australia, detailing everything from the delightful Norman church in the previous village to the colour of his new bootlaces, whilst attempts to make a simple telephone call from the village kiosk to a taxi firm ten miles away may continue to be completely frustrated by the mechanism's long-standing and inexplicable aversion to 10p or 20p pieces.

The Way turns right in the village on to a track which climbs out of the valley on to Cow Wold, heading north-westwards. There follows a quite delightful descent on good paths into Vessey Pasture Dale, with splendid views to the valley and the steep banks on each side. You then follow the dale in a direction just east of north, the ground rising steeply, and at the hilltop you turn right on to a track, heading eastwards and soon reaching the head of Deep Dale. This is well-named, with the steep banks on each side, dotted with small trees and bushes, plunging spectacularly to a narrow valley floor. Through the valley it is possible to view the ruined church of Wharram Percy, and an alternative route turns left off the main route to reach it, although it is easily reachable from the main path as well.

The main route continues along the hilltop and passes a strip of woodland to the left, while beneath your feet is Burdale Tunnel on the old Malton to Driffield railway line. Very soon the Way turns left on to a metalled road, from which there are tremendous views to the Derwent valley and beyond. Soon there is a junction with a track, and although the Way goes straight on, a left turn takes you along a path to the ruined village of Wharram Percy (the same path brings the alternative route back to the main route). Of all the detours off the Wolds Way, this one is especially recommended. The village once contained water mills, manor houses, and accommodation for workers on the land and their animals. Then, some 500 years ago, the landowners decided that more money was to be made from sheep than growing, and the peasants were thrown off the land. Only the church survived, but despite attempts at maintenance and restoration, it also crumbled and is now unsafe for worship, though parts of the eleventh-century tower and other later additions can still be seen.

You continue north-westwards along the track, then when this swings to the right, you go straight on along a footpath to reach Station Road, turning right to arrive in Wharram-le-Street (49.3), the church of which has a part-Saxon tower that is reputedly the oldest of any Wolds church. You turn left in the village on to the B1248, but by crossing straight over the B1248 and following the road, it is possible to visit the village of Duggleby. To the south-east of the village is Duggleby Howe, a gigantic round barrow which at 20ft high and 120ft in diameter is one of the largest of its type in

Britain. When excavated it revealed the cremated or buried remains of many bodies, together with the flint and bone implements of a late-Neolithic people. Duggleby Howe is situated on the B1253, and a few miles to the south-east along that road is Sledmere, the birth place of Sir Tatton Sykes.

Like his father before him, Sir Christopher Sykes, he was one of the greatest benefactors in the history of the Wolds, financing the building and restoration of numerous churches and other buildings in the area. His discovery of the fertilising value of bonemeal – he noticed the grass grew better where his foxhounds had gnawed their bones – also helped him to gain the epithet of Farmer's Friend. In West Heslerton church, close to the Way, there is a wall tablet with this simple tribute: 'Whoever now traverses the Wolds of Yorkshire and contrasts their present appearance with what they were cannot but extol the name of Sykes.' Famous as a jockey and pugilist, Sir Tatton was known as one of the 'three great sights of Yorkshire,' the others being Fountains Abbey and York Minster. His son was a hypochondriac who took his own cook with him on all his journeys to be certain of having the milk puddings he considered essential to his survival.

Duggleby to Staxton

The Wolds Way soon leaves the B1248, turning right and heading north. It crosses over the B1253, then shortly afterwards bears left to Wood House Farm and then right on to a track going uphill and north-eastwards. You pass Settrington Wood and then skirt another strip of woodland, going forward to a minor road crossing and the excellent viewpoint at Settrington Beacon, with good views across the Derwent Valley. Still heading north-east, you pass through an area of woodland, descend sharply and continue through open country. As the track swings to the north-west, the Way turns right along a path that heads south-east, offering views over a stream to the village of Wintringham (55.7). You turn left on to a track to reach the centre of the village, and then right, taking a road which leads past the large church. The church, one of the largest Wolds churches, has a Norman chancel and handsome Jacobean pews, but its finest feature is its stained glass, believed to be Flemish and dating from the fourteenth century, with 32 medieval saints filling the tracery lights of the aisle windows.

Continuing along the road beyond the church, the Way turns left and proceeds uphill through woodland, heading north, then leaves the woods and turns right on to a track heading east. For much of the next five miles you continue in an easterly direction, staying on top of a north-facing escarpment. Initially there is woodland to your left, but after crossing a road that leads northwards to West Heslerton the walking is more open, with excellent views across East Heslerton Brow to the Derwent valley and beyond.

If you have the time it may be worth detouring to West Heslerton, with its large stuccoed part-eighteenth-century Hall. In due course you arrive at, and turn left on to, a road heading downhill towards Sherburn (62.5), a pretty village with several fine old houses including the eighteenth-century Brewery House and Pasture House, a village cross presented by Sir Tatton Sykes the younger, and a part-Norman church containing several pieces of Anglo-Saxon sculpture. The Way does not enter the village but turns right on to a path just short of it. You turn right on to the next road to climb Sherburn Brow, and left on to a path which contours the Brow then drops and continues north-eastwards near the foot of the escarpment above Potter Brompton to reach a road leading down to Ganton. The Way turns left on to the road, passing the Victorian red brick Ganton Hall with its lovely parkland, and then turns right on to a path that skirts the village (65.5).

Like Sherburn, it is worth taking time to explore the village centre; its main street, with a stream running beside it, is lined with whitewashed chalkstone and pantile cottages dating back to the eighteenth century. From Ganton, the Way heads out into the country again, and after climbing back up the hillside on a succession of field-edge paths, you gain the top of the escarpment and head due east to reach the B1249. One is tempted to ask why the Way cannot simply remain above the escarpment from the West Heslerton road to this point, or indeed why certain stretches of other national trails are similarly circuitous in nature. Often this will be attributable to difficulties encountered with local landowners in the course of negotiation of rights of way, as happened in creating certain sections of the Wolds Way. The walker complaining that a certain section has been a little muddy or fiddly should regard his inconvenience as trifling compared with that endured by those negotiating at length to win that right of way in the first place, often well past the time when the future beneficiaries of their efforts would have retired to bed with their nightly ration of cocoa, Catherine Cookson and chocolate chip cookies.

Staxton to Filey Brigg

The Way crosses the B1249, but by detouring to the left along the road you will reach Staxton with its seventeenth-century Stirrup Inn and more attractive chalkstone houses, while to the right is Willerby Wold, with its long barrow, 4ft high by 133ft long. The Way heads just north of east from the B1249 and then south-east over Staxton Wold, passing round the edge of an RAF station. After what has been an unexceptional few miles, there is now a return to more traditional Wolds Way fare, with a succession of dry valleys to enjoy. You descend steeply into Cotton Dale, then turn left and climb steeply uphill again before proceeding north-eastwards above Lang Dale and, beyond a minor road crossing, Raven Dale. Because bulls run on the flat valley bottom, paths were specially created along the safer dale tops, although two steep descents and two very demanding climbs are still necessary on this section. It is interesting to compare these virtually bare green hillsides with the thickly wooded slopes much earlier in the route.

The Way drops down into Camp Dale and climbs out of it again, passing a small pond on the valley floor and now heading south-eastwards, *away* from the ultimate goal. There is then a further descent to Stocking Dale where you swing left up the valley, resuming a north-easterly course. This is the final dry valley of the Wolds Way, and with its plantations and steep banks it is one of the prettiest. Climbing to the head of the dale, and passing just below a strip of woodland, you emerge at a minor road. The Way crosses straight over, but a detour to the right along this road takes you to Hunmanby.

This is a most attractive little town with a twelfth-century church, many chalkstone buildings, two fine seventeenth-century houses (Batworth Cottage and the Old Manor House) and several eighteenth-century houses. Francis Wrangham, who was minister here in the early nineteenth century, was a great bibliophile and he often entertained the greatest of clerical eccentrics, Sydney Smith (himself once a Yorkshire parson), who came to borrow books from him. One assumes that Smith may have used some of them to assist him in his preaching, but he still adopted a somewhat fatalistic attitude towards the task of addressing his congregation, acknowledging that, 'When I am in the pulpit, I have the pleasure of seeing my audience nod approbation while they sleep!'

Having crossed the Hunmanby road, the Way follows a track past Muston Wold Farm, with superb views to the North Sea, Filey and Flamborough Head. The route then forks right and drops down to the A1039, turning right on to the road to reach Muston (75.2). The village boasts an early nineteenth-century hall and, at 8–9 Hunmanby Street, a chalkstone house with cruck framing – a rarity in the East Riding. Turning left in the village, you follow a path north-eastwards, crossing the A165 Scarborough–Hull road, then as you reach the outskirts of Filey you swing to the right to join the A1039 and follow it into the town centre (76.7).

Filey has had a long association with fishing, but its long sands have also turned it into a popular seaside resort. It contains a number of interesting features including the Norman church of St Oswald, regarded as easily the finest in the north-east corner of the East Riding, the early eighteenth-century houses of Church Street and the nineteenth-century Crescent which Pevsner suggests gives the town a 'distinctive, refined character.' It also boasts an old smugglers' inn of Old Filey, T'Aud Ship, complete with secret panels and hollow beams. The Way proceeds through the middle of the town then heads towards the beach, dropping down a flight of steps at the north end near the lifeboat station to reach Coble Landing, a popular mooring point for the distinctive flat-bottomed fishing craft known as cobles. To the right you can see the majestic headland of Flamborough, and to the left is the end of the Wolds Way at Filey Brigg.

The Way now heads resolutely for that objective, climbing on to the Pampletine cliffs which give fine views to Scarborough and beyond. It is a short walk along the clifftop to a junction of paths, where there is a splendid stone monument into which has been carved the names of various Wolds Way locations, thus giving you a chance to recall some of the highlights of the walk. The Way actually does turn left at this path junction and continues beside the sea to link up with the Cleveland Way just beyond Club Point. It is here that the Wolds Way ends (79.4). However, a far more satisfying conclusion to the walk is to turn right by the monument and walk along the clifftops to reach Filey Brigg itself (purists wishing to claim they have completed the whole trail can of course retrace their steps and then go out to the Brigg). The Brigg consists of a reef of rocks which juts into the sea for nearly a mile and when the seas are stormy, the sight of waves crashing against these rocks is indeed an awesome one. If conditions permit, it is possible to descend on to the reef. Those to whom its origins have been attributed include not only the Devil but the skeleton of a dragon that died after its jaws became glued together with Yorkshire parkin. Walkers wishing to celebrate their completion of the Way with a helping of this delicacy at one of the tearooms in Filey, please note.

SUMMARY OF PLACES OF INTEREST

Hull, Humber Bridge★, Welton, Welton Dale, Brantingham, South Cave, Comber Dale★, East Dale, North Newbald, Arras, Market Weighton, Goodmanham, Londesborough★, Millington Dale★, Huggate, Thixen Dale★, Thixendale, Deepdale, Wharram Percy★, Duggleby Howe, Settrington Beacon, Wintringham, Sherburn, Stocking Dale, Hunmanby, Filey, Filey Brigg★.

AMENITIES ON OR NEAR THE ROUTE

Hull★, Hessle, North Ferriby (L), Welton (L), Brantingham (L), South Cave, Goodmanham (L), Market Weighton, Millington (L), Fridaythorpe (L), Thixendale (L), Wharram le Street (L), Wintringham (L), Sherburn (L), Ganton (L), Staxton (L), Muston (L), Hunmanby, Filey★.

The Cleveland Way

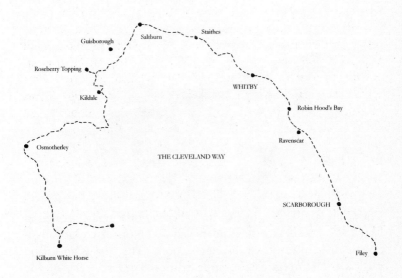

Length: 108 miles.
Start: Helmsley, North Yorkshire.
Finish: Near Filey Brigg, East Riding of Yorkshire.
Nature: A route of two halves; a traverse of the fringes of the North York Moors along the tops of the Hambleton and Cleveland Hills, then a section of coastal walking including some of the most spectacular cliff scenery on the east coast of England.
Difficulty rating: Moderate, but strenuous in places, particularly the Cleveland Hills.
Average time of completion: Between 7 and 10 days.

The Cleveland Way

The Cleveland Way is one of the older national trails, opened in May 1969. Rather like the Peddars Way and Norfolk Coast Path, it can be divided into two distinct sections. The first is an inland walk which includes the superb moorland scenery of the Hambleton and Cleveland Hills. The second is a coastal walk on which you will encounter not only excellent cliff scenery, but the bustling towns of Whitby and Scarborough, and beautiful villages including Staithes and Robin Hood's Bay. The route is extremely well signposted and well defined, posing no real technical demands, although considerable stamina is required to tackle some sections, especially that between Osmotherley and Clay Bank Top where there is a lengthy overlap with the Coast to Coast Walk.

The wildlife and plant life on the route contains the richness and variety one would expect from a walk that encompasses a tramp over splendid moorland and coastal scenery. The North York Moors provide three fine species of heather – ling, bell heather and cross-leaved heath – as well as cloudberry, crowberry and dwarf cornel, with their orange, black and red fruits. Grouse are plentiful, and you may also see the curlew, meadow pipit, merlin, common lizard and green-and-black caterpillar of the emperor moth, while the coastal section may bring sightings of the oystercatcher, plover, cormorant, tern, shag and dunlin.

What perhaps characterises the Cleveland Way is its splendid open walking and consequently wide sweeping vistas, both inland and on the coast, making binoculars a must. The factor most likely to spoil the walk in summer is a light mist known locally as 'roak', which drifts in from the sea on summer days and can reduce visibility quite significantly. In good weather, however, it is a most satisfying and enjoyable walk, and indeed if you still yearn for more when you reach the end, you can immediately join the Wolds Way which links up with the Cleveland Way. Whilst this is a potentially attractive proposition for the charity walker or national trail-bagger, you may, after giving the matter more serious consideration, regard the Wolds Way as somewhat anticlimactical to you after the glories of the Cleveland Way, especially when you find that your very last stretch of walking is through the suburbs of Hull.

Helmsley to the Kilburn White Horse

The Way begins in the charming town of Helmsley, the focal point of which is the ruin of a castle which was built in the early twelfth century although its oldest surviving buildings go back to around 1200. The marketplace in the town contains several attractive houses, some dating back to the sixteenth century, as well as a good range of amenities of which you would be well advised to take advantage as there is nothing more guaranteed until Osmotherley, a full day's walk away. The Way begins at an impressive monument with the national trails' acorn motif carved into it, this being reached by following a track heading westwards off the B1257 more or less opposite All Saints church. The Way then continues along this track, which becomes a pleasant footpath that gently rises through open country and follows the edge of a wood, still heading roughly westwards. There are fine views back to Helmsley and its castle ruin.

The Way continues to follow the path which temporarily enters woodland, dropping and then rising again to join a track and continue along the edge of a steep wooded escarpment, known as Whinny Bank. Soon, close to the site of a village rejoicing in the unusual name of Griff, you enter the wood and drop steeply down the escarpment to reach a road, turn left on to it, and follow it, coming to a bridge over the river Rye. Immediately before the bridge you should turn right to detour up to Rievaulx Abbey, a Cistercian foundation which was colonised in 1131.

There is more left standing at Rievaulx than at any Cistercian abbey in England except Fountains in the Yorkshire Dales, and although there is little remaining from the time of foundation, a great deal of the early thirteenth-century work still stands. Pevsner devotes eight pages of the North Riding volume of his *Buildings of England* series to Rievaulx, and his might well be regarded as the definitive, albeit scholarly guide, to its treasures. In a way, it is a shame that it comes so early in the itinerary, and walkers who at six or seven in the evening are still pounding the moors may regret the painstaking hours spent at Pevsner's behest seeking out chamfered buttresses and stiff-leaf corbels.

After crossing the Rye bridge you continue along the road, soon passing Hagg Hall on the left. Shortly after Hagg Hall the road bends sharply to the left, and just beyond the bend the Way turns right on to a track which passes beside three lakes, and then bears right to begin its passage towards an area of woodland marked on the map as Blind Side. However, soon you bear left off this track on a path through the woods, shortly turning right on a route which climbs out of the woodland and develops into a wider track that leads to the village of Cold Kirby. Its remote feel contrasts starkly with the lush, homely surroundings of Rievaulx.

The Way passes the nineteenth-century church of St Michael and proceeds through the village on a metalled road, turning first left on to a track. This leads to a path that in turn continues to the edge of a wooded area, then turns right, passing Hambleton House and coming to a lane. You turn left on to this lane and follow it to arrive at the A170 by the welcome Hambleton Inn, crossing straight over on to another lane before bearing right on to a path. This proceeds through woodland to emerge at the first highlight of the journey, the viewpoint of Sutton Bank. Suddenly, after walking through somewhat nondescript upland terrain, you are faced with a glorious panoramic view across a huge area of Yorkshire.

Here you have a choice. If pressed for time, you could immediately turn right to reach the A170 and cross it to begin the glorious promenade along the top of the escarpment which is the western rim of the wild Hambleton Hills. However, the definitive route of the Cleveland Way includes the detour along the tops of the cliffs of Roulston Scar, involving a left turn at Sutton Bank and a tremendous walk that leads to one of Yorkshire's more distinctive landmarks, the Kilburn White Horse. Although the views are stupendous – York Minster is clearly visible on a good day – you will be right above the horse and so unable to get a view of it that is as good as if you were seeing it from far below.

Indeed, when I walked the Way I was convinced I had been standing triumphantly on the horse's forelegs, but when I made a return visit two months later I found I had in fact been standing on its nose. The horse, dating back to 1857, is 314ft long and 228ft high, the outline having been cut by the village schoolmaster John Hodgson and his pupils. Teachers among Cleveland Way walkers might reflect that if the national curriculum and Ofsted had been around in 1857, the horse would probably never have been cut at all!

The Kilburn White Horse to Osmotherley

Having made the Kilburn White Horse detour, you now need to retrace your steps – no hardship in view of the magnificent scenery – to Sutton Bank (10), and then go forward to cross the A170, immediately beyond which is an impressive visitor centre. Then begins an exhilarating high-level march over the Hambleton Hills and along the top of the escarpment, with wild moorland and woodland to the right, and the great swathe of the Vale of York stretching out to the left. After passing high above Gormire Lake, the route follows a well-defined path that stays close to the escarpment edge, first alongside woodland, then past the impressive rocks of Boltby Scar, across a metalled road at Sneck Yate Bank, through a piece of woodland, and shortly thereafter on to a track that forks, the route taking the right fork past High Paradise Farm to reach an important crossroads of paths just beyond the farm.

The Way goes left to proceed north-westwards on an excellent track which passes along the right-hand edge of a forest and then strikes out on to open moorland, with Little Moor and Arden Great Moor to the right and Kepwick Moor to the left. You then curve gently northwards as you continue on to Whitestone Scar, between

Arden Great Moor and Kepwick Moor. Here you reach an important junction of paths, the Way heading left over Black Hambleton Moor, and again passing the right-hand edge of a forest, rising to over 1,300ft. Superb views now begin to open up ahead as well as to the left, with industrial Teesside clearly visible to the north.

Now the long descent towards Osmotherley begins. Shortly after leaving the forest behind, you drop down to a metalled road and, beyond that, a car park; bearing left here, you take a path which drops steeply down through the heather, passing to the right of two lakes and, at Oak Dale, joining a track leading to a metalled road. Crossing the road, you join a track that leads to Whitehouse Farm, beyond which the track turns into a path that heads westwards downhill to cross Cod Beck. There follows a climb through the woods and then a field walk, still heading westwards, into Osmotherley (21).

This is a delightful place, with attractive stone cottages round its triangular green and a church with a fine Norman south doorway. The steep streets of the village have cobbled pavements and grassy verges lined with trees and flowers. John Wesley, the founder of Methodism, preached in the eighteenth-century Methodist chapel; in North End, there is the old pinfold or pound in which stray animals were impounded until their owners paid a fine.

Wherever walkers stay in Osmotherley, they may well find fellow guests are doing Wainwright's Coast to Coast Walk, which meets the Way a mile north of the village. Those who have come from St Bees on that route will have accomplished over 140 miles, compared with the Cleveland Way walker's more modest 21.5, and may well therefore feel entitled to assume an air of smug superiority over those whose mileage has been so much less, reporting graphically and at great length about every hardship that has been fearlessly overcome, every hazard that has casually been brushed aside, every challenge that has almost contemptuously been negotiated, until the achievements of Roulston Scar and Black Hambleton are diminished to a level no greater than that felt on accomplishment of the daily lunch-hour stroll to the newsagents for a bag of Wotsits and a Pot Noodle.

Osmotherley to Live Moor

The Cleveland Way leaves Osmotherley by proceeding from the village green up North End, turning left on to Ruebury Lane and ascending gradually. The lane begins as a metalled road but becomes an unmetalled track that offers magnificent views westwards. You reach an area of woodland, immediately meeting a path that comes in from the left; the Way goes on ahead, but by turning left here you may visit Mount Grace Priory (see description of the Coast to Coast Walk). This is also the point where the Coast to Coast Walk meets the Cleveland Way and will continue with it for the next 14 miles, and the Lyke Wake Walk follows the same route for those miles. The Lyke Wake Walk was originally a 40-mile route along which local people used to carry the coffins of their deceased to bury them at sea. It has now become a challenge walk and people who complete it nowadays within 24 hours are eligible to join the Lyke Wake Club, membership of which entitles them to a small badge in the shape of a coffin!

The Cleveland Way, together with the other aforementioned routes, continues through the wood on a good path, heading north-eastwards to pass the television booster station on Beacon Hill. Soon afterwards, you emerge from the wood and swing in a more easterly direction. There follows a fine stretch of open walking across Scarth Wood Moor, the path losing height first gradually and then more rapidly, descending to reach a metalled road. The Way crosses straight over on to a very good woodland path, which drops down into the attractive valley of Scugdale. On arrival in the valley, you reach a gated lane and turn right, following another excellent path up the wooded valley for about three quarters of a mile, then turn left on to a path which crosses a tributary of Scugdale Beck and reaches a metalled road. You join this road, crossing Scugdale Beck immediately and climbing up to a T-junction with the Swainby–Scugdale Hall road at the hamlet of Huthwaite Green. The Way crosses straight over this road, taking a path to the right of a telephone kiosk up the facing hillside. In just under half a mile the Way turns sharply right up an extremely steep woodland path, emerging from the woods and striking out across Live Moor, heading eastwards.

The next six miles are the most exciting on the Cleveland Way, as the very good path, proceeding unmistakably and in a generally easterly or north-easterly direction, negotiates the Cleveland Hills, consisting of a succession of moors involving a number of lung-testing ascents and knee-jarring descents. The views throughout this sequence of climbs and descents are glorious; there are the wide plains, stretching for miles to the left, and on the right are the beautiful heather uplands of the North York Moors. The first ascent, to the 1,025ft summit of Live Moor, sets the scene, but although arduous it is by no means the toughest. Walkers may well be overtaken by those endeavouring to complete the Lyke Wake Walk in the quickest time they can, hopping nimbly and confidently both up and down the almost vertical slopes, unencumbered by rucksacks and clad in the lightest possible gear. Those burdened with heavy boots and burdensome packs may sadly conclude that exciting though it might be to cover the distance as quickly, any attempt on their part to do so might end with their entering a coffin rather than sporting one on their cagoules.

Live Moor to Guisborough Woods

From Live Moor the Way continues on over Carlton Moor, descending steeply off it to reach a metalled road. By detouring to the left down this road you will reach the pleasant village of Carlton, with its pretty Alum Beck, old cottages and sloping orchards and gardens, but the route continues on the obvious track over the road. Refreshments may be available here and even the fittest walker should take advantage of them, as there is nothing more for many miles. The Way then climbs on to Cringle Moor, described by Wainwright as the finest elevation yet reached along the escarpment, and you should pause at Cringle End near the summit where there is a view indicator and seat. There is another steep drop, another big climb to the summit of Cold Moor, another big descent, and then the finest climb of all, up on to Hasty Bank past the cluster of pinnacled rocks known as the Wain Stones, with some scrambling required to complete the ascent through the stones.

A superb high-level walk follows, and it is quite anticlimactical to drop steeply down to the B1257 just south of Clay Bank car park, marking the end of this wonderful sequence of ascents and descents. You should note that although the car park is well used, there are likely to be no amenities available and the nearest village, Great Broughton, lies a couple of miles to the north. After crossing straight over the B1257 there follows a long slog on to Urra Moor. The route, still extremely well-defined, continues in a south-easterly and then a more easterly direction, passing the 1,491ft triangulation point which marks the summit of Urra Moor, and inscribed stones known as the Hand Stone, the Face Stone and the Red Stone, thought to have been erected in the early years of the eighteenth century although there is some suggestion that they date back even further. Shortly beyond the Red Stone you reach a T-junction, meeting the clearly defined course of the old Rosedale Ironstone Railway (see description of the Coast to Coast Walk) and turning right on to it, very soon reaching the crossroads of paths known as Bloworth Crossing. Here, at last, the Cleveland Way parts company with the Coast to Coast Walk and the Lyke Wake Walk; the latter two routes go straight on, whilst the Cleveland Way goes left.

Proceeding along another excellent track, the Way heads north-westwards along the edge of the escarpment known as Greenhow Bank, then swings north-eastwards over Battersby Moor. You now enjoy splendid views as the track carrying the Way turns into a metalled road which descends steeply, swinging north-westwards again to pass Park Dyke, arriving at a T-junction with another road and going right along the road into Kildale (42). This is an obvious spot for a night's rest, being the first settlement since Osmotherley over 20 miles back, and walkers can sleep contentedly knowing there is the excitement of one of the best moments of the Cleveland Way: namely the ascent of the distinctive hill known as Roseberry Topping, early next day. Though well known as one of the most prominent natural landmarks in the North East and featuring in many of the panoramic views offered along the Cleveland Way, the quaint name given to this isolated conical hill may mean little to hikers and hillwalkers unfamiliar with the area who might well hazard a guess that Roseberry Topping might be either a garden fertiliser or a sickly-sweet flavoured synthetic cream that adorned the nation's Sunday dinner tables in the early 1970s.

The Way turns left in the village to head for the railway station, then immediately right along a lane, going under the railway and past Bankside farm, where you enter woodland. You follow the lane steeply uphill and at the brow of the hill you turn left, joining a track that heads westwards through the woods. You emerge on to Easby Moor and go forward, steeply uphill, to reach Captain Cook's Monument, in honour of the explorer who spent most of his childhood in the nearby village of Great Ayton. From here there are breathtaking views back to Kildale and the Cleveland Hills. Immediately beyond the monument you turn right along a path that heads north-eastwards, coming off Easby Moor to pass through woodland, descending briefly and then continuing along the west edge of Great Ayton Moor, passing along the eastern side of another patch of woodland. You then climb again and swing north-westwards, along a steep escarpment edge and then along the right fringe of Slacks Wood with the open moorland of Newton Moor to the right. Throughout this section of the Way there are magnificent views to the Cleveland Hills and the surrounding countryside.

At the top end of Slacks Wood there is a crossroads where there starts an official 'out and back' detour to Roseberry Topping, described as Yorkshire's Matterhorn. To make the detour, you take a left turn at the crossroads and then head just south of west to the gritstone-capped summit. The hill's terraced slopes have been caused by the alternation of adjacent beds of harder and softer rocks, making it a place of great interest for geologists as well as sightseers. The views are wonderfully wide-ranging, encompassing the moors, industrial Teesside, the villages of Great Ayton and Stokesley, and the town of Guisborough.

It is a real wrench to leave the summit and head back to the crossroads, going straight over and proceeding north-eastwards over Newton Moor and Hutton Moor along an obvious track with thick woodland to your left. There is no doubt that this section is something of a trudge, but patience is rewarded, for as you swing north-westwards to enter Guisborough Woods, you reach the rocky outcrops of Highcliff Nab, with superb views to Guisborough. It is possible to detour from here to visit the town; its most notable feature is its Augustinian priory, founded about 1120, although the oldest remaining features date back no earlier than the thirteenth century. St Nicholas church is worth seeing for its ornate Brus cenotaph, and the 1907 Methodist church must be inspected if only for the walker to decide if he thinks Pevsner was right to describe it as 'unforgivable'!

Guisborough Woods to Saltburn

Beyond the Nab you are faced with perhaps the least inspiring section of the Cleveland Way. You proceed initially through the long expanse of Guisborough Woods, passing an old quarry at one point, heading in a generally north-easterly direction along a good path, although care should be taken as there are numerous other paths in the wood. At length the woodland relents and you emerge into open land, arriving at a track. You turn left on to it, proceeding downhill, and soon turn right on to a path that heads eastwards through woodland to reach the A171 at Slapewath, the path seemingly going right past the village before turning sharply down to the road. The path can be muddy and the noise of the traffic on the A171 quite intrusive.

The Way turns left on to the A171 then shortly right on to a path that proceeds round the rim of a quarry to the left with woodland to the right. The old quarries hereabouts were once a lucrative source of ironstone and alum, which were first quarried here 400 years ago. Having rounded the quarry, you turn sharply right to head northwards with an area of woodland to the left, then right again to head north-eastwards past a triangulation point to Airy Hill Farm, joining a track here which leads down towards Skelton. You arrive at a road, going straight over and following a path over fields, turning right to follow a track briefly and then shortly left on a path that soon reaches the A173 in the centre of Skelton.

Skelton is not a particularly attractive village but does boast a fine late eighteenth-century house called Skelton Castle, reflecting the fact that there was a real twelfth-century castle here. Immediately south of the house is a remarkable old church with a three-decker pulpit, box pews and gallery, although in recent years it has fallen into disuse.

The Way crosses straight over the A173 through a modern housing estate – what a contrast to the glories of Roulston Scar,

Hasty Bank and Roseberry Topping! – and then from the north-east edge of the estate follows a path northwards through fields and into woodland. As the houses of Saltburn begin to appear, you cross Skelton Beck and pass underneath an extremely impressive brick viaduct carrying a freight railway, then stay on the left bank of the Beck through an area of woodland with more than one path from which to choose. With the suburbs of Saltburn encroaching, it is not quite such an idyllic scene as it might be, and the sense of being in a semi-urban environment may be accentuated by the presence of joggers.

Jogging is a late twentieth-century phenomenon which arose in response to concerns about the consequences for one's well-being of sedentary over-indulgent lifestyles. However, as you see overweight runners packed into ill-fitting tracksuits, sweat streaming from every pore, and an expression on their faces which suggests a recent encounter with the more zealous officials of the Spanish Inquisition, you may wonder why they do not resign themselves to an earlier but infinitely pleasanter demise in the comfort of their own armchairs.

Saltburn to Whitby

At length you reach the front at Saltburn (57), with the dullest part of the Cleveland Way and also any real route-finding difficulties now at an end; the second half of the Way consists of a straightforward walk along the finest section of the east coast of England. Saltburn not only offers a good range of amenities and rail connections, but is a cheerful little resort with a good stretch of sands and a pier that dates back to 1868. Crossing the A174, the Way joins a coastal path heading eastwards with the sea on the left, climbing past Saltburn Scar and Hunt Cliff where there is the site of a Roman signalling station built in the fourth century to warn of Anglian and Saxon pirates. There is then a drop to the dunes of Cattersty Sands and the village of Skinningrove, which with its vast ironworks is sadly is no more attractive than its name.

The Way then climbs again above Hummersea Scar and on past Boulby quarries, where ironstone, alum and jet have all been worked. The cliffs hereabouts, where it is said that the sixth-century Viking hero Beowulf is buried, are at 666ft the highest on the east coast of England, with excellent views and easy walking. After descending from the clifftops, the Way joins a track to pass through the hamlet of Boulby, continues alongside the cliffs of Bias Scar by means of a footpath, and then joins a metalled road to pass through Cowbar and arrive at the village of Staithes.

With its maze of cobbled streets running steeply up from the harbour, itself protected by the high cliffs of Cowbar Nab and Penny Nab, Staithes is one of the most picturesque settlements on the Way, although it has always been a tough working village with long-standing associations with the mining and fishing industries. Captain Cook, whose monument was seen several miles back, worked as an apprentice grocer in the village until he signed on as a cabin boy in a Whitby ship. There are several fine old stone buildings in the village, especially in the High Street and Church Street with its Georgian houses and rockery-girt cottages. Between these two streets run a number of quaint alleyways with most unusual names that include Gun Gutter, Slip Top and Dog Loup. The latter is just about 18 inches wide, and well-built or well-equipped walkers may proceed along it with some trepidation; after they have endured the rigours of Black Hambleton and the precipitous descents off Cold Moor and Hasty Bank, it would indeed be a savage irony for their conquest of the Way to be scuppered by becoming wedged between two stone walls.

Having left Staithes, the Way proceeds above the cliffs of Old Nab and on past the hamlet of Port Mulgrave with its harbour from which ironstone was once exported. Erosion is a serious problem on this stretch and walkers may be diverted from the cliff edge. You descend steeply to Runswick Bay, a holiday village which lacks the charms of Staithes (65), then walk along the beach for half a mile before climbing splendidly by a narrow beck and up some steep steps to regain the cliffs. From here you continue round the headland of Kettleness, which offers good views back to Boulby cliffs and forward towards Whitby.

The Way stays on the clifftop as far as Deepgrove Wyke, then drops steeply to join the course of an old railway, which was used to take steel products, fish and agricultural produce to the Middlesbrough area. You follow the old line to the village of Sandsend, where you join the A174 and proceed beside it through

East Row and alongside a golf course. Shortly beyond the clubhouse, you turn left on to a track which heads back towards the sea, and soon after passing under a footbridge, you bear right on to an obvious path that leads into Whitby (77).

This fishing port and seaside resort is an almost obligatory resting-place on the journey. Dominated by the remains of the thirteenth-century abbey – an earlier abbey was actually founded here in AD 657 – the town boasts a lively harbour and a jumble of steep alleyways and hillside cottages, converging on the River Esk which flows right through the town. Captain Cook lived in the town as a young man, and another noted navigator, William Scoresby, departed from Whitby for the Arctic whaling grounds. The parish church of St Mary, with its Norman tower, triple-deck pulpit and one of the most complete sets of pre-Victorian furnishings in England, is approached by the 199 Church Stairs from which there is a splendid view of the town.

The old streets are dotted with craft and antique shops, many of them offering items of jewellery made from jet, which is still found along the nearby cliffs. It comes from wood that has been washed out to sea, fossilised and then subjected to the pressure of water and silt. Those unable or unwilling to fill their rucksacks with pieces of jet may still find it hard to resist the allure of the cheaper merchandise that is found in profusion in the narrow streets of the town, from the 'Duck Or Grouse' sign that is an obligatory decoration for any low beam of which the purchaser may care to boast, to pieces of parchment bearing totally spurious family histories that have been ingeniously conceived in musty offices in Stoke Newington or Cricklewood.

Whitby to Newbiggin Cliff

Having climbed away from the Esk to leave Whitby near the abbey, you enjoy a splendid 7-mile walk to Robin Hood's Bay. Soon after leaving Whitby, you pass the cliffs of Saltwick Nab and Black Nab, with the picturesque Saltwick Bay nestling between them, and after an easy start, the going becomes more undulating. The cliff scenery is stunning and constantly fascinating; indeed the cliffs along the whole of the 20 miles between Whitby and Scarborough are a geologist's paradise. Shales, clays, sandstones and limestones all rise to the surface with their different colouring, the near-vertical limestone cliffs contrasting with the more rounded clay ones.

At Maw Wyke Hole the Cleveland Way once again overlaps with the Coast to Coast route, last seen at Bloworth Crossing on the moors, and both journeys follow the cliff path all the way to Robin Hood's Bay. Although there is a considerable amount of up-and-down work, the views out to sea are ample reward. Having proceeded in a south-easterly direction all the way from Whitby, the coast path swings south-west at Ness Point, from which it is a straightforward walk on to Robin Hood's Bay (84). Like Whitby, the village is a delightful jumble of narrow streets, passages and quaint old houses on a variety of levels, and is described as the most picturesque fishing village in Yorkshire. Though walkers attempting to reach Scarborough from Whitby in a day may feel the need to press on, it is an excellent place to stop and recharge the batteries.

The village is in fact the end of the Coast to Coast Walk, so Cleveland Way walkers should not be surprised to observe some impromptu celebrations from those who have successfully completed the 191 miles from St Bees. Of course, it could be that walkers ceremonially dipping their boots in the North Sea are just *starting* their tramp along Wainwright's famous route. Alternatively, they may have enjoyed going west to east so much that they have decided to immediately do it again in reverse, although they should remember the comment in a pub visitors' book that appeared in the TV series about the route: 'The walk to Robin Hood's Bay for an ice cream was lovely; it's the walk back to the car at St Bees that's killing me!'

Beyond Robin Hood's Bay there is more wonderful cliff scenery, but erosion has sadly taken its toll and you may be diverted away from the cliffs as far as Stoupe Beck Sands, where there is a brief gap in the massive stone stacks, before making the a long uphill slog to Ravenscar. A groundwork of streets was laid out here as part of a planned development which never materialised, although some buildings have been erected, including a large hotel dating back to 1774 and built on the site of a Roman signalling station. It now stands proudly on the cliffs, commanding splendid views in an unspoilt setting, almost exactly halfway between Whitby and Scarborough.

Beyond Ravenscar there follows a fine 10-mile walk to Scarborough, close to the cliffs most of the way, although at Beast Cliff the Way goes to the landward side of a strip of woodland, and at Hayburn Wyke there is a steep descent to a wooded valley with an attractive footbridge and waterfall. Emerging from the woods, the walking becomes more open and the lovely inlet of Cloughton Wyke, where the path dips down again, provides scintillating sandstone cliff scenery.

Excellent and straightforward clifftop walking follows, passing the headlands of Hundale Point, Long Nab, Cromer Point and Scalby Ness, but as you approach the latter you do become very conscious of the proximity of Scarborough. You descend to pass round the seaward side of Scalby Mills and beside North Bay, one of two large bays (the other being South Bay) that are separated by the promontory on which Scarborough's magnificent twelfth-century castle is built.

The Cleveland Way is not signposted through Scarborough (99), so you may choose whether to make a beeline for the onward route towards Filey and journey's end, or linger in the town which offers every possible amenity for the walker and holidaymaker, luxury hotels sitting easily with cheerful bed and breakfasts, smart restaurants competing for business with Macdonalds and Burger King. The town is full of fine buildings, most notably the parish church of St Mary which has twelfth-century origins, and the Grand Hotel, described by Pevsner as 'wondrous.' Its harbour is always busy, not only with pleasure craft but also traditional fishing vessels such as cobles and mules.

It has been said that Scarborough is a fishing village and seaside town rolled into one, and it is easy for the visitor to see why as he observes not only the quaint streets of the old town but also the traditional trappings of a holiday resort, from cockle stalls to amusement arcades. It will be a brave walker indeed who chooses to gamble part or all of his train fare home in the casino, in the full knowledge that the capricious turn of the roulette ball will determine whether his journey home next day is in the comfort of a first-class seat in a Pullman lounge or wholly dependent on a golden-hearted truck-driver magically appearing in the Esso Garage in Filey and responding favourably to his outstretched thumb.

The final leg of the official route resumes in Holbeck Gardens to the south of the town, not far from Holbeck Hall, a hotel which collapsed into the sea owing to a cliff slip in 1993. The Way, still following the coastline, rounds the headland of White Nab and passes along the landward edge of an area of woodland, descending to Cayton Bay. As you follow round the bay, you will note that the scenery is somewhat marred by the presence of a holiday camp as well as the nearby A165 road. Things improve, however, as you climb again and regain the coastline to pass Lebberston and Gristhorpe Cliffs, fascinating for their offshore reefs and layered rocks topped with crumbling boulder clay.

The official route shortly ends at Newbiggin Cliff, at the boundary of the old North and East Riding of Yorkshire (108). This also marks the start of the Wolds Way, which most walkers will wish to follow on into Filey. However, there is no proper sign or other landmark to show the end of the route, and it really is a desperately anticlimactical way to end a national trail of such beauty and variety. You may be reminded of the day you attended an afternoon concert featuring the London Philharmonic in a flawless rendition of the 1812 Overture complete with cannons and fireworks, from which you hurried away in order to see your next-door neighbour's nephew scraping his way through the Class 2A violin ensemble's version of *Popeye The Sailor Man* in the end of term entertainment provided by Merry Vale Junior.

SUMMARY OF PLACES OF INTEREST

Helmsley, Rievaulx, Sutton Bank, Kilburn White Horse★, Osmotherley, Live Moor, Carlton Moor, Cringle Moor, Cold Moor, Hasty Bank★, Rosebery Topping★, Saltburn, Boulby Cliffs, Staithes★, Whitby★, Robin Hood's Bay★, Ravenscar, Scarborough★, Filey Brigg.

AMENITIES ON OR NEAR THE ROUTE

Helmsley, Osmotherley, Kildale (L), Guisborough, Skelton (L), Saltburn★, Boulby (L), Staithes, Runswick (L), Whitby★, Robin Hood's Bay, Scarborough★, Filey★.

The Coast to Coast Walk

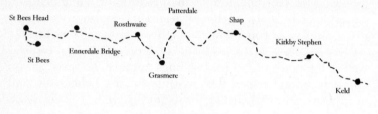

COAST TO COAST

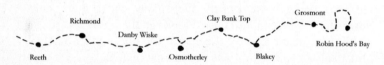

Length: 191 miles.
Start: St Bees, Cumbria.
Finish: Robin Hood's Bay, North Yorkshire.
Nature: A walk across Northern England from coast to coast, including sections of the Lake District, the Pennines, the Yorkshire Dales and the North York Moors.
Difficulty rating: Strenuous, occasionally severe.
Average time of completion: 2 weeks.

The Coast to Coast Walk

Whilst many long-distance footpaths owe their origins to a group of enthusiasts, the Coast to Coast Walk is without question the brainchild of a single individual, Alfred Wainwright, whose beautifully-illustrated guides to the Lakeland fells have become bestsellers amongst walkers and visitors to the Lake District. Having failed to enjoy his walk up the Pennine Way – at that time the only 'official' long-distance route in existence in England – he set about creating his very own long-distance route over kinder terrain. His stipulations were that it should be in the north of England, with which he was already familiar, and should have a definite start and finish point, thus providing a worthy objective for the walker whichever way he went. By drawing a line on a map between St Bees Head, one of the most spectacular points on the west coast, and the attractive village of Robin Hood's Bay on the same latitude on the east coast, he not only succeeded in meeting his self-imposed requirements but found a route between the two places that contained what he believed to be some of the finest scenery in Britain.

He finished the planning in 1972 and published a book describing the route in 1973. He expressed a hope that his planned path would avoid trespass or invasion of privacy. As it turned out, certain sections were found to cross land on which there was no public right of way, with the result that the many walkers who bought Wainwright's book and decided to follow his route were in fact trespassing in some areas! Where this happened, the National Park Authorities and other similar organisations were able to work together to re-route the walk over the nearest public rights of way, or arrange with landowners that Wainwright's original route could continue on a permissive basis. Wainwright was at pains to point out that his chosen route (which in any event incorporated a choice of paths at many points) was in no way the definitive crossing from coast to coast. The fact remains, however, that his route has been adopted by a vast number of walkers, doubtless encouraged not only by his much-reprinted 1973 guide but also his coffee-table companion volume published in 1987, which contained stunning colour photographs by Derry Brabbs, and Wainwright's own television series about the walk which appeared in 1990.

Moreover, the popularity of the trek has spawned two videos describing the route, and an array of merchandise for those wishing to acquire souvenirs of their adventure including postcards, plaques and certificates. So many people attempt the route that special maps have been designed for walkers, a Coast to Coast accommodation guide has been published, and baggage-carrying services are available for those who wish to walk in comparative comfort. It is now one of the most popular routes in Britain, beloved of walkers for its completely unspoilt scenery of tremendous beauty (it passes through three National Parks), immense historical interest, and great variety of terrain, animal life and plant life.

Although it is a challenging, demanding walk that requires physical fitness, proper equipment and good navigational skills, it is walked considerably more than a number of the national trails. Indeed, if forced to make the choice between the Coast to Coast or the Pennine Way, you may – on reading Wainwright's excellent companion guides to both paths – wish to opt for the former, particularly having seen Wainwright's parting observations about the latter: 'You won't come across me anywhere along the Pennine Way. I've had enough of it!'

St Bees to Blackhow

St Bees is a most attractive village from which to begin the walk; the Priory Church, built on the site of a seventh-century nunnery, has some features which date back to 1150 and there is a grammar school dating back to 1583. From the village centre it is a pleasant walk down the lane to the sea wall where the journey across England begins, and Wainwright suggests that as an opening ritual, walkers should dip their boots in the Irish Sea before getting going. There follows a splendid 4-mile cliff walk, heading initially (and perhaps incongruously) slightly west of north, following the clifftops for the most part and dropping down just once to the beautiful rock scenery of Fleswick Bay before rising again. The cliffs themselves, huge stacks of red sandstone, are magnificent and there are excellent views northwards to Whitehaven and beyond, and seawards to the Isle of Man. Once past St Bees Head and lighthouse, you swing round to the east and then leave the cliffs above Saltom Bay; your next sighting of the sea should not be for another ten days at least.

The route heads south-eastwards along well-defined tracks to the pretty village of Sandwith, but after leaving Sandwith there follows a rather fiddly four and a half miles, all the time heading south-east. You continue along narrow tracks, crossing two roads linking Whitehaven with St Bees, then descend and trudge across fields to pass under the Carlisle–Barrow railway close to Stanley Pond. You join another lane to climb out of the valley, cross the busy A595, and go on to reach Moor Row, half a mile east, by road and a portion of cycle track. You follow the Egremont road, heading southwards, out of Moor Row before turning left, heading eastwards across a field and then along a lane to reach Cleator (9). Turning left briefly along the A5086, you soon turn right to exit from this nondescript village of dull grey stone, descending to Blackhow Bridge and then following a lane to Blackhow Farm.

If you feel you have been spoilt by the excellent waymarking on the national trails you will already, less than ten miles into the Coast to Coast, realise that this route is far less well waymarked and you may, as you blunder anxiously around the outer recesses of Moor Row and Cleator with a big climb still to do that day, already regret your decision that the money required to purchase either Wainwright's guide or maps with the route plotted thereon was better spent on those two rounds in the St Bees hotel bar the previous night.

Blackhow to Honister

Beyond Blackhow Farm the walking improves with a stiff climb to the 1,131ft summit of Dent Fell, giving splendid views to the Isle of Man and to some of the Lakeland fells. Still heading east, the route drops from the summit to a forest, and in the absence of adequate waymarking, careful map reading is required to descend to Uldale. The route then bears left to emerge from the forest and head north-eastwards alongside Kirk Beck past the delightful ravine of Nannycatch Gate, with the slopes of Raven Crag and Flat Fell immediately to the left. You continue beside Nannycatch Beck, the valley narrowing as Flat Fell Screes are passed, and climb to a road beside the Kinniside Stone Circle, of recent rather than prehistoric origin. It is then a simple walk along the road, heading north, to the pretty village of Ennerdale Bridge (14), the gateway to Lakeland.

Turning right in the village, you follow the road towards Croasdale before turning right again down a road heading for Ennerdale Water, a clear path leading to the lake edge where you begin a splendid march along its southern shore. The going, on a rocky path, is quite rough, particularly as you negotiate the promontory known as Angler's Crag and pass a small headland known as Robin Hood's Chair. After passing through a small area of woodland you reach the eastern shore of the lake, and from there the route proceeds briefly north-eastwards through fields to reach a forest road. The going is then extremely easy, as the route continues south-eastwards along the road for four miles or so, past Low and High Gillerthwaite and through the massed conifers of

Ennerdale Forest roughly parallel with the River Liza. Gaps in the trees reveal superb views to Pillar and the awesome Pillar Rock on the right.

An *alternative* way leaves the main route just beyond High Gillerthwaite, turning left and climbing to the summit of Red Pike, then continuing south-eastwards along a magnificent ridge of mountains including High Stile, High Crag and Wainwright's own favourite, Haystacks. Passing the delectable Innominate Tarn, the alternative way continues in the same direction to the head of Loft Beck, where it meets the main route.

The *main* route, meanwhile, leaves the forest road almost immediately south of Haystacks, proceeding to that remotest and most romantic of youth hostels, Black Sail Hut. With Great Gable providing the backcloth, the setting could hardly be better, and on clear days the view from the window as the hosteller rises in the morning may well be felt to compensate for the lack of amenities a tired traveller might otherwise hope to meet after a long day's walking, whether this be Sky Digital in the bedroom or Rajput's Happy Tandoori Palace next door.

Beyond Black Sail Hut, you must be careful not to get sucked down to the valley bottom again but instead contour the hillside immediately beyond the hostel, there being no footpath to speak of. Eventually you reach and ford Loft Beck, then turn left to go parallel with it, following a badly eroded path very steeply uphill. This is the sternest climb yet, and good preparation for similarly tough work ahead. As you pause for breath, you should look back to the magnificent valley you are leaving behind, with Great Gable, Brandreth and Pillar soaring up beyond.

Eventually the ground levels out, and you reach a metal post marking the former Brandreth Fence, where the alternative route is united with the main route. Heading north-eastwards, the route then contours the hillside topped by Grey Knotts at a height of just under 2,000ft. The views are spellbinding; to the west can be seen the imposing summits of High Stile and High Crag, the less lofty but unforgettable Haystacks, and the twin lakes of Buttermere and Crummock Water, beyond which Grasmoor is clearly visible.

On a clear sunny day it is a place to linger, and the binoculars should be kept handy for sightings of golden eagles and peregrines.

Proceeding onwards, the route meets the Honister–Great Gable footpath and drops to an old tramway (*not* going forward to the old quarry road), turning right and heading due east downhill, initially gently and then precipitously. At length it emerges at the youth hostel and old quarry sheds at the head of Honister Pass on the B5289. You briefly join the road but soon forsake it to follow an old toll road running alongside it, and fleetingly returning to it. Walkers with blistered feet and knees still shaking from the precipitous descent off Grey Knotts can derive some passing *schadenfreude* from the sight of drivers attempting to manoeuvre their cars, people-carriers and caravans along this extremely awkward stretch of road, where one minor misjudgment can mean that only a piece of roadmanship regarded as overexacting even for those aspiring to join the Institute of Advanced Motorists stands between them and an unscheduled visit to Honest Pete's Motorscrap Heaven.

Honister to Grisedale Tarn

In due course the route turns right off the old toll road, negotiating a crude hairpin bend to drop down to Borrowdale and the pleasant and popular village of Seatoller. Turning left to proceed through the village car park, you join an attractive path that snakes through Johnny's Wood, with the River Derwent now visible to the right; the going becomes rough and a chain is provided at one point to negotiate an area of rocks. Soon after passing Longthwaite Youth Hostel, the Derwent is crossed and it is then a simple field walk northwards to reach Rosthwaite (28), the principal settlement of Borrowdale. With its green fields, attractive stone villages, a fine river leading to Derwent Water, and of course its mountain backcloth, Borrowdale is a magical place and the walker with time to spare may wish to enjoy the luxury of a bus ride to Keswick and back through the dale before continuing.

The route, having emerged just to the north of the village, crosses the B5289, turns left and then heads immediately right, soon branching off right to follow a well-defined path that heads south-eastwards, heading for Lining Crag and ultimately Grasmere. The going, past the delightful hamlet of Stonethwaite and alongside firstly Stonethwaite Beck and then Greenup Gill, is easy at first, but as you approach and pass Eagle Crag, which becomes less formidable as the height is gained, the gradient becomes stiffer. You will find pauses for breath become more and more necessary, but as you rest you can admire the view back to Borrowdale, a sight of bewitching beauty.

There is a steep scramble up on to Lining Crag, where hands as well as feet are necessary to make progress, but the reward is a stunning view to the northern end of the Lake District, including Bassenthwaite Lake and Skiddaw. The path becomes indistinct now, the direction only marginally east of south, as you cross a marshy area and pass the summit of Greenup Edge, marked by an iron stanchion. On a clear day the way ahead is obvious, a clear path being seen to head south-eastwards down the hillside to the head of Far Easedale Gill, with the prospect of Grasmere and its verdant surrounds beyond. If the summit of the pass is blanketed in mist, unless you are skilled in compass reading (and have a compass to hand), you must rely either on intelligent guesswork or prayers that out of the swirling white blanket may magically emerge a trusty walker who has undertaken the journey from Greenup Edge to Grasmere on a regular basis since 1957 and, better still, has a surplus of hot tea and Kendal Mint Cake in his knapsack.

After a rough descent to the head of the gill, Wainwright's recommended route turns left to climb on to the ridge immediately to the left, and proceeds to Grasmere via the ridge. The alternative is a straightforward descent on a path beside Far Easedale Gill, which is the obvious bad weather route. The ridge walk encompasses three mini-peaks, namely Calf Crag, Gibson Knott and finally Helm Crag; the going is not always easy, the path well-defined but weaving sinuously through the areas of grass and rock. The views are spectacular, and include Helvellyn, the Langdale Pikes, the long ribbon of water that is Lake Windermere, and even the sea. Of the three peaks on the ridge, Helm Crag is the noblest, with its intriguing and grotesque rock formations; indeed its summit rocks have been likened by some to a lady playing the organ!

There is a very steep descent southwards from Helm Crag into the valley to reach the path following the alternative route, and this in turn joins a road which leads into Grasmere (38). One of the major tourist spots in Lakeland, Grasmere is most famous for gingerbread, the annual August sports, and of course Dove Cottage, the home of William Wordsworth at the start of the nineteenth century. It is also a most useful place for replenishing supplies before heading resolutely north-eastwards towards Patterdale.

The route heads back along the same road used to enter the village but then turns right to follow a minor road past the youth hostel, and another turn right at a T-junction by Mill Bridge brings you to the A591 Keswick–Ambleside road. You cross straight over this road, and follow a clear path ahead to embark on the Grisedale pass route. The going is gentle at first, then below Great Tongue you have a choice between a long steady ascent or a shorter sharper one. The former is by way of path to the right of Great Tongue, alongside Tongue Gill and its impressive cascades. The latter proceeds to the left of Great Tongue, up an extremely steep grassy path running alongside Little Tongue Gill, then above a fringe of rocks the path levels out and swings to the right to meet the other path. Both then go forward to the summit of the pass, through a mass of rocks and boulders with the summit of Seat Sandal to the left and Fairfield to the right.

The summit brings with it an immediate view to the hitherto invisible Grisedale Tarn, the route proceeding along the right side of it to the base of Tarn Crag. Nearby is a rock known as Brothers Parting, where William Wordsworth said a last farewell to his brother John, the event being commemorated by verses on a tablet affixed. It seems a peculiar place for such a farewell to have occurred, but certainly more romantic and scenic, and infinitely more salubrious, than passport control at Gatwick Airport or bay 9 on Victoria Coach Station.

Grisedale Tarn to Kidsty Pike

Now you are faced with a tantalising choice. Straight ahead is Patterdale, and the main route proceeds easily and unerringly downhill through Grisedale, keeping Grisedale Beck to the left, with glorious views to Ullswater ahead. The path becomes a track and then a road that skirts Glemara Park; shortly after passing a road coming up from the left (in fact the Helvellyn alternative), the route turns right and follows a path through the park which emerges in the centre of Patterdale (46). An alternative track is by way of a right turn beside Grisedale Tarn, which provides a journey to Patterdale via the 2,756ft summit of St Sunday Crag, the path dropping down to meet the main route in Glemara Park.

The other alternative, for the adventurous walker, involves turning left by the tarn, ascending to skirt the 2,810ft summit of Dollywaggon Pike and then proceeding onwards to the summit of Helvellyn, one of Lakeland's Big Four at a summit of 3,118ft. It is then necessary to walk along the rocky ridge of Striding Edge, one of the most spectacular walks in the country, before dropping gradually to Grisedale to meet a road which in turn joins the road skirting Glemara Park referred to above. Whichever route is followed, you are likely to arrive in Patterdale feeling more than a little exhausted, only to be confronted with a huge mountainous barrier immediately before you.

Having turned right in Patterdale on to the A592, you soon turn left on to a road that crosses Goldrill Beck, going forward to meet a group of houses, bearing left and immediately right, taking a short climb which leads to a T-junction of paths. The route turns right here and begins an arduous climb south-eastwards along Boardale Hause, soon reaching a fork where it is important to take the right-hand path, which continues to climb steeply. It is a relief when the path levels out and you can enjoy magnificent views back to Helvellyn, Patterdale and Brothers Water.

There follows an exciting high level walk on an excellent path, reaching two forking paths at the head of Dubhow Beck and taking the lower of two. Soon the path swings round the northern end of Angle Tarn, a useful landmark in mist, and proceeds boggily but clearly by the eastern side of the tarn, rising slightly to Satura Crag. Here it is important not to veer eastwards on to Rest Dodd; the correct route, heading south-east all the time, stays close to a wall, descending slightly and then rising steeply towards the Knott, the ground still extremely juicy. The route aims for the Knott's eastern shoulder, the ground eventually levelling out and the going underfoot becoming clearer. Magnificent walking follows, with the summit of Rampsgill Head immediately to the east, and the 2,718ft summit of High Street straight ahead. The Coast to Coast does not make the climb to this fine peak, but at Twopenny Crag turns left and there is then a tremendous ridge march to Kidsty Pike, its summit clearly visible at the ridge end. To the right, and separating Kidsty Pike from High Street, is the great ravine of Riggindale.

The arrival at the 2,560ft Kidsty Pike marks a key moment on the walk; this is the highest point on the whole route, the last point which offers a grandstand view of Lakeland, and the beginning of the end of your association – on this trip – with the Lake District. On a clear day the views are magnificent, with many major Lakeland peaks including Hevellyn, Pillar, Coniston Old Man and Blencathra on show. On a wet or misty day you will simply be mightily relieved to have arrived here at all, and the thought that the weather forecasters are promising cloudless skies over the region for the next three days will merely add insult to the injury you feel that the weather during your three days in Lakeland has enabled you to see above an otherwise unremitting nine hundred foot cloud cover for a total period of twenty-three and a half seconds.

Kidsty Pike to Mazon Wath

Progress eastwards down to Haweswater Reservoir looks straightforward on the map, but the descent, after an easy start, is extremely steep; there are numerous drops requiring the use of hands as well as feet, if limbs are to survive intact. Eventually you reach the waterside and turn left to follow an excellent path by the west shore. After a brief climb to Birks Crag – the site of a British fort – and descent again, the going is very quick, with delightful surroundings including pleasant woodland and the impressive crossing of Whelter Beck. Eventually the steep hillsides to the left relent somewhat, and the path drops down to a road, but if you are heading for Shap and feel your day's work must be nearly done, you are sadly mistaken, as five miles of fiddly walking remain.

Soon after turning left on to the road, the route reaches the hamlet of Burn Banks and turns right along a path to reach a road crossing of Haweswater Beck. You cross to follow a path on the south side of the beck, heading eastwards. The path forsakes the beck, continuing eastwards then swinging south-eastwards to pass Rawhead, and north-eastwards over a metalled road to descend over common land to the pretty Lowther river bridge at Rosgill. The route turns sharp right along a path that passes near to the confluence of the Lowther and Swindale Beck, heading southwards to pass the farm at Good Croft and then crossing Swindale Beck by means of a charming packhorse bridge. A field path heading south-eastwards takes you uphill to a metalled road, and you turn left to follow it, shortly turning left again and walking downhill through a field – still heading south-east – to reach the imposing ruins of Shap Abbey, which dates back to the twelfth century.

Having endured a few miles of fiddly route-finding, you will be relieved to turn left on to a metalled road leading to the village of Shap (62) in just over a mile. At the end of this road, you turn right on to the main street (the A6 in fact) and into the village centre. Before the advent of the M6 the village served as a useful stop for motorists, as reflected by its wide range of amenities, but it now has the feel of a quiet backwater. Although there are good views back towards Lakeland, the pointed peak of Kidsty Pike being particularly prominent, it has little of architectural merit, the seventeenth-century market hall being the only building of real note in the village. It is remarkable however, for the length of its main street which may hold fascination for students of local history, socio-economic policy and town and country planning, but rather less fascination for the weary walker who, having walked all the way to the very bottom of the village in search of his night's lodgings, finds them to be situated at the very top.

The next 21 miles to Kirkby Stephen involve much easier walking over the limestone-rich Westmorland Plateau, but with a constant view to the fells, most notably the Howgills ahead and to the right. The route proceeds along Shap's main street, turning left opposite the King's Arms along a road. Soon you cross the main London–Glasgow railway, then strike south-eastwards, first along a lane, then a succession of field paths and tracks to the tiny hamlet of Oddendale, crossing a footbridge over the M6 and then passing a limestone quarry. At Oddendale the route swings southwards, going just to the east of a stone circle, then shortly after passing the walled enclosure and barn known as Potrigg, there is a left turn and you head in a more south-easterly direction again.

There follows a fine moorland walk along the side of Crosby Ravensworth Fell, the route well waymarked as it crosses an old Roman road and Lyvennet Beck and proceeds without difficulty to the Orton–Crosby Ravensworth road. There are two mini-valley crossings; at the second, a short detour to the right brings you to an ancient cairn described inaccurately as Robin Hood's Grave. On arriving at the road you could, if pushed for time, simply turn right and proceed to the cattle grid where there is a junction with the B6260 coming down from Appleby. However, Wainwright's recommended route involves crossing the first road and following a path that swings in a southerly direction to run between the two roads along a dry valley bottom, to reach the road junction. From here you may detour to the village of Orton by continuing along the B6260.

Orton is the only settlement of any size near the route between Shap and Kirkby Stephen; it is a charming village with tidy terraces of old cottages, a field serving as a village green with streams crossed by many little bridges, a church with a fine tower, and a former manor house built in the seventeenth century. However, the Coast to Coast itself does not visit Orton, but turns immediately left off the B6260. It proceeds along a grassy track and through a field to the east of Broadfell Farm, turning left on to a drive and left again on to a metalled lane which passes three more farms. Just beyond the last, a left turn takes you along a path to Knott Lane, crossing straight over to pass to the left of a prehistoric stone circle and across fields, heading east, to the farm at Acres. You turn left here and follow a lane past the farms of Sunbiggin and Stoneyhead Hall, and out on to Tarn Moor. You meet two crossroads of paths in close succession, turning right at each and proceeding downhill to a road. Having turned left along the road and passed Sunbiggin

Tarn, a favoured spot for waterfowl, you now have two very easy miles of road-walking.

The road heading north-east reaches a junction with a road heading south-east, and the route turns right on to that road (it is possible to cut the tight corner quite conveniently, saving a few minutes). This road passes the hamlet of Mazon Wath, then continues for a mile through moorland, reaching a cattle grid where the route turns left, eastwards, along a path. Walkers using the up-to-date edition of Wainwright's guide may be in for a rude awakening; having notched up mile 76 just south of Mazon Wath, they find themselves clocking it up again soon after leaving the sanctuary of the metalled road, with Kirkby Stephen still nearly seven miles away. The simple explanation is that Wainwright's original route was quite different from the B6260 to this point. The extra mileage may incite rebellion among the less stoical walkers in the party who believed that they were only required to walk 190, not 191 miles on this expedition. It should go without saying that Wainwright, being the purist that he was, would have precious little sympathy with their protests, their dark murmurings about the deployment of short cuts or even wheeled transport for a mile later on by way of compensation being as much of an abhorrence to his memory as the building of 100 new Wimpey Homes on the summit of Haystacks.

Mazon Wath to Ney Gill

Field walking now takes over as the route heads slightly south of east over Ewefell Mire (which is not as bad as it sounds) and past Bents Farm. It proceeds beside Bents Hill and alongside the prehistoric village settlement of Severals, of which there are few obvious traces. There is then an unexpectedly steep descent towards Scandal Beck, the path turning south-westwards to drop down to cross it by means of the charming Smardale Bridge. Turning left to head eastwards and then north-eastwards, the route initially follows a cart-track heading uphill, with fine views to an old railway viaduct. You should look out for the long mounds to the left of this section, known as Giants' Graves; they are not graves of giants, nor are they thought to be burial mounds. One theory is that they were platforms used for stacking bracken, another that they were coney-beds or rabbit warrens.

You continue on a clear path, heading north-eastwards and steadily uphill across the moorland of Smardale Fell and Limekiln Hill. The rewards for your efforts are your first views to the Eden valley, a sign that Kirkby Stephen is not far off. There is then easy downhill walking, still heading north-eastwards, to a metalled road. The route turns right on to it, almost immediately left on to another road, and shortly right on to a path, heading initially south-east and then north-eastwards downhill to pass underneath the Settle–Carlisle railway. Just to the right of the path, immediately beyond the underpass, are traces of the earthworks of another prehistoric settlement. Rather bitty but undemanding field-walking then follows, the route heading north-east and downhill to pass under two disused railways towards the Green Riggs Farm buildings. Here you take a right turn to join a lane that leads to the first of just two towns on the route, Kirkby Stephen (84), the lane emerging by the main street.

The town, with its wide range of amenities, is a most welcome halt on the journey. It is an attractive town too, with several Georgian houses including Winton Hall, built in 1726, and a thirteenth-century church dedicated to St Stephen, approached through a stone portico built in 1810 by a naval purser, John Waller. The church contains a stone carving of the Norse devil Loki, thought to be one of the earliest Christian symbols of the Devil in human shape.

For many years the town has also been the home of the Coast to Coast fish and chip shop, where in the BBC video Wainwright was seen tucking into a goodly portion of said fare, but one cannot rule out the sad possibility that in time it may have to swim with the irresistible tide of market forces and turn itself into the Coast to Coast Cybercafé, the Coast to Coast Craft Fayre, or even the Coast to Coast Mews, a block of luxury flats for retired town-dwellers who prior to purchase would have hazarded a guess that the Coast to Coast was either a firm of estate agents or a trans-Pennine bus company.

Having loaded the rucksack with provisions – there are no amenities available anywhere near the route for the next 23 miles – you leave Kirkby Stephen, bound for the halfway mark of the Coast to Coast at Keld, by following an alleyway off the marketplace down to cross Frank's Bridge over the river Eden. There follows a pleasant riverside walk eastwards, keeping the river to the right, and from here it is easy walking gently uphill through a field, still heading east, and then along a lane to the pretty village of Hartley. You cross a stream and reach a metalled road, turning right on to the road and following it uphill for just over two miles, past the somewhat unsightly Hartley Quarries. The going is extremely easy and it is undeniably good to get two quick miles under the belt before the real hard work begins.

Soon after passing Fell House Farm and crossing Hartley Beck, the metalled road peters out, giving way to an unmetalled track heading south-east past sheep pens. There follows a splendid march along an excellent track on to Hartley Fell, the views getting better all the time, with the summit cairns of Nine Standards excitingly visible ahead. Then, having reached 1,600ft, there is an important junction of paths for the watershed crossing that follows. In order to minimise erosion in the area, walkers between December and April are requested to omit Nine Standards but continue straight on along the bridleway heading south-east to 1,800ft, and then right along a path that proceeds past a wind shelter and south-westwards past potholes known as the Tailbrigg Pots to reach the B6270. The route turns left on to it, proceeding for a mile and a half before turning left again on to an unmetalled road which heads east to a shooting hut, from which a path is taken eastwards along the left bank of Ney Gill.

Walkers on the Coast to Coast between May and November should turn left at the important junction of paths referred to above, heading uphill along a very good path to reach Nine Standards, a group of cairns thought to be boundary markers or beacons and dating back several centuries. At 2,170ft, this is the highest point of the walk since Lakeland, and the views are tremendous, particularly across the Eden valley. A right turn and a short but exhilarating promenade along the hilltop brings you to Nine Standards Rigg.

Walkers between May and July will continue in the same direction to White Mossy Hill, then due south to a shelter and thereafter south-eastwards, heading steadily downhill in a south-easterly direction by Coldbergh Edge to meet the unmetalled road just east of the turn off the B6270 described above. Walkers between August and November will turn left, roughly halfway between Nine Standards Rigg and White Mossy Hill to head eastwards. The route is clearly marked by a line of posts as it negotiates a succession of hideous peat-hags, goes steeply downhill, swings south then south-east to follow a tortuously narrow, often very squelchy and constantly undulating path alongside Whitsundale Beck. Finally it leaves the beck to follow a slightly better path which in turn joins the Ney Gill-side path.

Whichever route has been followed, it is debatable whether you will feel the exciting attainment of Nine Standards and/or the crossing of the main watershed of Northern England to be an adequate pay-off for filthy gaiters, mud-splashed trousers and sodden socks and boots, and it would be hard not to sympathise with any walker who advocated a new all-the-year-round, all-weather, erosion-proof route from Kirkby Stephen to Keld, involving the peat-free and easily navigable B6270 throughout.

Ney Gill to Blakethwaite

The route fords Ney Gill soon after the reuniting of the three 'strands', and then continues eastwards to reach a narrow metalled road, turning left on to it to reach the farm at Raven Seat. After crossing Whitsundale Beck, you turn right on to a path which for the next couple of miles heads south-eastwards along the hillside, with splendid views to the beck on the right as it passes through a deep ravine. Having negotiated walled pastures just beyond Raven Seat, the walking becomes more open as it passes the huge sheepfold called Eddy Fold and drops down to Smithy Holme Farm and on along a cart-track.

As the track swings to the right to drop to the B6270, the route turns off left to run along a path parallel with that road but separated from it by the impressive limestone cliffs known as Cotterby Scar, and the River Swale which will never be far away over the next 30 miles or so. Looking down, a pretty waterfall called Wain Wath Force soon becomes visible. At length you reach a road and turn right on to it, then left on to the B6270, from which a clearly-signposted road leads into Keld (96), the halfway point on the Coast to Coast, and the point where the Coast to Coast meets the Pennine Way. It is also the gateway to the Yorkshire Dales National Park.

Keld consists of a small assembly of farm buildings and cottages, a hall and a chapel (rebuilt in 1860) all round or near a rustic square. Another chapel, a youth hostel and a few other buildings stand beside the B6270. The charm of the village lies not only in its pleasant buildings but also in its timelessness – the scene here has altered little in centuries – and of course, its magnificent setting amongst Pennine fells beside the River Swale. Wainwright comments that, at Keld, there is always the music of the water, and proof of this can be found in no less than four fine waterfalls close by: not only Wain Wath Force but Catrake, Kisdon and East Gill Forces.

Amenities are severely restricted; although there are a few bed and breakfasts as well as the youth hostel, there is no shop or pub in the village, and after the bustle of Kirkby Stephen the quietness and isolation is palpable. I selected a bed and breakfast a mile and a half north of the village (reached by following the Pennine Way) and was immediately struck by the remoteness and timelessness of the surroundings, somewhat rudely dispelled by the farm owner's teenage son who that evening whiled away a good two hours winning the Monaco Grand Prix and bringing about the bloody end of a ruthless serial killer by means of the PlayStation plugged into the television.

From the village square, a well-marked footpath heads south-eastwards, soon reaching another junction of paths where the route, now following the same course as the Pennine Way, turns left and drops down to cross the Swale. There is then a brief climb to a junction of paths with the beautiful East Gill Force immediately to the right. The Pennine Way bears left to head towards the Tan Hill Inn, whilst the Coast to Coast turns right to cross the water and follows a clear track south-eastwards, with splendid views to the Swale. You turn left off this track (at the time of writing this crucial left turn is not signposted and I suspect I will not have been the only one to miss it) and proceed past the ruins of the once handsome residence of Crackpot Hall; again it is important to take the upper of two paths beyond the ruins, proceeding north-eastwards to reach a bridge over Swinner Gill. The ruined smelting-mill here is just one of a number of old lead mine workings hereabouts, and several more reminders of the area's important industrial past will be seen in the next few miles. Many of the mines date back to the seventeenth or eighteenth centuries, but the industry collapsed at the end of the nineteenth century and farming has become the principal occupation in the area.

Having crossed the Gill by the bridge, the route continues eastwards, going steeply uphill beside another stream known as East Grain, but the rough walking soon gives way to an excellent track heading eastwards across the moors. The moorland scenery within the Yorkshire Dales National Park, and its bird life, are magnificent, and you should keep your eyes peeled for kestrel, merlin, lapwing, curlew and golden plover. It is a shame to leave this track at the point that it swings southwards towards Gunnerside. The route heads north-eastwards steeply downhill through grass and heather on a path that is far from obvious on the ground, and again signposting cannot be guaranteed.

Nearing the bottom of the narrow valley, you reach a much better track heading south-north, and you turn left on to it to head northwards up to the remarkable ruins of the Blakethwaite Smelt Mill, where you use a stone slab to cross Gunnerside Beck. The route then climbs steeply up the bank the other side, heading south-east towards a succession of hushes. A hush is a ravine that was cut by mineral prospectors to enable water, released from above, to strip the vegetation, thereby allowing the subsoil to be examined in the hope of finding a vein. More waggish walkers, particularly those used to controlling unruly schoolchildren, will not want to let slip the opportunity to say to their companions, 'Can we have a bit of hush, please,' whilst fans of The Carpenters will doubtless be unable to resist a quick burst of their 1976 single 'There's a kind of hush all over the world tonight'!

Blakethwaite to Reeth

Shortly before reaching further ruined mineworkings, you swing from south-east to east, the route climbing high into the moors directly away from the valley of Gunnerside Beck. The route here is most unclear on the ground, signposting is non-existent and prudent use of map and compass are essential to prevent the walker going badly off course (as I did). Assuming all is well, you soon join a track, heading east by the Old Gang Mines to cross Flincher Gill at Level House Bridge, and then south-east. You pass the distinctive tower and other ruins of the Old Gang Smelt Mill and continue on to Surrender Bridge, where you meet a road. You go straight over the road and after passing another ruined smelt mill, head north-westwards across a moor to negotiate the ravine of Cringley Bottom, dropping steeply to a beck and then rising equally precipitously, aiming for the squeeze stile. Once over the stile, there are three easy miles to Reeth along well-defined tracks heading south-eastwards and then eastwards across pastures, passing a number of farms. After the rugged moorland terrain, the surroundings now seem gentler as a gradual descent is made towards the Swale.

At length, you join a narrow lane which heads south-eastwards more decisively downhill, joining the B6270 and turning left on to that road to enter Reeth (107). Standing at the meeting point of Swaledale and the formerly industrial Arkengarthdale, and described as the capital of Upper Swaledale, the village consists of an assembly of grey stone houses round a large irregular green. Here is the confluence of the Swale and Arkle Beck – the meeting point of Swaledale and the formerly industrial Arkengarthdale. There are ample amenities here, with tourists well catered for by a number of hotels and tearooms.

The sight of a tea shop will gladden any walker's heart; a break from the rigours of a long hike to take tea may be most pleasant, particularly if the tea shop owner understands the needs of walkers and enjoys meeting and talking with them about their travels. Where this is so, it is likely that the thirsty hiker – quite unfussy about the quality of the brew provided it is hot and wet – will enter and be immediately bidden to sit wherever he wishes, with no pressure placed upon him to sample the culinary delights that may appear on the food menu. In certain establishments, however, particularly those wishing to boost revenue or attract a better class of customer, the sweaty traveller may be made to feel less than welcome. He may not only be forced to don a sleeved top and remove his muddy boots before the staff deign to speak to him, but may have to stand waiting while a properly-laid table is prepared for him. Having sat down, he will then be faced with the agonising decision between closely-prescribed set menus from which no deviation is permissible under any circumstances, the waiter or waitress making no attempt to conceal impatience as the already exhausted traveller endeavours to get his head round the relative merits of the Swaledale, Arkengarthdale or Dales Tea (*£1 supplement for smoked salmon sandwich, optional 10 per cent service charge added to all bills*).

Reeth to Danby Wiske

The route follows the B6270 south-eastwards out of Reeth, crossing Arkle Beck, and soon reaching Fremington. Here you turn left on to a minor road signposted for Marske, and in half a mile bear right on to another minor road which you follow for a mile as far as Marrick priory church. The original priory, thought to be either Benedictine or Cistercian, was founded in the 1150s and the church was built in 1811 out of materials from the priory, although the walls of the former chancel remain outside the church. At the church the route turns left off the road, and a good path is followed north-eastwards through attractive woodland to reach the pretty village of Marrick. The path leads to a road that follows through the village, turning right on to a road just past a house with a most peculiar sundial.

Very shortly you turn left to head north-eastwards and for just under two miles the walking is through a succession of fields, heading first downhill to the attractive cottage at Ellers and a charming bridge over Ellers Beck, then uphill to regain the Fremington–Marske road. Concentration is needed along this section, as the path is not clear on the ground and it is important to identify the stile or gate that will allow progress through to the next field. A useful marker is the 1814 monument to Matthew

Hutton, a 60ft obelisk just off route to the right not far from Hollins Farm beyond Ellers. Turning right on to the Fremington–Marske road, there is then a steep descent along the road to the lovely village of Marske, one of the prettiest on the whole route. The little church of St Edmund has a Norman doorway and some box pews; there is an eighteenth-century hall, a fifteenth-century bridge over Marske Beck, and several attractive stone cottages.

Ignoring the signposted Richmond road, heading off to the right, you continue on the road uphill past the church, turning right at a T-junction of roads on to another Richmond-bound road. This is followed for just under half a mile, after which the route turns right on to a path heading north-east to cross Clapgate Beck. It then goes steeply uphill, still heading north-east, to an unusual white cairn marking the junction of the path and a farm track, immediately below the dramatic limestone cliffs of Applegarth Scar. You head eastwards then north-eastwards along the track past a succession of farms, all with Applegarth in the title; the track is indistinct in places and there are a few stiles to negotiate, but just past East Applegarth Farm you join a much clearer track, heading into Whitcliffe Wood. You pass the steep slopes of Whitcliffe Scar on the left, and observe on the hilltop the monument known as Willance's Leap, commemorating the remarkable deliverance of a horseman who fell from the spot whilst riding in 1606.

Having passed through Whitcliffe Wood, heading south-eastwards, the track emerges to give a magnificent view of Richmond and the surrounding countryside. It is then a very easy and satisfying walk on to Richmond, the track becoming a road which proceeds unerringly downhill to this beautiful and historic town, with the best range of amenities on the walk. Wainwright invites walkers to tidy themselves up a bit as they approach Richmond in the hope of meeting a 'sweet lass of Richmond Hill' or two, but those who in the last 36 hours have sunk deep into peat bogs on Nine Standards and then floundered in ever-decreasing circles round the infamous hushes by Gunnerside Beck may have long since passed caring about their personal appearance, and will settle for making themselves sufficiently presentable to attend the town's chemist to be served much-needed additional supplies of blister pads.

Richmond (118) is a splendid town and indeed one of the most attractive towns in Yorkshire. It is dominated by the massive eleventh-century castle keep but there are many other notable buildings including the Georgian Theatre, one of the oldest in England, the medieval Holy Trinity Church which now houses the Green Howards' Regimental Museum, the fifteenth-century Greyfriars Gateway, and the eighteenth-century Culloden Tower in the 35-acre estate of Temple Lodge. The cobbled marketplace contains several fine eighteenth-century buildings including the Town Hall and the King's Head Hotel, and almost every street leading from the marketplace contains houses of historical interest.

The Coast to Coast Walk, taking whatever route through Richmond is desired, drops down to the fine eighteenth-century Richmond Bridge, crosses over and then turns left for a lovely walk beside the Swale, leaving the river as it curves to the left. You then proceed through a wood and past Priory Villas to reach the A6136 where you turn right. (Alternatively you may continue by the Swale to reach Station Bridge and turn right on to this road.) In half a mile there is a left turn along a lane leading past a sewage works, but there are good views over the Swale to the ruin of the twelfth-century Easby Abbey, described by Pevsner as one of the most picturesque monastic ruins in the county.

The route then follows a grassy bank heading south to reach the river at a sharp bend, and there follows a most picturesque woodland walk close to the river, followed by some fiddly field walking south-eastwards past the ruin of Hagg Farm. Eventually you reach the pleasant village of Colburn, which contains a rebuilt Tudor mansion and separate Manor Hall. After passing along its main street the route uses a mixture of tracks and footpaths to head eastwards, roughly parallel with the Swale.

At length you drop steeply to pass underneath the very noisy A1 and then continuing beside the Swale to Catterick Bridge. The original bridge dates back to the fifteenth century although the medieval structure is hidden by refacing and widening. You cross the bridge and continue by means of a path along the north bank of the Swale, bearing left to the B6271 as the river bends sharply to the right. You turn right along the B6271 then first right down a lane and shortly left along another lane to reach Bolton-on-Swale, crossing straight over the B6271 and heading for the church with its large and imposing tower of pale pink sandstone. The churchyard has a remarkable commemorative obelisk to a local man named Henry Jenkins who, if the wording on a black slab in the church is to be believed, lived to be 169. Moreover, he is reputed to have swum across the Swale when he was 100!

Having continued on the road past the church, the route turns right to follow a pleasant course south-eastwards through fields along a path beside Bolton Beck, first on its west bank and then its east bank, to reach a road at the hamlet of Ellerton Hill. You turn left on to the road and follow it. Here begins the generally-acknowledged low point of the Coast to Coast; for virtually all of the next eight miles the route follows tarmac roads, with no views to speak of, through a nondescript rural landscape at the northern end of the Vale of York known as the Vale of Mowbray. The road heads in an easterly direction, passing some woodland at Hodber Hill then, after going over a crossroads, it proceeds via Rawcar Bridge over Rawcar Beck to Streetlam. Here you have temporary relief from tarmac, the route turning right at a left-hand bend in the road to follow fields past West Farm, never far from the road which the route rejoins half a mile short of Danby Wiske (132).

The route carries on into the village, which one has to say sounds more picturesque than it is, although there is an interesting church with a Norman doorway, an early fourteenth-century chancel, a thirteenth-century north arcade and an early fourteenth-century memorial effigy. East of the church is the probably seventeenth-century Lazenby Hall which is worth a look if time is not pressing. In his books about the route, Wainwright makes great play of the fact that when planning the route he looked forward to a pub meal here but all he could get to eat was a bag of crisps from a surly landlord, and it was thus with delight that he was able to inform his viewers in the TV series that one could now obtain meals here that one inferred were fit for a king. When I arrived at the pub one lunchtime in late March however, I found it locked and deserted, which should serve as a caution to contemporary tarmac-crunchers against excessive drooling at the mouth at what may turn out to be empty promises of beef hotpot and steak and kidney pie.

Danby Wiske to Glaisdale

Beyond Danby Wiske you continue along the road in a vaguely easterly direction, crossing the main London–Edinburgh railway and soon reaching a fork in the road. The route takes the left fork to arrive at the A167 at the hamlet of Oaktree Hill (no amenities), while detouring right at the fork leads you to the town of Northallerton (lots of amenities) in two and a half miles. At Oaktree Hill, the site of the Battle of the Standard between the English and the Scots in 1138, the route turns left on to the A167 and shortly right on to a metalled lane. The long road walking section is over but scenically there is no great improvement. This is essentially farming, not walking country.

The lane soon reaches a metalled road; the path turns left on to it then immediately right to follow a mixture of farm roads and tracks eastwards past three farms, reaching another road. This time you bear right and shortly left to join a path which soon crosses the Northallerton–Middlesbrough railway line, heading north-eastwards. The route then goes sharply south-eastwards on a field edge, turning left on to a lane which proceeds north-eastwards past Harlsey Grove Farm and eventually to a metalled road. You turn right on to it, then at a T-junction of roads you go straight ahead eastwards on to a farm road heading to Sydal Lodge.

By this time, if you began the day at Richmond you will be feeling tired and drained from the many unrewarding miles walked today, but there are now good views ahead to the Cleveland Hills which will spur you on as you use a field path to proceed over the River Wiske to the ruins of Brecken Hill farm. You now join a farm track, which follows field edges, first in one direction then another, passing two more farms, and finally arriving at a road on to which you turn right to reach the extremely busy A19, which like the Cleveland Hills will also have been evident for some time. There is no bridge and you must take your life in your hands as you cross straight over and proceed south-eastwards along the minor road immediately opposite, to reach the twin villages of Ingleby Arncliffe and Ingleby Cross (141).

The road drops down to the A172 Thirsk–Stokesley road, crossing straight over and proceeding south-eastwards, heading uphill to reach Arncliffe Church and Hall. The church was rebuilt in 1821 except for the Norman west doorway, and inside there are box pews and two fourteenth-century effigies. The Hall was built in 1753–4, and contains two rooms with some of the most spectacular rococo plasterwork in the country.

Beyond the Church and Hall, a farm is passed and the lane turns sharp right; the Coast to Coast goes straight on through a field into woodland, reaching a forest road. You turn right on to the forest road, heading south-westwards close to the edge of the forest with lovely views through the trees. In just under a mile the forest road swings sharply left, at which point a path leading to the right provides a detour to the fourteenth-century Mount Grace Priory, described by Pevsner as the best preserved Carthusian monastery in England. The Coast to Coast, however, swings left with the forest road, then almost immediately right, gaining height all the time. Very soon there is a T-junction of paths, and the point at which you meet the Cleveland Way. Both Coast to Coast and Cleveland Way go left, but by detouring to the right you can reach Osmotherley (described in Cleveland Way chapter).

From the T-junction there is a substantial overlap with the Cleveland Way. The chapter devoted to the Cleveland Way fully describes the next section, via Beacon Hill, Scarth Wood Moor, the attractive valley of Scugdale, the hamlet of Huthwaite Green, and the ascent on to the Cleveland Hills. There is a real roller-coaster walk over Live Moor, Carlton Moor, Cringle Moor, Cold Moor and Hasty Bank before the final big ascent on to Urra Moor and the joining of the old Rosedale Ironstone Railway. It is at Bloworth Crossing that the Cleveland Way parts company with the Coast to Coast, the former turning left off the old railway while the latter (with the Lyke Wake walk) goes straight on, following the old railway.

The railway was constructed in 1861 to convey high-grade iron ore mined on the Rosedale hillsides some way to the south-east, and although passengers were occasionally carried, the line was only ever used by freight trains. However, ironstone production declined after the turn of the century and the line shut in 1929. The old trackbed now allows fast, easy walking for the next five miles, negotiating a number of bends before heading more resolutely south-eastwards. There is fine moorland scenery all around, the heather a quite magnificent sight when in full flower in the summer, and to the right there are excellent views down the more verdant valley of Farndale. Birds to look out for are the curlew, merlin and grouse, the latter easily identifiable with its cries of 'Go back! Go back!' Wainwright writes that this section is pure delight to walkers with youthful minds who can imagine themselves speeding along in charge of a locomotive, although if by now you are feeling the effects of your long day's march over the Cleveland Hills you may wish you really were.

Four miles beyond Bloworth Crossing the track comes on to High Blakey Moor, swinging to the left to pass round the head of Blakey Gill, and here the Lion Inn comes into view; this is indeed a welcome sight for those who have walked from Ingleby Cross or Osmotherley today. Soon after the track has swung to the right again beyond Blakey Gill, you leave it by turning left and climbing slightly to reach a metalled road immediately beside the Lion Inn (162). Turning left on to the road at the inn, you follow the road for a mile, bearing right by the Margery Bradley boundary stone to follow a distinct but rough path across moorland.

In due course you reach another road, at a monument known as White Cross or Fat Betty, and you then turn right to follow this road. Shortly the road bends right, but the route goes straight ahead along a very boggy moorland path, soon rejoining the road as it curves round to the left. Almost immediately you turn left along *another* juicy track and reach *another* metalled road. A quick look at the map will show that all the walking from the Lion Inn to this point can be undertaken by road, and this may indeed be the best option in wet weather, with Wainwright describing both off-road sections as 'revoltingly slimy!'

You turn left on to the road and follow it, but after half a mile you branch right on to a clear path heading eastwards past Trough

House, and there follows a grand walk on a good path that passes round the head of Great Fryup Dale. The sight on the map of Great Fryup Head may conjure a mental picture either of a larger-than-life character in a children's pantomime, or of some senior government administrator whose task is to ensure statutory minimum standards of nutritional quality of cooked food, especially that served to ravenous Coast to Coast walkers at breakfast time.

Once past Great Fryup Head the track swings to the north-east and crosses Glaisdale Moor, reaching a road. You turn left on to this road and follow it for about a mile, again heading north-eastwards and enjoying fine views to Great Fryup Dale to the left and Glaisdale to the right. Just before a white Ordnance Survey column, you branch off to the right along a good track across Glaisdale Rigg, heading north-eastwards and eventually descending towards Esk Dale. The walking is as fast and easy as that between Bloworth Crossing and the Lion Inn, with good views to both Glaisdale and Esk Dale. The track becomes a road and you go forward on this road to meet a T-junction of roads, at which you turn right to pass through the village of Glaisdale.

The main part of the village is strung out along a steep hillside, commanding splendid views down into the deep wooded heart of Esk Dale, and as you descend towards the river Esk along the road you will note terraces of typically Victorian cottages, built to house workers at the village's three blast furnaces. At length you reach the railway station on the left, leaving the road just before the railway bridge and turning right on to a woodland path. By passing under the bridge, however, you can view Beggar's Bridge; one of the best-known landmarks in this part of Yorkshire. A packhorse bridge, built in 1619 and unaltered ever since, it is said to have been built by Thomas Ferris, a poor youth who used to wade or swim over the Esk to court the daughter of the squire of Glaisdale. The squire did not approve of the liaison so Ferris left the dale to seek his fortune. He returned a wealthy man, married the girl and built the bridge to symbolise their love and to enable later generations to cross the river dryshod. Not that that would presumably have deterred Henry Jenkins from taking a celebratory one hundred and sixtieth birthday dip had he fancied a change from the icy waters of the Swale.

Glaisdale to The Hermitage

The route now heads south-eastwards on a beautiful path through East Arncliff Wood, with both river and Whitby–Middlesbrough railway visible through the trees. After a mile you reach a metalled road, and turn left on to this road to proceed across the Esk into Egton Bridge, the lush meadows and trees presenting an amazing contrast to the remote moorland you passed only an hour or so back. The village contains many pretty cottages, an imposing manor house, and the nineteenth-century Roman Catholic Church of St Hedda with a richly decorated altar made in Munich, and fine tableaux depicting the Stations of the Cross. The Postgate Inn, a useful stop for weary walkers, is named after a local priest, Father Nicholas Postgate; hanged in 1679 for baptising a child into the Roman faith, he was one of England's last Catholic martyrs. Like Glaisdale, the village also has a useful railway station on the Whitby–Middlesbrough line. Just before the church you turn right off the road to proceed eastwards along the estate road of the manor; this was once a toll road, and a list of charges still stands at the toll bar by the estate road, easily visible (but thankfully not applicable) to today's walkers.

Keeping the meandering River Esk to your right, and remaining on the estate road, you swing to the left, pass under the railway and continue north-eastwards to reach the Egton–Grosmont road. You turn right along the road, shortly crossing the Esk and soon reaching Grosmont (176). Apart from the nineteenth-century church of St Matthew, containing what Pevsner describes as a 'fussy' interior, there is little of architectural interest amongst the austere grey stone buildings of the village. Grosmont's main feature of interest is the railway station that marks the northern terminus of the North York Moors Railway which runs down to Pickering via Goathland. It has been re-opened as a preserved steam railway after being axed from the main rail network many years ago.

There is no doubt that the sight of steam locomotives – of which arguably the most impressive is the Sir Nigel Gresley – pulling majestically out of the station, is a thrilling one, but the steam buff in the party who looks forward to a full afternoon off from Coast to Coast walking not only to travel the length of the line but to examine, in minute detail, the full range of rolling stock in the adjoining sheds, may have to yield not only to the demands of a tight walking schedule but to the sensibilities of those for whom only fifteen more miles of walking, a journey home and a couple of nights' sleep separate them from unwilling re-acquaintance with the daily joys of the 8.16 from Catford.

Grosmont has a reasonable range of amenities, though at the time of writing has no pub or restaurant serving evening meals. The route sticks to the main road through the village and, having crossed the railway, follows the road as it climbs extremely steeply uphill. You reach a right fork, and take this, climbing a 1 in 3 gradient, and soon swinging sharp right, ignoring a left turn. From the lushness of Eskdale you now suddenly find yourself on the moors again, climbing to the 900ft height of Sleights Moor. The road goes forward to meet the A169 Pickering–Whitby road, but the Coast to Coast turns left just under half a mile short of the junction and follows an often soggy moorland path north-eastwards to meet the A169 and crosses straight over it on to a bridleway (the 1998 edition of Wainwright's guide shows a slightly different route here).

The route then follows the bridleway eastwards, heading downhill; in due course it becomes a lane, and then meets a road coming in from the left; you join the road continuing eastwards to drop down to the delightful hamlet of Little Beck in a wooded valley. A stream (amazingly called Little Beck) is crossed, and almost immediately afterwards the Coast to Coast route turns right off the road to take a path heading south-eastwards through woodland, keeping Little Beck to the right. The path is quite undulating, and although well-defined it can be extremely muddy.

In just under a mile after leaving the road, the path rises to reach the Hermitage, a huge lump of rock out of which an impressive stone shelter has been carved. The going now gets easier, and soon you will see the magnificent waterfall of Falling Foss to the right, its wooded setting enhancing its charms.

The Hermitage to Robin Hood's Bay

The path passes immediately to the left of a building known as Midge Hall, near the waterfall, and crosses a footbridge over May Beck, where the route bears left, keeping the beck to the left. You cross a wide track, then continue beside the beck before fording it and proceeding on a path that keeps May Beck immediately to the right. You continue near May Beck, heading south-eastwards, and at length reach a metalled road beside a car park. Turning left on to the road, you stay on it for half a mile or so, turning right off it just beyond New May Beck farm. You proceed on a path that heads north-eastwards over Sneaton Low Moor and then due north to reach the B1416. Turning right here, you follow the road for a little over quarter of a mile before turning left on to a path and striking out across the moors once more on a well-defined path that is marked by a line of posts.

In due course, the moorland gives way to pastures, and as this happens you swing slightly west of north, descending through fields to reach a lane which you follow to meet a road. You follow it north-westwards to a junction, and here turn right on to a metalled road that proceeds past Mitten Hill Farm and across the A171 to reach Hawsker. The attractive village has a useful range of amenities although so few miles now remain that you may be happy to press on. You exit from Hawsker along a road that is signposted to Robin Hood's Bay, and very soon, when the road bends to the right, you proceed straight on down a lane to Seaview caravan site. If you are tired, you may in fact be tempted to proceed straight along the road, attempting to satisfy your protesting conscience by saying that you will still have walked from coast to coast, and if traces of guilt remain you can rest assured that a later return to walk the neglected final section will provide a good excuse for a pleasant weekend away, especially if it can be planned to coincide with a visit of the in-laws.

The lane continues past the Seaview caravan site, and tremendous excitement now awaits as you descend past another caravan site (Northcliffe) and then along a clear path north-eastwards to arrive at the North Sea. The excitement is enhanced by the tremendous cliff scenery of Maw Wyke Hole immediately to the left. On reaching the cliffs you turn right and again join the Cleveland Way for the final miles to Robin Hood's Bay. The next two miles are exhilarating as you follow a well-defined coast path on a platform high above the North Sea, and as you round Ness Point, you see journey's end ahead. It is without doubt the finest ending to any of the routes described in this book, all the more so because the objective has been so well-defined from the start – a walk from coast to coast.

At length the path leads to a road which proceeds past rows of houses to reach a T-junction with the road that has come from Hawsker. The route turns left on to this road, and then shortly left again down a road that leads into the main village street of Robin Hood's Bay (191). This descends precipitously through the old part of the village, and straight down to the North Sea, where your first task must be to obey Wainwright's command and place your boot into its salty waters. As Wainwright himself says, 'by this ritual you will have completed a walk from one side of England to the other.' Robin Hood's Bay, as well as marking the end of the walk, is an extremely picturesque spot in its own right; it is a maze of steep streets and passages with houses on many levels, and the old church of St Stephen has some splendid features including box pews, three-decker pulpit and gallery. There are many places to obtain celebratory refreshments, and a wealth of attractive little shops, several of which sell Coast to Coast souvenirs – little mementos of a magnificent walk across England.

Before staggering back up the hill to catch a bus back to Whitby or Scarborough – from where there are excellent bus and rail connections to all parts of the country – you may be tempted, as I was, to obtain a certificate of successful completion of the walk. In fact, these are rather *too* easily available, and the walker who proudly produces his completed and independently verified log of the journey in the back of his Wainwright guide and waits in the queue to present it in exchange for a lovingly hand-printed parchment and word of congratulation for defying the elements and accomplishing the 191 miles, may be somewhat mortified to see customers ahead of him paying less than two pounds for precisely the same piece of merchandise, clad in equipment which suggests that the only walking they have done that day is the two hundred yard stroll from the pay and display car park.

SUMMARY OF PLACES OF INTEREST

St Bees, Dent Fell, Ennerdale Water, Black Sail, Haystacks★, Borrowdale★, Stonethwaite, Helm Crag★, Grasmere, Grisedale Tarn, Brothers Parting, Helvellyn★, St Sunday Crag, Patterdale, Angle Tarn, Kidsty Pike★, Haweswater, Shap Abbey, Robin Hood's Grave, Orton, Smardale Bridge, Kirkby Stephen, Nine Standards★, Keld★, East Gill Force, Blakethwaite/Old Gang Smelt Mills, Reeth, Marrick Priory, Marske, Richmond★, Bolton-on-Swale, Mount Grace Priory, Live Moor, Carlton Moor, Cringle Moor, Cold Moor, Hasty Bank★, Rosedale Ironstone Railway, Great Fryup Head, Glaisdale, Egton Bridge, Grosmont, Falling Foss, Robin Hood's Bay★.

AMENITIES ON OR NEAR THE ROUTE

St Bees, Sandwith (L), Moor Row (L), Cleator (L), Ennerdale Bridge (L), Seatoller (L), Rosthwaite, Grasmere, Patterdale, Shap, Orton (L), Kirkby Stephen★, Keld (L), Reeth, Marske, Richmond★, Catterick, Bolton on Swale (L), Danby Wiske (L), Northallerton★, Ingleby Cross (L), Blakey (L), Glaisdale, Egton Bridge (L), Grosmont (L), Hawsker (L), Robin Hood's Bay.

The Pennine Way

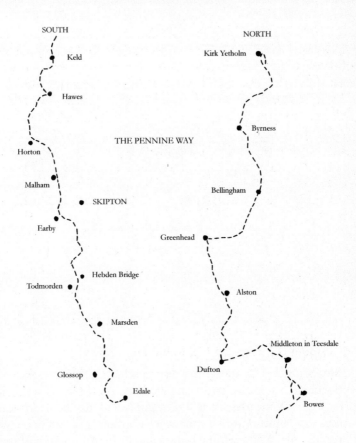

Length: 270 miles.
Start: Edale, in Derbyshire.
Finish: Kirk Yetholm on the Scottish border.
Nature: A walk up the Pennine and Cheviot ranges of northern England, through some of the wildest and most remote upland terrain in the country.
Difficulty rating: Severe.
Average time of completion: 3 weeks.

The Pennine Way

The Pennine Way is the father of all long-distance footpaths in Great Britain. It is the oldest and arguably most famous trail of the British Isles and although not the longest, it is the most technically demanding and the most satisfying to achieve. It also has the most chequered history. Seventy years ago, much of the land over which the present route passes was strictly private. Understandably, many countryside lovers at that time were wanting far greater access to areas of outstanding natural beauty, and in 1932 thousands of them deliberately flouted the laws of trespass by walking in the hills around Kinder Scout, which now forms the southern end of the Pennine Way. The Kinder Trespass caused considerable embarrassment to the Establishment, whose attitudes to walkers were considerably less sympathetic than they are today. Then in 1935, one Tom Stephenson wrote an article in the *Daily Herald* which proposed a continuous route across the Pennines. It took a further 16 years for his suggestion to gain ministerial approval, and after that came lengthy and often bitter negotiations with local landowners before the route was complete. Finally, in 1965, a ceremony on Malham Moor marked the official opening of the long-distance route linking Edale, in the Peak District, with Kirk Yetholm on the Scottish border.

The route has become extremely popular over the years – so much so that there has been very considerable erosion in some areas, resulting in re-routing and extensive path repair. Purists could argue that it is not a true Pennine Way in that firstly it starts some way into the Pennine range and finishes in the Cheviots, well beyond the Pennines, and secondly it does not keep to the main Pennine watershed (the highest ground of the Pennine chain where both west-flowing and east-flowing watercourses begin), but often descends to lower-lying ground on either side. However, it is the variety of landscapes that make the route so interesting and rewarding, ranging from the peaty moorland of the Peak District and the Cheviots to the dramatic limestone outcrops of Malham; from the noble splendour of Hadrian's Wall to the pastoral charm of Wensleydale, and from the formidable heights of Great Dun Fell and Cross Fell to the awesome falls of Hardraw and High Force.

Each type of landscape brings its own distinctive wildlife and plant life. On the moors you will walk amongst bogbean, marsh cinquefoil, cotton grass, crowberry and bilberry, be bidden by the grouse to 'go back' and watch as curlews, golden plovers and hen harriers hover overhead. The limestone country of Yorkshire offers purple saxifrage, juniper and hart's tongue fern, and on entering the primrose and cowslip-clad pastures of the Dales you may spot a merlin on a fence post, scanning the surroundings for potential prey.

If you examine the crags of Hadrian's Wall you may find bell heather, rock-rose, wild thyme and tormentil while ring ouzels and jackdaws fly around you, and you may be accompanied on your journey through the Cheviots by skylarks and meadow pipits. The encounters with civilisation bring their own rewards. The Pennine Way has been called a giant pub crawl, and even small communities along the route offer everything the walker needs, from sumptuous bar meals washed down by real ale, to the shelf in the convenience store offering the latest hi-tech foot powder, blister cream or other supposed remedy which even though it may not do the slightest bit of good, will at least make hikers feel better about putting their boots on again next morning.

The pub crawl does of course come at a price, and not just the cost of a few pints of beer. The Pennine Way is a very considerable undertaking, requiring a great deal of planning and preparation, and experience of hill walking and navigation. Most walkers will need three weeks to complete it, and that in itself calls for a high level of fitness as well as proper advance planning and an adequate financial outlay. It is very important not to be so carried away with the idea of 'doing the Pennine Way' that you lose sight of your own personal limitations. If you possess neither camping equipment nor navigational skills (including the ability to use a compass) you should think very seriously about whether to attempt the route, especially if you are on your own.

It is true that the walk is not quite the formidable proposition it once was. Many of the worst surfaces have been replaced by proper flag paths; bag-carrying services vie with each other to provide the best deal for transporting your rucksack or luggage from one accommodation to the next; mapping of the Way seems to improve year by year, with numerous excellent maps and guides available to try and help you not to put a foot wrong; and the mobile telephone makes it much easier to summon assistance if required.

Nevertheless, the terrain is tough, and demands the utmost respect. Whilst many sections of the route are well-signposted and follow good firm paths, there are as many others where not only the signposting, but the path itself, is non-existent, and the Way itself is either over steep hills and fells or across treacherous moorland wildernesses where slimy quagmires wait eagerly to suck in not only your boots but most of the lower half of your body. In bad weather, you can lose all sense of direction and what, in good weather, might be a straightforward walk across a field to a stile may turn into a nightmarish struggle that sees you floundering spectacularly off course. There is no shortage of accommodation along the Way but there are long stretches with none at all, including the first sixteen and the last twenty-nine miles.

These rather gloomy comments are not intended to deter would-be walkers but to serve as a warning, and if you are adequately prepared, you will enjoy a unique walking experience to be treasured forever. That said, much will depend on the prevailing conditions; some walkers, despite having the best possible protection from the elements, have been known to give up after less than ten miles, beaten back by the sheer awesomeness of Kinder, whilst rumours abound of hikers accomplishing the whole route with consummate ease despite carrying minimal equipment and supplies. I have even heard a story of one man completing the walk clad in a suit and carrying an umbrella, doubtless with a rolled-up copy of *The Times* under his arm as well.

Edale to Snake Road

The Way starts in the pretty village of Edale, a popular centre for walkers, and easily accessible from other parts of the country with its convenient railway station on the Sheffield–Manchester line. To get to the start of the route, you need to make your way to a cluster of buildings known as Grindsbrook Booth, by the Old Nag's Inn, a justifiably popular watering-hole. You turn westwards away from the buildings, along a lane, then proceed gently over fields, slightly south of west, to the hamlet of Upper Booth, from which you turn right on to a metalled road, follow this as far as Lee House, heading north-westwards, and then continue along a good path in the same direction. At length you reach the stiff ascent on to Kinder, known as Jacob's Ladder. It derives its name from a certain Jacob Marshall, a packhorse driver who is said to have scrambled up the hill by the shortest route so he might have time to smoke a pipe while his ponies took a more gentle but far longer ascent! Above Jacob's Ladder you continue westwards along a wide path beside a broken wall, turning right to Swine's Back, then right again to head just east of north. You pass Edale Rocks and the triangulation point at Kinder Low – 2,077ft high! – and, enjoying fine views to the Derwent valley, proceed beside the escarpment crest, passing through an area of boulders and gravel to reach the magnificent Kinder Downfall.

As you head towards the Downfall, you have on your right the amazing Kinder plateau, an awesome wilderness of featureless, largely pathless, peat moorland and one of the most frightening tracts of country you are ever likely to see. The peat is actually an accumulation of black, undecayed plant debris which formed as a result of a 2,000-year period of wet weather in prehistoric times. It is unpleasant to walk on, holds huge quantities of rainwater, and, to make matters worse, erosion of the peat has produced 'hags' or steep-faced islands, separated from their neighbours by 'groughs' or watercourses which cut through the peat and invariably run straight across the walker's direction of travel. The Way used to proceed to the Downfall directly across the plateau, having ascended from Edale by way of Grindsbrook Clough, until serious erosion problems forced the route to be diverted on to what was formerly just a bad weather alternative. Even in good weather progress could be painfully slow, as detours were necessary to avoid the worst sections, and in rain and mist the experience could become life-threatening.

I shall never forget taking this route, reaching the plateau and gasping with horror at the terrain that stretched in front of me. Every step across the plateau was dogged with uncertainty – there was no path to speak of – and real fear that a false move would see me sink out of sight forever. It was only by joining a party of students that by trial and error I found my way across it, though I cannot pretend I was at all faithful to the correct route. The current route, however, poses no such problems, and in clear conditions the Downfall should be reached without difficulty. In windy conditions and when the waters are in full spate, this is a truly spectacular sight, the wind causing the water to be blown high into the air above you.

At the Downfall you change direction, heading north-westwards through more boulders and gravel, dropping to Ashop Head and climbing again to Mill Hill, where you swing north-eastwards again and continue in this direction for three miles to reach the often snowed-up A57 Snake Road via Glead Hill and Featherbed Moss.

This walk is now straightforward, as an excellent flag path (a line of flagstones) has been laid for walkers, but in days gone by this section was one of the most treacherous on the whole route, and many hikers – particularly those who had struggled over the old route on the Kinder Plateau – have called it a day here. Barry Pilton, writing in *One Man and His Bog*, recalls meeting a man on Kinder who told him that the Snake Road was where 75 per cent of all walkers gave up the Pennine Way, 'when the hypothetical path crosses a very real bus route!'

Snake Road to Crowden

You cross straight over the Snake Road (the unusual name is derived from the presence of a serpent in a local family crest) and continue north-eastwards. You cross an old packhorse route of Roman origin called Doctor's Gate, then proceed along a shallow trench known as Devil's Dike, swinging slightly west of north to ascend towards the 2,060ft Bleaklow Head. At the time of writing, parts of this path have been flagstoned, but not all, and the going, across further peat moorland, can be most unpleasant in places. Having decided, whilst floundering across Featherbed Moss, that I would join the ranks of the first-day Pennine Way failures, I met another Pennine Way walker hereabouts, and my spirits – as well as the conviction that in his company I might be able to complete day one at least – rose considerably as we tackled the Bleaklow ascent together. Each time our feet went down we could not tell how far they would go, and we both sank to our knees on more than one occasion, but by means of a succession of tall wooden posts we kept to the route and arrived at Bleaklow Head.

Close by are the Wain Stones, an extraordinary formation of grit stone that resembles two faces engaged in a kiss. The rock from which the grit has been created is known as millstone; isolated blocks of coarse millstone have been scoured and shaped quite grotesquely by the wind and weather, resulting not only in the Wain Stones but many other curiously-formed outcrops on these soggy moors. Bleaklow Head, set in the midst of another peaty wilderness, is certainly not one of the scenic highlights of the Way, and the principal emotion of walkers who successfully make it is likely to be relief rather than pleasure. Beyond Bleaklow Head you swing north-eastwards briefly, then turn north-westwards, beginning the long descent into Longdendale.

The route swings westwards to follow the north bank of Wildboar Grain, soon reaching its confluence with Torside Clough, crossing this watercourse and continuing just north of west, initially contouring Clough Edge then turning in a more northerly direction to drop steeply to the Longdendale valley floor. Dropping to a farm road, you turn left on to it and follow it as far as the B6105 Woodhead–Glossop road, crossing straight over this on to a causeway that separates Torside Reservoir on your right from Rhodeswood Reservoir on your left. Having passed both reservoirs, you turn right on to a well-defined track through woodland, heading north-east across the A628 and then remaining roughly parallel with that road and the north-west-facing fringe of the Torside Reservoir.

The Way shortly turns left off the track to head north-westwards towards Laddow Rocks, but by detouring on along the track you reach the youth hostel at Crowden (15.5). This is the first accommodation opportunity since leaving Edale sixteen miles back, and a place for walkers to lick their wounds and exchange stories of the first day of their big adventure. I introduced myself to two other Pennine Way walkers here and we decided to join forces for the rest of the walk.

It is at Crowden Youth Hostel that the efficiency of the baggage-carrying services will be tested for the first time, as walkers hope to be reunited with their luggage, rather like airline passengers after a flight. On days of particularly unpleasant weather, however, one cannot rule out the awesome possibility that – unlike at the airport, where passengers wait in vain for luggage that has not arrived – there will be baggage at the youth hostel that remains unclaimed. It will be left to the hostellers who have safely arrived at Crowden to speculate whether the owner has disappeared irretrievably into one of the blacker and more glutinous peat-hags on Bleaklow, or took one look towards the sullen mist hanging over the upper reaches of Jacob's Ladder and decided that walking conditions underfoot would be rather better in the Peace Gardens in Sheffield or the Piccadilly Plaza in Manchester.

Crowden to Standedge

Having rejoined the route, you have an easy enough start, proceeding north-westwards towards the impressive gritstone formations that are known as Laddow Rocks. To your right is Crowden Great Brook, which is never far away as you follow a good path, crossing Oakenclough Brook and climbing steadily. Beyond Laddow Rocks you swing north-eastwards and continue in that direction towards Black Hill, striking out on to open moorland; for a while you follow the left bank of Crowden Great Brook, then proceed along a flag path to Dun Hill and thence to the summit of Black Hill. This used to be another quite ghastly stretch of the route, but although the horrors have been somewhat mitigated by the flag stones, the 1,908ft Black Hill itself remains a peaty morass around a triangulation pillar. Indeed, the Royal Engineers triangulation team had such a difficult time erecting the pillar that the summit has been nicknamed Soldier's Lump!

Even in pleasant conditions, the surroundings are hardly hospitable or indeed especially aesthetically pleasing, but in wet or misty weather, it is a place to escape from as quickly as your legs and the terrain underfoot will allow you to. There are actually plans to re-route the Way to avoid the summit, which may or may not have come to fruition at the time of publication of this book. Alfred Wainwright, author of the *Pennine Way Companion* that many walkers use to guide them up the route, advises you that before resuming the journey from Black Hill you should 'make sure there is nobody in the vicinity sinking out of sight and in need of help!' I myself fell victim to the peat on Black Hill; despite having no rucksack to weigh me down, an innocently-taken step through the cotton grass saw me shoot downwards into a sea of filth. My immediate fear was that I would lose my boots, but somehow I managed to haul myself to safety and decided that if I could cope with this, I could cope with the rest of the Pennine Way. I did.

From the summit you head northwards then swing north-eastwards downhill past Black Dike Head, before turning north-westwards along a flag path which continues downhill. You cross over Black Dike and Dean Clough, then climb slightly, crossing Reap Hill Clough and arriving at the A635 Holmfirth–Greenfield road. (Fans of *Last of the Summer Wine* may like to note that the series is shot in and around Holmfirth, some four miles along this road to the right.) You turn right on to the road and follow it briefly, then turn left on to the Meltham road. Wainwright wrote in an early edition of his *Companion* that on sunny summer weekends a gentleman by the name of Mario would sell ice cream at this road junction. Certainly there was no sign of Mario at the time I wrote this book, and I could only assume that, depending on his willingness or otherwise to forsake the warm-hearted folk of West Yorkshire, he was plying his trade in the balmier and less peaty resorts of the Mediterranean.

Shortly after joining the Meltham road, you turn left on to an excellent path that proceeds north-westwards downhill to Wessenden Lodge. This is a welcome break in the struggle across peat moorland. You keep the reservoirs of Wessenden Head and Wessenden to your left, with a fine backcloth of hills behind, as you descend to the Lodge, set snugly amongst the trees, but just before reaching the Lodge you turn left and follow the western end of Wessenden Reservoir, then swing right to follow a narrow but reasonably good path uphill to a waterfall. You cross the water immediately below the fall and, without losing height, swing north-eastwards on what is still a well-defined path.

On a separate expedition, I walked as far as the waterfall after a period of extremely wet weather. The flow of dirty water cascading from above was immense, and even at its easiest point the crossing looked not so much uninviting as downright dangerous. It may be possible in such conditions to retrace your steps, scramble down the bank, and ford the brook as it drops down towards Blakeley Reservoir, shinning up the other side to pick up the north-eastward path, but I personally did not fancy it!

The path, now high above the brook, swings north-westwards and follows alongside Blakeley Clough, heading slightly uphill. You cross the Clough but continue along the bank, with the water to your left, now heading just south of west up on to Black Moss.

As the ground levels out, the Way turns right and proceeds in a generally north-westerly direction, passing between Black Moss Reservoir and Swellands Reservoir, and thereafter following a flag path downhill to the A62 at Standedge Cutting (26). It is at Black Moss Reservoir that you will be reunited with the course of the former route, which proceeded north-westwards from Black Hill and from the A635 followed a dismal course through a peat wilderness, of which White Moss was the worst section.

Wainwright reminds his readers that there is a good Lancashire word that well describes the ooze of mud and mire so prevalent on this first section of the Way, namely 'slutch'. To quote Wainwright: 'Say it slowly, with feeling, and you have the sound of a boot extricating itself from the filthy stuff.' Indeed, walkers who have struggled off Black Hill to find there is still more torment to come may wonder if one of our friend Mario's concoctions was a Slutch Puppie, a glutinous brown lump with a deceptively firm topping but impossibly gooey underneath.

Standedge to Hebden Bridge

With the next easily accessible accommodation some 11 miles further up the route, many walkers will turn right along the A62 and then a minor road down to Marsden, some three miles away; refreshments and accommodation may also be available by following the A62 to the left. The Way proceeds north-westwards from the A62, initially along a sandy track and then uphill on to Millstone Edge where, among the rocks, you will find the Ammon Wrigley Memorial Stone, named after a much-revered writer and local poet.

Still heading north-westwards, progress is initially very straightforward as you walk along a dry track on the edge of an area of peat moorland, swinging briefly north-east at Northern Rotcher before turning north-west again, this being your general direction all the way to the A58. You continue over the moors, dropping to Oldgate Moss, then after passing Little Moss you cross the A640 Milnrow–Huddersfield road, and proceed upwards to Rapes Hill, descending and then rising again to White Hill. The going could be quite juicy as you come off White Hill, but improves as you go forward to the A672 Oldham–Halifax road by way of Axeltree Edge.

Crossing straight over the A672, you pass Bleakedgate Moor Wireless Telegraphy station and very shortly after that you cross the M62 trans-Pennine motorway beyond which you head via Slippery Moss and Redmires to Blackstone Edge. This section, passing over more hideous peat moorland, has been greatly improved in recent years but it used to be a diabolical stretch of route. On the occasion I walked it, one of my new-found walking companions became completely stuck here, requiring assistance to be extricated; fortunately, as my rucksack was being conveyed by van, I was able to take his rucksack for a while, but it was not surprising to hear him later confess that this experience caused him to consider giving up altogether. In his *Companion*, Wainwright has written little comments at the foot of each page summarising the walking for that particular page of text; the bottom of the page including Redmires bears the comforting prophecy that, 'You will question your own sanity!'

The huge boulders of Blackstone Edge provide a welcome contrast to the peat moorland, and from now on the going becomes a great deal easier. You head northwards on a good path as far as the Aiggin stone, an old guide stone, then turn left along a Roman road and shortly right on to a path that curls round Blackstone Edge moor, alongside a watercourse known rather unromantically as Broad Head Drain. You then head downhill to the A58 Littleborough–Halifax road (34). You bear right on to the A58 then shortly left, proceeding north-westwards along a reservoir road for some three miles, passing firstly Blackstone Edge reservoir, then the reservoirs of Light Hazzles and Warland. The going is the easiest so far, and there are excellent views to the town of Littleborough and its surrounding hills; after the great wildernesses experienced further back, it is somehow reassuring to know that civilisation is not too far away.

Finally, just beyond Warland Reservoir, you turn right and proceed first just south of east then north-eastwards alongside Warland Drain. The imposing monument of Stoodley Pike should now be clearly in view and, leaving Warland Drain at Langfield

Common, you head north-eastwards towards it, along a good clear track. At Withens Gate you pass a track leading to Mankinholes Youth Hostel, a useful stopping-place for those for whom a further three-mile slog to the flesh pots of the Calder Valley is too much.

The Way continues on to Stoodley Pike, a monument 125ft high which was built in 1856 as a replacement to a monument constructed following the defeat and exile of Napoleon. There is a viewing balcony inside, offering an excellent panorama on a half-decent day. From Stoodley Pike you head eastwards, then swing north-eastwards and begin to descend into the Calder valley, hitting a farm road at Lower Rough Head, and proceeding north-westwards through Callis Wood – the first area of woodland since the start of the route – to cross the Rochdale Canal and river Calder and reach the A646 (42). Two towns lie within easy reach of the Way at this point: Todmorden three miles to the left, and Hebden Bridge a mile to the right. Of these, Hebden Bridge is the more interesting, its mills and grey terraced houses recalling the area's proud industrial past, and it could now almost be described as a giant museum piece.

It is an easy walk on from Hebden Bridge to the fascinating village of Heptonstall with its narrow streets of dark stone houses, the lovely cobbled Weavers' Square, and a sixteenth-century Cloth Hall. The village was once the centre of the handloom weaving trade and one could easily visualise the packhorses clattering through the little thoroughfares, having struggled up from the Calder. The octagonal Methodist church, founded by John Wesley in 1764, is one of the oldest Methodist churches, while the Anglican church of St Thomas dates back to the 1850s, having been built to replace a much older church that suffered heavy storm damage. I was amused to read that the vicarage is built on the site of a cockpit – not the pilot's seat in an aircraft, but an area used in the Napoleonic Wars for cockfighting!

Hebden Bridge to Top Withens

Two fairly mediocre miles follow, as you undertake the long climb out of the Calder valley. You turn right on to the A646 then shortly left, passing under the Bradford–Manchester railway and following a track roughly north-westwards uphill past Dew Scout Farm. Just beyond the farm you turn sharp right, then shortly left uphill past Popples Farm and Scammerton Farm, heading just west of north. You cross a metalled road, continue northwards over Pry Hill, descending to cross Colden Water and climbing again, picking up a lane that leads north-westwards into Colden, which sadly is no prettier than its name. Crossing another road, you continue north-westwards along a partially walled footpath to Long High Top, swinging north-eastwards to Mount Pleasant farm. Here you reach Heptonstall Moor with some relief, and strike out north-westwards across the heather moor, crossing over Clough Head Hill. The going is excellent, with walkers further motivated to make fast progress by the prospect of the Pack Horse Inn which is now imminent!

After a 2-mile walk across the moor, you turn sharp right to continue just east of north, past the eastern edge of Lower Gorple reservoir, across and then along the east bank of Graining Water, and forward to a metalled road at Widdop. By detouring right you will reach the Pack Horse Inn, but the Way goes left, following the road north-westwards, shortly bearing right on to a reservoir road, heading north-eastwards – your direction of travel almost all the way to Ponden Hall. You then proceed past two of the Walshaw Dean reservoirs, keeping the first of these to your right (note: a diversion to the opposite side of the reservoir may be in force) then cross a dam and proceed immediately beside the second, keeping it to your left. Before reaching its top end, however, you turn right, away from it, and head on to the open moors, climbing quite steeply initially, but being rewarded with a fine moorland march, enjoying excellent views back to Stoodley Pike. You pass Withins Height, having gained 1,000ft since the Calder valley, and go forward to a now ruined house named Top Withens, which is reputed to have inspired Emily Brontë when she wrote *Wuthering Heights*.

The Brontë Society have since placed a plaque on the wall of the ruins reminding literary pilgrims that the buildings, even when complete, bore no resemblance to the house she described as Wuthering Heights, but it may have been in her mind when she wrote of its setting. There is something undeniably romantic about the windswept moorland scenery that surrounds Top Withens and which has inspired so many twentieth-century writers, film-makers and musicians, and the contemporary walker taking in these uncompromising surroundings can almost hear the anguished outpourings of Laurence Olivier and Merle Oberon or, if less culturally inclined, the fiery screechings of Kate Bush.

Top Withens to East Marton

Beyond Top Withens you begin to descend, following an excellent track past Upper Heights Farm, then turning left to follow a path past the farms of Buckley and Rush Isles, now heading north-westwards – your direction of travel virtually all the way to Thornton in Craven. Just beyond Rush Isles Farm you reach a junction with a lane on to which you turn left, but by detouring right and then right again on to a road, you reach Haworth and its Parsonage, home of the Brontë sisters. The town's steep main street is most attractive, although fearfully busy at holiday times, the crowds attracted not only by the Brontë connection but by the Keighley and Worth Valley Railway, where the film of *The Railway Children* was made. The Way, however, eschews the delights of Haworth and having joined the lane beyond Rush Isles Farm it proceeds alongside Ponden Reservoir to Ponden Hall (53), a fine seventeenth-century farmhouse which is reputed to be the inspiration for Thrushcross Grange, another important location in the novel *Wuthering Heights*.

Beyond Ponden Hall the Way continues along a path which, having passed the head of Ponden reservoir, arrives at the Colne–Keighley road. You turn left on to this road then shortly right, proceeding uphill through fields parallel with Dean Clough and then along a walled farm track, turning left on to another road at Crag Bottom. You follow this road to the left then at Crag Top turn right, striking out across Oakworth Moor and Ickornshaw Moor, the outstanding landmark on which is the 1,453ft Wolf Stones, just to the left of the route on the moor's south fringes. Flagstones have helped to ease what used to be quite an arduous passage over this moorland.

As the Way continues across the moor it gradually descends, and as you lose height you should look out on your right to the gritstone summit of Earl Crag, decorated by two impressive monuments. You proceed somewhat circuitously round a number of ruins just beyond Andrew Gutter – a reminder of the sad decline of agricultural communities in the wake of the Industrial Revolution – but after passing Lumb Head Beck progress is straightforward, along a walled path which arrives at the A6068. You turn left on to it and shortly right to follow a path into the village of Ickornshaw, one of four little villages all strung together but with precious few amenities. In theory you could turn right on to the village street and then left at a T-junction into Gill Lane, passing the pretty Cowling church and the eastern end of the hamlet of Middleton. The Way, however, turns left off Ickornshaw village street almost at once, and follows a field path past the western end of Middleton to reach Gill Lane. You follow Gill Lane as far as the hamlet of Gill, and at the delightful Gill Bridge you turn left and strike out across rolling fields and meadows, climbing all the while. There are good views back across Cowling to the monuments on Earl Crag.

You reach a metalled road, turning right and then immediately forking left to follow another road downhill, soon turning left again on to a path that drops to Surgill Beck. There is a climb to Wood Head Farm at which you join a lane that leads to the lovely village of Lothersdale (61), where picturesque cottages are grouped round an old textile mill in a wooded valley. There is a useful pub here where you can celebrate the end of twenty rather bitty miles' marching and look forward to some really great walking ahead. I recall one particularly cruel twist of Fate that befell a Pennine Wayfarer walking this stretch a day or two ahead of us; having survived the rigours of Bleaklow, Black Hill *et al*, she was forced to abandon her walk after being bitten by a dog on Ickornshaw Moor.

Dogs can be somewhat unsettling for long-distance walkers as it can never be predicted until the last minute whether they will studiously and disdainfully ignore you, sniff inquisitively and often noisily but harmlessly around you, or start tearing large chunks out of you. As a particularly aggressive-looking specimen bounds towards you, the promise of the owner (who more often than not appears incapable of controlling a hibernating tortoise, let alone a German shepherd) that he 'won't hurt you' may well appear as comforting and reassuring as the words 'No Ripoff's Garranteed' on the flier recently dropped through your letter box by Baz n Dave Perfect Plumbing Limited.

You leave Lothersdale along a lane heading northwards from beside the inn, but when the lane peters out you continue uphill, keeping alongside a wall, in due course reaching the Colne–Skipton road. You cross over it and briefly join a lane, which ends at Hewitt's farm, and again you keep alongside a wall, going forward on to Pinhaw Moor and arriving at the 1,273ft Pinhaw Beacon, a really fine viewpoint with spectacular views to Airedale and the town of Skipton. With some reluctance you set off again, actually heading a little south of west to pick up a quarry road. Here you return to north-westward travel, going forward on the quarry road to meet a road junction, and proceeding straight across to join the metalled Elslack road. Follow it over Elslack Moor; to your right is one of the largest patches of woodland seen so far on the route, containing the tiny Elslack reservoir. After about half a mile you bear left, initially across the rather juicy moorland of Park Hill and then through pleasant pastures, descending all the time.

At Brown House you pick up a farm road which passes under the old Colne–Skipton railway to reach the A56 at the pretty village of Thornton in Craven (65), the gateway to one of the lowest-lying and gentlest sections of the route. Thornton in Craven offers a reasonable range of amenities, and by turning left on to the A56 you will in a mile and a half reach the little town of Earby, which has many more. The Way crosses more or less straight over the A56, initially following Cam Lane and then proceeding through fields, veering slightly west of north as it passes Langber Hill and arrives at the Leeds and Liverpool Canal.

In the nineteenth century this enjoyed extensive industrial use, but like many canals in other parts of the country, it has now been revived as a tourist attraction, populated by pleasure craft. A quite delightful walk north-eastwards ensues along the towpath, and there is the possibility of a detour to the pretty village of East

Marton, though with only two miles walked beyond Thornton in Craven, it may be too early in the day to patronise the village inn. To reach East Marton you will need to get on to the A59, which crosses the canal by means of an unusual double-arched bridge, the extra arch being needed to facilitate the passage of the busy roadway above. Those who kept their cameras firmly in their rucksacks whilst battling with the peat moorland further south may feel disposed to deploy them in these rather more congenial surroundings to capture this distinctive feature.

The camera is an obvious means of storing up one's walking memories, but sadly it is not a foolproof method. Bad light or over-exposure may ruin some shots, rainwater may clog the apparatus and spoil the whole film, or the thoughtless photographer, having taken 36 magnificent snaps, finds his genius has not extended to remembering to insert the film in the first place. The biggest irony, of course, is when having sent off the film to the developers, the processing company muddles two sets of prints and the walker's breakfast is enlivened, not by three dozen breathtaking vistas of the rugged Pennines, but by seemingly endless shots of total strangers grouped round a cake clumsily decorated with the words 'Happy 80th Doris' in wobbly pink icing.

East Marton to Fountains Fell
Shortly beyond East Marton the route bears right and now heads in a north-easterly direction to Gargrave. Soon after leaving the canal you pass round the edge of a small woodland area and turn right on to a lane, then as the lane swings left you leave it and continue north-eastwards over pasture. The Way is not clear on the ground and there are numerous gates and stiles, making progress slow and potentially confusing in mist. You follow briefly alongside Crickle Beck and then climb gently on to Scaleber Hill, where there is a good view to Airedale with the welcome sight of Gargrave immediately ahead. You soon turn right on to a farm road and follow this across the railway – the famous Skipton–Carlisle line – then immediately after crossing the railway, you turn right along a path that takes you into Gargrave (70). This is an obvious stopping-place, with shops, refreshments and accommodation; despite having

walked only five miles since breakfast, my fellow walkers and I could not resist stopping here for cream doughnuts bought from the village bakery!

Having crossed the river Aire and the busy A65, you leave Gargrave by way of West Street, following a lane that heads north-westwards towards Bell Busk. You pass an area of woodland known as the Mark Plantation, and at the end of it you turn right, continuing in a north-westerly direction through open country, again with no obvious path on the ground, on to Eshton Moor. After crossing the moor you arrive at the river Aire, and from here virtually all the way to Malham the Way follows alongside the river, heading northwards through the meadows. Initially you stay on the left bank, looking northwards, then at Newfield Bridge you switch to the right bank, soon reaching the little village of Airton. Delightful walking through meadows and parkland, still on the right bank, takes you to the pretty village of Hanlith, with its mill and millpond. You turn right beside Hanlith Bridge along a lane, but soon turn left and return to the river which you follow as far as Malham (77). With more than seventy-five miles and the less rewarding parts of the route behind you, confidence should now be soaring, and indeed it is said that if you make it to Malham you will complete the whole route.

Hopefully the easy walking you have done from Thornton onwards will allow you time to linger in this remarkable village, historically famous for its sheep sales, and boasting a fine assembly of limestone cottages, many of which are several hundred years old. Walkers' needs have been well catered for by the Buck Inn and the Lister's Arms, which has the date 1723 above the doorway, and today the village offers a full range of amenities, catering as it does for not only walkers but tourists and geologists.

Close to Malham are two remarkable limestone features, namely Malham Cove and Gordale Scar; Malham Cove, a cliff 280ft high, will be seen by Pennine Way walkers heading northwards from the village but a detour is needed to visit Gordale Scar, a mile eastwards. This is a massive cleft in towering and overhanging limestone walls, with waterfalls plunging down a ravine 250ft deep in places. Suddenly, all the geology they tried to teach you at school comes breathtakingly to life, as you see it for real rather than in the pages of an insufferably tedious textbook, the reading of which as early evening homework served as a poor substitute for a cup of hot Bovril in front of *The Perils of Penelope Pitstop*.

Leaving Malham, you begin innocuously enough by following the Settle road north-westwards, but soon turn right to follow alongside Malham Beck and head inexorably towards the formidable limestone cliffs of the Cove, from which the beck emerges. Shaped as it is like a section of an immense amphitheatre, it appears to be an impenetrable obstruction to progress, being almost intimidating in its scale and steepness. It is worth walking to the base of the cliff, where there once poured a waterfall higher than Niagara. However the Way leads you to the left to follow a stepped path to the top, where another surprise awaits you in the form of a magnificent limestone pavement which you follow parallel with the cliff edge before turning left and heading north-westwards again. Those without a head for heights would do well to stay well back from the cliff edge, as it is unprotected and dangerous; furthermore, the pavement itself is uneven and should be walked on with care. With those caveats in mind, you will find this to be the most exhilarating walking on the route so far.

Having turned left, you proceed over what is known as the Dry Valley, an area of lush green grass overshadowed by weathered limestone formations. You swing north-eastwards among the rocks of Comb Hill, and pass Water Sinks, where the stream that has issued from Malham Tarn further north disappears underground. Shortly you arrive at a metalled road, turning right on to it, and shortly left on to a path that heads just east of north to another road. You turn left on to this road, and follow it as it swings north-westwards round the edge of the National Trust-owned Malham Tarn, a serene and beautiful piece of water, and one of only a small number of natural lakes in Yorkshire. Situated amongst limestone, which does not hold surface water, the Tarn is only able to exist because it lies on a bed of Silurian slate which is impervious to water.

In the woodland that borders the lake, and passed by the Way, is Malham Tarn House, now a field study centre and reputedly the place that Charles Kingsley, who often stayed here as a guest, was inspired to write *The Water Babies*, one of the best-loved children's stories of all time, published in book form in 1863. Not far beyond Malham Tarn House, just before Water Houses, you turn right and head northwards through open country, keeping a wall to your left. In a mile, near Stanggill Barn which is beyond the wall to the left, you head north-westwards to pick up a farm road, turning right on to it and following it to the hamlet of Tennant Gill. You then begin the long and arduous ascent of Fountains Fell, heading north-westwards all the way.

Fountains Fell is not the loveliest of mountains – its side has been disfigured somewhat by old mine workings, of which only one colliery building remains – and there is no great satisfaction in reaching the extensive fell top. The igloo-shaped colliery building, and two tall cairns, referred to as stone 'men' by guidebooks, are the only real features of interest as you near the summit. The early part of the climb is quite easy, but as you climb towards and then pass the 2,000ft mark, crossing a number of watercourses including Tennant Gill itself, the limestone gives way to millstone grit and the going, although never very steep, becomes rougher underfoot. Indeed in very wet conditions, with soggy or flooded ground, you may be in very real danger of becoming a water baby yourself. Unlike with Charles Kingsley's Tom, however, it is hard to see what moral lessons you might learn, other than a reminder of the truth of the proverb which broadly speaking dictates that you only have yourself to blame if you choose to walk the Pennine Way, not in a pair of £129.99 water-resistant Gortex boots available from the specialist outdoor retailers in the Queen's Plaza, but in a pair of £9.99 water-welcoming boots you bought from the market stall in Corporation Road.

Fountains Fell to Horton in Ribblesdale

The view north-westwards from the summit of Fountains Fell, when you finally get there, is dominated by Pen-y-Ghent, which is the next major objective. You leave the summit cairn and head slightly south of west, descending rapidly, then turn north-westwards to follow alongside a wall, soon arriving at a metalled road, turning left on to it and following it south-westwards, passing Rainscar House. At a cattle grid you turn right and walk north-westwards up to the buildings of Dale Head farm, then beyond the farm you continue north-westwards along a good path that is bound for Horton. The Way too is destined to reach Horton, and in bad weather there may be merit in following this path all the way. However, at the limestone crater known as Churn Milk Hole, the official route bears right to begin the ascent of Pen-y-Ghent, one of the highlights of the Way.

The ascent is fairly gentle to begin with, but as you gain height the going becomes very much steeper, and it is an exciting scramble through the boulders of limestone and gritstone to the grassy 2,273ft summit. On a clear day the view is absolutely fantastic, with several mountains and hills visible, including Pendle Hill, the Howgill Fells, Whernside and Ingleborough. These last two, with Pen-y-Ghent, make up what are known as the famous Three Peaks, the conquest of which in a single day's journey is now an established challenge walk of 24 miles. For Pennine Way walkers, however, it is downhill all the way to Horton, with no more climbing required.

You head just north of west and begin your descent, which is initially very steep, then at 1,900ft – look out at this point for the purple saxifrage in the springtime – you turn almost due west, making slightly gentler progress downhill through the grass and heather. As you do so, you pass Hunt Pot, a limestone pothole which is only 15ft long but 200ft deep, and you should take great care as you look down into the abyss. Just beyond Hunt Pot you swing a little north of west to reach a rough walled lane known as Horton Scar Lane, then turn left, south-westwards, on to the lane, and follow it to Horton (92). However, by detouring right at the point you reach the lane, you will soon reach another, more spectacular pothole known as Hull Pot, only 60ft deep but 300ft long, and boasting a waterfall after heavy rain.

Horton (or, to give the village its full title, Horton in Ribblesdale) is not a tourist honeypot like Malham behind you, or Hawes, just ahead; although it boasts an ancient church and views of the river Ribble, its workmen's cottages and Victorian terraces remind you that this has for a long time been an important quarrying area. The setting of the village is tremendous, with Pen-y-Ghent rising up on one side and Ingleborough on the other, and there is opportunity for rest and refreshment in the village. Those wishing to call a temporary or permanent halt to their Pennine Way walk here may note that the village also has as a useful railway station on the famous Settle–Carlisle line.

Arguably the village's most celebrated rendezvous point is not the pub but the Pen-y-Ghent Café, the base for many rigorous walking expeditions including the Three Peaks Walk. After we had walked here from Malham safely and in glorious sunshine, our tea and Kit-Kats were consumed in a celebratory frame of mind, but one could well imagine would-be climbers and fellwalkers sitting here over mugs of stewing tea for hours on end, waiting with growing frustration for the rain and mist to relent, with nothing to do but read the papers and exchange inconsequential banter with other equally anguished souls. Such a fate is certainly hard on the keen walker who has got up on a weekend morning at 5 a.m. to drive to Horton, leaving his wife and family in the comfort and warmth of their beds, especially when his long drive home is overshadowed by the prospect of having to confess to them that his most satisfying achievement of the day was solving the Dingbats puzzle in the *Mail on Sunday*.

Horton in Ribblesdale to Hawes

Having reached Horton, the Way turns right on to the village street, and shortly right again up another walled lane known as Harber Scar Lane, heading just east of north and then northwards, steadily gaining height. You keep a wall to your left and proceed along a lovely packhorse road, the going straightforward and comfortable. You pass more potholes including Sell Gill Holes, which open into a 210ft deep underground chamber, an open chasm called Jackdaw Hole, the ominously-named Cowskull Pot, the 180ft Pen-y-Ghent Long Churn, and beyond that, Canal Cavern. You continue just east of north over Rough Hill, then turn left, off the packhorse road, and proceed in a roughly westerly direction to the buildings of Old Ing, where you turn sharp right on to the Settle–Hawes packhorse road, proceeding most pleasantly just west of north, passing Dry Laithe Cave, otherwise known as Calf Holes.

You go forward to the sixteenth-century bridge crossing of Ling Gill; just below the bridge, the water cascades down a spectacular limestone gorge which is visible from the Way. From the bridge, you continue northwards, uphill, to Cam End, where your route meets the Roman road from Ingleton to Bainbridge, and at this important junction of old roads you turn right and continue over Cam Fell, still gaining height; you are now proceeding north-eastwards, your direction of travel all the way to Hawes. It is appropriate that, as you head towards the 1,800ft contour, this stretch should be known as Cam High Road.

This section also forms part of the Dales Way, a walk of some 95 miles from Leeds to the Lake District. I walked the Dales Way myself a few years ago, and found it to be a pleasant walk, but it is undoubtedly far less challenging or rewarding than the Pennine Way or Coast to Coast, and many walkers may feel frustrated that with so many wonderful hills and mountains in view, the route involves so much pounding along the flat. The section that overlaps with the Pennine Way is actually the best bit! There are superb views from here on a good day, including the Three Peaks and the Dent Head viaduct on the Settle–Carlisle line. The Dales Way goes off to the right but the Pennine Way, passing the 100-mile mark, continues to a farm road, turning left on to it and then, in around half a mile, left off it to proceed along West Cam Road, a wide grass path or 'green road'.

You soon contour the west slopes of Dodd Fell, remaining at just under 1,900ft throughout. The going is straightforward and, in good visibility, quite delightful, but in poor conditions, it can be anything but. Alan Plowright, in his homage to Wainwright entitled *Plowright Follows Wainwright*, recalls arriving at Dodd Fell at 2.30 a.m. on the infamous Fellsman Hike, a 61-mile challenge walk incorporating eight peaks, to be completed in 24 hours. He had to find a checkpoint on or near the summit but because the checkpoint official's light had failed, he had spent a full hour blundering around in the pitch darkness trying to locate it before giving up and bedding down. When dawn broke, he saw the checkpoint only 50 yards away. The things people do for pleasure . . .

Beyond Dodd Fell you head for the unpleasantly-named Ten End Peat Ground, forking right at a junction of paths here (left provides a more direct route for Hawes which may be preferred in bad weather). Now you begin to descend, slowly at first, then more rapidly, with the beautiful prospect of Wensleydale opening out before you. The path becomes less distinct as you follow first the left side, then the right side, of a wall, in due course reaching Gaudy House and joining Gaudy Lane. When this ends at a junction of lanes, you cross over and follow field paths to a housing estate at the western edge of the village of Gayle. You pass through the estate, turn briefly left on to the Gayle–Hawes road, then bear right along a path which shortly arrives in the little town of Hawes itself (106.5).

Hawes is an obvious stopping-place on the Way, with an excellent range of amenities and a chance to stock up on supplies and enjoy a few creature comforts. It has many visitor attractions, including the Dales Countryside Museum, a traditional ropemaker's, and a creamery that offers a fine range of home-produced Wensleydale cheeses for sale. Pennine Way walkers who feel able to take a couple of days out, or feel they have done enough, or possibly both, may wish to use Hawes as a base for exploring the lovely Wensleydale countryside with its pretty villages among the lush green meadows, and impressive hills towering behind.

Hawes is one of only very few tourist traps visited by the Pennine Way, and while some may dislike the place for that, it is undoubtedly useful for the purchase of postcards and presents. However, with other equally pressing matters to attend to, such as boot drying and food buying, the walker can be forgiven for being rather more hasty and less selective than might otherwise be the case when deciding which particular 'Present From Wensleydale' to choose to take home, and the recipient should perhaps not be too surprised to turn the box upside down to find that the confection in question originated not in the sweet air of the verdant Yorkshire Dales countryside, but in an industrial estate in the suburbs of Bradford.

Hawes to Thwaite

You leave Hawes by following the road heading northwards off the A684, signposted to Hardraw (some maps say Hardrow, some say Hardraw, but let's not call the whole thing off – this is one of the best bits!). You could simply walk to Hardraw along this road, but the Way uses a path to cut a corner, then soon turns left off the road and wanders north-westwards through the pastures to arrive in the village. You turn left on to the road to cross the bridge over the stream, but by entering the Green Dragon Inn beside the bridge, and paying an entrance fee, you can walk out to the magnificent Hardraw Force. Seen at its best after heavy rainfall, this is England's highest waterfall above ground, and a quite incredible spectacle, the water cascading 100ft over a tree-clad limestone ledge. Although notices forbid it, many cannot resist the temptation to walk round immediately behind the fall, in the tiny space between the cascade and the cliff face. All I can say is that you do so at your own risk!

Back on the Way, having crossed the bridge by the pub, you turn right and proceed north-westwards along a walled lane on to Bluebell Hill, effectively the start of the long, laborious climb to the summit of Great Shunner Fell. At Bluebell Hill you lose the walls but continue on a clear track. The going is excellent as far as Little Fell, but here you leave the track, bearing right to head just west of north and then swinging northwards on a much more indistinct path. As with Fountains Fell, the going gets rougher and peatier as you gain more height, but the reward on a clear day is a fantastic view back to Wensleydale and beyond. Finally you swing north-eastwards to reach the 2,340ft summit of the fell, the highest ground reached so far. On days of good visibility this is one of the highlights of the walk; we reached the summit in pouring rain with no views to speak of.

Great care is needed to identify the correct route as you begin descending, heading north-eastwards through an unpleasant sea of peat, although flagstones help mitigate the worst sections. Some two miles after leaving the summit, you swing south-eastwards, and reach a walled lane, which makes for firmer going as you drop down to the B6270, turning right to little village of Thwaite (117). It was here that my companions and I found sustenance – as well as the opportunity to dry out – at the Kearton Restaurant; named after Richard and Cherry Kearton (both male!), two well-known naturalists who came from the village. The restaurant has long been a favourite stopping-place for walkers.

One of the pleasures of walking the Pennine Way is meeting other hikers and swapping experiences, and from such meetings can come friendships and possibly even romance. The unattached male traveller, having taken a shine to a similarly eligible lady walker he met whilst walking the Way, may repair contentedly to his hostel bed that night to enjoy dreams of a true walkers' wedding, enhanced by rucksack-shaped wedding cake and followed by a honeymoon spent bagging a few dozen Munros together. Sadly, the course of true love will not often run so smoothly. If they meet again having completed their Pennine journey, they may well find conversation that flowed so naturally on the magnificent heights of Pen-y-Ghent or by the sparkling cascade of Hardraw rather harder to come by in the British Home Stores cafeteria in Reading. Of course, it may be that the letter written by the would-be suitor suggesting a post-walk meeting is never replied to, and the writer is left not knowing whether his anxiously-penned epistle has been misplaced en route to its intended recipient, or has been used by her to wipe the last traces of cow-dung off the sole of her left boot.

Thwaite to Bowes
The next section is quite magnificent. Leaving Thwaite, you head north-eastwards, uphill, to reach the hamlet of Kisdon, then just before Kisdon Cottage you bear left and begin a tremendous walk, initially just east of north and then swinging north-westwards, towards Keld. You proceed along a limestone shelf amongst trees, bracken and grass, while to your right is a steep slope leading down to the river Swale. A little less than half a mile short of Keld and just beyond Birk Hill, a detour to the right takes you to the beautiful Kisdon Force. The Way does not go quite as far as the centre of Keld, but turns right and drops steeply to cross the Swale and then climb, again steeply, up the other side with the spectacular falls of East Gill Force to your right. For the drop down to the Swale and the climb back up again, you will be overlapping with Wainwright's

Coast to Coast Walk, described elsewhere in this book. Many walkers will wish to detour to Keld (120), where accommodation is available.

Originally, Keld was a Viking settlement, and its name comes from an old Norse word for a well or a spring; it is not only a picturesque place, its sturdy cottages of grey stone blending beautifully with the surrounding hills and woodland, but it has a timeless and enduring quality which is somehow very reassuring. Having passed East Gill Force, you wave goodbye to Coast to Coast walkers who turn right to cross the stream just above the Force, while you turn left and proceed north-westwards past the buildings of East Stonesdale, then heading just west of north, you gradually climb out of the dale on to the moors.

For a while the going is excellent, and there are lovely views back to Keld and its surrounds. Having crossed Lad Gill you swing north-eastwards, still gradually climbing, and although the Way hereabouts is sometimes unclear and a little juicy underfoot, you will be spurred on by the thought of reaching the Tan Hill Inn. At length it comes into view, and your pace will surely increase as you head towards it; although you may only have walked four miles from Keld, you will surely want to halt awhile at this Way-side pub (124), which is also the highest pub in England, at 1,732ft. Historically it has served as an important centre of industrial and commercial activity, being the meeting of four trade routes, as well as an obvious place of rest and refreshment for moorland travellers. Many of the patrons would have come from the numerous collieries nearby, all of which are now abandoned, with derelict airshafts the only surviving evidence of the mining activity.

Having refreshed yourself at the Tan Hill Inn – we spent a full two hours chatting by its roaring open fire – you turn briefly right on to a road, then almost immediately left to proceed north-eastwards and gradually downhill across Sleightholme Moor. You follow alongside Coal Gill Sike for a short while, then are joined by Frumming Beck and later Sleightholme Beck to your left, eventually reaching Sleightholme Moor road and turning left on to it, following it to the buildings of Sleightholme. The walk across Sleightholme Moor is boggy and unpleasant, and you may in fact be tempted to stick to the road all the way, using the Arkengarthdale road as far as Cocker, then picking up Sleightholme Moor road. This is a logical bad weather alternative, although Wainwright severely reminds us that 'strictly this isn't doing the Pennine Way.'

Having passed the buildings of Sleightholme, the Way shortly forks left on to a path which proceeds north-eastwards to Trough Heads Farm, crossing Sleightholme Beck at Intake Bridge. At Trough Heads Farm you have a choice between the main route and the Bowes loop, the latter involving two extra miles but a chance to visit the village of Bowes. The *main* route forks left to turn north-westwards and proceeds in that direction over heather and grass towards the A66, passing over the river Greta by means of a natural limestone bridge, known as God's Bridge. A tunnel is used to pass under the A66 – in bygone years, walkers had to walk across this very busy trans-Pennine road – and you then embark on a singularly uninspiring 4-mile trudge across open moorland, still heading north-westwards. You begin by crossing Bowes Moor and passing the ruins of Ravock Castle, then having gone over Deepdale Beck you rise gently to the 1,402ft Race Yate, before descending over Cotherstone Moor to reach a road just south of Clove Lodge. You turn left on to the road and follow it past the lodge.

The *Bowes loop* route forks right at Trough Heads to proceed northwards then eastwards, passing the farms of East Mellwaters, West Charity Pasture and Lady Mires, proceeding roughly parallel with the Greta. At Lady Mires you briefly join a road which you could follow all the way to Bowes, but the loop route soon turns left on to a path that goes forward to cross the Greta and head north-eastwards to Swinholme (if, owing to high water, the Greta is impassable, you will have to follow the road all the way to Bowes). You briefly join a lane here, but soon turn right and proceed eastwards through the fields to reach Bowes.

Bowes to Langdon Beck

Bowes has two features of interest; it is dominated by its huge Norman castle keep, and is also the site of a Roman fort, of which some of the ditches are still visible. There is also the possibility of refreshment and accommodation in the village. You leave Bowes by following the main street westwards then turning sharp right over the A66 by a footbridge, following the metalled road north-westwards across the moors as far as West Stoney Keld. The loop route goes forward on a track to the ruined farmhouse of Levy Pool then continues north-westwards across drab moorland, passing the 1,274ft millstone outcrop of Goldsborough, and shortly afterwards reaching the Cotherstone–Clove Lodge road. You could just turn left on to that and be reunited with the main route at Clove Lodge in less than a mile, but the official loop route crosses the road and proceeds to East Friar House, turning left and following fiddly paths to reach the road and join up with the main route a little further north of Clove Lodge.

You may well feel, particularly if the weather has been unkind, that it would have been better to have stuck to the main route in the first place, especially if you were seduced there solely by Wainwright's suggestion, in his *Companion*, that 'you once knew a girl who lived at Bowes', and found that that girl was now heavily pregnant with her fifth child and living in an eighth floor council flat in Lower Edmonton.

You should proceed triumphantly down the road to Blackton Bridge in Baldersdale (135 via *direct* route), knowing that you have reached the halfway point on the Pennine Way. Having crossed Blackton Bridge over the river Balder, with Blackton Reservoir immediately to your right, you swing just north of east to go forward to Birk Hat Farm. You then swing just west of north, passing High Birk Hat Farm, and having crossed a metalled road linking Balder Head with Romaldkirk, you proceed on to Mickleton Moor. The Way swings more northwards to reach the farm at How, then proceeds down to Grassholme reservoir in Lunedale, turning left on to a metalled road to cross the water and continue north-westwards along the road to the hamlet of Grassholme. Shortly you turn right and proceed over pastures, just west of north, to the B6276 Brough–Middleton in Teesdale road. You cross straight over on to a track that starts out north-westwards, then climbs north-eastwards, your direction now all the way to Middleton in Teesdale.

Beyond the buildings of Wythes Hill the track disappears and you strike out over open fields, continuing to climb; the fields give way to heather and bracken and as you reach the top of the rise, you are treated to a lovely view across Teesdale, which is ample reward for the tedious miles tramped since Tan Hill. To the right is the walled and reputedly haunted plantation of Kirkcarrion, the site of a large tumulus. It is all downhill now, and you can enjoy a quite delightful walk on springy turf to reach the valley at the village of Middleton in Teesdale. The Way turns left on to a cart-track just before the bridge over the Tees, but most travellers will wish to detour into the village which lies across the bridge (141).

Middleton in Teesdale, which boasts an excellent range of amenities, is a pretty village of sandstone houses and whitewashed cottages. Standing amongst tall trees that overlook the village is Middleton House, one of the village's more imposing buildings and former headquarters of the Quaker-owned London Lead Company. The building is now a shooting lodge, but a memorial to the London Lead Company remains in the village in the form of a blue and white memorial fountain, which was erected in 1877. Another feature of interest is the sixteenth-century detached belfry just to the north of the parish church; the belfry retains one of its three original bells, which is rung by using both hands and a foot!

The next eight miles are sheer joy. Navigation is easy and uncomplicated as the Way proceeds chiefly north-westwards beside the Tees, following it upstream. The early walking is not so much spectacular as pleasant, as the Way proceeds through the meadows beside the tree-lined river, passing Scoberry Bridge and Wynch Bridge, soon after which you meet Low Force, a succession of splendid mini-waterfalls. The river bed between Scoberry Bridge and Low Force is wide, with numerous rocky islands and platforms, many carpeted with flowers, while columns of dolerite rock – formed as a result of seismic activity some 300 million years ago – guard the riverbanks. Beyond Low Force, as you pass Holwick Head Bridge, the surroundings get even better. The trees around the river become more profuse, with junipers attractively clothing the slopes, and the noise of the river is noticeably louder.

Then comes the magnificent cascade of High Force. Although it is not the highest waterfall in the country, its thunderous surge of water makes it the biggest, as the Tees, after proceeding from its source on Cross Fell (which you will visit some 30 miles further on), suddenly crashes over a band of shale down a 70ft drop into a wooded gorge surrounded by deep foliage and dolerite rock. It is a truly awesome sight, and, like Hardraw, is seen at its best after wet weather. So there is something to be said for all the Pennine Way rain after all.

The final three miles from here to Langdon Beck are somewhat anticlimactical; you deviate away from the Tees a little at Bracken Rigg and climb on to High Crag, then join a farm road at Cronkley Farm and return to the river at Cronkley Bridge. You cross the bridge and turn left, proceeding alongside the Tees to the point where it is met by its tributary, Langdon Beck. The Way then simply continues along the riverbank, but this time the bank of Langdon Beck, keeping it to the left as far as Saur Hill Bridge (149). The route crosses the bridge, but by detouring right here you soon reach Langdon Beck Youth Hostel. This is a useful stopping-place for those covering the Middleton to Dufton section in two days, since only the strongest walkers can hope to manage it in one day. We arrived at the hostel in excellent shape, knowing that Dufton was well within our capabilities next day, and such was our relaxed mood that we enjoyed some keenly-contested games of chess that evening.

No self-respecting bed and breakfast or youth hostel should be without a stock of games and puzzles to while away a long evening and to keep one's mental as well as physical faculties exercised. Naturally enough, they will not be at the top of the owner's list of maintenance priorities, and users should not be surprised to find papier mâché models masquerading as rooks and bishops in the box of chess pieces, or a jigsaw representation of the Arc de Triomphe which is missing 200 square metres of blue sky, the front half of a green Citroën, and the legs of half a dozen gawping Japanese tourists.

Langdon Beck to Garrigill

After crossing Saur Hill Bridge you begin walking towards Dufton. Remarkably, your general direction of travel for this section is south-westwards, effectively taking you further away from your ultimate objective. A straightforward walk over grassland brings you back to the Tees, which you now follow upstream for some two and a half miles, keeping the river to your left. Almost at once you pass the farm at Widdybanks, and can look across the river at this point to Cronkley Scar, a hill of jagged rock rising majestically beyond the fast-flowing waters. The riverside walk which follows will pose no navigation problems but does require some scrambling over boulders and scree around Falcon Clints. We stopped at one point along this part of the walk to admire a remarkably docile grouse; this bird, with its distinctive 'go back' call, is a common sight on the Pennine moors, and with many of these moors being used for grouse-shooting during the season, there are sometimes path diversions.

The riverside walk comes to a dramatic climax with Cauldron Snout, a magnificent cataract crashing down through the rocks on a channel of dolerite. You clamber through the boulders that border the cataract until you reach and cross a bridge high above the cascades, although before making the crossing you may wish to detour further upstream to inspect the infamous Cow Green reservoir, the construction of which in the 1960s caused huge controversy. Its stark concrete dam wall, which can be seen from the Pennine Way, sits most uncomfortably with the tremendous surroundings and the natural exuberance of the waterfall directly below. Having crossed the bridge, the Way leaves the Tees and follows a farm road as far as the farms of Birkdale, running parallel with Maize Beck, a tributary of the Tees. Anticlimax now sets in, as having left Birkdale you ford Grain Beck and embark on a section of nondescript peaty moorland; this used to be one of the more infamous sections of the Way, but in recent years it has been improved and you should have few problems.

Two miles from Birkdale you arrive at Maize Beck and proceed briefly along its north bank. You now have a choice: you may either ford the beck after roughly half a mile of beckside walking, and proceed just south of west along a cairned route to High Cup Plain, or, if the waters are too great, you proceed on beside the beck as far as the footbridge near the impressive limestone formations of

Maizebeck Scar, then beyond the footbridge you turn sharply south-westwards to High Cup Plain.

Whichever route you take, your labours will soon be rewarded by your arrival at High Cupgill Head and what is perhaps the greatest moment on the whole walk. Suddenly, with no warning, the featureless moorland comes to an end, and the ground falls spectacularly away in front of you to reveal a fabulous view of the Vale of Eden with the mountains of Lakeland towering up behind. This is High Cup, consisting of a sweep of sheer whinstone cliffs to the right and the left, and, immediately ahead, a huge basin of grass and scree through which High Cup Gill flows. Some refer to this whole scene as High Cup Nick, but do so incorrectly, as the Nick is merely a cleft in the escarpment.

The Way follows the right-hand sweep of cliffs, passing a pillar of basalt known as Nichol Chair and making a magnificent descent along a cairned route that arrives just below Peeping Hill. The views are stupendous, and on a good day you can see the Galloway hills in southern Scotland as well as Lakeland peaks. As you pass the old quarries and profusion of holes and pots you may be reminded of the descent from Pen-y-Ghent to Horton.

You turn briefly north-west, then join a lane which swings just south of west and proceeds past Bow Hall Farm into the lovely village of Dufton (162), whose squat sandstone cottages, set round a spacious green, make a delightful sight. With refreshment and accommodation available, it is an obvious stopping-place for Pennine Way walkers, as there is nothing now on offer for nearly twenty miles. One piece of trivia that walkers may swap as they enjoy their evening drink in the village is that Dufton was the home of the cobbler who gave his name to Nichol Chair. He is reputed to have mended a pair of boots on the top of the slender basalt pillar, despite the apparent lack of room for both his tools and his backside. Work must have been more fun before the advent of Health and Safety inspectors . . .

Despite the attractions of Dufton, an early night is advisable as you now have a very long and tiring day ahead. Having arrived in Dufton further from your ultimate objective than you were at Langdon Beck, you waste little time making up the 'lost' ground, heading resolutely north-eastwards all the way to Knock Fell. Inevitably, it is also uphill all the way, your having lost so much height on the descent from High Cup. After leaving Dufton you head initially for Coatsike, then continue along a lane to the old farmhouse of Halsteads and having crossed Great Rundale Beck, you proceed along a walled track, climbing steadily. The climb is enlivened however by lovely views to the Eden valley as well as to the very distinctive summit of Dufton Pike.

Gradually the gradient becomes stiffer, as you ford Swindale Beck and continue roughly parallel with it, passing Knock Hush, one of a number of watercourses that were created artificially for the purpose of scouring vegetation with a view to seeing what minerals lay in the subsoil. Coast to Coast veterans may remember seeing some hushes in the moors above Swaledale. You leave Swindale Beck and haul yourself past the distinctive cairn known as Knock Old Man and up to the 2,604ft summit of Knock Fell, comfortably higher than any ground covered so far. The views make the effort well worthwhile, and there is even better to come.

You swing north-westwards, your direction of travel all the way to Cross Fell, and now are faced with three further peaks in succession, each preceded by a slight dip and then a brisk ascent. The walking is generally extremely good underfoot, and as most of the hard climbing has now been done, the lungs will not be greatly tested any further. The main problem is likely to be bad weather; these very lofty summits attract violent air currents that are the source of a local meteorological phenomenon known as the Helm Wind which can produce some very unpleasant conditions indeed. When low cloud or mist come down, navigation could be a serious problem.

The first of the three peaks is the 2,780ft Great Dun Fell, easily identified even in bad weather by its radar and weather stations and its very conspicuous 'golf ball' which is visible from as far away as Helvellyn in the Lake District. The 2,761ft Little Dun Fell, which follows, is quite uncluttered, and you may wish to pause on the summit before tackling the final peak, Cross Fell, which at 2,930ft is the summit of the Pennine Way and provides tremendous views to Lakeland. If you are blessed with good weather you may feel your walk to reach this point, particularly in the final stages, has been almost too easy, but when the mist or rain have closed in you will have a real struggle to locate the path to the summit in what is a huge featureless grassland area.

No less difficult, but crucially important, is locating the route off the summit; this heads north-westwards and steeply downhill to meet a cairned path, actually an old corpse road, on to which you turn right and which you follow north-eastwards all the way to Garrigill, nearly eight miles away. You will notice the profusion of old mineworkings as you proceed on your way, and you should look out also for the bothy or shelter known as Greg's Hut which you pass soon after joining the corpse road.

The going is now very easy and straightforward on an excellent track through the heather, although the lovely views to the Eden valley have been left behind. One interesting feature of this section is the accumulation of blue crystals of fluorspar, a non-metallic mineral which, although regarded as waste material in lead mining, has been used in steel manufacture. You may even be tempted to pick a few crystals off the track and take them home as an unusual souvenir of your walk, although it would be prudent not only to secrete it carefully but remember to deal with it at journey's end. It would be all too easy, in the excitement of completing the walk, to forget that bits of the stuff were still sitting at the bottom of a fleece jacket pocket or rucksack and liable either to go shooting down the washing machine's waste water pipe into eternal oblivion, or take up permanent residence inside your camera, battery shaver or toothbrush.

Garrigill to Greenhead

At length the corpse road becomes a walled lane, still descending, and drops down to the South Tyne valley, arriving at the village of Garrigill (178.5), a pretty village, and a welcome one too, being the first settlement since Dufton to offer accommodation and refreshment. However, some walkers may still prefer to press on to Alston. The Way turns north-westwards at Garrigill, joining a road that proceeds through the village and out the other side, going roughly parallel with the South Tyne. Soon, however, you turn right on to a path that follows the riverbank, keeping the river to your right. After just over a mile of delightful riverside walking you switch to the opposite bank, briefly leaving the river and heading across a number of fields past the farms of Sillyhall and Bleagate, the gentle pastoral landscape quite a contrast to the wilds of Cross Fell.

You then return to the river and, keeping it to your left, go forward into Alston (183) which, built along a steep cobbled street with side streets of stone houses, is claimed to be the highest market town in England. The town has all the amenities a walker could want, including not only ample refreshment and accommodation facilities, but banks and, at the time of my visit, a laundrette. I also came upon the famous Alston bottle shop and enjoyed browsing amongst the collection of something in excess of 8,000 bottles, although the man who had accumulated this extraordinary collection, Arthur Roland, claimed not to drink anything except tea.

The seventeen miles beyond Alston rank as among the most tedious on the whole route, with no great scenic rewards and plenty of opportunity to lose yourself. You proceed out of Alston pleasantly enough, on a path that keeps the South Tyne close to your right, but then branch off north-westwards, away from the river, passing Harbut Lodge and proceeding across fields, over the A689 and forward to Gilderdale Burn. A little beyond the farm at Harbut Law the 'official' route takes the walker round effectively three sides of a square to get to Gilderdale Burn, but a direct short cut across the fields is available. Beyond Gilderdale Burn you join a cart-track, continuing north-west then swinging north-eastwards past the grassy ramparts of the old Roman fort at Whitley Castle, and arrive at the farm at Castle Nook, where you are reunited with the A689.

You cross the road and swing north-westwards again, proceeding through a number of fields and passing the little hamlet of Kirkhaugh. The path is often indistinct on the ground but you can be guided by the course of the old Haltwhistle–Alston railway which you keep to your right. As the A689 comes in from your left, you again eschew tarmac to swing under the old railway, by means of a viaduct picturesquely bathed in woodland, and proceed alongside Thornhope Burn. Now the South Tyne comes in from the right, and, having passed the meeting of Thornhope Burn with it, you briefly follow the South Tyne upstream until you reach your friend the A689 again. At last you are allowed the privilege of a walk alongside it, soon reaching the pretty but amenity-less village of Slaggyford (189).

You leave the A689 by turning right up a lane that proceeds parallel with the old railway, then having crossed Knar Burn, pass underneath the railway once more and head uphill slightly away from it, still heading north-westwards. The Way passes the buildings of Merry Know then swings north-eastwards and downhill, crossing the A689 again and arriving at the hamlet of Burnstones. The walk from Slaggyford to Burnstones is fiddly and can get very muddy, and it may be possible to follow the old railway track as an alternative, as we did. We turned right on to the road at Burnstones and found refreshment at the Kirkstile Inn at Knarsdale a short way down the road. However, the Way bears left at Burnstones, and there then follows the fastest walking of this 17-mile slog, as you proceed first northwards, then slightly west of north, along the Maiden Way for two and a half miles.

This is an old Roman road linking Kirkby Thore in the old county of Westmorland with a fort near Hadrian's Wall. It is a pleasant moorland march, the route being very easy to follow and largely clear on the ground, with a parallel wall or fence to guide you. Having proceeded in a straight line along the Maiden Way, crossing Lambley Common, the Pennine Way then swings north-westwards to reach the disused Lambley Colliery and enjoys one final meeting with the A689. It is improbable that walkers will feel moved to shed any tears over this last farewell, unless of course they have been religiously following it ever since their first meeting with it that morning, having worked out that that was by far the easiest and most painless method of making progress. With both Pennine Way and A689 walkers having enjoyed nearly three miles' straightforward walking since Burnstones, morale is likely to be high, and even the more staid walkers in the party are likely to be amused rather than annoyed when asked what does the maiden weigh.

After some excellent walking from Burnstones, there is now a profound deterioration. Wainwright calls this section 'uninteresting' and I think he was being kind! From Lambley Colliery you proceed just west of north across featureless pasture, reaching the barn of High House and briefly swinging north-eastwards to cross Hartley Burn by a footbridge. This is a pleasant enough spot, but beyond, as you proceed north-westwards, there is a dismal section of fiddly field walking, passing the buildings of three farms, some of them ruinous. Beyond the third farm, Greenriggs, you cross over the twin moors of Round Hill and Wain Rigg, passing just to the east of the triangulation point on Black Hill; this is rather less dire than its namesake further south, but no lovelier. There is no path as such, and a compass is essential in mist.

Continuing north-westwards you arrive at Gap Shields, swinging north-east, and with some relief you pick up a track here, bearing right on to it and following it slightly south of east, then a little north of east. Looking at the map you appear to have covered two sides of a triangle since escaping from Wain Rigg, but near some old clay pits you swing north-westwards and then decisively north-eastwards, following a good cart-track to cross the A69. Crossing over, you continue north-eastwards to reach what is called the vallum, a broad ditch which served as an old military boundary, then turn right to walk by the vallum as far as a road linking Gilsland with Greenhead (200).

Most walkers who have come from Alston today will have had enough and will be ready for a bed at Greenhead, which lies just a quarter of a mile away and offers refreshment and accommodation. There is cause for triple celebration here. You have clocked up 200 miles on the Pennine Way, you have reached one of the best sections of the route (namely the walk along a section of Hadrian's Wall), and you have now reached the end of the Pennine Range. Of course all this presupposes that you have found your way off Round Hill and Wain Rigg without difficulty, and that you are not tottering around these foothills in ever-decreasing circles, your sense of desperation bringing on hallucinatory visions of a gap appearing amidst the squelchy grass to be magically filled, to the sound of trumpets and the crackling of fireworks, by the sudden dramatic advent of the A689.

Greenhead to Bellingham

The next ten miles are tremendous, and make up for the sad tramping you have experienced since Lambley Colliery. Beyond the Gilsland–Greenhead road, you swing north-eastwards, immediately reaching Thirlwall Castle, a fortified tower-house almost 700 years old but ruined for at least the last 300 years. Heading eastwards – your principal direction of travel all the way to Rapishaw Gap – you follow a section of Roman ditch to reach Walltown Quarry, then join a road heading for the farm at Walltown. After half a mile or so of road walking, you bear sharply left, uphill, to reach Hadrian's Wall at Walltown Crags.

The Wall was a Roman frontier system built under the direction of the emperor Hadrian between AD 122 and 126 to mark England's northern boundary and to prevent tribes such as the Scots and the Picts from launching raids into northern England. It was skilfully built to take advantage of the lie of the land. Some of it, including the section that you will walk, was constructed on serrated dolerite crags of the Whin Sill (a seam of igneous dolerite that runs across northern England), providing a barrier that was partly natural and partly man-made.

Thousands of troops defended the Wall; sixteen forts, plus some smaller intermediate fortifications were built to accommodate them, and in addition there were guardposts, known as milecastles, and turrets that served as watchtowers. Fragments of some turrets can still be observed today. The Wall remained an effective defence for well over 250 years, seeing some bloody conflict, although it was breached in AD 197, 296 and 367–68. It was finally abandoned in about AD 383, and now, where once Roman soldiers stood, there are huge ridges, topped by stone blocks, rising out of largely remote deserted countryside. Some parts of the Wall can now be seen rising to eight or nine feet high, with fragments of the defensive fortifications still remaining, whilst in other places the Wall has dwindled to virtually nothing. The Pennine Way follows the Wall for eight miles, and they are eight tough miles, faithfully following the ridge with its ups and downs, and occasional rocky scrambles; the irregular formations of dolerite have little sympathy for tired legs! The reward, however, is a grandstand view of the north Pennines and Cheviots, and the thrill of having the Wall itself immediately beside you.

Just under two miles from Walltown Crags you reach the remains of a fort known as Aesica, then continue past Burnhead, briefly joining a road before proceeding on to Cawfield Crags. You descend to a road at Caw Gap then rise again on to Winshields Crag, at 1,230ft the highest point on the Wall. This is all superb walking, with glorious panoramic views stretching as far back as the Solway Firth, and no difficulties underfoot or with navigation. Shortly beyond Winshields Crag you reach the B6318 (207.5) where a right turn leads you to the Twice Brewed Inn and the Once Brewed Youth Hostel. The inn got its name from the belief that the ale supplied there was fermented twice to give it added strength, while the hostel owes its name to a remark made upon its opening to the effect that it was hoped nothing stronger than tea, brewed only *once*, would be consumed there!

Tea is of course a life-saver for weary walkers but how they gain access to it at the end of their day will vary greatly. A huge pot of piping hot tea, accompanied by a plate of cakes, brought to the tired traveller whilst he reclines in a deep armchair, is an answer to every hiker's prayer. Less welcome is the hotel room where the guest is left to make his own, and is forced to grapple with the intricacies of a jug kettle with a somewhat temperamental element, so that a full 15 minutes after trying every combination of knob and button that the apparatus boasts, the would-be tea-drinker is still not sure if he has actually managed to switch the thing on at all.

From the Once/Twice Brewed turning you continue along the Wall over Peel Crags and past Crag Lough, then climb on to Hotbank Crags. Just beyond these crags is Rapishaw Gap, where you leave the Wall, but by continuing via Cuddy's Crags and Housesteads Crags you reach the Roman fort of Housesteads. Also known as Vercovium, it ranks as one of the finest Roman hilltop fort remains in Great Britain. Even if you do not detour to Housesteads, the view from Rapishaw Gap towards Cuddy's Crags and Housesteads Crags is superb and worth photographing before you leave the Wall for the last time. Now anticlimax sets in. You turn left at Rapishaw Gap to head in a vaguely northerly direction, sometimes just east and sometimes just west of north, across a rather nondescript landscape of open grassland and heather. To your right is Broomlee Lough, and ahead is Wark Forest. Having passed just to the east of the farm at East Stonefolds you plunge into the forest, where you stay for most of the next five miles.

This is generally acknowledged by Pennine Way walkers as an unwelcome interlude, the dreary conifers of Sitka and Norway spruce packed tightly together so as to ensure minimum light and maximum claustrophobia. Fortunately progress is fast and straightforward on a wide well-defined track, and there are two interludes of open country as you proceed north-eastwards. There is also a standing stone called Comyns Cross, a product of Arthurian legend, towards the end of the first 'break' in the woodland.

Having emerged from the final tranche of forest, you continue north-eastwards across grass moorland and arrive at Warks Burn. Beyond Warks Burn, which is extremely picturesque, there is a pleasant but fiddly and rather unexciting walk across pasture dotted with old farmsteads. At Low Stead you join a road and follow it north-eastwards to a T-junction of roads, crossing straight over and following a path that continues north-eastwards to Houxty Burn. You cross the burn and ascend north-eastwards on to Ealingham Rigg, doubtless suppressing a snigger as you pass the buildings of Shitlington Hall and then proceed over Shitlington Crags.

Shortly you reach a walled cart-track, turning right to follow it, and head briefly just south of east, enjoying good views to Bellingham and the valley of the North Tyne from here. After barely half a mile you turn left off the cart-track and proceed across some rather boggy pasture, initially going north-eastwards then swinging north-westwards, descending into the North Tyne valley. At length you arrive at the B6320, turning left on to the road and following it over the river into Bellingham, pronounced 'Bellin-jam' (225). The little town has a wide main street and marketplace flanked by sturdy buildings of grey stone, and there are many places available for refreshment and accommodation. Indeed this is the last place on the whole route where provisions are readily obtainable, and there are still over 40 miles to go. So make sure you leave Bellingham with a full rucksack!

Although most of the buildings are nineteenth-century, the parish church of St Cuthbert dates from the twelfth century, and its stone roof was to guard against marauding bands of sixteenth-century cattle thieves known as Border Reivers. Such nefarious activity has of course been consigned to the history books, and so apparently peaceful is this town now that one suspects that even a conviction for dropping a crisp packet in Bellingham's main street would be sufficient to make headline news in the local paper and prompt a flood of correspondence from readers bemoaning the breakdown of standards of discipline and demanding the immediate return of National Service.

Bellingham to Clennel Street

The walk from Bellingham to Byrness is not one of the best sections on the Pennine Way. However, the day can be improved by a detour, right at the start, to a superb waterfall called Hareshaw Linn, a 30ft cascade into a rocky chasm surrounded by towering cliffs and woodland, situated a couple of miles north of the centre of Bellingham. Annoyingly, it is necessary for you to retrace your steps to Bellingham before continuing. The start of the walk towards Byrness is easy enough, consisting of a straightforward walk along the West Woodburn road and then a farm road, heading north-eastwards and uphill to the farm at Blakelaw. You then swing in a more northerly direction and proceed across grass and heather moorland, gradually gaining height and veering to the north-west to pass Hareshaw House and Abbey Rigg, where there is an old colliery.

The Way crosses the B6320 Bellingham–Otterburn road and you now begin one of the least inspiring sections on the northern half of the route, consisting of a walk across marshy grass and heather through featureless moorland terrain. In bad weather you will almost certainly need a compass to steer you along, as there are virtually no landmarks. Initially you proceed uphill just east of north on to Lough Shaw, then swing west of north to pass the 1,183ft summit of Deer Play, where on a good day there is a fine view to the Cheviots, and beyond Deer Play you proceed north-westwards to the 1,167ft summit of Lord's Shaw. Beyond Lord's Shaw there is a descent to the Gib Shiel–Troughend road, and now things get easier.

Having crossed the road, the Way once again strikes out north-westwards over the moors, but there is now the reassurance of a fence to your right, and this stays with you all the way to Redesdale Forest where you will join a road. Initially you skirt the western edge of Padon Hill but it is worth detouring to enjoy the tremendous views from the 1,240ft summit with its pepperbox monument commemorating Alexander Padon, a Scottish Covenanter who held open-air services here.

The Way loses height beyond Padon Hill but then climbs to the 1,191ft Brownrigg Head; this can be quite an arduous ascent, especially in bad weather. Your moorland tramp is almost over however, and after a squelchy descent off Brownrigg Head you enter the massive Redesdale Forest, turning right at Rookengate on to a metalled road and pounding north-westwards along it for three and a half miles as far as the hamlet of Blakehopeburnhaugh. As we passed through we decided that living in a place with one of the longest names in Great Britain must be a mixed blessing; whilst acknowledging that it undoubtedly provided a useful conversational gambit for the locals, we could not help wondering how many of them had succumbed to writer's cramp simply in the process of completing a driving licence application form.

The road walking temporarily ends just beyond Blakehopeburnhaugh, at the bridge crossing of the river Rede. Immediately beyond the bridge you turn left on to a path that proceeds quite delightfully along the riverbank north-westwards as far as the farm at Cottonshopeburn Foot. Continuing north-westwards, the Way crosses the Rede again and follows a forest trail towards Byrness, crossing the river one more time to enter the village (241), originally established to accommodate construction workers building a nearby reservoir, and then adopted as a Forestry Commission village to facilitate the management of Redesdale forest. In recent years it has become a useful place of refreshment for road travellers on the busy A68, which passes right through the village. It is also an almost mandatory stopping-place for Pennine Way walkers, being the very last settlement on the route where amenities of any description are available, though even these amenities are limited.

Ahead is a very tough 27-mile march across the Cheviots to Kirk Yetholm (29 miles if you include the detour to the Cheviot) with no shelter or refreshment, and although it is possible to detour off the route to obtain accommodation, the detour is a long one. Many walkers will hope to do the whole walk to Kirk Yetholm in one go, starting as early as five or six in the morning. In the circumstances it is unlikely either that sleep will come easily that night, or that even the most competitive Scrabble player in the party will that evening quibble unduly about a deviation from the rules that has somehow enabled both 'Blakehopeburnhaugh' and 'Cottonshopeburn' to mysteriously appear on the board.

Your problems begin almost immediately with an awkward and steep ascent out of the village through the trees, heading north-eastwards on a forest path which when we walked it was by no means obvious. With some relief you emerge on to the 1,358ft Byrness Hill, swinging north-westwards past Saughy Crag and then northwards to Windy Crag. Heading just east of north and continuing to gain height, the Way then continues across the open moor, but navigation is assisted by a fence running alongside you to the left. You proceed past Ravens Knowe then, descending, swing west of north and go forward on to Ogre Hill where you cross the border into Scotland. The Way crosses the border fence and heads northwards away from it, then swings eastwards, passes over Coquet Head and crosses back over the border fence to Chew Green, the site of Roman camps; these camps were a stopover on Dere Street which was an old Roman road linking York with Scotland. The Way then swings north-westwards and proceeds just east of north to follow Dere Street, passing just to the east of the 1,664ft summit of Brownhart Law.

You then stay alongside the border fence for a little under a mile, passing the site of a Roman signal station. This is tremendous walking with no navigational problems and sweeping views across some of the loneliest countryside in the British Isles. The Way then leaves the security of the fence, striking out north-eastwards for two miles through trackless, albeit cairned moorland terrain; becoming reunited with the fence just south-west of Lamb Hill. The ground can be very wet underfoot, although beyond Lamb Hill the going improves.

Now things get easier as you proceed confidently beside the fence for just over two miles, heading north-eastwards past the 1,677ft Lamb Hill, uphill to the 1,842ft Beefstand Hill and forward to the 1,812ft Mozie Law. The Way then moves a little away from the fence but stays parallel with it and continues eastwards to pass Foul Step, then, proceeding a little south of east, rejoins the fence. You continue alongside the fence, heading just south of east, then cross the fence and swing eastwards to climb to the 2,034ft Russell's Cairn, which unless you are detouring to the Cheviot is the halfway point between Byrness and Kirk Yetholm.

Russell's Cairn consists of a mound of stones that are of Bronze Age origin; the hill on which it stands is called Windy Gyle, an appropriate name if ever there was one, because the wind can blow ferociously hard on this exposed Cheviot summit. The views are magnificent, from what is the highest point on the ridge so far. Beyond Windy Gyle you continue north-eastwards beside the border fence for over four miles, keeping the fence to your right on your descent to Clennell Street and thereafter keeping it to your left.

At Clennell Street (255.5) you have the opportunity to break your journey by detouring to the left to Cocklawfoot (two miles) or to the right to Uswayford (one mile); you may be fortunate enough to obtain accommodation at either. It is the logical place to leave the route if you have decided to split the Byrness–Kirk Yetholm walk into two days, especially as there are no further convenient opportunities to leave the ridge. Some walkers have booked accommodation at Uswayford but have then decided to continue on to Kirk Yetholm anyway without stopping.

If you decide to join their number, common courtesy dictates that you phone to cancel your booking. It would indeed be regrettable if a search party was sent out into the Cheviots in pitch darkness to attempt to locate a supposedly benighted walker who is in fact merrily celebrating his completion of the route in Kirk Yetholm and who, if asked whether Uswayford meant anything to him, would scratch his head and hesitantly reply that it sounded as though it might be a fictional non-league football team that inflicted a shock FA Cup third-round defeat on Melchester Rovers.

Clennel Street to Kirk Yetholm

Beyond Clennell Street the walking gets tougher, and although there are no navigational difficulties, thanks to the fence, there is a lot of climbing on surfaces which can be atrocious. You pass Butt Roads (certainly no roads) at 1,718ft, continue to Kings Seat (again, neither king nor seat) at 1,743ft, then climb to Score Head at 1,910ft where the going does become extremely difficult. Peat-hags bring back unpleasant memories of Bleaklow and Black Hill, but added to that is a climb of almost inhuman severity to the 2,419ft west top of Cairn Hill. The relief at reaching this summit is quite indescribable, particularly for walkers who are missing out the Cheviot and who can now begin marching north-westwards towards Auchope Cairn and downhill to Hen Hole. However, for the sake of completeness if nothing else, many hikers will wish, as we did, to make the detour to the Cheviot, up and back on the same path, involving a return trip of just under three miles north-eastwards via the 2,545ft top of Cairn Hill.

This used to be one of the most fiendish parts of the whole Pennine Way, consisting of a trudge along a wide whaleback ridge on an appalling peaty surface with peat-hags just waiting to engulf the walker who had hitherto survived everything the Pennine Way could throw at him. Despite the fact that we had all entrusted our rucksacks to the baggage-carrier for this section, and were thus carrying less weight, two of us sank majestically into the peat en route for the summit; one of these unfortunates was in it up to his waist and required the assistance of two people to help him out. We literally had to crawl our way to the summit column, at 2,676ft the highest ground since leaving Cross Fell, and found an extraordinarily disappointing view. We fought our way back to the main route, our consciences squeaky clean but our clothes precisely the opposite. Things have now changed for the better, and walkers who detour to the Cheviot can enjoy proceeding along a proper flag path.

On return to the main route, you now proceed north-westwards across very squelchy terrain as far as the 2,382ft Auchope Cairn, an important moment on the walk, for not only does the surface underfoot greatly improve but there is no higher ground to come, and the worst of the walk from Byrness is behind you. You may wish to stop here for some celebratory refreshment, although creature comforts seem as far away as at any point since pulling away from the A68. Walkers who may have been going for some seven or eight consecutive hours now may well feel the need for a 'comfort break' of a more personal nature, but will have no alternative other than to cast away their pride and relieve themselves in the open air, taking care to note the direction of strong winds.

Beyond Auchope Cairn, the Way proceeds north-westwards – the direction of travel all the way to the end – and, still keeping immediately to the right of the border fence, moves confidently downhill on a good track passing just to the south of the impressive Hen Hole, a narrow ravine and waterfall flanked by huge cliffs, the unusual formations resulting from glacial retreat 10,000 years ago. A brief detour is needed to visit the Hole and if time is pressing, you may feel it to be a bridge – or waterfall – too far. There is then a tough climb to the Schil, the last summit on the Way at 1,985ft; this ascent seems particularly cruel after what has gone before, but there is a splendid view from the summit and if you opt for the low-level route from Black Hag there is now no more serious climbing to be done. From the summit, the Way descends rapidly, crossing the border fence and pulling away from it, proceeding round the western edge of the 1,801ft Black Hag.

Here you have a choice of routes. You may either turn left off the ridge and descend along a far from obvious path that takes you past the ruin of Old Halterburnhead to the farm at Halterburnhead, joining a road here that takes you safely to the end of the national trail at Kirk Yetholm. This used to be the official way but is now more of a bad weather alternative to a higher-level path that is now designated as the main route. This continues along the ridge, maintaining a height of well over 1,000ft and returning to the border fence as it proceeds by way of Steer Rigg and climbs to White Law. Beyond this summit, you remain beside the border fence, but now begin to lose height and soon bear left, away from the fence, descending more quickly. If you are not totally absorbed in the effort of keeping going at this late stage, look out on your right hereabouts for the concentric ramparts of an Iron Age hill fort on Green Humbleton.

At length you reach the road that has come up from Halterburnhead and are reunited with the alternative route, a simple mile of road walking now taking you to journey's end at Kirk Yetholm. The last mile is always the hardest of all, especially for those who have walked all the way from Byrness in a single day, but as the houses of Kirk Yetholm and its nineteenth-century village kirk come closer, tiredness is forgotten and replaced by great excitement and a real sense of achievement. Reaching the Border Hotel in the village (270 including Cheviot detour) is a really marvellous moment for even the most hardened hiker, and following congratulations all round, there can be few better ways of celebrating successful completion of the walk than a few drinks and perhaps a meal in the hotel. We obtained a free drink here courtesy of Wainwright, having presented our *Pennine Way Companions* as evidence that we had done the complete walk, but I cannot say if that tradition will persist by the time you read this.

What is certain, however, is that as you linger in the charming village and then catch a bus from nearby Town Yetholm back to civilisation, you will bask in the satisfaction of having risen to a formidable challenge, that of walking not only the most famous but also the toughest long-distance route in Great Britain. It may well rank as one of your greatest life experiences. But, as Wainwright so rightly says, the satisfaction is intensely personal and cannot be shared, and you can expect no acclaim from others, let alone any press recognition, for what you have done; one glance at any newspaper you chance to read as you make your way homewards should suffice to convince you that you are far more likely to attract media immortality by activity that is rather less time-consuming and labour-intensive, be it gatecrashing a Royal garden party dressed in nothing but a pair of luminous lime-green ankle socks, or being summarily expelled from the Big Brother house after residing there for precisely thirty-seven minutes.

SUMMARY OF PLACES OF INTEREST

Kinder Downfall★, Wain Stones, Ammon Wrigley Memorial, Stoodley Pike★, Top Withens, Ponden Hall, Lothersdale, Pinhaw Beacon, Leeds and Liverpool Canal, Malham, Gordale Scar★, Malham Cove★, Dry Valley, Malham Tarn, Fountains Fell, Pen-y-Ghent★, Hull and Hunt Pots, Sell Gill Holes, Cam High Road, Hawes, Hardraw Force★, Great Shunner Fell, Swaledale, Keld, East Gill Force, Tan Hill Inn★, Bowes, Low Force, High Force★, Cauldron Snout, High Cup★, Dufton, Cross Fell, Alston, Thirlwall Castle, Hadrian's Wall★, Housesteads★, Hareshaw Linn, Chew Green, Brownhart Law, Russell's Cairn, The Cheviot, Hen Hole, The Schil.

AMENITIES ON OR NEAR THE ROUTE

Edale, Crowden (L), Marsden★, Hebden Bridge★, Haworth★, Lothersdale (L), Thornton in Craven (L), Earby, Gargrave, Malham, Horton in Ribblesdale, Hawes★, Thwaite (L), Keld (L), Bowes (L), Baldersdale (L), Middleton in Teesdale, Dufton, Garrigill (L), Alston★, Greenhead (L), Once Brewed (L), Bellingham, Byrness (L), Kirk Yetholm (L).

The South West Coast Path

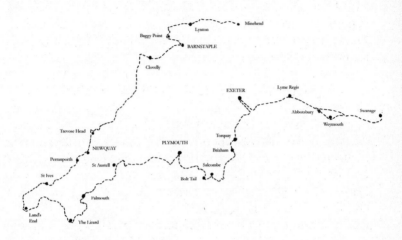

Length: 613 miles.
Start: Minehead, Somerset.
Finish: South Haven Point, near Poole, Dorset.
Nature of terrain: A walk round the often rugged and spectacular coastline of the south-western counties of England, covering the entire coastlines of Devon and Cornwall, and sections of the coastline of Somerset and Dorset.
Difficulty rating: Strenuous, severe in places.
Average time of completion: 6 to 8 weeks in aggregate.

NB: All mileages assume the most direct routes are taken. Separate mileages are given for alternatives to seasonal ferries. No alternative routes, or mileages for these alternatives, are given in respect of ferries used by the Coast Path that run all year.

The South West Coast Path

The statistics speak for themselves. This enormous coastal trek is a truly awesome logistical challenge for any walker, however fit or experienced. Yet foot-travellers whose ambition it is to complete all the big walks in Great Britain will at some stage have to rise to it and in doing so put to one side their fears and prejudices about the sea, whether they arise from viewing too many of marine disaster movies such as *Titanic* or *The Poseidon Adventure*, or simply stem from an outbreak of queasiness on the Isle of Wight ferry at the age of eight and a half.

The glorious coastal scenery of Somerset, Devon, Cornwall and Dorset, with high cliffs, quaint villages, cosy harbours, sandy coves and dramatic peninsulas, acquired popularity with holidaymakers and walkers long before any suggestion was raised of a continuous coast path. The idea of joining up the numerous existing rights of way along these coasts to create an unbroken route came from a wartime committee of the Ramblers' Association. It was given official blessing in the National Parks and Access to the Countryside Act of 1949, and thereafter each of the four county councils involved set about designating and waymarking the route. Progress was slow, and although most of the necessary work had been done by the end of the 1970s, there were still some sections that required negotiation at that time. Even at the time of writing, although a continuous route is available to walkers, not all the work has been done to provide a true coastal route throughout, and in one or two places it is necessary to detour to existing rights of way inland to maintain the continuity.

The fact is, however, that no two walkers will follow exactly the same route for a number of reasons. There are some 'cul-de-sacs' to headlands that involve detours, and which may be omitted if time is pressing; for example, the Lulworth–Kimmeridge section of the Dorset coast is only open at certain times and an official inland alternative is prescribed. Some river and estuary crossings may be undertaken by ferry, and whilst many of the ferry trips are actually incorporated into the official route, even some of these do not operate out of season, and lengthy foot detours may therefore be necessary (suggested alternatives to seasonal ferries are shown in italics, but you may prefer to use taxis if short of time – I assure you it is not cheating!). Often there is a choice of path along the clifftops, with no suggestion as to which, if any, is the definitive one.

You would be unwise to lose any sleep over having cut a sizeable corner rather too liberally, and could in any event respond to any suggestion of cheating by pointing to the fact that 150 or 200 yards missed in the context of 613 miles' walking is statistically insignificant. I wish I could have seen it that way when, having discovered I had missed the tip of Chynhalls Point near Coverack in Cornwall during a long weekend's walk, my conscience tortured me all the way home and forced me into a round trip of nearly 550 miles in the car, for no more than twenty minutes' extra walking. Extravagant things, consciences . . .

Unless you are incredibly fit and in the fortunate position of having sufficient time and resources available, it is unlikely that you will even contemplate trying to complete the South West Coast Path in one go. It is very easy to break it down into sections, and because communications with the rest of Great Britain are so good, you will have little difficulty in breaking off and starting afresh at a later time. The added advantage of a number of separate expeditions is that you can see the effects of each season on the coastal scenery. Summer is on the face of it the best time to be on the Coast Path, with seasonal ferries running, accommodation and refreshment easily available almost everywhere, and the best chance of settled sunny weather. However, springtime offers a dazzling array of colourful plant life, autumn can bring wonderfully crisp clear days with incredibly wide-ranging views, and those brave enough to walk sections of the route in winter can gaze with awe as the seas, driven by south-westerly gales, crash majestically against the rocks and cliff-faces.

Your walk needs to be planned with care, especially if you wish to walk the Lulworth–Kimmeridge coastal section and use the seasonal ferries, but having made the necessary enquiries and arrangements, you will find many of the hazards that are present on some of the other long-distance routes to be absent on the South West Coast Path. Most of the larger villages and towns on the route are well served by public transport, thus allowing considerable flexibility in planning your itinerary. Amenities are extremely plentiful, even out of season, although it is wise to enquire about accommodation in advance during the winter months.

You will have little difficulty with route-finding, although you need to be careful to take the correct turning out of the towns and villages along the way. The simple advice, if you are walking from Minehead, is to keep the sea on your right! Furthermore, the ground underfoot is usually very pleasant to walk on, especially on the clifftops. Assuming you do decide to break up the South West Coast Path into sections, the hardest aspect will be the amount of up-and-down work. Do not think it is simply a case of ascending serenely on to the clifftop in the morning and gently descending in the evening. There are numerous breaks in the cliffs, with coves, combes, valleys, harbours and inlets, necessitating a very large number of drops and climbs, and although the scenic rewards are tremendous, the effort required is colossal. It has been calculated that on the entire walk you will cover 91,000ft of ascent – three times the height of Mount Everest!

The whole route abounds with magnificent plant life and wildlife. The first part of the path, along the Somerset coast, traverses the fringes of Exmoor, famous for its ponies and also red deer which can often be seen in winter, especially in the oak woodland areas through which you will pass. The coastal heath round North Hill attracts stonechats and Dartford warblers, whilst further on you may see peregrines, ravens, shelducks, herons, egrets, redshanks and golden plovers. The Braunton Burrows in Devon host rare plants such as sand toadflax and water germander, while the sea around Lundy Island, clearly visible from the north Devon coast, has been designated a marine nature reserve and the island itself is host to some 40 species of bird breed. Many clifftops of Cornwall are decorated with tiny flowers such as spring and autumn squill, kidney vetch, thrift and bladder campion, while above you hover fulmars, kittiwakes, and lesser black-backed and herring gulls. Look out too for puffin, guillemots and razorbills on some of the small offshore islands. Off the Land's End peninsula, where gulls and auks breed along the cliffs, you may see grey seals and possibly even orcas and dolphins, whilst on the Lizard peninsula there is a remarkable variety of plant species rarely found elsewhere, including long-headed clover, pigmy rush and hairy greenweed.

On many parts of the Dorset and south Devon coast, especially the Exe estuary, you may see winter flocks of avocet, shoveler, wigeon, teal, brent geese, grey plover and ringed plover, whilst the spectacular cliffs around Lulworth Cove in Dorset support a wonderful range of butterflies and orchids. Even very near the end of the route, on the cliffs round Durslton Head, you will see shags, guillemots, kittiwakes or fulmars. Birdwatchers in the party will of course wish to train their binoculars in the hope of sighting rare and exotic feathered visitors from other climes, but others in the group, having studied the map and seen there are six more vertical ascents to do before lunch, may well be forgiven for being more anxious to move onwards, even at the risk of being accused of not knowing their hoopoe from their shag.

Minehead to Croyde

The South West Coast Path begins at Minehead and you will be heading in a generally westerly or south-westerly direction all the way to Land's End. Minehead is a pleasant and popular seaside resort; Quay Town, the oldest part of Minehead, has a harbour dating back to 1616. You start your adventure by climbing steeply out of the town on to North Hill, an area dotted with prehistoric mounds, using one of two alternative routes, the stiffer one proceeding via the ruins of Burgundy Chapel. Although there is a clifftop alternative, the official route from North Hill follows a path some way back from the cliff edge across an area of heathland, passing just to the north of the 1,013ft Selworthy Beacon. A detour is possible to the left here to visit the Beacon and also the beautiful thatched village of Selworthy.

You continue to Bossington Hill, passing Hurlstone Point and dropping down to the lovely Hurlstone Combe, proceeding through the combe to the pretty village of Bossington, which lies slightly inland. You then strike out towards Porlock Bay, and it is a straightforward walk beside the bay to reach the hamlet of Porlock Weir (9). As you proceed beside the bay, you pass just to the north of Porlock, with its small whitewashed houses and ample amenities. Beyond Porlock Weir you enter an extensive area of woodland, soon reaching the Norman Culbone Church, which is just 12ft wide and is claimed to be the smallest medieval church in England. A colony of lepers lived hereabouts in the Middle Ages and would follow services through a window. Beyond Culbone the walk is easy and quick, continuing through the woods and dropping to Yenworthy Combe, going forward to Sisters' Fountain with its distinctive cairn and slate cross, and a most refreshing spot in the heat of summer.

You now leave Somerset and enter Devon. Lovely walking follows, the route proceeding through the beautiful woodland of the Glenthorne Estate, seen at its best in spring when the rhododendrons are in full bloom, and past a woodland lodge with its magnificent gate-pillars topped with wild boar heads. The walking becomes more open, with bushes and shrubs replacing the trees, and consequently much better sea views. You proceed past Wingate Combe, with its attractive waterfall, and go on down to Caddow Combe where there is a splendid view to the lighthouse on Foreland Point, the most northerly headland on the whole route; you should certainly detour to the lighthouse, from which there are glorious views across the Bristol Channel to south Wales.

Beyond Caddow Combe you rise to Butter Hill, coming within sight of Countisbury church, then follow a path that runs parallel with the A39 down towards Lynmouth. Shortly before reaching the village you go away from the A39 to make a wooded zigzag descent, then make a zigzag ascent to reach Lynmouth's neighbour Lynton (22). The ascent involves three crossings of the water-powered Lynmouth Cliff Railway, which provides a rather easier link between the two places if you feel you have done enough climbing for one day. Lynton is a Victorian resort, whilst Lynmouth has attractive thatched cottages as well as a picturesque harbour and promenade. In 1952 a freak storm flooded the village, resulting in the loss of 31 lives and the destruction of 100 homes.

Superb walking awaits you on the journey from Lynton to Combe Martin. You begin with an easy walk below Hollerday Hill to the famous Valley of Rocks, a remarkable dry valley surrounded by craggy outcrops, the most spectacular being Castle Rock, thought to be the result of glacial activity 10,000 years ago. Some road walking follows as you pass the Christian retreat centre at the mock-Gothic nineteenth-century Lee Abbey, and go forward to Woody Bay, through a predominantly wooded landscape.

Beyond the bay, however, the woodland ends and you join an exposed cliff path which takes you to Highveer Point. Here you turn inland to round the gaping chasm of Heddon's Mouth, the cliffs falling away below you to a narrow channel of water before rising up equally precipitously beyond. You descend cautiously to cross the water just above Hunter's Inn, then climb steeply back up to the clifftop west of the Mouth. Tremendous walking follows as you negotiate East Cleave and North Cleave, then contour the northern edge of Holdstone Down, descend to Sherrycombe and climb very steeply to Great Hangman. At 1,043ft it is the highest point on the whole route, and there are fantastic views that include the Gower peninsula in south Wales as well as miles of Devon countryside.

You then pass by Little Hangman, offering further great views, and drop down to Combe Martin (35), which boasts one of the longest village streets in the country, extending as it does for some two miles along the A399. There are many typically Devon cottages with slate roofs and walls painted in a range of colours, and the church, which is at least 700 years old, is renowned for its 99ft tower with battlements and tiers of gargoyles. The village's most unusual feature is the Pack o' Cards Inn which originally had four storeys, 13 doors and 52 windows, representing card suits, cards in a suit, and cards in a pack respectively. It should come as no surprise to learn that it was built by a gambler!

A predictably stiff climb out of Combe Martin is followed by a succession of small headlands and inlets; having passed the mock-Gothic Watermouth Castle and the attractive harbour at Watermouth, you go on round Widmouth Head and Rillage Point, interspersed by Samson's Bay. Beyond Rillage Point the route temporarily joins the A399, then bears right to make a zigzag climb to Beacon Point and Hillsborough, from which you can enjoy a fine view of Ilfracombe before descending to enter it.

Built round its old harbour, Ilfracombe (40) is the largest seaside resort on the north Devon coast, with all the amenities you could wish for. I arrived here one freezing January afternoon after walking from Lynton, and of all the misfortunes that befell me that evening I could not decide which was worst out of the long uphill detour to find my hotel, the newly-formed split right down my waterproof trousers, the central heating system in the hotel breaking down, or the absence of a decent crossword puzzle in my Sunday paper.

The first part of the route from Ilfracombe westwards, known locally as the Torrs Walk, consists of a zigzag climb up to a lovely grassy area known as Torrs Park, from which straightforward up-and-down walking on well-defined paths takes you to the pretty village of Lee. Here you briefly join a metalled road, dropping steeply to Lee Bay and then climbing back on to the cliffs for a superb 4-mile march to Morte Point via Bull Point and its lighthouse, Damagehue Point, Rockham Bay and Whiting Cove.

Until it levels out near the end, the coast path is constantly undulating, often plunging to sea level to meet grotesquely-shaped rocks that are constantly pounded by the surging surf, and the surroundings are further enriched by streams and waterfalls on the slopes. The last part of the walk is magnificent, as the ground levels out and a superb path, hugging the cliff edge with a grandstand view of the rock pavements and pillars below, brings you to Morte Point, with its spectacular jagged ridge of slate. It came as no surprise to me to learn that the wild waters off this headland have seen numerous shipwrecks. Beyond Morte Point the walking remains enjoyable but rather less spectacular, as you proceed to the sprawling holiday village of Woolacombe (48) with its jumble of hotels, boarding houses, shops and holiday homes.

Beyond Woolacombe you continue beside the dunes of Woolacombe Bay and then, having passed the hamlet of Vention, you strike out westwards towards the prominent headland of Baggy Point. The walking is certainly bracing, and with westerlies blowing in off the sea it seem like an endless trudge, but the reward, on reaching the Point, is a fantastic view which on a clear day can include Lundy Island and even the Milford Haven oil refineries of Pembrokeshire. Having rounded the Point, the last scenic highlight for some time, you have a straightforward descent to Croyde Bay (53). This is popular holiday country but in January I found the amenities hereabouts sadly limited; my keenly anticipated hot lunch consisted not of the hoped-for plaice and chips in a cosy bar next to a roaring fire overlooking the surging seas, but was in fact limited to a microwaved steak pie purchased from the Woolacombe village deli, and consumed at some speed on a bench near the bus stop before I lost all feeling in my fingers and toes.

Croyde to Westward Ho!

The walk onwards from Croyde to Westward Ho! is the most unexciting of the whole trail, and if you are pressed for time you should consider omitting it. It begins pleasantly enough, the route following alongside the B3231 Croyde–Braunton road with excellent views across Saunton Sands. The route does not cross the sands but having left the B3231 proceeds on to Braunton

Burrows nature reserve. The Burrows are huge sand dunes clothed with tufts of grass, and are exceedingly difficult to walk on, but thankfully the route follows a wide track through the middle of the reserve, emerging at an area of mud and sand on the edge of the estuary of the river Taw. An official detour takes you through the Burrows along a boardwalk to view the meeting point of the Taw and Torridge estuaries. Once the estuaries have met, they form a single channel of water that flows into the bay, marked on the map as Barnstaple or Bideford Bay. Tantalisingly, you can look across this channel towards Appledore, no more than a mile away as the crow flies, but to get there on foot will require a good five hours' walking.

The route turns left to follow the estuary inland, soon swinging left again alongside the river Caen, a tributary of the Taw, and, keeping Braunton Marsh to the left, follows the Caen to Velator on the edge of the sprawling community of Braunton. It is mechanical, uninteresting walking, and you may well regret your decision not to take the bus into Barnstaple. At Velator you reach the course of the old Braunton–Barnstaple railway, turn right on to it and follow it all the way into Barnstaple. At first the walking is fast, if tedious, with the busy A361 close by to your left; about the most interesting thing is the sight on the map of a village just the other side of the A361 with the splendid name Heanton Punchardon. In due course, however, the Taw reappears to your right, and you follow alongside it as far as Barnstaple (69). Although this is comparatively dull walking, you are unlikely to be on your own. This section, along with much of the north Devon coastal section of the route, coincides with the 180-mile Tarka Trail named after the eponymous hero of Henry Williamson's much-loved novel. The riverside walk is also ideal for a gentle family stroll.

Barnstaple is the largest town in the northern half of Devon, as well as one of the oldest towns in Great Britain, and until the Taw silted up, it once boasted an important harbour. Its heyday was in the eighteenth century, and it still has a largely Georgian centre. One of the most pleasant parts of the town is an eighteenth-century colonnade named Queen Anne's Walk, while St Anne's Chapel dates from the fourteenth century and once housed the grammar school that educated the poet John Gay, author of *The Beggar's Opera*. The town is an obvious place to stock up with provisions and also has a useful station with trains to Exeter.

You cross the Taw by means of the 16-arched Long Bridge which dates from the thirteenth century, and after a brief road walk, join another piece of old railway, this time the former Barnstaple–Bideford line. You are now walking along the south side of the Taw estuary, although you are often separated from it by grassland or marshes, and there are excellent views to Braunton Burrows and Baggy Point. A little way beyond Lower Yelland the route briefly forsakes the old railway to hug the riverbank by means of some rougher tracks and at one point a trudge through sand dunes, but at the village of Instow it regains the railway and passes a superbly restored signal box and platform.

At Instow you reach the point where the Taw and Torridge estuaries meet, and can look directly across to Saunton Sands and Braunton Burrows. Now it is the Torridge that impedes progress; a seasonal ferry across the river to Appledore is available, but otherwise you must continue along the old railway, underneath the A39 and its impressive bridge crossing of the river, and on to the old Bideford station. Immediately beyond this, you cross the Torridge by means of the 677ft long Bideford Bridge, with 24 arches that are all of varying lengths, and proceed into Bideford, the chief port of north Devon between the sixteenth and eighteenth century, with narrow streets that contain many seventeenth-century buildings.

Beyond the town you proceed beside the estuary along a rough sea wall – a breach in the wall necessitates an inland high-tide diversion – then proceed past the Appledore shipyard into Appledore village, which is as charming as its name suggests, with quaint narrow streets of trim cottages and Georgian houses. It has a long association with fishing, and the largest covered shipbuilding dock in Europe was opened here in 1970. At Appledore you arrive at the meeting point of Taw and Torridge for the third and last time, then follow the south side of the 'combined' estuaries to the mouth. At long last you have reached the open sea again and, having gazed with satisfaction across to the huge white blob of Saunton

Sands Hotel, you now swing left to proceed by Northam Burrows to Westward Ho! (86).

Although this section will not have been of great interest, at least there will have been no shortage of places of refreshment; my elevenses consisted of a Mars Bar in a restored railway carriage that is housed at Bideford's old station, and in true British Rail tradition, the chocolate coating of the bar was well past its best. Recalling the line from *The Two Ronnies*, I suppose it would have been tempting, if somewhat undiplomatic, to ask the staff if the 70p for coffee was per cup or per slice . . .

Westward Ho! to Bude

Beyond Westward Ho! the cliff walking resumes in earnest and the first climb brings a delightful view forward to Clovelly and Hartland Point and out to Lundy Island. The lungs are certainly tested as you proceed on to Abbotsham Cliff and Green Cliff, then descend to the sea before a steep climb through a hazel and hawthorn thicket to Higher Rowden. A respite follows, as beyond Peppercombe you follow a delightful path through the oak and birch of Sloo Wood, with foxgloves adding constant splashes of colour. There is a steep descent to sea level at Buck's Mills followed by a very tough climb and then a pleasant but unspectacular walk along field edges, separated from the sea by thick woodland.

At length you pick up the Hobby Drive, a clearly defined track that follows a somewhat serpentine course through the woods. It leads you to Clovelly (97), one of the showpiece villages of England, consisting of a tiny harbour at the foot of a single steeply-inclined cobbled street of stunningly attractive snow-white flower-decked cottages. It is a massively popular tourist haunt, so be warned!

Now ten unforgettable miles await you. Initially the walking is easy as you keep a fairly level course through the woods but much closer to the sea, and glimpses through the rhododendrons reveal superb views, most notably at the quaintly-named Gallantry Bower viewpoint. Having passed the ornate early nineteenth-century Angels Wings viewing shelter you plunge to the sea at Mouth Mill, close to the impressive arched Blackchurch Rock. You rise again then drop to the modest Windbury waterfall past a riot of foxgloves and scabious, then pull clear of the woods and follow an open stretch along field boundaries close to the cliffs of Exmansworthy, Gawlish and East and West Titchberry. There are views back as far as Morte Point from here, and you should make the most of them, for soon you arrive at Hartland Point and swing in a much more southerly direction, losing the panorama of the Morte Point–Braunton coast you have enjoyed for so many miles.

Tremendous walking ensues, as you drop to the waterfall below Upright Cliff and climb again, following a remarkable hanging valley known as Smoothlands, to Damehole Point. Here a glorious view opens up ahead, while all around you are fascinating rock formations with much to interest the geologist. There is then an exposed and difficult scramble on to Blegberry Cliff, a descent to Blegberry Waterfall and a particularly severe climb to Dyer's Lookout. Gentler walking brings you to a road leading eastwards to the village of Stoke, while immediately seawards is Hartland Quay (107), a tightly-packed weather-beaten group of buildings including a museum that stand defiantly between sea and cliffs. Like many little settlements on the Cornwall or Devon coast, this is an exciting place to be in winter, as you stand watching the angry seas, whipped up by force nine gales, pound the harbours and surrounding cliffs. This of course assumes that you have got there safely in the first place, unimpeded by washed-away roads near Taunton, or twigs on the line at New Malden.

Beyond the Stoke road you soon pass to the landward side of the huge sheer cliff known as St Catherine's Tor, then descend to the superb cascade of Speke's Mill Mouth before climbing on to Swansford Hill with dramatic views back to the Tor and Hartland Quay. Flat clifftop walking follows, the main hazard being the frighteningly close proximity of the path to the cliff edge round Milford Common. A track leads left to the hamlet and youth hostel of Elmscott, while the route goes forward to join a road that leads to Embury Beacon and the cliffs guarding the north side of Welcombe Mouth. So far so good. Then the real work begins, as you negotiate a succession of massive combes: Welcombe Mouth, Marsland Mouth (where you enter Cornwall), Litter Mouth, Yeol Mouth, St Morwenna's Well, the Tidna, Stanbury Mouth,

Duckpool, Warren Gutter and Sandy Mouth. Each involves a steep, often perilous drop down a narrow path, sometimes but not always stepped, then a footbridge crossing over a narrow stream, followed by a back-breaking climb to regain the lost height.

Just before the Tidna you can detour to Morwenstow and its part-Norman church; its most famous parson was Robert Hawker, who championed the celebration of Harvest Festival and who would often repair to a cliff-edge driftwood hut close to the coast path to write poetry and enjoy a spot of opium.

Beyond the Tidna comes an outstanding promontory viewpoint at Higher Sharpnose Point, whilst at nearby Lower Sharpnose Point are the huge satellite tracking dish aerials of Cleave Camp which will remain visible for miles. Just above Duckpool, close to Steeple Point, is a fine view up the partially wooded Coombe Valley, but you will notice how much less wooded the combes are generally than in Somerset or north Devon. Beyond Sandy Mouth it is a much easier walk into Bude with just one innocuous descent to Northcott Mouth and climb on to Maer Cliff.

Bude (121) is a popular surfing resort with a wealth of places advertising bed and breakfast, but the sign outside will tell you nothing about what lies within. You may be offered a hot drink in a comfortable lounge on arrival and then shown to an immaculately-decorated bedroom with large springy bed, invited to make yourself at home and asked to elect your breakfast time next morning. Or you may be ushered briskly into a cheerless room, be curtly informed that breakfast is between 8.00 and 8.15 a.m., and be left to contemplate the dire retribution that awaits if you as much as dare to breach any of the 28 regulations posted on the wall, which proscribe everything from wearing walking boots on the carpets to eating custard creams in the room after 9.45 p.m.

Bude to Boscastle
Straightforward clifftop walking takes you on from Bude to Widemouth Sand, but then things get tougher. Coastal erosion round Great Wanson and Millook means that you must undertake two very considerable climbs by road, although there is some fine clifftop walking round Bridwill Point between these two ascents,

with good views back to those satellite dishes. Having left the road, you enjoy easier walking on the approach to Dizzard Point, with just one short drop into a beautiful wooded combe. However, beyond Dizzard Point the walking gets harder again, with a descent from Chipman Point being followed by a very stiff climb to Cleave. From here you strike out towards Castle Point and follow a piece of massive whalebacked and heather-topped headland, with tremendous views that stretch as far as Hartland Point. There is then a descent to the stream of Aller Shoot, a severe climb to the cliffs of Pencannow Point, and a descent to the pretty cove of Crackington Haven. This is roughly halfway from Bude to Boscastle and a good place to stop for rest and refreshment, as the seven remaining miles to Boscastle offer no facilities.

They are seven unforgettable miles, starting with a climb to the majestic rugged headland of Cambeak and then a steady uphill trudge past rocks called the Strangles to the 732ft High Cliff, the most elevated cliffs in Cornwall. There is a near vertical descent from here, followed by a climb up the side of the landslipped Rusey Cliff along a twisting narrow path, with the sea to your right and precipitous slopes of gorse, heather and bracken to your left.

At length you regain the clifftop at Buckator and proceed easily on past Fire Beacon Point, Beeny Cliff and on to the Pentargon inlet with a quite splendid cascade. Another climb brings you to Penally Hill where you have your first view of Boscastle, and it is then a steady descent down the cliffside to this beautiful village (137). Its harbour is the only shelter for miles along the north Cornwall coast, the narrow inlet snaking between high slate cliffs to a small stone jetty that was once used for exporting slate and grain. The village itself, with its narrow streets of slate cottages, lies half a mile from the harbour in the picturesque Valency Valley, and with its museum of witchcraft and multitude of craft and gift shops selling everything from leathers to curses, has given up without a struggle to the tourist trade. Thomas Hardy, who loved this area, was inspired hereabouts to write his novel *A Pair Of Blue Eyes*. The only novel I could have been inspired to write after my walk here from Bude would have been *A Pair Of Red Legs*, from sunburn that gave me such agony when my lower limbs touched anything, that in any event I doubt I would have got past page one.

Boscastle to Port Isaac

More tremendous walking awaits between Boscastle and Tintagel. You leave Boscastle and pass the headland of Willapark, its white coastguard building standing high above the southern entry to Boscastle harbour; curiously, further on in this section there is another headland called Willapark which gives fine views back to Hartland and the ubiquitous satellite dishes. Highlights as you proceed include the view out to Long Island, a spectacular tower of rock rising from the sea and a favourite gathering place for puffins, and the Ladies Window, a natural rock archway high above the sea. For me the best feature of this section is Rocky Valley; reached by a steep descent, it consists of a river guarded on either side by lush green banks, punctuated in spring with pockets of cow parsley, while immediately above stand rock stacks with almost surreal arrangements of jagged outcrops, ledges and faces.

From there you go forward to Tintagel, obtaining excellent views to this historic site firstly from the second Willapark and then Barras Nose, this being the last piece of headland before you drop to Tintagel Haven. To your right is the island promontory, reachable by bridge, known as Tintagel Head on which stand the ruins of Tintagel Castle that date back to the twelfth century. Excavations have revealed evidence of a Celtic monastery on the site, and legend has it that King Arthur was born and held court here or hereabouts. The village of Tintagel, formerly known as Trevena, is just off the route, and offers plenty of amenities; features of interest include the old post office building that dates from the fourteenth century, and the Norman church of St Materiana which is much closer to the route.

Very easy clifftop walking now takes you past Dunderhole Point and Higher Penhallic Point to Trebarwith Strand where it is advisable to seek refreshment, as the five miles on to Port Isaac are tough. You begin with a colossal ascent, a big descent to the combe at Backways and strenuous climb up again, then after a brief respite you must negotiate three very steep-sided combes in succession, past Dannonchapel, Barrett's Zawn and Ranie Point. At Barrett's Zawn look out for an adit, or tunnel cut into the rock to allow easy access to the beach for the purpose of slate quarrying. At times the path is so steep and the ground so crumbly that hands as well as feet may be required!

After Ranie Point things get easier, with one gentler combe, St Illickswell Gug, to negotiate before a brisk canter past Port Gaverne, once an important centre for the export of slate quarried nearby into Port Isaac (150). This is a wonderful, typically Cornish seaside village, with narrow alleys of slate-built cottages quaintly arranged above a busy harbour. A fellow guest at my bed and breakfast that night claimed to have picked up a radio station broadcasting in Cornish, apparently untroubled by the fact that the last Cornish speaker, Dolly Pentreath, is thought to have died in 1777.

Port Isaac to Newquay

The section from Port Isaac to Polzeath begins with an excellent and straightforward march round the headlands of Lobber Point, Varley Head and Kellan Head, from which you descend slightly inland to the small and totally unspoilt village of Port Quin, which lies at the end of a charming natural harbour. Towards the end of the nineteenth century its entire male population was lost when its only fishing vessel came to grief at sea. The western edge of the harbour is guarded by Doyden Point, close to which is a folly known as Doyden Castle. You pass the folly as you return to the cliffs and enjoy a great walk past Trevan Point and two delectable inlets, Epphaven Cove and Lundy Beach, the latter lying at the sea end of a wooded valley. Lundy Hole, just beyond, is a collapsed cave where you can look through a massive natural rock arch to the foaming sea far below.

The Coast Path continues round Carnweather Point and round the neck of the twin headlands known as the Rumps where there are Iron Age fortifications and splendid views to the Mouls, a rocky island where seabirds regularly congregate. Next is Pentire Point, one of the best viewpoints on the north Cornwall coast; I am told that when conditions are right, even the Cleave Camp dishes may make an appearance! There follows a long and steady descent to

Polzeath, a sprawling village with a popular beach and ample facilities. Now you leave the coast for a while to follow a section of the Camel Estuary, beginning with an easy walk round Trebetherick Point to Daymer Bay and passing the golf course at St Enodoc, although you should detour across the golf course to the church with its slightly angled thirteenth-century spire. The poet John Betjeman is buried in the churchyard and you may recall the words of his poem which were inspired by this place:

> Paths, unfamiliar to golfers' brogues,
> Cross the eleventh fairway broadside on
> And leave the fourteenth tee for thirteenth green,
> Ignoring Royal and Ancient, bound for God.[1]

A weary trudge over the dunes round Daymer Bay is followed by an easy passage round the edge of Brea Hill, topped by Bronze Age tumuli, and further dune walking takes you to Rock where it is necessary to use the ferry (year-round, save winter Sundays) to cross the estuary to reach Padstow (162). A seventh-century monastery was founded here by St Petroc and Walter Raleigh presided as Warden of Cornwall from the town's Court House. Its narrow streets of stone cottages and lovely harbour have a typically Cornish charm, somewhat shattered on May Day with the Obby Oss, a pagan celebration of the departure of winter. If you arrive in Padstow on May Day, having now walked 162 often very tough miles, you might be well advised to smarten up, for fear that the revellers take you for some fearful pagan monster and force you to suffer the painful consequences.

From Padstow you head back towards the coast, rounding St George's Cove and a large sandy expanse which includes the treacherous Doom Bar, where 300 craft, including three lifeboats, have perished. At the round tower of Stepper Point you reach the mouth of the Camel Estuary and enjoy a fine coastal walk to Trevone. You pass the grotesquely-shaped Merope islands, which are actually headlands that have become separated from the

---

[1] John Betjeman, 'Sunday Afternoon Service in St Endoc Church, Cornwall', *Collected Poems* (1958, John Murray).

mainland, and after a steep descent and climb past the limestone cliffs at Porthmissen you come to the headland of Roundhole Point and a massive collapsed cave, taking the form of a huge hole in the ground on the headland itself. You descend from Roundhole Point to the village of Trevone then negotiate a succession of bays including Newtrain, Harlyn and Mother Ivey's.

The coast path stays close to the shore, only really rising significantly to round Trevose Head and its lighthouse, but soon dropping to Booby's Bay, the veritable treadmill of the sands round Constantine Bay, and then Treyarnon Bay. These are all honeypots in the summer months and the walking itself is tame stuff. However, you then return to the cliffs and pass a number of long thin coves, enjoying the variety of colours; the yellow of wild buttercups, pink of the foxgloves, lush green of the clifftops, severe grey of the rocks, soft azure of the sea, and creamy white channels of foam with the tides. You descend to another little resort, Porthcothan (174), but ascend again to enjoy a tremendous cliff walk to Park Head, with the fascinating but highly dangerous Trescore islands nearby and views back to Trevose Head.

Just beyond Park Head are the Bedruthan Steps, a sequence of large rock islands constantly pounded by the sea, and said to be used by the giant Bedruthan as stepping stones: of these, Queen Bess Rock was said to resemble the profile of the monarch until a rock fall in the 1980s, while Samaritan Island was named after a ship wrecked just off it in 1846. A well-signposted route gives you access to a grandstand view of the Steps, but venture out to them at your peril! The walk on to Newquay is a walk of contrasts, with magnificent headlands topped with prehistoric forts and views inland to china clay spoil heaps being interspersed with descents to sea level and the tourist spots of Mawgan Porth, Watergate Bay and Whipsiderry.

After rounding Trevelgue Head you proceed past Porth and a number of mini headlands, using a mixture of paths and roads to arrive in Newquay itself (184), a town with a proud fishing and mining history and now the biggest and most garish resort on the Cornish coast. I was fortunate to stay in a superb bed and breakfast where a fellow-guest extolled the virtue of organised walking. I remain ambivalent about this; whilst a guide will ensure you don't get lost and will draw your attention to features of interest, it must be irksome for the whole party to be forced to stop or worse, backtrack, simply because some wretched soul thinks they may have left a bag of postcards behind at the last pub stop 45 minutes ago.

Newquay to Hayle

Leaving the unsubtle joys of Newquay, you proceed round Towan Head, with excellent views across Newquay and its bay, and past Fistral Beach, renowned as the best surfing beach in the country. The route avoids the headland of Pentire Point East but skirts the western edges of the sprawling village of Pentire to arrive on the banks of the Gannel, a tidal river. There is a seasonal ferry at high tide, and a choice of summer or winter foot crossings, the latter requiring an extensive and unwelcome diversion upstream along the shores, and not usable for two hours or so round high tide.

Once over the Gannel you proceed seawards alongside it, passing Crantock Beach and Rushy Green and passing through the dunes to return to the coast at Pentire Point West. You round this headland and then proceed past the cove and lagoon of Porth Joke, known locally as Polly Joke, going forward to Kelsey Head where you can look out to a National Trust-owned island called the Chick. There is a tough stretch of dune walking from here past Holywell Bay and on to the village of Holywell (189); I remember the café here for the refusal of staff, after serving me food and drink, to top up my water bottle, on the pretext that their supply was metered!

Beyond Holywell you climb on to the cliffs to round Penhale Point and pass an army camp, then continue to Ligger Point, from where there are good views ahead to the Perran Sands. You drop to these sands, which at low tide you can follow all the way to Perranporth, whilst at high tide you will be forced to endure a treadmill through the dunes. A brief detour inland across the dunes will take you to St Piran's Oratory, a sixth or seventh-century chapel and one of the country's oldest Christian buildings.

Beyond Perranporth (195), another popular holiday destination with a good range of amenities, you enter what was serious tin-mining country, with a number of old mining shafts nearby as you round Cligga Point, although in recent years tin-mining in Cornwall has ceased completely. Beyond Cligga Point, the walking is straightforward on flat cliff tops, but there follows a steep descent to Trevellas Cove, then a big climb and further drop to Trevaunance Cove. From here it is an easy walk to St Agnes, once the centre of a flourishing tin-mining industry and today a pleasant village of sturdy slate and granite cottages, with old miners' cottages standing in a stepped terrace known as Stippy-Stappy. Trevaunance Coombe itself has had three harbours since 1632, all destroyed by the sea. The surroundings are certainly majestic, though evidently lost on two walkers who, as I passed them on my descent, were engrossed in discussion, not on the subject of the beauty of the surroundings or the awesome power of the sea and its delicate ecological relationship with the coastline, but about railway halts in the Cotswolds.

Progress beyond Trevaunance Cove is initially excellent, past St Agnes Head with excellent views to the Bawden Rocks, otherwise known as Man and his Man, where guillemots and razorbills often gather. The views from the heather-clad clifftops are excellent, extending as far as Trevose Head. In due course you reach the nineteenth-century Wheal Coates engine house, a relic of the mining industry; engine houses drove the mining machinery and pumped water from the mine shafts. You drop steeply to the inlet at Chapel Porth, then climb up on to Mulgram Hill to get an excellent view of the engine house and the other workings of Wheal Coates mine. There is then fast walking on a good level path, followed by a descent to the unremarkable village of Porthtowan, which is flanked by numerous old mineworkings, and indeed you will see more evidence of mining activity as you proceed towards Portreath.

Much of this next section is quite easy, passing the perimeter fence of the Nancekuke defence area, but there are a couple of steep drops and climbs including a tricky descent to Sally's Bottom! You swing round the edge of Gooden Heane Cove, the path just inches from the sheer cliff edge, then descend to the village of Portreath (208), once a busy port and now a popular holiday village.

From here you climb to the lovely cliffs of Western Hill, with good views back to Gooden Heane Point and forward to Navax Point and Godrevy Point.

The combes emerging at Porth-cadjack Cove and Bassett's Cove and their attendant drops and climbs slow progress a little, but once you get on to Reskajeage Downs the walking is good and quick. Highlights include the clifftop Crane Castle of Iron Age origin, and a great vertical chasm known as Hell's Mouth. As a road runs parallel with the coast path hereabouts, these are popular spots. Superb walking takes you out to Navax Point and then Godrevy Point, with grandstand views to Godrevy Island and its now unmanned nineteenth-century lighthouse that inspired Virginia Woolf's novel *To The Lighthouse*.

On a nearby reef, many of the personal effects of Charles I were lost in a severe shipwreck on the very day of his execution. Rounding Godrevy Point, you now begin the walk round St Ives Bay, enjoying fine views to St Ives, but beyond the golden sands of Godrevy Cove anticlimax sets in, the route being forced inland to cross the Red River, so named because it once discharged huge quantities of red mining residue into its waters. You must then follow a road to reach Gwithian, and for four miles beyond you have to tramp through a large area of dunes, passing the holiday complex of Hayle Towans. The route is well waymarked and avoids the worst peaks and troughs but after the glories of Godrevy you will feel much like you did last Christmas when having sat through three mesmerising hours of *Schindler's List*, you found yourself tuned into the rather less captivating *Santa Meets The Teletubbies*.

Hayle to Land's End

At length you reach Hayle Estuary where there is a tantalising view across to Lelant and St Ives, but with no ferry available you must endure a tedious walk round the edge of the estuary. You begin with a grim trudge through a sorry industrial landscape to arrive at the nondescript village of Hayle (220), joining a road that takes you out of the village and across the river Hayle. Immediately beyond the crossing you fork right along a road which leads you into the village of Lelant, then as the main road bends left, you go straight ahead, north-eastwards, to the rough granite church of St Uny. Here you leave the road and cross the golf course, passing underneath the St Erth–St Ives branch line and across the dunes along the seaward side of the railway, with the pleasant prospect of St Ives Bay immediately to your right.

You continue round the headland of Carrack Gladden, with the railway still to your immediate left, and arrive at Carbis Bay, where you climb away from the sea, crossing the railway and following roads towards Porthminster Beach. You cross to the seaward side of the railway once more and go forward into St Ives (225). The official route follows the bay right round to St Ives Head, also known as St Ives Island, rounding the headland and going on to Porthmeor Beach, but it is perfectly possible to cut through the town to reach Porthmeor Beach rather more quickly.

St Ives has a long history as a fishing port, has supported a flourishing pilchard fishery for many years, and is a magnet for visitors with its narrow cobbled streets of stone cottages, sandy beaches, picturesque harbour, beautiful bay and views seawards to Godrevy Island. It is very popular with artists too, and many galleries have opened in the town, including a Tate Gallery.

Leaving St Ives, you embark on a much wilder and more exciting stretch of coastline. The terrain can be boggy but the coastal scenery is majestic as you proceed past the headlands of Clodgy Point, Hor Point, Pen Enys Point, Carn Naun Point and Mussel Point; from Mussel Point there are good views to the Carracks, a group of islands where seals can be seen. You proceed on past the steep Tregerthen and Tremedda cliffs on to Zennor Cliff, a granite headland towering 200ft above the sea. Just beyond this point you can detour to the granite village of Zennor with its megalithic burial chamber known as Zennor Quoit, a museum with many exhibits relating to tin-mining, and the twelfth-century St Senara's Church. The church has a bench end which commemorates the mermaid who supposedly enticed the squire's son, and tenor in the village choir, out to sea and a watery death. How very inconsiderate of her; chorus tenors are like gold dust . . .

From Zennor Cliff you continue past Pendour Cove, Porthglaze Cove and Treen Cove, with its old mine building, to the magnificent

Gurnard's Head. The route cuts round the neck of the headland, but a detour to the headland and its promontory fort, Trereen Dinas, is strongly recommended. As you stride out to the next major headland at Pendeen Watch (238), the terrain continues to be juicy underfoot, but the scenery remains tremendous, with the coves of Porthmeor, Halldrine, Porthmoina and Portheras to your right, and the impressive Bosigran Cliff providing a splendid viewing platform just beyond Porthmeor Cove. Shortly before Portheras Cove you can detour slightly inland to visit the lonely church of St Bridget at Morvah with its fourteenth-century tower.

From Portheras Cove you stride out to Pendeen Watch with its lighthouse that dates back to 1900 and was established because other lighthouses along the coast were sometimes concealed by high cliffs. Between Pendeen Watch and Cape Cornwall, the next significant headland, there is a vast amount of evidence of tin-mining activity, with an abundance of disused mines, while just beyond Trewellard Zawn, at Levant mine, there is a restored beam engine, and close to Botallack there are two restored engine houses.

Shortly beyond the fort of Kenidjack you reach Cape Cornwall, the only piece of headland in England to be called a cape, and once believed to be England's most westerly point, although Land's End has since been given that distinction. You do actually move slightly east of south as you ascend to the next headland, Gribba Point, but after some splendid clifftop walking past Polpry Cove and Aire Point you follow the sands round the lovely Whitesand Bay and swing south-westwards again to reach Sennen Cove (247). The thirteenth-century church of St Sennen in the village of Sennen, a short detour inland from here, is the most westerly in England.

From here you climb on to Mayon Cliff and proceed, high above the sea, past Maen Castle promontory fort to Dr Syntax's Head, then having rounded the headland you can stand on the granite cliffs, gaze out to the Longships Lighthouse and find you have literally reached Land's End. There is no more land ahead of you and you must now turn eastwards to continue, this time along the *south*-facing coasts of south-west England.

Land's End has become hideously commercialised, a big theme park having opened here in recent years, but it is still a magical place. Though you will have covered some 250 miles to get here from Minehead, many walkers hereabouts will have been tackling the rather longer trek from one end of the British Isles to the other; you may even see one such poor walker hobbling feebly nearby, blisters obviously wearing down his iron resolve – and wish him well for his remaining 875 miles to John o'Groats.

Land's End to Porthleven

Having rounded Dr Johnson's Head and begun the long eastward trek towards Poole, your next major objective is Gwennap Head, where you will swing from south-east to north-east. The broad coast path maintains a fine clifftop course, past Nanjizal Cove, Pendower Cove, Folly Cove and the inlet of Porth Loe, and the headlands of Carn Lês Boel, Carn Barra, Black Carn and Carn Guthensbrâs. Just before Gwennap Head is the holed headland of Tol-Pedn-Penwith, which is certainly worth a detour. Having rounded Gwennap Head you proceed past the small village of Porthgwarra and on to Porthcurno with its magnificent Minack Theatre, an open-air theatre that was begun in the 1930s and constructed in classical Greek style, with seating cut cleverly into the cliffs so that audiences can enjoy not only the play but the superb marine backdrop. You continue round the inlet of Porth Curno, at the eastern end of which is a granite block known as a 'logan' rock, estimated to weigh about 65 tons, which 'logs' (rocks) at the slightest touch. In 1824 it was pushed over the cliff by a party of sailors; the incident caused such an outcry that Lieutenant Goldsmith, the ringleader, had to reposition the rock at his own expense!

You proceed on past Cribba Head to the quite delightful hamlet of Penberth and its tiny cove, guarded by an impressive assembly of rocks and boulders, then on past the inlet of Porthguarnon, the charming wooded cove of St Loy, and the headlands of Merthen Point and Boscawen Point. You drop down to Lamorna Valley to round Lamorna Cove, then having passed the old granite quarries round Carn-du, you begin the long walk round Mounts Bay.

The next few miles see a return to civilisation as you follow a well-defined path past Kemyel Point and Penzer Point into

Mousehole (pronounced Mouzel), a pretty fishing village with houses of grey granite looking out on to a little harbour. On 23 December each year, fishermen gather to eat Stargazy Pie, made with whole fish whose heads poke out through the crust; the feast commemorates one Tom Bawcock whose catch of fish supposedly once saved the village from starvation. It is a straightforward walk now, following a road into Newlyn, an important fishing village, and continuing into Penzance (264). The town boasts some excellent eighteenth-century houses, and gardens with sub-tropical plants. One of the most famous Penzance residents was Humphrey Davy, inventor of the miner's safety lamp, and a statue of him stands outside the imposing market house in Market Jew Street.

An easy 3-mile walk beside railway and road takes you from Penzance to Marazion, with great views to St Michael's Mount, to which access is possible from Marazion. Separated from the mainland by a tidal causeway, it is dominated by its superb castle, much of which dates back to the fifteenth century, and built on the site of a twelfth-century Benedictine monastery. Having left Marazion, a straggling but most attractive village with old cottages and winding streets, you begin heading resolutely south-eastwards to the Lizard.

The walk on to Perranuthnoe is uninspiring, beginning with a road walk to Trevenner and then a section of beach walking, but beyond Perranuthnoe there is better walking with fine views towards the Lizard. Acton Castle, an eighteenth-century castellated mansion, is just a short way from the coast path to your left as you approach Cudden Point. Having rounded the point, you soon reach Prussia Cove, named after a notorious smuggler who was known by his followers as the King of Prussia. The secluded Cornish coves were perfect spots to land contraband; Bessy's Cove hereabouts was once a landing place for smuggled brandy and named after the keeper of a nearby beerhouse.

You then proceed past Kenneggy Cliff and its mine dumps, round Hoe Point and forward to the extensive Praa Sands and village of the same name. Good cliff walking on to and round Trewavas Head takes you past further engine houses, one of which, Wheal Prosper, is owned by the National Trust. The coast between Megliggar

Rocks, just beyond Trewavas Head, and Porthleven is liable to landslips, so follow signs carefully – and watch your feet – as you proceed past Tregear Point to Porthleven (277), once an important seaport, as indicated by the eighteenth-century Harbour House and nineteenth-century West Wharf. The 1890 Wesleyan chapel inspired the verse, 'They built the church upon my word as fine as any abbey; and then they thought to cheat the Lord and built the back part shabby!'

Porthleven to Coverack

Beyond Porthleven there is a tough stretch of beach walking round the edge of the Loe, Cornwall's biggest natural lake. Having passed Loe Bar, a thin piece of land separating the Loe from the sea, you join a more comfortable path, passing the memorial to the hundred victims of an 1807 shipping disaster, and continue past Gunwalloe Fishing Cove. You proceed past Halzephron Cliff to Church Cove, and the fifteenth-century church of St Gunwalloe which, though close to the sea, is sheltered from it by a bluff. From there you continue to Poldhu Cove then climb steeply over Angrouse Cliff before descending to Polurrian Cove. Another climb takes you past a huge hotel, from which you descend to Mullion Cove (284) and its little harbour. This is one of the loveliest coves on the whole route, surrounded as it is by immense jagged cliffs and enjoying excellent views to Mullion Island.

There is a steep climb up from the Cove and there follows an incredible 6-mile walk to the Lizard via Predannack Head and Vellan Head, the coast path staying on the cliff edge almost all the way, with just one big drop and ascent round Kynance Cove. The cliff formations are remarkable, with numerous huge crevices and caves, and so many intriguing names: Ogo-dour Cove, Pengersick, Ogo Pons, Gew-graze, Pigeon Ogo. I noticed one rock formation between Predannack Downs and Kynance that was shaped just like a human head. Gone are the trim fields and neat village communities, to be replaced by a gaping wilderness of heather and grass.

Eventually you reach Lizard Point (290), turning eastwards, now walking on the southernmost stretch of land in Great Britain and passing the Most Southerly Café, although the gimmickry of Land's End is thankfully absent. Of more interest perhaps is the Lizard Lighthouse, built in 1751, and the Lion's Den, a huge hole in the cliffs caused by a collapsed sea cave. Further amenities are available in the nearby village of Lizard, and having made the detour inland you may also wish to inspect the pretty church of St Winwallo at nearby Landewednack. The Coast Path goes round Bass Point then starts heading north-eastwards, soon passing Hot Point. Lovely clifftop walking follows, with only minor undulations, taking you past the lifeboat chute at Kilcobben and on to the Devil's Frying Pan, a funnel-shaped depression leading to a remarkable rock arch between two cliffs. Just beyond is Cadgwith, almost your definitive Cornish fishing village with a busy harbour and whitewashed thatched cottages.

Having descended to the village, you return to the clifftop for a time, then descend to Poltesco, site of a former serpentine works, and Kennack with its ugly caravan park just beyond. However, having passed the sands there and ascended to the cliffs, you enjoy an outstanding walk via Carrick Lûz and the delectable Beagles Point to Black Head, with stunning views almost throughout and exceptionally beautiful spring flowers. There are a number of tough descents and ascents, Downas Valley being the most gruelling, and the slippery serpentine stone makes it hard to maintain footholds.

Beyond Black Head the walking becomes less strenuous but still interesting, with a good clifftop march followed by a visit to the fortification on Chynhalls Point and a walk round Dolor Point into Coverack (301), a pretty village that lies just short of the halfway mark on the route. You may wish to celebrate with a cream tea, hoping that your celebratory feast consists of home-baked scones, home-clotted cream and home-made jam, and not home-frozen Co-op scones, home-chilled Asda squirty cream and plastic pots of jam that have languished for the last five months on the shelf of the nearest cash-and-carry.

Coverack to Falmouth

You leave Coverack along a lane followed by an ill-defined path which stays almost at sea level to round the aptly-named Lowland

Point, beyond which you must negotiate Dean Quarries before coming to Godrevy Cove. You proceed along part of the beach, with views out to sea to the infamous Manacles rocks which have seen many shipwrecks, then go inland to the pleasant hamlet of Rosenithon before descending steeply to the village of Porthoustock. A coast route is available from here, past the now unused quarries round Pencra Head and Porthkerris Point, although at high tide you will need to stick to a track beyond Pencra Head that leads to roads which you follow to Porthallow. Both routes provide fine views to Falmouth and are superior to the long-time official route which snakes tamely along inland roads and paths past the hamlet of Trenance.

From Porthallow there is much better walking on a well-defined cliff-edge path to Nare Point, beyond which you go along the south bank of Gillan Creek round the twin villages of Gillan and Flushing. There are lovely views across the creek to the church at St Anthony-in-Meneage. Unless the creek can be waded (one hour either side of low tide) you must continue along the bank, a rather muddy and fiddly trudge, to the hamlet of Carne, and you are then able to follow roads round to the north side of the creek to continue. From here, the route proceeds past the church and out to Dennis Head, from which there are fantastic views across Falmouth Bay to Falmouth, St Mawes and St Anthony Head lighthouse.

Having rounded the headland, you now begin a golden walk along the south bank of the Helford River, through mostly wooded and far less rugged surroundings, and with lovely views across the river. Soon you reach Helford (314) with its lovely whitewashed thatched cottages and the very popular Shipwright's Arms. From Helford you cross the river by seasonal ferry to Helford Passage. *[Alternative route, 9 miles: head westwards from Helford along a lane, then southwards on a metalled road through Kestle to reach a T-junction. Turn right and head westwards along roads to Mawgan. Turn right in the village to arrive at the B3293. Follow this north-eastwards through Gweek to Naphene Downs. Turn right to follow metalled roads eastwards via Nancenoy, Polwheveral and Porth Navas to Helford Passage.]*

From Helford Passage you proceed seawards along the north shore of the river, passing the pretty village of Durgan and the stunning gardens of Glendurgan nearby, and the fifteenth-century church at Mawnan that stands in the lovely National Trust-owned Mawnan Glebe. You then pass the river mouth and begin the walk round Falmouth Bay, rounding the attractive Rosemullion Head and enjoying fine forward views over the bay as you continue and descend to the popular Maenporth Beach. A brisk climb takes you on to Pennance Point, having rounded which you begin the long walk out to Pendennis Point.

On the headland is Dennis Fort, a Tudor defensive blockhouse, and Henry VIII's Pendennis Castle. Road walking then brings you to Falmouth (324), a busy port and the terminal of the ferry to St Mawes which you must use to continue your journey. Save for winter Sundays, it is a year-round ferry service, but if for any reason it is not running you have three options: a 34-mile road walk, a financially crippling taxi, or a day spent initially lingering over a lazy breakfast then pottering the narrow sun-soaked streets, enjoying fresh lobster at a cosy low-beamed restaurant, or ice cream at a pavement café . . . it's your decision.

Falmouth to Gorran Haven

Having crossed Carrick Roads by ferry to the lovely St Mawes and its castle, also built by Henry VIII, you immediately need to use a seasonal ferry across the Percuil river to St Anthony on the Roseland peninsula. *[Alternative route, 6 miles: follow the A3078 out of Mawes north-eastwards via St Just in Roseland, crossing the river at Trethem Mill then turning right along a minor road to Tregassa. Turn right here on to a minor road that proceeds just west of south via Gerrans and Bohortha to reach St Anthony-in-Roseland.]* You soon pass the twelfth-century church of St Anthony-in-Roseland with its Norman south doorway, and connected to the nineteenth-century Place House, from which you stride out to St Anthony Head and its nineteenth-century lighthouse, and Zone Point with its fine views back across Falmouth Bay. At this point you bid farewell to Falmouth Bay and enjoy an easy walk along flat cliff-top paths to the village of Portscatho, followed by a walk round the edge of Gerrans Bay to its eastern end at Nare Head.

Initially the going from Portscatho is straightforward as you pass by the beaches of Porthcurnick and Porthbean, and then, beyond Creek Stephen Point, those of Pendower and Carne. Tougher walking follows as you then ascend to the cliffs, drop steeply to Paradoe Cove and then climb again to round Nare Head, with fine views from the headland. It is now a strenuous walk beside Veryan Bay to Portloe, the next village; having passed Rosen Cliff you have a near vertical descent, a mighty climb above Parc Caragloose Cove, and another big drop past Manare Point and Jacka Point to reach Portloe (337), a comparatively unspoilt and beautifully kept fishing village with a tiny harbour. Two miles west is Veryan with its thatched whitewashed circular cottages, said to be Devil-proof as there were no corners where Satan could lie in wait!

Enjoyable but tough clifftop walking past Caragloose Point takes you to the attractive twin villages of West and East Portholland, and a mile further on you reach Porthluney Cove. Close by is the majestic nineteenth-century Caerhays Castle, designed by John Nash who was also responsible for Brighton Pavilion and Buckingham Palace. You return to the clifftops, the slopes clad with bracken and outcrops of rock, then after dropping to the wonderfully unspoilt Hemmick Beach, you begin your assault on Dodman Point, which lies at the far eastern end of Veryan Bay and is one of south Cornwall's most prominent headlands. Although the ascent from Hemmick Beach is tough, the view from the memorial cross at the Point itself is tremendous, with a whole new coastal vista opening out to the east, including the broad sweep of St Austell Bay. There is then a long and difficult descent to Maenease Point, beyond which is the village of Gorran Haven (345) where you will no doubt hope for a meal after so much tough walking. The upside of Cornwall being so popular with holidaymakers is the easy availability of inexpensive cafés and takeaways, but the downside is that these eateries can be somewhat tacky with excruciatingly corny names. To liven up a dull walk, you may like to think what name you would give to your own seaside chippy: My Plaice, The Cod Piece, For Goodness Hake, or even Come Fry With Me.

Gorran Haven to Looe

There is terrific cliff walking from Gorran Haven on to Turbot Point, down to Colona Beach and round the neck of the Chapel Point headland, where you begin walking round Mevagissey Bay. It is necessary to follow roads to pass into and through the undistinguished village of Portmellon and continue to Mevagissey, a picturesque fishing village with a lovely harbourside which can get very choked with visitors and cars in summer. Some up-and-down walking sees you round Penare Point and pass the ruins of Portgiskey, soon arriving at Pentewan with its huge caravan park, but from here you face a much more demanding section, with a number of steep climbs and descents. Early on there is a refreshing interlude at Hallane where a gushing stream meets the path in woodland before cascading into the bay, and shortly thereafter you round Black Head with its fine view over Mevagissey Bay. You now begin the walk round St Austell Bay, enjoying rather easier walking as you pass the wooded cove of Ropehaven, but there follows one of the most savage switchbacks on the whole route. Gentler walking follows as you pass the popular beach of Porthpean and follow the clifftop round the edge of Duporth village, shortly reaching Charlestown (356).

Its late eighteenth-century harbour, once extremely important for the export of local ore and china clay and containing two magnificent tall ships, is bordered by lovely old cottages, and was the setting for the BBC's popular *Poldark* series. The market town of St Austell lies just a mile further inland; the town has a long association with the china clay industry, hence the mountainous white spoil heaps, known as the Alps, which can be seen in the neighbourhood. You continue round Landrion Point and alongside the extensive sands of Carlyon Bay with its massive eyesore of an entertainment centre. Then you have to negotiate, in quick succession, the Par china clay works, the residential sprawl of Par village, and a big caravan park at Par Beach. You return to the cliffs, meeting the Saints Way which crosses inland Cornwall, then drop to Polkerris. Its little assembly of cottages in a narrow valley make a picturesque sight, but the surroundings are sadly dominated by the china clay works and the village can get terribly crowded in summer.

From Polkerris you ascend steeply through woodland and now enjoy a fine cliff walk to Gribbin Head with its distinctive red and white striped daymark, built in 1832. Rounding the headland and leaving St Austell Bay behind, you soon reach the delectable Polridmouth Cove, behind which is a serene lake, beautiful woodland and a road leading to Menabilly, a mansion that dates back to 1710 with gardens famous for sub-tropical plants. Menabilly was the home of the novelist Daphne du Maurier for many years and was the Manderley of her famous novel *Rebecca*. An easy field-edge walk is followed by a glorious promenade to Fowey (366), past the rocky Coombe Hawne, Henry VIII's St Catherine's Castle, and pretty Readymoney Cove.

From the cove, with its lovely views across the water to Polruan, you proceed along a road up the west bank of the river Fowey into the town of that name. Once one of England's busiest ports, it boasts an early fourteenth-century church, streets containing many sixteenth and seventeenth-century houses, and a lovely harbour that is now a haven for pleasure craft. You cross the river by ferry to reach Polruan, which has a charming waterfront, quaint narrow streets, and a partially ruined square harbour-fort dating back to the sixteenth century.

Having climbed out of Polruan you return to the cliffs, rounding Lantic Bay and its twin beaches of Great Lantic and Little Lantic, and stride out on to Pencarrow Head from which there are tremendous views that extend as far back as Dodman Point. Beyond Pencarrow Head you proceed round Lantivet Bay, passing the gorgeous Lansallos Cove, a paradise of soft golden sands surrounded by formidable rock faces; look out for a rock cut lane used by farmers to facilitate the transport of seaweed from the beach. To your left you can see the tower of the fifteenth-century church of St Ildierna, easily reachable from the coast path and containing some fine sixteenth-century carved bench ends.

There is now some tough up-and-down work but the way ahead is clear, the views superb and the cliff scenery majestic, most notably the natural arch on Raphael Cliff; at times the only sounds are those of the sea caressing the rocks and perhaps the warning tones of the bell buoy. Beyond Raphael Cliff the going is easier, with an exhilarating promenade high above the sea and then a descent to Polperro, a gem of a village, with elegant Georgian houses, the famous House on Props (a house supported on wooden stilts and overhanging a brook), higgledy-piggledy narrow streets of cottages adorned with flowers, and a quite beautiful harbour.

Although the coast path from Polperro on to Talland round Downend Point and by Talland Bay can be very crowded in summer, the crowds tend to thin out as you follow the cliffs to the promontory of Hendersick, looking ahead to St George's Island which will remain visible on and off for the next sixty miles. Beyond Hendersick you follow the cliff path round the edge of Portnadler Bay, joining a road near Hannafore Point and following it into West Looe (378), from which a road bridge takes you over the river Looe into East Looe. The towns offer contrasting forms of nourishment for the visitor; on my Sunday evening visit in August, West Looe Methodist Church offered community hymn singing and the route to eternal salvation in the Lord, while East Looe offered hot pasties and clotted cream toffees.

Looe to Plymouth

Undistinguished walking follows, as you pick your way round the housing developments and holiday complexes at Plaidy and Millendreath, but east of Millendreath the scenery improves with some pleasant woodland, good views back to St George's Island and the added attraction of Murrayton Monkey Sanctuary. You descend again to the twin villages of Seaton and Downderry, then after a stiff climb you must follow the B3247 forward to Portwrinkle, although it is hoped that this lengthy road walk will be replaced with a proper coast route. I found Portwrinkle (386), despite its quaint name, to be an uninspiring place with limited amenities, and the route beyond it is little better; initially there is a good climb up to the cliffs, alongside a golf course, but you are then forced back on to tarmac by the Tregantle firing ranges, rejoining the B3247 near Trethill Cliffs and remaining on it to pass round the inland side of the danger area.

Once past the ranges you branch off right along a minor road which takes you back to the cliffs. You stay on the road through the straggling village of Freathy and for about a mile beyond it, before bearing right on to a path which snakes its way along the hillside amongst a vast profusion of holiday chalets. It is a relief to fight clear of them and proceed round Polhawn Cove and Queener Point to reach Rame Head. With its chapel ruin standing on cliffs 300ft above the sea, this is the last major Cornish headland on the route and a significant landmark.

Rounding the headland, you proceed just north of east past Lillery's Cove, with only a short detour being required for you to reach the part-thirteenth-century church of St German, built all of rough slate. You go forward to Penlee Point, where you get your first view of Plymouth Sound, then head up the west side of the Sound and away from the open sea, walking through a predominantly wooded landscape to reach the attractive twin villages of Cawsand and Kingsand with their streets of quaint cottages looking out over Cawsand Bay, an inlet of the Sound.

Beyond Kingsand you proceed on round Cawsand Bay to enter Mount Edgcumbe Country Park. The original sixteenth-century house of Mount Edgcumbe was burnt out during the Second World War, but the magnificent grounds survived intact and contain some interesting features including an eighteenth-century folly ruin and a splendid Orangery. You proceed through the grounds to Cremyll (399) for the short journey across the Sound back into Devon and the huge port of Plymouth, easily the largest conurbation on the route. You will have to turn your hand to all types of urban skills that you will have neglected while tramping through deepest Cornwall, such as walking along pavements rather than the middle of the road, remembering your PIN for the cashpoint, and finding a seat in Burger King that isn't immediately adjacent to a party of 23 six-year-olds.

Plymouth to Bigbury-on-Sea
Although Plymouth was badly bombed during the Second World War, there is still much to see in the city. If you get to look at nothing else, try to visit the Hoe, a level headland and esplanade overlooking

the Sound, with many monuments including a statue of Francis Drake who reputedly played bowls here while waiting for the onslaught of the Spanish Armada, and Smeaton's Tower, an eighteenth-century lighthouse. Elsewhere are ramparts of the seventeenth-century citadel, the Devonport dockyard and naval base, and the ancient Barbican area with its quaint narrow streets.

The route is not signposted through Plymouth; to continue onwards you firstly need to cross the river Plym using the Laira road bridge, then follow roads and paths through the suburban communities of Oreston and Hooe to reach Turnchapel which lies on the southern shores of Cattewater, the stretch of water linking the river Plym with the Sound. Here the route resumes with a climb out of Turnchapel, and proceeds round the neck of Mountbatten Point, to reach the cliffs above Jennycliff Bay, an eastern inlet of the Sound, with tremendous views back to the city and across the Sound to Rame Head and Mount Edgcumbe. The route continues down the east side of the Sound, with easy walking on low cliffs and no sense that you are so close to a great city.

You pass Bovisand with its marine training school and holiday camp, go round Bovisand Bay to reach the rocky Andurn Point, and proceed past Renney Rocks on your right and the village of Heybrook Bay to your left. Beyond Heybrook Bay you pass round the gunnery ranges of HMS *Cambridge*, where an inland detour may be necessary if firing is in progress. To your right, as you proceed past the ranges, is a great expanse of rock that tapers off at Wembury Point, and just out to sea beyond the Point is a prominent rock island called Great Mew Stone. Beyond the ranges it is easy walking alongside a rocky shoreline to Wembury church (413), beautifully situated on the hillside looking out to Blackstone Rocks on the shores of Wembury Bay. The route climbs high above the bay and you enjoy a splendid walk through the bracken with grandstand views to your next obstacle, the river Yealm. You drop down to Warren Point, situated on the riverbank, and a seasonal ferry crossing takes you across to the wooded east bank.

[Alternative route, 10 miles: return to Wembury church and follow minor roads northwards via Wembury village, Knighton and Hollacombe Hill, then turning eastwards via Spriddlestone to reach the A379. Follow this

road eastwards through Brixton. A mile or so beyond Brixton turn right on to a road heading via Puslinch to the B3186. Turn right on to this road then first left via Bridgend and Noss Mayo to rejoin the route.]

The route turns right but by going left you soon reach the pretty village of Noss Mayo, situated alongside a tributary of the Yealm, looking across to Newton Ferrers on the other side. It is popular with the boating and fishing fraternity, its relaxed atmosphere epitomised by a notice I saw displayed in large letters in the village that read, 'Old fishermen never die – they only smell that way.'

From the east bank of the river, the Coast Path proceeds along a track well above the Yealm, following it south-westwards to Mouthstone Point where the river flows into Wembury Bay, and then swinging south-eastwards again to continue beside the open sea. Having paused for a moment above Mouthstone Point to enjoy superb views back to Rame Head, you proceed on along a wide cliff path which is in fact a nineteenth-century carriage drive cut by Lord Revelstoke, a local landowner. Enjoying fine views ahead across Bigbury Bay to Bolt Tail, the next major headland, you go on past Stoke Point and follow the edge of a strip of woodland to reach Stoke, where it is worth detouring down a steep hill to view the ruined fourteenth-century church of St Peter the Poor Fisherman.

Beyond Stoke the walking gets tougher, with a particularly steep descent and climb to St Anchorite's Rock, set impressively on a hilltop some way back from the cliff edge. From the Rock there is another big drop to the delightful inlet at Bugle Hole with a jumble of rocks set against a stern backcloth of steep gorse-clad cliffs, then follows a steady climb back on to the cliffs overlooking the mouth of the river Erme. The view up the estuary is quite magnificent. You descend to Mothecombe Beach, then after a climb through woodland on Owen's Hill, you walk down to a slipway that provides the river crossing point to get over to Wonwell Beach. No ferry is available, and it is necessary for you to wade across the river, which you can do safely up to one hour either side of low water. Tide times are widely advertised enabling you to plan your arrival time carefully, but if you have time to spare you could detour to the pretty village of Mothecombe where refreshments may be available.

[Alternative route if the tides are unfavourable, 7 miles: proceed northwards along minor roads from Mothecombe via Holbeton to Ford, then follow a lane past Hole Farm to a footpath that heads north-eastwards, just west of Flete, to reach the A379. Turn right to follow the A379 over the Erme at Sequer's Bridge. Shortly beyond the bridge turn right on to a minor road heading southwards to Great Torr. Turn right at Great Torr on to a lane that heads south-westwards to Wonwell Court, from which a path runs to Wonwell Beach.]

Assuming you complete the crossing safely, you arrive on Wonwell Beach and stride confidently on past Muxham Point, giving you a lovely view back up the Erme, then embark on a very tough but exhilarating cliff walk to Challaborough. There is a good deal of up-and-down work but the rewards are unforgettable vistas of coves, rocks and often sheer cliff faces, including the shiny Dartmouth slate at Ayrmer Cove, as well as splendid views out across Bigbury Bay to Burgh Island. You drop to the popular holiday village of Challaborough, immediately beyond which is the little town of Bigbury-on-Sea (427).

It is certainly worth detouring to Burgh Island, reachable across the sands from Bigbury-on-Sea at low tide and by sea tractor at high tide, and offering fine views from its hilltop. One should imagine that bed and breakfast owners at Bigbury-on-Sea are quite used to Coast Path walkers arriving either very early or very late depending on the state of the tide when they reached the Erme, although they could be forgiven for being rather less tolerant of hikers who turn up on the doorstep at midnight having spent all evening in a Bigbury-on-Sea pub, having accomplished the journey from Mothecombe several hours earlier by wading into nothing moister than a local minicab.

Bigbury-on-Sea to Dartmouth

The Coast Path now leaves Bigbury Bay and begins wandering up the west side of the Avon estuary. A rather fiddly climb out of Bigbury-on-Sea beside the B3392 gives a fine view across the estuary, and you then follow the Avon inland, descending to the hamlet of Cockleridge. Just beyond Cockleridge you go down to the riverbank for a seasonal ferry crossing to Bantham on the opposite bank. At low tide and in calm conditions it is possible to wade the river with extreme care, but this is not recommended.

[Alternative route, 7 miles: return to the B3392, following it north-eastwards to the inland village of Bigbury, turning right along a tidal road that follows the bank of the Avon to Aveton Gifford. Turn right on to the A379 here, cross the river then immediately turn right on to a lane heading for Stadbury Farm. A footpath then takes you south-westwards beside the Avon to Bantham.]

Having reached Bantham you may either go right out to Hams End, where you can gaze across a wide expanse of sand to the mouth of the Avon, or cut across the neck of this little headland.

The Coast Path, now following Bigbury Bay again, then heads south-eastwards beside Thurlestone golf course, beyond which there is a less inspiring interlude round an inlet of the bay, with some large hotels dominating the scene, although things improve as you continue past Beacon Point and Woolman Point. Soon you get to to the cosy sandy beach of Hope Cove, guarded by impressive outcrops of rock, while immediately adjacent are the twin villages of Outer Hope and Inner Hope (433). From Inner Hope, a particularly lovely village with a square of thatched whitewashed cottages and a backcloth of wooded hills, there is a brisk climb to Bolt Tail, which offers stunning views across Bigbury Bay and right back to Rame Head and beyond. You now enjoy a magnificent cliff walk south-eastwards, passing another stunning viewpoint at Bolberry Down, and descending to Soar Mill Cove, an exquisite narrow inlet with a golden sandy beach, guarded by steep clifftops and rocky outcrops.

Having regained the height lost, it is a marvellous walk on to Bolt Head along gorse and bracken-clad hillsides and down a grassy gully, and from Bolt Head, an important wartime lookout point with good views across to Prawle Point, there is quite an exciting rocky scramble round Starehole Bay to Sharp Tor. Called the Courtenay Way, it was cut in the nineteenth-century to provide ease of access for visitors to Bolt Tail. From Sharp Tor you continue to chart a precarious course along the side of steep-faced cliffs, now following the west side of the Kingsbridge estuary, passing the magnificent gardens of Overbecks then following roads into

Salcombe (440). Originally a shipbuilding town with a castle built by Henry VIII, it is now a somewhat exclusive yachting and boating centre with little sympathy towards long-distance hikers. Indeed my February request of various bed and breakfasts for a one-night August stay as a Coast Path walker could scarcely have been met with more contempt if I had said I was to be spending a celebratory week in the area having been crowned Halitosis King of Llandrindod Wells.

An all-year ferry takes you from Salcombe to East Portlemouth, and there ensues a brief road walk to Mill Bay before an excellent cliff walk to Prawle Point, initially following the east bank of the estuary before proceeding more resolutely eastwards with the sea to your right. A narrow but unmistakable path weaves its way along the cliffs, with a dramatic drop to the sea on one side, and impressive rocky outcrops on the other; rocks along this section of coast include Pig's Nose, Ham Stone and Gammon Head! Beyond Gammon Head there is an almost sheer drop to Maceley's Cove, which like Soar Mill Cove is a lovely golden carpet standing between two towering columns of rock.

You go on to Prawle Point, the southernmost headland in Devon, providing tremendous views back to Bolt Head and forward to Start Point, then beyond the headland you enjoy rather easier walking, much of it along field-edge paths close to the shore round Langerstone Point and beside Lannacombe Bay. However, having passed Lannacombe Beach there is a much more strenuous walk to Start Point along a narrow ledge through the crags, before the lighthouse road allows an easier passage round the great schist outcrops of the headland to the Point itself. From here there are fine views across Start Bay which you will follow for some miles. You go back down the lighthouse road then descend steeply to sea level to reach Hallsands, consisting of a holiday complex and an old village that was ruined when, as a result of nearby shingle-dredging a century ago, it lost its natural sea defences and was exposed to the elements. It is certainly worth detouring to visit the ruined houses.

You continue past Tinsey Head and forward to the straggling village of Beesands, from which it is easy walking past the lake of

Widdicombe Ley and Beesands Quarry to reach the busy and useful village of Torcross (453). There follows a walk along a shingle path beside Slapton Sands, used in 1943 for D-Day preparations by USA troops, but beyond Strete Gate you are forced away from the sea, there being no coast route available, using a number of lanes on the inland side of the A379 via Strete, Blackpool and Stoke Fleming.

Just before Little Dartmouth you turn right off the road to return to the coast, and enjoy a good cliff walk past Combe Point and Compass Cove to the mouth of the river Dart at Blackstone Point where there is a footbridge over a dramatic sea-washed gully. There is now a pleasant walk up the west side of the Dart, passing the ruins of the fifteenth-century Dartmouth Castle and its neighbouring church of St Petrox with lovely views over the estuary. Road walking then takes you into Dartmouth (463); recalling Gammon Head and discovering that this district is known as South Hams, perhaps you should celebrate your arrival with a bacon sandwich!

Dartmouth to Torquay

Dartmouth, famous for its naval college, is a lovely town and boating resort, with many fine old buildings including a restored row of seventeenth-century houses on granite pillars known as the Butterwalk. The Coast Path uses the year-round ferry to Kingswear to cross the Dart, then beyond Kingswear comes one of the toughest sections of all. The up-and-down walking begins almost at once as you proceed through a wooded landscape by the east side of the Dart, enjoying fine views across to the castle, to reach the Dart's real mouth at Inner Froward Point with its Second World War lookout buildings.

Having enjoyed the view to Start Point you continue on past Outer Froward Point and Pudcombe Cove, walking immediately below the beautiful gardens and woodland of Coleton Fishacre but still high above the sea. From here to Sharkham Point via Scabbacombe Head and Crabrock Point the walking is often very severe, with particularly tough ascents from the intervening Scabbacombe Sands and Man Sands, and some awkward descents which can be very slippery in wet weather. Beyond Sharkham Point the walk out to Berry Head round St Mary's Bay is marginally easier but quite fiddly, and it is good to reach the headland with its country park, lighthouse and Napoleonic War fort.

Now you look out across Tor Bay, and its string of seaside resorts dominated by Torquay on the Bay's north side. You descend from Berry Head to sea level and soon arrive in Brixham (474), consisting of an early Victorian town centre and a fishing harbour where there are a number of early nineteenth-century houses. A stone on the quayside commemorates the landing of William of Orange here in 1688. You proceed past Churston Cove and Fishcombe Point and through woodland as far as Elberry Cove, then go round Churston Point to arrive at Broad Sands, but are then forced inland by the Torbay and Dartmouth railway, proceeding beside the line along the edge of Goodrington and as far as Goodrington Sands. You walk alongside the sands then climb briskly to Roundham Head before descending to the promenade of the very popular resort of Paignton.

No sooner have you left Paignton than you join the road taking you into Torquay (482). This is Devon's largest resort, created largely in the nineteenth century, and with its stuccoed villas and sub-tropical trees and flowers, the nearest thing to a French Riviera resort in Britain. Many parts of the town retain a Victorian character but all the unsubtle trappings of a modern resort are there. On the Saturday night I was there in August, the town was packed with diners and clubbers, some dressed to kill in short skirts and high boots, others happy to amble the streets in vest tops, shorts and sandals. Wherever you stay in Torquay, you must just hope that the hotel you have chosen does not come complete with a waiter who responds to your inquiries with the single word '*Que?*' and a manager who goosesteps into the foyer and urges you not to mention the war.

Torquay to Exmouth
Fiddly but not unpleasant walking takes you via Daddyhole Cove and Meadfoot Beach away from the centre of the town, with good views across the bay to Berry Head, from which you go forward to the grotesquely-shaped piece of headland known as Hope's Nose

at the very end of Tor Bay. Rounding the headland, you now begin the walk alongside Babbacombe Bay, some woodland walking taking you past Black Head to Anstey's Cove. A climb on to Walls Hill is followed by a descent to the beaches of Babbacombe and Oddicombe, beyond which you pass Petit Tor Point and follow a principally wooded course with limited sea views past Watcombe to Maidencombe. You are, however, at last emerging from the outskirts of Torquay.

The walk from Maidencombe to Shaldon is very tough, with a number of severe climbs and descents, and the hilltop views are often partially obstructed by trees, but the last rise brings a superb view to the river Teign and beyond, and a rapid descent from here brings you to the Ness, a tall tree-clad outcrop of sandstone at the mouth of the river. It is then a short walk to Shaldon from where a ferry journey takes you across the water to Teignmouth (493), one of Devon's oldest seaside resorts with many buildings dating back to the Georgian and early Victorian eras.

From here to Holcombe you follow the sea wall, with the railway immediately adjoining it on the landward side. The railway, part of the London–Penzance line, is one of the most spectacular pieces of line in the country, with massive railway tunnels cut into the rocks. At high tide the sea wall is unusable and you must proceed inland along paths and then by the A379 to Holcombe. The main route leaves the sea wall just outside Holcombe and joins up with the other way in the village, and you then remain on the landward side of the railway, initially heading seawards to proceed parallel with it before retreating slightly inland on the approach to Dawlish. You join a minor metalled road and follow it to the A379, bearing right into a park and following the sandstone cliff edge before descending on a zigzag path and arriving by the boat cove near Dawlish town centre.

Partly Regency in character, Dawlish was a favourite town of Jane Austen, and Dickens made it Nicholas Nickleby's birthplace. An easy walk along the sea wall once more – or along the landward side of the railway at high tide – takes you to Dawlish Warren which boasts a large nature reserve but also a profusion of caravans and chalets. Walkers who look coldly upon holiday centres such as this might care to ask themselves whether their upset springs not so much from concern about the disfigurement of the coastline as the annoyance they feel when stuck for 12 miles on a main road behind a caravan or camper van driver unable or unwilling to top 22mph. Or of course it could just be a pathological aversion to *Hi-de-Hi*.

At Dawlish Warren you leave the sea wall and begin walking up the west bank of the Exe estuary, following a metalled road through the village and then on via Eastdon and Cockwood. Just beyond Cockwood you pick up the A379 which takes you on to Starcross, famous for its pumping house that formed part of Brunel's ill-fated Atmospheric Railway. At Starcross you can, during the summer, catch a ferry across the Exe to Exmouth where the true coastal walk resumes, but at other times it is necessary to continue up the side of the Exe to Topsham to cross the river there.

You leave the A379 to proceed along a minor road, with the railway to your immediate right and the lovely Powderham Park on your left, boasting a heronry and a castle that has been the home of the Earls of Devon since 1390. Having passed Powderham Church the road swings sharply left, but you go straight ahead on a track, cross the railway with extreme care and strike out on a path that continues alongside the estuary, and then beside the Exeter Canal which is separated from the estuary by an area known as West Mud. Soon you reach the ferry and use it to cross the estuary to Topsham. *[Alternative route if the ferry is unavailable, 4 miles: retrace your steps briefly and follow a minor road westwards to reach the A379 just east of Exminster, following it over the estuary to Countess Wear, turn right here and follow the road to Topsham.]*

Topsham, for a long time an important port serving the nearby and easily accessible cathedral city of Exeter, is a pretty village with graceful Georgian houses and a genteel air; I remember stopping here for a cream tea and being asked to choose from a jam list! There is no Coast Path route as such down the east side of the estuary to Exmouth, and you may prefer to take the train. If you want to walk it, follow a minor road eastwards out of Topsham to Marsh Barton, joining a footpath and then a lane to bring you to the A376 at Ebford. Turn right on to the A376 and follow it through

Exton, then beyond the Royal Marines' barracks, turn right down a minor road to Lympstone, a pretty village of thatched cottages and Regency villas and once a fishing port from which boats sailed as far as Greenland.

At Lympstone you can then follow the East Devon Way, which hugs the railway on one side and the estuary sands on the other, soon bringing you into Exmouth (512). You have now negotiated your final river obstacle of the route. Whilst you may feel that the ferry crossings have disrupted the continuity of the walk, you may still be in a better position than the purist you met at the start, who has flatly refused to resort to any mechanical aid on his journey and who, as you enjoy Exmouth's delights, is still picking his mud-splattered way round the creeks of deepest Cornwall with as much chance of finding a path or a bridge as being attacked by a swarm of killer Cornish pasties.

Exmouth to West Bay

Exmouth, for a time the home of Lady Nelson, is the oldest resort in Devon, renowned for its red sandstone cliffs and bathing beaches, with buildings dating back to the eighteenth century. The Coast Path resumes at Maer Rocks just to the east of Exmouth, and you can choose whether to cut through the town centre or walk out to the Point where you can see across to the Dawlish Warren nature reserve, before leaving the estuary behind and following the waterfront to Maer Rocks. You ascend to the cliffs above Sandy Bay and pass through an extensive holiday park before going forward to the triangulation point and viewpoint of West Down Beacon and descending to Budleigh Salterton, a pleasant resort with a number of eighteenth-century houses.

Just beyond the town you detour briefly inland to cross the Otter estuary, beyond which it is easy walking along low clifftops past Brandy Head and Smallstones Point to Ladram Bay, a small inlet with striking sandstone stacks rising impressively behind. There is then a climb to High Peak with its Iron Age hill fort, and soon after that you pass the tremendous viewpoint of Peak Hill, at just over 500ft above the sea. There follows a very steep descent to Sidmouth (525), a town of fine Regency and Victorian buildings, and a tough ascent out of the town on to Salcombe Hill Cliff. This is followed by a big drop to Salcombe Mouth, another big climb to Dunscombe Cliffs, a plunge right down to the beach at Weston Mouth, and a massive ascent to Weston Cliff with tremendous views that extend back to Sidmouth and Budleigh Salterton and across large areas of Devon countryside.

There is temporary respite with a level walk along Coxe's Cliff, and you briefly lose sight of the sea as you proceed through woodland just south of the lovely village of Branscombe. Easily reachable from the route, it contains thatched cottages, a thatched smithy that has been working since the fifteeenth century, and St Winifred's Church with a Norman tower and three-decker pulpit.

You drop down to the sea again at the trippery Branscombe Mouth, then to reach Beer, the next village, you have a choice of routes. You may follow the top of Hooken Cliffs, offering superb views as far ahead as Portland Bill, or take the path through the undercliff area, formed as a result of a landslip in 1790, and now a fine centre of insect, butterfly and plant life. Both routes unite at Beer Head, the most westerly chalk headland in the country, from which it is a straightforward descent to the seaside village of Beer.

A name like that could not fail to cheer a thirsty walker on a hot day, although the real ale enthusiast walking the Coast Path may be no less tolerant of poor quality ale in his seaside hotel than in his local at home, perhaps being moved to remark that he would have had a great time if his bathwater had been as warm as his beer, his wine as chill as the waiter who served it, and his port as mature as the fungus sprouting from his bedroom skirting board.

From Beer you briefly return to the cliffs but soon drop down to the inlet of Seaton Hole and then, depending on the tide, follow the beach or a road on to the bustling resort of Seaton (534). You use the B3172 to cross the river Axe – a detour up this road brings you to the lovely thatched village of Axmouth with a church containing medieval wall paintings – then branch off along a track which skirts the inland side of a golf course, soon turning seawards on to Haven Cliff. You then proceed along a path through an undercliff created on Christmas Eve 1839 by a slip of an estimated eight million tons of rock. Virtually this entire walk is through dense woodland, and although you will not get lost, there are no landmarks to tell you where you are, and it can feel claustrophobic with very restricted sea views through the veritable jungle.

Emerging from the woods, you leave Devon and enter Dorset, and almost immediately arrive in Lyme Regis (542). Once an important port – Edward I used its harbour during his wars against the French and a number of ships departed the harbour to fight the Armada in 1588 – it is now a popular resort with strong literary associations. Having enjoyed a stroll along the Cobb, a massive breakwater sheltering the harbour, and ambled along the pretty narrow streets of craft shops and cafés, you head for Charmouth, using a coastal route that opened as recently as 1996 after severe erosion problems had previously forced it well inland.

You pass Charmouth and then proceed on to the cliffs again, further cliffslips having created a no-man's land of vegetation and rock between you and the sea, and ascend to Golden Cap, at 626ft the highest cliff on the south coast. There is a steep descent to Seatown, a big climb to another excellent viewpoint at Thorncombe Beacon, a further drop to the sea at Eype's Mouth, then yet another ascent to West Cliff before a drop to West Bay (551). It is a 2-mile walk from here to the attractive town of Bridport with its fine Georgian buildings and fifteenth-century almshouses; for centuries it has thrived on the rope-making industry, and the pavements used to be 'rope-walks' that were laid out for twisting and drying the cord and twine. West Bay itself comes as something of an anticlimax so soon after the timeless charm of Lyme Regis, with many of the less welcome concessions to the holiday industry, and one suspects that Meryl Streep's brooding stares and wistful gazes as the French Lieutenant's Woman, so effective when set against the Cobb and the restless sea immediately beyond, would not carry quite the same gravitas if behind her stood nothing more stern and uncompromising than a mobile doughnut stand.

West Bay to Lulworth (coast route)
You climb steeply from West Bay on to East Cliff, then are forced inland, descending to cross the river Bride at Burton Freshwater, a short detour here bringing you to Burton Bradstock, a lovely village

with 300-year-old thatched cottages and a fourteenth-century parish church. The route ascends on to Burton Cliff, then drops to Cogden Beach, where you begin a long walk by the shoreline. Progress is initially reasonably good, as you keep to the landward side of a strip of water named Burton Mere, but you are soon forced on to the shingle of what is known as Chesil Beach, arriving soon at West Bexington. *[Here an inland alternative to Osmington Mills begins, described later.]*

After some more shingle walking you join a surfaced lane that brings you to within half a mile or so of the western end of the Fleet. This is a lagoon separating the mainland from the long, thin, blue-clay reef of Chesil Beach whose massive shingle wall, in places 35ft high and 150 yards wide, consists of pebbles thrown up by the stormy seas and increasing in size from west to east. It extends as far as Portland and although it could be followed, it is an extremely tough walk, especially in bad weather. The official Coast Path veers to the landward side of the Fleet, contouring Chapel Hill topped by the fifteenth-century chapel of St Catherine, and skirting Abbotsbury (560) with its lovely thatched cottages, massive tithe barn built on the site of an eleventh-century abbey, and swannery which is seen at its best during the hatching season in late spring. East of Abbotsbury you are forced well inland even of the Fleet, proceeding through heavily farmed land to pass over Merry Hill then swinging southwards past Wyke Wood to return to the Fleet at Rodden Hive.

Progress is now very easy as you follow a clear level path beside the Fleet, incorporating numerous inlets and mini headlands, but always separated from the open sea by the great shingle wall of Chesil Beach. There may be a brief inland diversion at Tidmoor Point if there is firing on the Chickerell rifle range. You pass the Royal Engineers camp and, with views to the isle of Portland on your right and the suburbs of Weymouth now encroaching to your left, you proceed to Ferry Bridge. Here you cross the causeway linking Weymouth and Portland, swing from south-east to north-east and follow a rather fiddly course along a mixture of roads, greens and narrow paths snaking between houses and the sea to enter Weymouth itself. Although not part of the Coast Path, there is a coastal route round Portland, which despite containing military installations and a young offenders' institution, provides some fine walking, especially if you feel that the 574 miles you have already done is not enough.

Weymouth (574) is a pleasant seaside town with a large sandy beach, an attractive harbour, and many fine old buildings including Georgian and early Victorian houses and also Tudor cottages, and as you approach the harbour you will pass the impressive Nothe Fort, which was built as a defence against Napoleon. Beyond Nothe Fort you turn sharp left down to the harbourside, to cross the water by means of the Town Bridge, then follow the harbour seawards again and return to the seafront at the Esplanade. You leave the town, following Weymouth Bay beside the A353 coast road which you leave at Overcombe, following Furzy Cliff past Bowleaze Cove and then striking out to Redcliff Point. Pleasant and undemanding cliff walking takes you on to Osmington Mills, where the inland alternative from West Bexington (see below) rejoins the main route. Thirsty walkers will be delighted to note that the Coast Path here passes right through a pub garden!

You continue along gentle cliffs to Ringstead Bay, passing close to the site of what is now the deserted village of Ringstead, the ruin of which, according to legend, was brought about by French pirates. At Ringstead Bay the walking gets a lot tougher, with a big climb to the coastguard cottages of White Nothe, at 548ft the highest point attained since Golden Cap. From here to Lulworth the scenery is truly magnificent, the Coast Path following the tops of sheer limestone cliffs high above the sea with some very steep climbs and descents, and tremendous viewpoints from the summits of Swyre Head and Hambury Tout. Between these two hilltops there is a depression from which you have a perfect view of Durdle Door, a natural arch of limestone and one of the most photographed coastal features in the country.

A long descent from Hambury Tout brings you to Lulworth (586), a popular village of attractive cottages and shops built on the edge of Lulworth Cove, a quite remarkable natural inlet with two arms of Portland and Purbeck stone almost encircling the water. It is here that, if you have made the right arrangements, you now have the enticing prospect of a quite fantastic 7-mile coast walk to Kimmeridge. However, owing to Army activity, this walk is only usually available at weekends and holiday periods, and outside those times you will be forced to take a very tame inland walk instead (see below). Unless, that is, you have the sufficient time and resources to while away up to five days in and around Lulworth, or are immediately able to hire a set of clothes and generate a set of false documents that will fool officials into believing you are a senior army officer with orders to cease all firing practice forthwith. Might just be easier to come back another day . . .

West Bexington to Osmington Mills (inland route)

The inland alternative from West Bexington to Osmington Mills (18 miles in all) follows a portion of the South Dorset Ridgeway, a prehistoric route with one of the biggest concentration of round barrows (burial mounds) in Britain. If you opt for the Ridgeway alternative, you proceed inland up West Bexington village street then steeply uphill to meet the B3157 on Limekiln Hill, turning right to follow the road. You pass an old limekiln that has been restored by the National Trust, then go forward to the Iron Age hill fort of Abbotsbury Castle. Leaving the B3157, the route continues eastwards across White Hill, immediately above Abbotsbury, then after crossing a metalled road, goes past a stone circle on to Portesham Hill.

You cross another metalled road and soon reach the restored Neolithic (pre-Bronze Age) Hell Stone burial chamber, then enter an area of woodland and swing north-eastwards to arrive at the Hardy Monument. Built in 1844, this is named not after the novelist Thomas Hardy, but Admiral Thomas Hardy, Nelson's flag-captain at Trafalgar, and immortalised in Nelson's reputed last words, 'Kismet, Hardy' or as some are wont to say, 'Kiss me, Hardy!' The views from the monument are tremendous, extending right out to Weymouth and the sea beyond. It is then an easy walk south-eastwards on a good path over Bronkham Hill and Corton Down, passing a massive succession of Bronze Age (2200–650 BC) round barrows and with fine views to Maiden Castle to the left. First occupied 4,000 years ago, and fortified in the Iron Age, Maiden

Castle is one of the largest earthwork fortifications in Europe, its perimeter extending more than two miles and its terraced ramparts rising to more than 80ft.

You cross the B3159 just north of Upwey, then swing southwards on a lane parallel with the A354 Dorchester–Weymouth road, soon crossing this and proceeding eastwards over Bincombe Down. Swinging southwards, you drop steeply to the pretty village of Bincombe, then head south-eastwards to climb on to Green Hill, passing just north of the hill fort of Chalbury. From this point you veer north-eastwards, climbing steadily to West Hill which again is dotted with round barrows, then go south-eastwards again, dropping steeply down towards Osmington. You can now look back on West Hill and see a white horse cut into the hillside in recognition of the many visits to the area made by George III during his reign.

The route joins a lane which soon reaches the pleasant thatched village of Osmington, crosses the A353 and takes a gentle climb and descent through fields, returning to the sea at Osmington Mills. Here the inland alternative ends; certainly it makes a change from coastal walking but lovers of the sea and the cliffs may feel all the round barrows to be rather too much of a good thing, particularly if they have already sampled something genuinely prehistoric five nights back, to wit the toast served up by Mrs Golightly in the Belle Vue Guest House.

Lulworth to Kimmeridge

The *main* route climbs out of Lulworth, with tremendous views to the cove, and descends to the Fossil Forest, consisting of lumps of rock which contained tree stumps from a forest that existed well over 100 million years ago. Here, fortunate walkers will pass through the gates into the restricted zone. The route through the area is guarded by yellow boundary posts and frequent warning signs, but despite this is totally unspoilt by development, and the absence of farming, owing to the military activity, has produced a wilderness landscape that is most unusual on the south coast of England. Beyond Fossil Forest and the grotesque formations of Mupe Rocks, there is a massive climb round Mupe Bay on to

Bindon Hill with awesome sheer chalk cliffs. You drop to the tiny cove of Arish Mell, steep chalk cliffs zealously guarding its entrance, then have another back-breaking climb to the Iron Age hill fort at Flower's Barrow and a huge drop to Worbarrow Tout, from which there are tremendous views back across Worbarrow Bay to Bindon Hill. There is then another big climb on to Gad Cliff, where you should detour to Tyneham. Having been evacuated in 1943 as part of the Allied invasion plans, the villagers never returned, and Tyneham is effectively a ghost village with ruined houses adjacent to a pretty green and pond, although the church is lovingly maintained and the school has been furnished to look just as it did before the evacuation.

A high level walk takes you from Gad Cliff on to the tremendous viewpoint of Tyneham Cap, from which you begin descending towards Kimmeridge Bay. You go round the more modest headland of Broad Bench and pass the Kimmeridge oil well, leaving the restricted area and rounding Kimmeridge Bay, passing close to the tiny grey limestone village of Kimmeridge. If your timing has gone awry and the coast route is unavailable, the most direct alternative (still entailing an extra six miles or so) is to follow the B3070 via West Lulworth, Lulworth Camp and East Lulworth to West Holme, turning right on to a road that heads past East Holme to Stoborough, turning right again to follow a road southwards to Creech, and following metalled roads south-westwards and south-eastwards through Steeple to reach Kimmeridge. Worse, the B3070 is sometimes closed beyond East Lulworth, in which case the only way round is north-westwards along roads to Coombe Keynes and Wool, where you can pick up a road heading eastwards via East Stoke to West Holme. Or at Wool you can pick up a taxi, cursing the vital day you wasted back in Penzance trying to find a shop that stocked your preferred brand of insect repellent.

Kimmeridge to South Haven Point

From Kimmeridge (593) you ascend past the ornate Clavel Tower, built in 1820 as a folly and later used as a coastguard lookout, and some excellent walking follows on cliffs known as Kimmeridge Ledges, the Coast Path proceeding high above the sea and often perilously close to sheer drops. You pass Rope Lake Head and the delightful waterfall and woodland at Egmont Bight, then climb steeply to the limestone peak of Houns-tout Cliff. Cliff slips have resulted in the diversion of the coast route away from the sea round Chapman's Pool and into the valley of Hill Bottom instead, but having risen from Hill Bottom you swing southwards to follow parallel with the coastline once more, negotiating a tough descent and climb at Emmett's Hill and going forward to St Aldhelm's or St Alban's Head, some 354ft above the sea. Before you round the headland it is worth detouring to visit the square twelfth-century St Aldhelm's Chapel, and pausing to admire magnificent views which can extend as far as Portland.

Now you proceed north-eastwards, initially on the limestone cliffs but then dropping to the combe at Winspit, from where it is an easy detour to the pretty village of Worth Matravers with cottages of Purbeck stone and a church with some fine Norman features. Beyond Winspit, you return to the cliffs, passing plenteous evidence of quarrying activity as you proceed on via Seacombe Cliff towards Durlston Head. At Dancing Ledges a swimming pool was cut into the limestone slabs by quarrymen almost a century ago, and further on you meet the Tilly Whim Caves, consisting of large black holes in the steep limestone cliff face, the name being derived from a quarryman called Tilly and a kind of crane called a Whim.

As you approach Durlston Head you enter Durlston Country Park, passing Anvil Point with its lighthouse, visitor centre and folly known as Durlston Castle, built around 1890 by one George Burt. You round Durlston Head, the cliffs hereabouts hosting a wide variety of seabirds, then descend to Peveril Point with its coastguard station and enter Swanage (605). It is a pleasant resort, the most striking architectural feature being the town hall, another gift of George Burt. The town hall is worth visiting for its remarkable seventeenth-century façade, an example of the City of London style of the period which Pevsner curtly describes as 'overwhelmingly undisciplined!' Then again, Swanage is a holiday resort after all . . .

From Swanage you return to the cliffs, climbing on to Ballard Down with its five small bowl barrows – circular Bronze Age burial mounds – and enjoying a splendid walk along the tops of the virtually sheer chalk cliffs. Soon you reach the Foreland, also known as Handfast Point, where you look down on the dramatic assortment of crumbling chalk stacks of Old Harry rising from the water. If you feel sufficiently daring you can follow a perilous course along a narrow ridge towards the first of them, but it would be a pity to slip to your grief so close to the finishing line! Then you swing westwards and descend on a wide track, enjoying fine views to Bournemouth and beyond, soon arriving at the pretty village of Studland, with a lovely little Norman church and popular pub.

The last two and a half mile stretch of the national trail consists of a walk either along the beach or through the dunes beside Studland Bay, keeping the Studland Nature Reserve to your left. Part of the sands bordering Studland Bay has been designated a nudist beach, and in summer you may feel somewhat overdressed in your T-shirt and shorts. You continue on the sands round Shell Bay to arrive at the ferry terminal at South Haven Point, where the official Coast Path ends (613). The Sandbanks chain ferry will convey you from here across the mouth of Poole Harbour for a long walk or interminable bus ride into the centre of Bournemouth, where you will merge into the holiday crowds with no-one to reward or even recognise what, if you have walked all 613 miles, is a truly stupendous achievement.

If you have come to love the coastline and the constant presence of the sea, perhaps the best reward you could give yourself is a relaxing week's beach holiday where you can sit contentedly on your hotel veranda without the thought that the nearest refreshment is an excruciating thirty-minute tramp away over shingle, that the nearest accommodation a body-battering twelve steep-sided combes away, and that the next stage of your holiday cannot be realistically achieved without the help of a ferry across the bay which is not due to run again for another four and a half months.

SUMMARY OF PLACES OF INTEREST

There are hundreds on the Coast Path but to my mind these stand out as being of special interest:

Foreland Point, Valley of Rocks, Great Hangman, Morte Point, Clovelly, Hartland Point, Higher Sharpnose Point, Morwenstow, Castle Point, High Cliff, Boscastle, Rocky Valley, Tintagel, Port Isaac, Lundy Hole, Pentire Point, St Enodoc, Padstow, Merope Rocks, Bedruthan Steps, Godrevy Point, St Ives, Zennor, Pendeen Watch, Cape Cornwall, Land's End, Minack Theatre, Mousehole, St Michael's Mount, Mullion, Lizard, Helford River, Falmouth, St Anthony Head, Caerhays, Dodman Point, Mevagissey, Charlestown, Gribbin Head, Fowey, Pencarrow Head, Polperro, Rame Head, Mount Edgcumbe, Plymouth, Erme Estuary, Burgh Island, Bolt Head, Salcombe, Prawle Point, Start Point, Dartmouth, Brixham, Torquay, Dawlish, Exmouth, Ladram Bay, Weston Cliff, Branscombe, Hooken Cliff, Lyme Regis, Golden Cap, Abbotsbury, Chesil Beach, Weymouth, Durdle Door, Lulworth Cove, Bindon Cliff, Tyneham, St Aldhelm's Head, Old Harry.

AMENITIES ON OR NEAR THE ROUTE

Minehead★, Porlock, Lynmouth, Lynton, Combe Martin, Ilfracombe★, Woolacombe, Croyde, Braunton, Barnstaple★, Bideford★, Appledore, Westward Ho!, Clovelly, Bude, Boscastle, Tintagel, Port Isaac, Polzeath, Padstow, Trevone, Newquay★, Perranporth, St Agnes, Portreath, Hayle, St Ives, Mousehole, Penzance★, Marazion, Porthleven, Lizard, Coverack, Helford, Falmouth★, Gorran Haven, Mevagissey, Charlestown, Par, Fowey, Polruan, Polperro, Looe★, Cawsand/Kingsand, Plymouth★, Bigbury, Hope, Salcombe, Stoke Fleming, Dartmouth★, Brixham★, Paignton★, Torquay★, Teignmouth★, Dawlish, Dawlish Warren, Topsham, Exmouth★, Sidmouth★, Beer, Seaton, Lyme Regis★, West Bay, Weymouth★, Lulworth, Swanage★.

Offa's Dyke Path

SOUTH

• Clun

NORTH

Knighton

• Prestatyn

RHYL

Kington

• Bodfari

OFFA'S DYKE PATH

• Llandegla

Hay on Wye

• HEREFORD

Llangollen

Oswestry

Llanymynech

Monmouth

ABERGAVENNY

Welshpool

Chepstow

Montgomery

Sedbury

Newtown

Length: 178 miles
Start: Sedbury Cliffs, near Chepstow.
Finish: Prestatyn, on the North Wales coast.
Nature: A coast to coast walk following the English/Welsh border based on the eighth-century Offa's Dyke earthwork.
Difficulty rating: Moderate to strenuous, but many easy sections. Some strenuous sections could become severe in bad weather.
Average time of completion: 2 weeks.

NB: The distances given assume that the longer (riverside) route is taken between Brockweir and Bigsweir. The upland route is shorter by 1 mile.

Offa's Dyke Path

Offa's Dyke Path is one of the most satisfying national trails to attempt and accomplish. It runs right up the border between England and Wales, from south to north, and it is a true coast to coast route, starting from the shores of one wide band of water, the river Severn, and finishing on the shores of the Irish Sea on the coastline of North Wales. Unlike the Pembrokeshire Coast Path, where after 180 miles of walking you are only 30 miles away from where you started, the successful Offa's Dyke walker will really sense that something quite momentous has been achieved. Moreover, on its way from south to north shore, the route follows virtually all that remains of Offa's Dyke, a most remarkable historical feature.

The Dyke was apparently constructed by the Mercian king Offa, the most powerful of all the Anglo-Saxon kings, reigning from AD 757–796; his empire stretched across much of central and southern England and, latterly, East Anglia. The purpose of the

Dyke was to mark an agreed, definite frontier between his kingdom of Mercia and the Welsh kingdoms to the west of it. There had been numerous border disputes and fluctuations for several hundred years, but peace was finally achieved in 780 and it was in 784 that work began on the Dyke. Although many historians believe that its purpose was primarily to serve as a frontier marker, it also enabled trade between Mercia and Wales to be controlled, and may have prevented or hindered cattle raids. Moreover, it has been suggested by Frank Noble, who played a prominent part in establishing the national trail, that the form and siting of the Dyke points to its main purpose being a defensive one.

Whatever its purpose, it was – and still is today – an awesomely impressive construction. Though each owner of the land through which the Dyke was to run had responsibility for the work on their section, the dimensions were similar throughout; the earth bank of the Dyke was on the whole 6ft high and 60ft wide, and it was always ditched. It covered a distance of 149 miles. Remarkably, 1,200 years later, 81 miles of the Dyke were still standing, and it was suggested that these remains could become the basis of a long-distance path.

Following sterling work by the Offa's Dyke Association, 1971 saw the opening of a route which aimed to follow as much of what remained of the Dyke as was feasible, and at the same provide a continuous coast to coast walk along, or very close to, the whole of the border between England and Wales. The result is a journey which provides a fascinating exploration of our past, and wonderfully contrasting and unspoilt scenery from beginning to end. On no other national trail is there such diversity.

Many sections could be accomplished by the most ill-equipped novice, but as many again will impose the greatest technical demands on even the hardiest traveller. One aspect common to every stretch of the route, besides the bilingual signposting ('Llwybr Clawdd Offa –Offa's Dyke Path'), is the ubiquitous stile – there are hundreds – but this should not detract from your enjoyment of the variety of surroundings. There are moors and mountains, forests and pastures, switchback hills, gentle riverside strolls, canal paths and aqueducts. There are also many chocolate-box villages and towns, and in fact you are never very far from places of habitation or amenities which are plentiful throughout.

The only sort of walking that is lacking is sustained coastal walking, but some travellers may not object to this. Indeed, the aspiring Offa's Dyke walker who has just completed the South West Coast Path or the Pembrokeshire Coast Path, on being told that this next walking assignment involved further cliff-edge marching, might well feel like the theatre-goer who, having staggered back to his car after an interminable performance of one of the lengthier operas in Wagner's *Ring* cycle, switches on his car radio to be greeted with the announcement that the next musical offering will be an uninterrupted transmission of *Madame Butterfly* in Italian.

Sedbury to Bigsweir

The start of the walk is at Sedbury Cliffs, on the English side of the border. If you have arrived at Chepstow by public transport, the easiest and pleasantest way to get to the start is actually to cross the river from the town centre, join the national trail and simply follow it backwards to the beginning! It is worth pausing upon reaching the start, marked by an inscribed stone, so you may enjoy the fine views down and across the Severn estuary; this is the widest stretch of water you will see until you reach Prestatyn nearly 180 miles away. Nearby is the magnificent Severn Bridge, opened in 1966, with its enormous centre span of 3,240ft. This is the older of the two Severn crossings. Then you turn your back on the Severn and head back towards Chepstow, proceeding slightly north of west alongside a fragment of the Dyke. It is good to see it making an appearance at once, as if reminding you of the over-riding theme and purpose of the journey.

You cross B4228 Beachley–Sedbury road, and the route continues in broadly the same direction, descending through a field to reach a housing estate which boasts an Offa's Close and Mercian Way. At length you reach the banks of the river Wye and swing right to follow a path high above the river and reach another area of housing, turning left briefly on to the B4228 and left again on to a path which meets the A48 (2). There is easy access from here across the Wye to Chepstow, a town full of interest with steep medieval streets, a sixteenth-century gatehouse, and an impressive castle begun by the Normans in 1067 and finished during the thirteenth century to defend a strategic bend in the Wye.

Beyond the A48, the route follows a mixture of paths and lanes running alongside the B4228, heading north-eastwards away from Chepstow. The highlight of this section is Wintour's Leap, a superb viewpoint on steep limestone cliffs high above the Wye. The route continues by the B4228, briefly proceeding to the east of it, before returning and at last leaving it for good at Dennel Hill, turning left to pass through the magnificent woodland on the eastern side of the Wye. The woodland opens out to give exquisite views to the Wye and in particular the remains of Tintern Abbey. The best viewpoint is at Devil's Pulpit, a small limestone outcrop from which it is said the Devil tried to corrupt the monks at Tintern.

It is possible hereabouts to pick up a path leading down to the ruins of the abbey which was founded in 1131 by Cistercians. It was a victim of the dissolution in 1536, although the abbey church with its rose window is almost intact. Having passed the Pulpit and swung eastwards, you leave the woods, swing sharply to the west and go downhill to reach Brockweir. You may either choose to follow alongside the Wye to Bigsweir Bridge (11.5), or take a shorter but tougher route across St Briavels Common, with the Dyke clearly visible in places. This route starts with a brief walk along a metalled road heading north-eastwards, then follows a long woodland climb on a stony track, the reward being a sensational view back to the Severn Bridge and beyond. Flatter walking ensues, then a massive descent through woodland and an easy valley walk to Bigsweir.

The Wye valley is a naturalist's paradise; the waters attract kingfishers, dippers and herons, while in the woodland areas – themselves a happy mixture of lime, oak, ash and beech – the observer may spot buzzards, woodpeckers, sparrowhawks and tawny owls. The Wye round Bigsweir is particularly noted for its glasswort, and the woodland walker in spring should look out for wood anemone, wood sorrel, dog's mercury and violets. Incidentally, this is the only section on the national trail of any length where a choice of route exists. Having done and greatly enjoyed both, I think I would commend the longer but flatter valley route to the comparatively inexperienced walker who is getting acclimatised to the demands of a long-distance walk, as I was when I first walked the route. It did not help, of course, that my Chepstow hotel cooked breakfast had been limited to a flabby fried egg and two sad sausages.

Bigsweir to Monmouth

At Bigsweir Bridge the route turns right on to the A466 but then bears almost immediately right again on to a metalled road and shortly left on to a path, climbing steeply through woodland and then following the right fringe of the woods past Coxbury Farm. It is tough going but soon comes the reward in the form of a lovely walk through Highbury Wood, high above the Wye on the stony ridge of the Dyke. Progress northwards is easy and fast, and it is a shame to drop down to Lower Redbrook (15) and bid farewell to the Dyke, which will not be seen again for well over 50 miles. The village does offer refreshments, and when I visited I had the choice between the unusually named Fish and Game pub, or the Little Chef.

The route turns right to follow the A466 briefly, then soon turns right again, joining the B4231 Newland road (entering Wales at this point) and climbing steeply. Shortly the route bears left on to a farm track and proceeds north-westwards, still climbing initially through open fields and then through woodland to reach the Kymin. At 800ft, this is a wonderful viewpoint; immediately below is Monmouth, but well beyond the town in the distance you will observe the very distinctive hill known as Skirrid Fawr, which will often be seen for the next 20 miles or so. Close by the viewpoint is the Naval Temple, built in 1800 to commemorate a number of late eighteenth-century admirals. There is then a steep descent to Monmouth, initially along a path that, heading north-west, drops into further woodland, keeping the metalled access road to the left. The route swings round to join the road briefly before bearing left again along a path that leads to the A4136, which you then follow to the left to cross the Wye and arrive in the town (18.5).

Monmouth contains many Tudor and Georgian buildings, including several fine inns, and is a lovely place to spend some time. Among the many buildings of note are the Georgian Shire Hall, built in 1724, a museum devoted to Nelson, the ruins of an eleventh-century castle, the preserved seventeenth-century Great Castle House which became the headquarters of the Royal Monmouthshire Engineer Militia in 1875, and a two-storeyed gatehouse that was built in 1260 as one of four medieval gates into the town. The gatehouse is built on Monmow Bridge, the only Norman fortified bridge that survives in Great Britain; the river Monmow, over which the bridge passes, flows into the Wye just south of the town. The town also boasts statues of Henry V, who was born in the castle, and Charles Rolls, of Rolls Royce fame.

Despite this wealth of treasures, it is clear that some walkers passing through it will continue to keep more basic concerns at the forefront of their minds. One Offa's Dyke Path traveller, when invited to pass comments about Monmouth for an Offa's Dyke Association newsletter, simply wrote, 'The better of the two fish and chip shops shuts at 9 p.m.'!

Monmouth to Pandy

By contrast with what has gone before and what awaits later, the next section of the walk, from Monmouth to Pandy, is a gentle journey through peaceful rolling countryside. Whilst it is very pleasant, it could not be described as spectacular, although the 1,596ft summit of Skirrid Fawr, becoming increasingly prominent as the walk continues, is a constant feature of the landscape. Having proceeded south-westwards down the main street of Monmouth, the route turns right on to the B4233 Abergavenny road, and shortly left on to the metalled Watery Lane. As the road bends sharply left – shortly before terminating at Bailey Pitt Farm – you turn right on to a path that soon enters King's Wood, climbs quite steeply, and heads just south of west, picking up a track that descends gently to a metalled road just east of Hendre Farm. You turn right on to the road, then just beyond the farm buildings turn left to follow a path through fields heading north-westwards, keeping the river Trothy – another tributary of the Wye – on your left. Close by is the site of the now obliterated thirteenth-century Cistercian Grace Dieu abbey.

On reaching a road you turn left on to it and immediately cross the Trothy, then soon turn right on to a path which continues through rolling pastures, with the Trothy now to your right. The path swings from north-westwards to just south of westwards, and stays very close to the water to reach a hamlet which rejoices in the splendid name of Llanvihangel-Ystern-Llewern. The little church is dedicated to St Michael of the Fiery Meteor, which conjures up images of fire-and-brimstone rhetoric traditionally beloved of Welsh non-conformist chapel preachers, although its setting could hardly be more peaceful or idyllic. You cross a metalled road here and go south-westwards on a path through fields, in due course reaching another road, turning left on to it and following it steeply downhill. Then you bear right and head north-westwards, passing directly in front of an imposing house called The Grange and crossing an area of orchard before reaching another road, turning right on to it and following it to Llantilio Crossenny (27.5).

This is near enough the halfway mark between Monmouth and Pandy, and offers a perfect incentive to rest weary limbs, in the form of the Hostry Inn, which has a reputation for excellent beer. There has been an inn here since the fifteenth century. When I walked here from Monmouth, alone, I recall meeting another lone walker near Hendre Farm and, assuming he was happy to have a bit of temporary company, I joined him for a little while. As we walked, I sensed that he would have preferred to stay on his own, and we duly continued at our own paces.

It is of course difficult for walkers, when they meet with a solitary hiker travelling their way, to know whether this trekker is walking alone by choice or whether he would in fact like some company. The lone traveller will not be best pleased if, having been on the point of discovering his true place amidst the natural and spiritual order of the universe, his train of thought is derailed by a succession of conversational banalities introduced by his new companions on any subjects from fierce farmers to broken bootlaces, while the walker or walkers who have cajoled him into joining them will not exactly be overjoyed when they find their new acquaintance has all the carefree ebullience of a Moscow bus inspector on a freezing February Monday morning.

From Llantilio Crossenny, the route strikes out marginally north of westwards through open country to the little settlement of Treadam, then turns right to follow a track northwards to White Castle, the highlight of the Monmouth–Pandy section. It was one of three border castles built as a defensive triangle to guard the border land against Welsh raids, and although the round-towered stronghold of White Castle is now a ruin, it is nonetheless a most impressive one. The route then heads north-westwards again through very pleasant open farmland to reach the B4521 at the intriguingly-named hamlet of Caggle Street, turning right on to the road. Just past the little village chapel you turn left and continue north-westwards, initially along a path and then a metalled lane, through Old Court, then beyond this hamlet you turn right up a path leading to the hilltop village of Llangattock Lingoed. The Hunters Moon Inn, which was built in the seventeenth century, has changed little since, and there is also a pretty church which dates back to the thirteenth century. The route leaves the village on a path heading north-westwards through open country and, soon after leaving the village, there is a delightful narrow wooded valley or dingle to negotiate. Having lost some height from Llangattock Lingoed, a steep climb is required to bring you within sight of Pandy.

Continuing north-westwards, you reach a metalled road immediately north-east of the hamlet of Great Park and join a footpath just the other side, leading you to a lane which shortly reaches another metalled road. There follows a descent north-westwards along a path, keeping the little village of Wern-Gifford on your left, to the village of Pandy (35) on the busy A465 Abergavenny–Hereford road in the valley of the river Honddu. If you have spent the day hiking here from Monmouth, this descent represents a fine climax to the day's march; it is an easy and not excessively steep downward incline through fields, with the giant Skirrid Fawr towering to the left and the Black Mountains directly ahead. Pandy offers a good range of amenities, as does the neighbouring village with the splendid name of Llanvihangel

Crucorney, which boasts an Elizabethan manor house and fine gardens.

It is at Pandy that you will wish to pay particular attention to the weather forecast for the next day, for immediately ahead lies the assault on the Black Mountains, a much tougher proposition than anything encountered so far. I had the good fortune to arrive at Pandy during a spell of settled summer weather, so was able to spend a relaxing night here without worrying about what next day would bring; my contented evening stroll was enlivened by a football match that was in progress on the village playing field. With the peak of Skirrid Fawr gazing benignly down on the Honddu valley and across to the Black Mountains, the setting was bewitching indeed and an obvious distraction to away players who, mesmerised by its beauty, could be forgiven for losing concentration in defence and gifting the home side a few soft goals.

Pandy to Hay on Wye

An early start and a good breakfast are essential for walkers aiming to reach Hay on Wye from Pandy in one day, for there is no refreshment or proper shelter of any kind until you get to within a mile of Hay. The start is deceptively innocuous. You take a path heading westwards away from the A465 at the south end of Pandy, crossing the river Honddu and the Abergavenny–Hereford railway almost immediately, and reaching a narrow metalled road. You follow this westwards through the hamlet of Treveddw then cut off a sharp corner in the road, rejoining it further on and following it to a crossroads, turning right. Having climbed quite steeply, you promptly descend again, before branching off left on to a path just before the hamlet of Tre-wyn. By this time you may feel a little like a taxi-ing aircraft waiting for its take-off slot. However, having joined this path, you begin the ascent to Hatterrall Hill, and the crest of a magnificent mountain ridge which you will follow all the way to Hay Bluff and beyond.

It is a stiff climb, and also a long one. Do not be deceived by a trig. point at just over 1,500ft; it is only on Hatterrall Hill at 1,740ft that the crest is properly gained and the gradient eases, but in fact you will continue to gain height gradually; the highest point of the ridge being some 2,300ft about a mile and a half from its northern end. In fine clear weather, this ridge walk, lasting some ten miles, is one of the most thrilling walks you will ever accomplish. With only sheep and Welsh moorland ponies for company, you pass through totally unspoilt heather moorland, dotted with bilberry and crowberry; to your left you gaze across the formidable Black Mountains range, and to your right across a massive area of beautiful border countryside.

Between your ridge and the higher peaks of the Black Mountains lies the enchanting Vale of Ewyas. It is possible to drop down to this valley not far beyond Hatterrall Hill – although it will be a tough climb back up again – to visit the village of Llanthony with its twelfth-century Augustinian priory, while further up the valley at Capel-y-ffin, easily reached by road, there are the remains of the more recent Benedictine abbey of St Anthony. You could stay on the metalled road from there all the way to Hay if you did not fancy trying to find your way back up to the ridge again.

If the weather is bad, you may in fact have second thoughts about tackling the ridge at all; the ground is liable to turn into an instant quagmire, and the terrain is so exposed and so prone to low cloud and mist that without proper equipment you could be in some danger. If you decide against it, it is simple enough to follow the A465 south-westwards to Llanvihangel Crucorney where you will pick up the road that runs to Hay via Llanthony and Capel-y-ffin.

Walking the ridge in fine settled weather, I met another Offa's Dyke walker who carried nothing but a stick, flask and guidebook and informed me his wife was carrying his equipment by car. She had met some other walkers whose kit up until then had been carried by taxi, and she was now ferrying their luggage as well, which consisted of bulky suitcases and holdalls. It would have been intriguing to follow their progress if motorised transport for their baggage had been unavailable at some time during their walk!

It is of course something of a risk to entrust one's equipment to the local taxi service when walking a national trail. While one hopes that there are not too many drivers who would stoop to helping themselves to the contents of the bags or rucksacks assigned to them, one can never be entirely easy in one's mind that the driver will locate the exact accommodation at which he has been asked to leave the luggage in question. Few things will be more disconcerting for the exhausted walker than to arrive at Oaklands Cottage in Church Road where he has booked for the night only to find, six telephone calls later, that his bags have been deposited at Oaklands House in Church Lane which he passed some seventy-five minutes ago.

You continue along the top of the ridge, gradually gaining height, following not only the eastern edge of the Brecon Beacons National Park, but also the border between England and Wales. A triangulation point is situated at the spot where the ridge reaches 2,000ft, but you continue to climb to 2,306ft, the highest point on the whole of the national trail. To the right, as you proceed, is a parallel ridge and the 2,100ft summit of Black Hill, while to the left is the 2,260ft summit of the Twmpa, separated from your ridge by the Gospel Pass which is followed by the metalled road between Capel-y-ffin and Hay. It is a justifiably popular motor route but the ridge walk is a thousand times better.

Having passed the ridge summit, and descended sharply by about 100ft, you then have a choice. You may either veer slightly left along a path which soon arrives at the trig. point of Hay Bluff (48.5) and continues to a road which you then follow to the right. Alternatively, you may pass round Hay Bluff, leaving it to your left and following a path that arrives a little further down the road. The former course is to be recommended, since Hay Bluff is a wonderful viewpoint and a place to linger on a clear day. After following the ridge for so many miles, you suddenly see it falling away in front of you and are treated to a breathtaking panorama across the lovely Radnor countryside, with fine views to Black Hill and the Twmpa.

Sadly, beyond Hay Bluff you must begin your descent. The early part of it is spectacular; you drop 600ft in half a mile, although the steepness is mitigated for walkers by a carefully constructed path which, for erosion prevention, should be followed rather than cut round. In due course you reach the road, where you will see a prehistoric stone circle over the road as you reach it, and possibly, as I did, a rather less than prehistoric ice cream van.

You turn right on to the road, the path of the alternative route meeting the road a little further along. As the road bends slightly right, you leave it by bearing left on to a field path heading slightly west of north, and this general direction is maintained all the rest of the way to Hay. The path skirts the western edge of Tack Wood, briefly joining a track at Cadwgan Farm before heading out into open fields again, with Hay on Wye now directly ahead of you. You drop down steeply to arrive at a metalled road, bearing left on to it, then turn right to enjoy a very pleasant pastoral walk into the town (53), with the beautiful waters of Cusop Dingle to your right. Once a border fortress – the town is built right on the border, and boasts Norman castle ruins and thirteenth-century town walls – it is now one of the loveliest old towns in Britain, combining bygone charm with an impressive range of amenities and an abundance of fine shops and restaurants.

It is known as a book town, for in 1961 one Richard Booth opened a huge second-hand bookshop here, many other bookshops have opened since, and a major book festival is held here every year. Bibliophiles can find books on every conceivable topic, from rolling stock on the Fenchurch Street–Southend line down the ages to inter-war Northern non-league football, and you can be sure that if there is insufficient room in your rucksack, traders will post your chosen book home for you. Even those without a literary bent may succumb to the array of reading matter on offer, and keen walkers wishing to round up the party next morning for the next stage of the hike should not be surprised to find at least one of their number sitting in a dusty corner of the children's bookshop flicking nostalgically through the pages of *Billy Bunter's Postal Order* or the 1972 *Beano* annual.

Hay on Wye to Hill Farm
It is with some reluctance that you will leave Hay, although if time is available it is worth detouring one mile up the B4351 to the pretty village of Clyro, where the famous diarist Francis Kilvert was curate from 1865 to 1872. Having left the town, the route follows the left bank of the Wye, heading just east of north, then heads slightly away from the river and proceeds north to cross the

A438. From here you get a fine view back to Hay and the Wye valley. You turn right to walk beside this busy road but soon turn left and head north-westwards on a path that goes along the edge of Bettws Dingle, a deep wooded valley with a waterfall. It is a lovely shady spot on a hot day, although there is an eerie feel about the lines of closely packed conifers. A substantial climb through the woods, still heading north-westwards, brings you to a minor road where you turn right.

The route follows the road to a T-junction, and turns right here, following the road until, shortly before Catworthy Court, the road bends to the right. You turn left here on to a path which meets another road at Cae-Higgin and then turn left again to follow this road briefly. Just before Cwm-yr-eithin the route turns right on to a farm lane that heads northwards. You gain further height here, but the reward, as you look back, is a superb view back to the Black Mountains, Hay Bluff and the Twmpa.

You cross another metalled road and head north-westwards towards Newchurch, soon passing the 1,167ft summit of Little Mountain to your left, which although modest compared with Hay Bluff, is still well over 800ft higher than the Wye valley that you forsook a few miles back. It is easy to detour to the summit, on which stands the site of a Roman camp. Beyond Little Mountain you drop very steeply towards the buildings of Gilfach-yr-heol. Just before them you bear right on to a lane and follow it to reach the pretty village of Newchurch in the valley of the river Arrow. When you reach the B4594 you turn right on to it and pass through the village. You then turn right again, this time on to a path heading north-eastwards and, climbing steeply again, continue on to Disgwylfa Hill, reaching 1,250ft. This is wonderful walking on springy grass with glorious views across miles of totally unspoilt countryside.

You begin to descend and drop down to a crossroads of paths where you turn left, soon reaching Hill Farm and, beyond that, a metalled road. Still maintaining a height of over 1,000ft, you turn right on to the road. At Hill Farm, at the time of my visit, there was a welcome water tap provided for walkers, and some amusing doggerel extolling the benefits of this free refreshment.

Like blisters, thirst is one of the great enemies of the long-distance walker, and opportunities to refill the water bottle, whether from a convenient drinking-water tap or mountain stream, should not be spurned lightly. Of course, many people with businesses or indeed homes close to the route will be only too pleased to replenish the liquid supplies of gasping hikers, though it takes an especially thick-skinned traveller to make the request at an off-licence or other shop that sells bottled waters, without actually making any purchases there. Those of a more timid disposition, or in a village with no shop, may be reduced to that most desperate of measures, the tap in the village public convenience, but may be disappointed there too, either because the sink is too small to fit the bottle beneath the tap, or because there is a new-style, vandal-proof handwash providing a flow of tepid fluid so feeble that by the time the bottle is full, you could either have hitched a lift to the nearest supermarket and back, or dug your own well on the village green.

Hill Farm to Burfa

Having turned right on to the road beyond Hill Farm, you shortly turn left along a path that heads northwards to a metalled road a little way east of Hengoed, then having crossed the road you proceed on a path heading north-eastwards past Stonehouse Barn and a disused quarry. You drop very steeply to reach a metalled road, and turn left on to this road, following it to the village of Gladestry (63). You then turn right on to the B4594 to pass through the village, in which the Royal Oak pub offers the first on-path refreshments since Hay. Even though the town of Kington is only a few miles away, it is worth stopping at Gladestry, as in order to reach Kington you must tackle Hergest Ridge which means another substantial climb, this time up to almost 1,400ft.

Having proceeded through the village on the B4594, you turn right on to the Huntington road and shortly left on to an excellent path which, heading north-eastwards, ascends on to the bracken-clad ridge. Although perhaps lacking the grandeur of the ridge between Hatterrall Hill and Hay Bluff, this is marvellous open walking. The ridge, where once a racecourse stood, is blessed with a lovely grass surface, making progress very easy, and there are tremendous views in all directions, stretching up to 30 miles on a clear day.

Having proceeded north-eastwards to gain the top of the ridge, you then swing eastwards to make the descent. With some reluctance (unless the weather is bad) you drop down off the ridge to meet an area of forest to your left, and at the edge of the forest you join a metalled road which you follow eastwards to arrive in Kington (67.5), on the English side of the border. To your right, as you follow this road, are Hergest Croft Gardens which have a fine variety of trees and shrubs and in summer provide a rainbow display of azaleas and rhododendrons.

Kington is a small market town on the banks of the river Arrow, which you last saw at Newchurch. There has been a settlement here since Norman times but virtually nothing here remains from that era. However, the town does boast a large thirteenth-century church and late Victorian clock tower, but arguably the most charming corner is a row of well-kept whitewashed stone cottages looking out on to Back Brook, a tributary of the river Arrow. You will see these cottages on your way out of the town. Though the town certainly lacks the interest of Monmouth or the charisma of Hay, it is a hospitable place, with plenty of shops and ample facilities for eating, drinking and sleeping. My bed and breakfast host not only offered me delicious warm home-made bread but also, as I arrived on a scorching August afternoon, a dip in his paddling pool that he had filled for his three small children.

To exit from Kington it is necessary, having passed Back Brook, to cross the busy A44 that bypasses the town to the north, and head north-westwards to Bradnor Green, initially on a lane and then a path which climbs very steeply. Having passed Bradnor Green you cross what is the highest golf course in England at well over 1,000ft, and though care is needed as you cross the fairways, the views are once more astonishing. The route, still heading north-westwards, stays well to the east of the nearby 1,282ft summit of Bradnor Hill, then swings north-eastwards to climb on to Rushock Hill. This is quite demanding but exhilarating walking. It is on Rushock Hill that you are reunited with the Dyke for the first time since Lower Redbrook, and for much of the next 70 miles you will be walking either along or beside it.

You turn left to follow the Dyke, briefly heading westwards and passing a trio of eighteenth-century yews named the Three Shepherds. Soon you reach the 1,230ft summit of Rushock Hill, providing views that stretch back to the Black Mountains, before beginning a big descent, passing to the left of the picturesquely-named Knill Garraway Wood. You then turn right, heading northwards, keeping to your left the summit of Herrock Hill, which is just a few feet lower than Rushock Hill. Now you descend rapidly, swinging westwards again just beyond Herrock Cottage and following a lane through a small patch of woodland to reach the B4362 at Lower Harpton, where you return to Wales.

You turn right and follow this road for a few hundred yards as far as the ancient Ditchyeld Bridge which crosses the Hindwell Brook, although motor travellers use a more modern bridge beside it. A signpost here points the way to such delightfully-named places as Evenjobb and Presteigne. The national trail turns left on to the road signposted for Evenjobb, but soon leaves it, turning right on to a path that skirts the western edge of a large area of woodland. Having 'lost' the Dyke shortly before Lower Harpton, you are now reunited with it, and begin one of the finest sections of Dyke-side walking on the route.

As you swing to the left to head decisively north-westwards on to Evenjobb Hill, you pass a settlement known as Burfa, while in the woods to your right is an Iron Age fort known as Burfa Bank. At Burfa the route passes a magnificently restored timber-framed house, which was the home shared by the late Kathy and Ernie Kay, pillars of the Offa's Dyke Association. The name of the house, parts of which date back 600 years, is Old Burfa, which is certainly one of the quainter names you will have encountered on the route, and may indeed sound to the less discerning follower of popular culture like the name that might be ascribed by Sid James to a dilapidated touring vehicle in one of the *Carry On* movies.

Burfa to Knighton

Beyond Burfa it is quite delightful walking on to Evenjobb Hill. You cross a metalled road just east of the village of Evenjobb then proceed through Granner Wood, heading north-eastwards. You swing north-westwards, emerging from Granner Wood and climbing in open country towards another area of woodland called the Hilltop Plantation, just to the east of the farm at Pen Offa. You pass a summit of 1,218ft within the plantation, then, still heading north-westwards, drop down into open country to meet a metalled road. Crossing it, you turn north-eastwards and head in a virtually straight line quite steeply downhill towards the Lugg valley. The Dyke is clearly visible for much of the journey from Burfa to the Lugg valley, and makes a splendid spectacle, while views to the west are quite magnificent.

As you continue northwards towards Knighton and beyond, you may find the route following the top of the bank, but often the bank is so thickly laden with trees and other vegetation that progress along the top of it is not feasible and the path proceeds beside it instead. At the bottom of the hill you reach another metalled road which you cross, heading north-eastwards over pleasant meadows to cross the river Lugg and climb gently to arrive at the B4356 at Dolley Green. Three miles or so to the east, along the road, is Presteigne, an attractive town with several black and white timbered cottages and Georgian houses; no fewer than 30 of its present buildings were once inns!

Having turned right on to the B4356 at Dolley Green (75.5), the route almost immediately turns hard left, and begins to climb again. It proceeds initially north-westwards along a lane before turning north-eastwards and ascending steadily on to Furrow Hill, picking up a track briefly before turning sharp right and shortly left to follow the Dyke over Hawthorn Hill. At 1,300ft this is the highest ground since Hergest Ridge, with excellent views all around; Presteigne can clearly be seen to the south-east, and on a clear day it is possible to see back as far as the Black Mountains.

Still maintaining a height of well over 1,000ft, the route turns slightly west of north to cross the B4355 Norton road and shortly afterwards turns right on to it. Soon you reach a junction with the

B4357, and you turn left on to this road, reaching the hamlet of Rhos-y-meirch and bearing right on to a narrow minor road then immediately right on to a path which proceeds slightly east of north, following the Dyke to Knighton. You pass just to the west of the prettily-named hamlet of Jenkin Allis, and the 1,066ft summit of Ffrydd, then drop very steeply, passing the edge of a golf course (walkers who have spent the day coming from Kington will remember *starting* the day crossing a golf course) and then through a small section of Great Ffrydd Wood. At the bottom of the hill the B4355 is crossed, and it is then a short walk to the main street of Knighton (81).

Known in Welsh as Tref-y-Clawdd or the Town on the Dyke, because stretches of the Dyke can be seen around the town, it boasts a number of seventeenth-century houses round a marketplace, another prominent Victorian clock tower, a little railway station on the Swansea–Shrewsbury line, and plenty of shops and accommodation. It is often trumpeted as the halfway mark on the national trail, but it is still some eight miles short of halfway.

Of particular interest to the walker in the town is Offa's Dyke Park, containing the stone that commemorates the opening of the national trail here in 1971, and the Offa's Dyke Information Centre. The centre contains a formidable array of literature about the route and the Dyke, and is the headquarters of the Offa's Dyke Association, which does tremendous work in promoting and maintaining the route. The Association will also issue badges for those who can verify they have walked the route from end to end, while its newsletters, available at the Centre and in many other places on the path, contain fascinating stories of individual endeavour and ingenuity in completing the walk. Indeed the enterprising fundraiser should carefully peruse them before satisfying himself and his sponsors that he really *is* the first person to be travelling from Sedbury to Prestatyn backwards by pogo stick with a rucksack containing nothing but two lumps of concrete.

Knighton to Churchtown

The next section, from Knighton to Brompton Hall, is the toughest of the whole route, but it is also very rewarding. Several splendid stretches of the Dyke are still in evidence and the border countryside is absolutely delightful, with tremendously varied plant life and wildlife. Walkers should keep an eye out not only for foxes and rabbits but also weasels and polecats, while the spring brings plentiful amounts of primroses and early-purple orchids. At Knighton you cross back into Shropshire, and much of this section will be on the English side of the border.

The start is deceptively easy, as the route drops to the river Teme which skirts the northern fringes of the town, then turns left to follow the south bank of the Teme north-westwards on a path, and crosses the railway and river. Almost immediately beyond the river you go over a metalled road, then climb very steeply on to Panpunton Hill. Initially you head north-eastwards, then on Panpunton Hill turn north-westwards – this will be your direction of travel as far as Llanfair Hill – and embark on a splendid high level promenade, following the Dyke as you go. From Panpunton Hill you continue on to Cwm-sanaham Hill, with views across the Teme valley to the site of Knucklas Castle, an Iron Age fort.

There follows a precipitous descent to a metalled road at Selley Hall, then after crossing the road you regain the lost height quickly and proceed past Garbett Hall, where a water tap should be available, on to Llanfair Hill, now rising to 1,400ft. You are able to walk along the bank of the Dyke here, and there is a real feeling of being on top of the world, with fantastic views across miles of lovely countryside. You reach a metalled road, turning right on to it and now heading slightly east of north. The road arrives at a crossroads where you turn right again, then almost immediately left to leave the tarmac and embark on another big descent to Lower Spoad, this time walking parallel to the Dyke. At Lower Spoad you reach the B4368, and by turning right on to this road you can detour roughly four miles to Clun.

There has been a settlement here since the Bronze Age, making it one of the most ancient in the country; the little town contains a fine Norman castle ruin, many houses dating from the seventeenth century, and a late eighteenth-century town hall. Even today, it remains a peaceful little place in beautiful surroundings. The poet A. E. Housman immortalised Clun and its neighbour villages in his poem *A Shropshire Lad*, writing that 'Clunton and Clunbury, Clungunford and Clun, are the quietest places under the sun.' Locals claim that this rhyme is older than his poem and that in earlier versions the adjective 'quietest' was varied to 'prettiest,' 'wickedest' or 'drunkenest'!

There is brief respite for the walker as the national trail, having crossed the B4368, proceeds across the meadows adjoining the river Clun, and over the river itself. Having crossed the river, beside which is the beautiful half-timbered farmhouse of Bryndrinog, you rise and shortly reach another metalled road, just east of the village of Newcastle, which contains a useful pub. I reckon this road crossing to be the halfway point of the national trail (89). Then, after going straight over the Newcastle road and refreshing yourself from another route-side tap, you head north-eastwards on to Graig Hill.

This is an ascent of almost inhuman severity. The Dyke, bedecked with larches, climbs with you, and droll walkers may crack that this section of the Dyke must have been planned by King Offa on one of his 'off-a' days! There follows a rather easier descent, the route coming down to cross three lanes in close succession just west of Mardu near the hamlet of Upper Mount where there is also an attractive pond. Swinging north-westwards, you proceed up a little valley through a small patch of woodland, then turn north-eastwards and climb steeply up to another metalled road at Hergan. Crossing the road brings no respite; you continue to climb as you head northwards to Middle Knuck, temporarily sharing your route with that of the Shropshire Way which has come up from Clun.

Beyond Middle Knuck the climbing temporarily ceases, and after crossing a metalled road you descend steeply through woodland, heading slightly east of north, towards the delectable hamlet of Churchtown (92). As you approach the hamlet, the woods suddenly clear to give you the prospect of an open downward incline, dotted with trees and given added summer colour by patches of rosebay. Snugly nestling in the valley with a hill rising steeply behind is the church of St John, and you drop down to meet it. It is a lovely place to stop and take stock before embarking on the next climb, although despite its suffix 'town' the hamlet boasts no amenities whatsoever. However, its somewhat inappropriate name may set you thinking about other place names on the route and their aptness. Is there a new castle in Newcastle, do they make hay in Hay, or are dollies found on Dolley Green?

From this come all sorts of possibilities which might well find favour with the Offa's Dyke Association newsletter editor, or fellow walkers along one of the less mesmeric stretches of the route. In fact, the insomniac Offa's Dyke walker might do worse than use the sleepless night hours to devise a quiz based on place names on or along the route, inviting the reader to think where along the route to find a world class snooker player (Hendre), an English Second World War hero (Montgomery), a town that rhymes with a famous children's author (Knighton), a village famous for its brown ale (Newcastle), or a village that goes with Andy to produce a much-loved children's programme?

Churchtown to Four Crosses

Having crossed straight over the metalled road by the church, you head just west of north and tackle perhaps the most gruelling ascent of all as you climb on to Edenhope Hill, which some say offers the best view on the entire walk. In winter the path gets very muddy, and in the summer it is crumbly and stony; when the latter conditions prevail, as they did when I walked it, you should be careful where to put your feet for fear of inadvertently creating a miniature landslide as I managed to do. Reaching a metalled road, you cross it and descend quite steeply to the river Unk, then ascend again through Nut Wood, heading north-westwards. This is the last big climb for a good few miles. You emerge from Nut Wood into fine open countryside, passing another pond, and for a while you pass along the ditch of the Dyke. You soon cross a lane that carries the Kerry Ridgeway, and by detouring right on to this lane you can reach Bishop's Castle, which contains some fine Tudor buildings and an eighteenth-century town hall. However it is four miles away and you may wish to press on to Montgomery, especially as no more climbing is needed to get there.

Having crossed the lane, back now in Wales, you descend, slightly east of north, enjoying really lovely views to the Vale of Montgomery, with Corndon Hill dominating the scene to the north-east. You reach a metalled road, turn left on to it and pass through Cwm, then continue north-westwards, follow the road to a sharp right hand bend and continue straight on along a path that continues in the same direction through Mellington Wood, with Mellington Hall to your right. In due course you reach a driveway, turn left on to it, and almost immediately come to the B4385 Montgomery–Bishop's Castle road.

Continuing in the same direction, you turn left on to this road and having crossed the Caebitra river, returning to England, you arrive at a crossroads with the A489 Newtown–Church Stoke road. There is a most welcome pub here, named the Blue Bell Inn (96). The hard graft is temporarily over, and immediately ahead of you is some easy, level walking through fields and woodland. Having crossed the A489, you straight away turn right on to a path which immediately passes Brompton Hall then follows an almost straight line north-westwards for the final three miles to the Montgomery road. The path faithfully follows not only the course of the Dyke, clearly visible through this section, but also the English/Welsh border. As you near the B4386, the next road crossing, you get a lovely view to Montgomery, and indeed having arrived at the road (99), you have only a 1-mile detour to the left to reach it.

Montgomery is a beautiful little town, with a church dating from the sixteenth century, a Georgian square, some attractive half-timbered houses, and the hilltop ruins of a thirteenth-century castle, although an earlier castle was built here by Roger de Montgomery in 1072. There are majestic views across the Vale of Montgomery from beside the ruins of the later construction.

After my long, hot walk from Knighton I felt I deserved a cream tea and found myself presented with a huge plate of barely digestible teacakes and scones, the crumbly texture of which invited comparison with the soil on the climb up from Churchtown. Having staggered out of the tearoom I met up with my bed and breakfast hostess who was running a market stall in the town hall. On being informed by her that her husband would be round soon with the car to get home, and thus inferring transport was to be offered to me, I patiently waited until the aforesaid vehicle arrived. I watched it being meticulously loaded with unsold produce and folding tables, until the horrid realisation dawned that there was to be no room in the car for me. Defeated, I had to trudge off to the guest house unaided, feeling not a little foolish.

The next section of the route begins as easily as the previous one finished, since, having crossed the B4386, it continues along the flat in a north-westerly direction. You ford the river Camlad, returning to Wales, and then cross over a metalled road before swinging slightly east of north to walk alongside the B4388 just east of the village of Forden. You cross the A490 Welshpool road, and strike out north-eastwards on a path that proceeds through Kingswood and arrives at a narrow lane. Joining this and continuing north-eastwards, you embark on an upland area known as the Long Mountain, and although this sounds formidable, the going is not especially difficult. You climb very steeply then turn left into a forest, following the route carefully, as it is is essential not to lose your way amongst the numerous tracks in the trees.

Forest walking is not to everyone's taste, but there are breaks in the trees giving fine views north-westwards to Welshpool. There is also a lake called Offa's Pool which sounds historic and romantic, but it is simply part of the waterworks system of the Leighton Estate through which you are now travelling. As I walked through these woods I had a particularly clear view of a buzzard, and emerging from the wood I met a huge flock of pheasant congregating on the path.

If all goes well you arrive at a narrow metalled road at Pant-y-bwch, join a path the other side and head eastwards then north-eastwards to reach Beacon Ring, rising to well over 1,300ft, with a triangulation point and an Iron Age hill fort at the summit. This is another tremendous viewpoint, with splendid views to the Severn valley and the Shropshire hills, and you should make the most of it, for there will be no better view for the next 15 miles at least.

Continuing north-eastwards, the route skirts the eastern fringes of the Cwmdingle plantation, then turns north-westwards and drops down to the Severn valley at Buttington. The descent is not especially steep, but it is messy with numerous stiles and fields to be negotiated, and a couple of very brief stretches of lane walking. At length you reach the B4388 Montgomery road at Buttington (108.5) and are temporarily reunited with the Dyke, which you lost in the forest, but of which beyond Buttington you will see little for some 12 miles. However, I was consoled by the presence, at Buttington, of the Offa's Dyke Business Park. Sadly there was insufficient time to explore the park for signs of an Offa's Dyke Carpet Warehouse, Offa's Dyke Bankrupt Electrical Wonderland or even a discount store named Offa's Offers.

Having turned right on to the B4388, you soon turn off to the left to cross the the Shrewsbury–Aberystwyth railway line and reach the A458 Shrewsbury–Dolgellau trunk road. Turning left on to it, you immediately cross the river Severn, which of course you last saw at Sedbury back at the start of your walk. The route then turns right on to a path, but by continuing along the A458 you will reach Welshpool in just under a mile. Welshpool, which has a useful rail link to Shrewsbury, is an attractive market town with some fine Georgian buildings, although its finest feature is Powis Castle, dating back to the late thirteenth century, and containing quite exceptional gardens.

Returning to the national trail, the path from the A458 heads north-eastwards across meadows to the ghastly A483, a trunk road that links the north and south Wales coasts, which you follow briefly to the right before turning left to walk beside the Shropshire Union Canal. This is a lovely towpath walk alongside what is a significant environmental success story. Built in the late eighteenth century during a canal boom, it fell into disuse with the advent of the railways to the area, but has now been restored for the benefit of walkers, wildlife enthusiasts and barge travellers. In many ways it is a shame not to be able to follow the towpath all the way to Four Crosses (where the national trail does pick it up again) but presumably in deference to the course of the Dyke, the route leaves it at Pool Quay.

Crossing the A483 and still heading north-east, you instead embark on a walk along an embankment on the west side of the Severn, which is part of the Severn flood defence system. It is pleasant but hardly breathtaking stuff; the highlights, for want of a better expression, are the three Criggion radio masts and the sight of the Breiddens across the river, a range of heavily quarried hills rising to 1,200ft. Near Trederwen the route leaves the riverside, turning hard left then right to proceed briefly through intensely farmed countryside, temporarily rejoining the Dyke. You cross the B4393 and shortly afterwards arrive at Four Crosses where, having crossed another B road (an arm of the B4393) you are forced to renew your acquaintance with the A483, following it through the village.

Four Crosses to Oswestry
When the route was opened the A483 was followed for the next mile and a half to Llanymynech, but now the path turns left just beyond Four Crosses on to a metalled road, and then right to pick up the towpath beside the canal again. You follow this north-eastwards on its east bank, until the B4398 comes in to meet it, and it is a straightforward road walk to Llanymynech (119). The towpath section is lovely; there are sturdy brick bridges, lovingly restored locks and mile posts, pleasant views and no traffic noise, but the undoubted highlight is the aqueduct over the river Vyrnwy. Llanymynech has a wide variety of eating places – the one I chose came complete with soap opera repeats on a big-screen TV – but there is little of architectural interest in the village. Students of old railways may note that this was the site of an important railway junction, with the Oswestry–Welshpool line meeting branch lines from Llanymynech to Shrewsbury and Llanfyllin. Indeed you will have crossed the course of the first of these lines just east of Pool Quay and again at Four Crosses, which incidentally is one of the defunct stations immortalised in the song *The Slow Train* written by Michael Flanders and Donald Swann.

There are of course certain dangers in letting old railway enthusiasts in the party loose in and around a place like Llanymynech, for fear that in their quest to see what remains of old lines they will unreasonably hold up the progress of the uncommitted. Of course, non-devotees may be happy to have an excuse to while away an hour or two in blissful idleness, leaving their more fanatical brethren to shin up or down vertical embankments, vault over barbed wire encrusted five-bar gates, and be chased through lengths of barely penetrable undergrowth by hungry Rottweilers.

At the crossroads in the village, which sits right on the English/Welsh border, you turn left on to the A483, then as the road bends right you turn left up a lane, and immediately right on to a path that climbs on to Llanymynech Hill. You head initially north-westwards then swing north-eastwards, briefly rejoining the Dyke as you round the edge of a golf course. Route-finding is a little fiddly, so follow the waymarks carefully. There are excellent views from the hillside, notwithstanding the fact that the elevation is nothing like as lofty as some of those encountered south of Montgomery. Llanymynech Hill has been mined for both copper and limestone; the hillsides show ample evidence of this, and as you swing north-westwards and drop very steeply, you cross the old Tanat valley mineral railway line. Having crossed the A495 you shortly turn left on to a lane that passes through Porth-y-waen, proceeding a little north of west, then at Cefn-y-blodwel you turn right on a path which leads towards Nantmawr (despite the Welsh sounding name, you are back in Shropshire). You soon turn right on to a metalled road to enter the village – a straggling collection of houses tightly packed into a little valley – then shortly bear left up a path that heads north-westwards through fields and woodland to the summit of Moelydd. Despite its comparatively modest height of 935ft, there are tremendous views to the Berwyn Mountains to the west and the Shropshire hills to the east.

Swinging north-eastwards, you descend again, using a lane to pass by Ty-canol, then when this lane reaches a metalled road, you cross straight over and proceed along a path to Trefonen, crossing a charming brook in the shade of some trees at a field edge. You join a road that proceeds along the south edge of Trefonen, but soon turn left and head just west of north along a path that skirts the east side of the village, soon rejoining the Dyke.

Continuing in the same direction, you rise then, having crossed the Croesau Bach–Oswestry road, drop very steeply by road to the Morda valley. This is a lovely spot, and there is the added bonus of a pub, formerly a mill, at this point. After what has been fiddly walking all the way from Forden, it is good, once you have climbed out of the valley, to enjoy a lovely stretch of path through Candy Wood and then across common land beside a disused racecourse to the B4580 road (128), heading initially just west of north, then just east of north. The views, through the gaps in the trees, are again delightful, and there is plenty of Dyke to see.

By detouring right on to the B4580, in two miles you will reach Oswestry, a picturesque market town, which although largely rebuilt in the nineteenth century, has a number of seventeenth-century houses including Llwyd Mansion. There is also a part-Norman church, an early fifteenth-century grammar school (since converted into cottages) and castle ruins within a public park. My bed and breakfast host was a 60-year-old widower, but far from having become a sad recluse, he led an incredibly active lifestyle. If he was not raising money for charity with cabaret acts, he was bopping the night away in Oswestry's hottest nightspots. Indeed he was preparing to go out for a night on the town as I returned from my takeaway evening meal, and I was not a little relieved that the aroma of his powerful aftershave completely nullified the less pleasing stench of fried food fumes that still lingered on my T-shirt.

Oswestry to Llandegla
Though the Dyke continues over Baker's Hill, the national trail north of the B4580 prefers to follow a road that proceeds round the east side of it. At Carreg-y-big, however, the route turns left off the road and there follows a really fine section of path walking, initially northwards and then just east of north, following both the Dyke and the English/Welsh border for roughly four miles. Only at Orseddwen is the route briefly diverted from the Dyke on to a nearby track, but it soon rejoins it and proceeds along the western edge of Selattyn Hill before descending to cross the B4579 at Craignant.

The route then climbs out of the valley, but before descending to the next major valley, that of the Ceiriog, there is a dramatic section at Nanteris involving a very steep wooded descent and climb almost immediately afterwards. This section has been less than affectionately described by walkers as the 'dirty dingle' although there is now a fine wooden stairway so progress is not quite so awkward now as it was. The descent to the Ceiriog is slow but rewarding, the route following the bank of the Dyke, and there are fine views ahead to the sandstone walls of Chirk Castle.

On arrival in the valley, you cross two roads in quick succession, and after crossing the second of these, the B4500 Chirk–Glyn Ceiriog road (133), you join a lane which climbs steeply out of the valley and heads north-westwards to Crogan Wladys. You then swing north-eastwards along alternate sections of footpath and metalled roads to drop to the A5 and the Vale of Llangollen. You are now back in Wales and will stay there for the rest of the journey.

This section, which provides good views to the countryside and communities in and around the Vale, skirts the western edge of the grounds of the fourteenth-century Chirk Castle, whose massive rectangular structure has unusually wide battlements, round towers at each corner and a fifth tower over the gateway. Inside the castle there is some fine sixteenth-century decorative work and some Stuart portraits which include Charles I and Charles II. The castle and grounds are open at certain times, and a permissive route is sometimes available which would allow you to follow a portion of the Dyke through the grounds. Though remnants of the Dyke are still in evidence north-east of here, this is the last bit of Dyke walking you will do on your journey.

You cross the A5 and follow a path to the A483, turning left on to it to cross the Llangollen branch of the Shropshire Union Canal, then turn immediately left again to follow the canal towpath on its north side. There is easy access across the canal to the amenities of Froncysyllte (137) if they are required. This is delightful walking, culminating in the magnificent Pont Cysyllte aqueduct. Designed and built by Thomas Telford and William Jessop between 1795 and 1805, it carries the canal across the river Dee, at a height of 120ft above it. The route continues alongside the canal over the aqueduct, the towpath side protected from the long drop to the Dee by railings, although vertigo sufferers can cross the Dee on a much lower bridge.

Immediately beyond the canal there is a pub; unsurprisingly this is very popular with canal users as well as walkers. Indeed the thirsty walker, laden with heavy rucksack and boots, who arrives at the pub after a tiring hike from Oswestry, may be somewhat peeved to be kept waiting at the bar behind the narrowboat traveller, shod in nothing heavier than deck shoes or flip-flops, and whose most strenuous outdoor activity that morning has consisted of hopping briefly ashore for the Sunday papers and fresh supplies of sunblock.

Just beyond the aqueduct, the towpath walk ends and the route bears left to pass through the little village of Trevor, soon reaching the A539. After briefly following that road to the left, the route turns right to head north-westwards into the Trevor Hall Woods, climbing steeply, and you should follow the signposts carefully amongst the packed conifers. Near the north-west tip of the woods, you reach a narrow metalled road. I was absolutely parched when I arrived here, and was mortified to see a signpost saying 'Cream teas half a mile' with the signpost pointing in the opposite direction!

Your way is to the left, north-westwards, along the road. Though seasoned walkers dislike tramping on tarmac, this particular march, along a rugged hillside, is a joy; to the left are fine views to the Vale of Llangollen, with the town of that name clearly visible further up the valley, and you can see the Berwyn Mountains rising up impressively behind. To the right, Trevor Rocks enhance the ruggedness of the scene, and soon to your left is the magnificent sight of Castell Dinas Bran, perched on a steep hillside and bypassed by the route. Once an Iron Age hill fort, a castle was built here in the thirteenth century for the princes of the Welsh kingdom of Powis, and although it is now a ruin, many of the walls and towers survive. It is certainly worth climbing it if you have the energy.

You continue along the road, looking down on Valle Crucis, a Cistercian abbey founded in 1189, and then at Rock Farm you turn right off the road on to a path to enjoy a tremendous walk along the western slopes of the limestone Eglwyseg Mountain, which at its highest rises over 1,640ft. The path follows a ledge cut into steeply-packed scree with the craggy upper slopes of Eglwyseg forming an impressive sight to the right, while to your left is an area of forest called the Foel Plantation, and ahead are views to the summit of Cyrn-y-Brain, around 1,850ft high. Swinging slightly north of east, you arrive in a secluded area of woodland and meet a road by an attractive stream; this lovely little oasis in such wild country is known as World's End (144.5).

You go northwards up the road through the woods, heading steeply uphill, and emerge on to open moorland, continuing slightly east of north, then as the road begins to bend more to the right, you turn left to follow a path across the heather moor. This is some of the highest ground covered on the path since leaving the Black Mountains behind, with an elevation of well over 1,500ft. Heading north-westwards, your path enters an area of thick woodland and descends. After wet weather this path can be extremely muddy, and even in a time of drought, when I walked it, it was very spongy, although boardwalks cover the worst sections. There is quite an eerie stillness about the woods, and even in bright sunshine the conifers produce dark shadows across the path.

At length you emerge at the hamlet of Hafod Bilston and having crossed a metalled road you proceed, still north-westwards, along a path through fields to reach the A525 Wrexham–Ruthin road. You cross it and follow a lane north-westwards, almost immediately crossing the A5104 Bala–Chester road, and continuing into Llandegla (148.5) which, like Pandy, is the prelude to a sustained section of remote high-level walking, and an obvious place for an overnight stop.

My bed and breakfast hosts were also in charge of the village shop, which explained their insistence that I breakfast between 7 and 8 a.m. (on a Sunday) and their rushing me through my meal at a speed which suggested long years of experience working at restaurants with special pre-theatre sittings.

Llandegla to Moel Fammau

Barely 30 miles separate you from journey's end, but you are now confronted by the formidable Clwydians, a range of heather-clad and, in parts, afforested hills of Silurian sandstone overlooking the Vale of Clwyd, some topped by Iron Age hill forts. Unlike the walk over the Black Mountains, where there was one big climb only, the traverse of the Clwydians involves numerous ascents and descents, making it an altogether tougher proposition. Leaving Llandegla, you proceed north-westwards on the floor of the valley of the river Alyn, through pleasant farmland. You turn westwards to cross the B5431 then soon afterwards begin to climb, following a path initially north-westwards then south-westwards to a metalled road at the splendidly-named settlement of Tyddyn-tlodion, and turn right to follow that road just west of north. Soon you reach a five-pronged junction of lanes and paths. Your route is more or less straight ahead, again just west of north, keeping an area of woodland to your right.

Now you begin your tramp over the Clwydians in earnest, passing over the hills of Moel y Plâs and Moel Llanfair, swinging briefly north-eastwards, then heading north-westwards again to negotiate Moel Gyw. As might be expected, there are two substantial uphill trudges but you are rewarded with splendid views. As you pass over Moel y Plâs, you can admire Llyn Gweryd lake in its delightful setting to the south-east, with woodland guarding its southern and western shores, while on your left you will look down to the Vale of Clwyd, a broad expanse of rolling countryside, which will remain in view throughout your traverse of the Clwydian range. On this southern section of the range there are especially good views to the town of Ruthin which boasts a ruined castle and fourteenth-century church. Beyond Moel Gyw there is a drop to the A494 (154.5) with road links to Mold and Ruthin; the roadside pub marked on some OS maps is now a motel, which may be a disappointment to some walkers, and stir up recriminations amongst members of the party who were misled into believing refreshments would be available. It is more than a little appropriate, therefore, to see that a few miles north-east from here on the A494 towards Mold is a place called Loggerheads.

The national trail turns right on to the A494 then shortly left on to a path heading north-eastwards through fields as it contours the next hill, Moel Eithinen. Then, as if tiring of these lower slopes, it bears left at a crossroads of paths and climbs steeply north-westwards to skirt the southern edge of Foel Fenlli, which boasts an Iron Age hill fort on its summit. The avoidance of the summit itself is for erosion prevention rather than a desire to give walkers an easier time!

Beyond Foel Fenlli the route swings north-eastwards, descending steeply to reach a narrow metalled road at Bwlch Penbarra. It is marvellous walking; the northern Clwydians form a splendid spectacle ahead, the Vale of Clwyd stretches out below, and at your feet lie acres of heather which form a blaze of colour in late summer. There is a car park at Bwlch Penbarra where refreshments are often available. However, at the time of my visit, I decided that officialdom was clearly frowning upon Offa's Dyke walkers being lured to such hedonistic diversions as ice cream vans, for the kissing gate that stood between the path and the van was too narrow for both my rucksack and myself to pass through!

Having crossed the road, you proceed initially north-westwards, then north-eastwards, climbing all the time, towards the climax of the walk along the Clwydians, namely Moel Fammau, or Mother Mountain, and the mother of all the Clwydians at 1,818ft. The climb is on a good wide path and the views are still excellent. At the summit of Moel Fammau (158.5) is the Jubilee Tower, built in 1810 to mark the golden jubilee of George III, and though it was never finished and fell into disrepair, some restoration work has been done. The views are incredible; not only should you enjoy the neighbouring Clwydians and your new friend the Vale of Clwyd, but the Wirral is clearly visible from here, and on good days it may be possible to make out Snowdonia and even Liverpool Cathedral. Bwlch Penbarra, the launching pad for day walks to Jubilee Tower, is just an hour's drive from Merseyside, and the walker on the slopes of Moel Fammau is likely to hear as many Scouse accents as Welsh ones, although it would be a brave hiker to openly confess hereabouts that he found one as impenetrable as the other.

Moel Fammau to Henfryn Hall

You drop down very steeply off Moel Fammau as you head north-westwards on to Moel Dywyll, then swing slightly east of north to skirt the summit of Moel Llys-y-coed. There is another dramatic plunge to a metalled road, heading north-westwards, and indeed that will be your direction of travel all the way to Bodfari, where most walkers who have started that morning from Llandegla will wish to call it a day. Crossing the metalled road you climb again, keeping the summit of Moel Arthur and its hill fort to your left, then drop down again to another metalled road and after crossing it you embark on your last significant climb this side of Bodfari to the summit and hill fort of Penycloddiau. A large coniferous forest has been cultivated on these slopes, and the route passes along the eastern fringes of it on the way up. The views back down the Clwydians are majestic – it is especially satisfying to identify the Jubilee Tower, which is now a mere speck in the distance – and you can also look down on the historic town of Denbigh in the Vale of Clwyd. You are spared the ascent of Moel y Parc, the last really spectacular hill in the range, which lies straight ahead, but instead the route chooses to bear left, just north of west, round the base of the hill.

There follows a long and anticlimactical descent on a path which swings in a more northerly direction to reach a metalled road near the Grove Hall. You turn left on to the road and follow it briefly, then as the road bends south-westwards, you continue westwards on a path which crosses the river Wheeler and reaches theA541 at Bodfari (166). You are now barely 100 feet above sea level. Refreshments are available here although it would be wrong to set one's expectations too high; I made a beeline for a house advertising teas and found this consisted of a vending machine at the back of a shop!

The route turns right on to the A541, following it briefly, then bears left up a lane, crosses a metalled road and continues north-westwards on a path, climbing steeply. You turn right to head north-eastwards round the eastern edge of another hill fort at Coed Moel-y-Gaer, then bear left, just west of north, to meet a metalled road. Crossing it, you join another road that heads uphill, just east of north. Having passed St Michael's of the Fiery Meteor many miles back, and almost felt the fire-and-brimstone message such a dramatic dedication seems to carry, it may appear somewhat ironic that the map should announce that at this stage of the walk you are proceeding through Sodom.

Whatever temptations of the flesh arose in the area that gave rise to the name Sodom, there seems little to beguile you over the next few miles, in terms of scenery or amenities. In fact, this last stretch of the national trail is an anticlimax. Leaving the road at a kink in its otherwise unerring north-easterly direction, you bear left on to a footpath and proceed north-westwards, skirting the summit of Cefn Du. North-westwards is now your direction of travel all the way to the A55. Beyond Cefn Du you pick up a metalled road, which you follow to a road junction, where you turn left then immediately right on to another road. At the next junction you bear left on to a path which contours the southern slopes of Moel Maenefa then drops dramatically to reach a metalled road.

You turn left down the road, then just before St Beuno's College bear right to contour the hillside, soon bearing left at Maen Efa to drop down to the A55. This is the main trunk road across North Wales, carrying traffic from the Midlands to the holiday paradises of Llandudno and Colwyn Bay, and the busy port of Holyhead; the national trail bears right to proceed briefly alongside it before thankfully using a footbridge to cross it. From the footbridge it is a short walk into the village of Rhuallt (170.5), the only habitation of any consequence between Bodfari and journey's end, and offering refreshment at the Smithy Arms. You exit from the village along a metalled road heading north-westwards as far as Brynllithrig Hall, then turn right and proceed north-eastwards, climbing again to reach a metalled road at Bodlonfa. This climb, on to the slopes of Mynydd y Cwm, is arduous indeed, but you can be reassured that there is nothing worse to come.

Turning left on to the road, you follow it through an area of woodland. Where this ends, you turn right on to a path that heads initially just east of north, then north-westwards across two metalled roads and past some old mine workings, and over the hill known as Marian Ffrith, the last Clwydian on the route. The northernmost Clwydian, Moel Hiraddug, lies off the path to the north-west. Having descended to Tyddyn-y-cyll you change direction, heading north-eastwards, still going downhill. You cross a road, then at Bryn Cnewyllyn bear eastwards to Marian Mill Farm, swinging north-westwards past a waterworks through a patch of woodland at Henfryn Hall.

Henfryn Hall to Prestatyn

Beyond Henfryn Hall you reach a metalled road, following it briefly to your right before turning left on to a path that soon reaches the A5151 at Ty Newydd. Crossing it, you head north-westwards along field paths, interspersed with a small road section, to Bryniau, situated just to the east of the viewpoint of Graig Fawr. Now journey's end is within sight. After so many miles of nondescript trudging, you ascend the slopes of Coed yr Esgob and are treated to a splendid march along the top of cliffs around 700ft high, looking down on the town of Prestatyn and the Irish Sea. This area is a nature reserve and a lovely climax to the walk, with views which on a good day stretch as far as Snowdonia and Anglesey.

At length you drop down off the hilltop and into the town of Prestatyn. You then follow a succession of roads north-westwards which head unerringly into and out of the town centre, and down to the sea, the road to the seafront rejoicing in the unusual name of Bastion Road. Fittingly enough for the end of Offa's Dyke Path, Prestatyn was the northern end of the Dyke, though all traces of the earthwork have now disappeared from the area. The town, a popular holiday resort with four miles of fine beaches, is a very pleasant place to end your walk from Sedbury, but before you start to relax you must walk to the stone at the end of Bastion Road and close to the seashore, marking the official end of the route (178).

Immediately adjacent is a splendid Offa's Dyke Centre where you may be invited to sign a book to certify your completion of the walk and purchase appropriate souvenirs. Staff at the Centre will also be happy to provide the necessary verification for the purposes of obtaining a special badge awarded by the Offa's Dyke Association to those who complete the walk. Despite the somewhat anticlimactical final miles, it is with a heavy heart that most travellers from Sedbury will head back to the town's railway station to commence the homeward journey, having enjoyed a walk that is so full of history, great scenery and wonderful variety. At least, however, you will have your memories to sustain you, to say nothing of the thought of receiving the Offa's Dyke Association badge, or indeed the parcel from that little bookshop in Hay that is awaiting you at home, containing priceless copies of a dust-jacketed *Trouble at St Judes* and a first-edition *Fly Fishing* by J. R. Hartley.

SUMMARY OF PLACES OF INTEREST
Chepstow, Devil's Pulpit, Tintern, The Kymin, Monmouth★, White Castle, Skirrid Fawr, Llanthony Priory, Capel-y-ffin, Twmpa, Hay Bluff★, Hay-on-Wye★, Clyro, Little Mountain, Disgwylfa Hill, Hergest Ridge★, Hergest Croft Gardens, Rushock Hill, Herrock Hill, Burfa, Presteigne, Hawthorn Hill, Knighton★, Cwm-sanaham Hill, Llanfair Hill, Edenhope Hill, Montgomery★, Beacon Ridge, Shropshire Union Canal, Vyrnwy Aqueduct, Llanymynech Hill, Moelydd, Oswestry, Chirk Castle★, Pontcysyllte Aqueduct, Castell Dinas Bran, Eglwyseg, World's End, Foel Fenlli, Moel Fammau/Jubilee Tower★.

AMENITIES ON OR NEAR THE ROUTE
Chepstow★, Redbrook, Monmouth★, Llantilio Crossenny (L), Pandy, Hay-on-Wye★, Gladestry (L), Kington★, Knighton★, Clun, Newcastle (L), Bishops Castle, Montgomery, Forden (L), Welshpool★, Four Crosses (L), Llanymynech, Trefonen (L), Oswestry★, Chirk, Froncysyllte, Trevor, Llandegla (L), Bodfari (L), Rhuallt (L), Prestatyn★.

The Pembrokeshire Coast Path

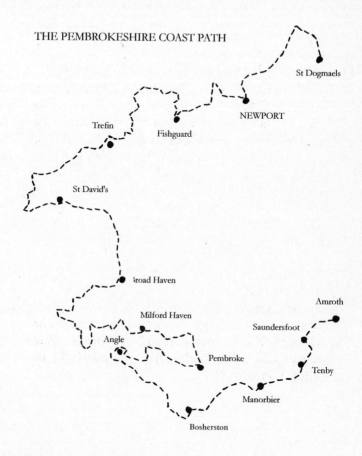

THE PEMBROKESHIRE COAST PATH

Length: Between 175 and 185 miles, depending on choice of route.
Start: St Dogmaels, near Cardigan.
Finish: Amroth, near Saundersfoot.
Nature: A walk along the often rugged and spectacular coastline of the Welsh county of Pembrokeshire.
Difficulty rating: Moderate to strenuous.
Average time of completion: 2 weeks.

The Pembrokeshire Coast Path

The Pembrokeshire coastline has always been regarded as an area of great historic and scenic interest. In 1952 it was designated as a National Park, and a suggestion was made that a continuous path along the coastline be available to walkers. The idea received enthusiastic support, but it was not until May 1970 that the route opened, largely due to the need for negotiation with landowners, who were not always cooperative. Even upon opening, the route was not continuous; the crossing of the Cleddau estuary south of Milford Haven on foot was not possible until the opening of the Cleddau Bridge in 1975. Now however, with continuity assured, the route offers some of the best coastal walking in Britain, with a tremendous variety of coastal scenery.

This variety is as a result of the area's rich and colourful geological past. The southern end of the walk will, for example, reveal rocks of old red sandstone, coal measures and carboniferous limestone; those were all sedimentary rocks which were legacies of the Upper

Palaeozoic era, deposited on the surface of the land by the actions of the sea. All these rocks are over 300 million years old. Further north, you will find examples of much older rock of Precambrian origin, that is up to and over 1,000 million years old. Much of this is made up of sea floor sediments, but some rock is as a result of lava and compressed ash of volcanoes that erupted at least 600 million years ago. Then, 400 million years ago, a series of collisions took place between the mobile continental plates which raised the mountains of North Wales and twisted and folded the horizontal rock layers of north Pembrokeshire into the grotesque shapes of grits and shales that make the coastline so fascinating for today's visitor.

The first settlers arrived in the area in around 5000 BC, but it was the Iron Age dwellers, moving in 2,600 years ago, who were the first to leave their mark on the landscape. They did this by means of a succession of defensive promontory forts of which there remains much evidence today. In the years following the departure of the Romans – who had a negligible effect on Pembrokeshire life – Christianity flourished in this corner of Wales; St David is the most famous of a large number of devout monks and ascetics who lived and worked in the area. The cathedral of St David's, though not strictly on the route itself, is the principal architectural highlight of the region.

The Norman invasion and subsequent colonisation of south Pembrokeshire by English-speaking settlers led to the so-called 'Landsker' or divide between the English-speaking peoples of that region, and the largely Welsh-speaking peoples of the north. That can still be traced today; Welsh is heard more often in north than in south Pembrokeshire, and the place names tend to become more Anglicised as progress southwards is made. By way of example, in the early stages of your journey south you will pass Pen yr Afr, Pwllygranant, Careg Yspar and Trwyn y Bwa, all offering a challenge to your Welsh pronunciation skills; 150 miles later, you will have to get your tongue round nothing more taxing than East Moor Cliff, Swanlake Bay and Bubbleton.

The combination of majestic scenery and Iron Age and Christian relics is reason enough to visit the Pembrokeshire coastline, but there are many other attractions for the walker. Most notably, there is an abundance of wildlife and plant life. Heather, gorse and bracken are constant features, while spring yields generous quantities of snowdrops, daffodils, primroses and cowslips, and carpets of bluebells and foxgloves. Seagulls are in evidence at every step of the walk, but they are joined by many other seabirds including gannets, razorbills, guillemots, fulmars and choughs. Choughs, with their glossy blue-black plumages and red legs, are plentiful in Pembrokeshire despite going into decline elsewhere. Seals can also be seen, particularly in the autumn breeding season.

The walking, although demanding at times, poses no serious technical challenges; because the route keeps largely to the coastline, route finding is rarely a problem, with a clear well-defined coast path. Although the region is wonderfully unspoilt, there are many towns and villages on or near the route, so there will be no difficulties in finding food or accommodation, and public transport links are excellent. The most remarkable aspect of the walk is that, although at over 175 miles from end to end it is one of the longer national trails, the distance from start to finish as the crow flies is only 30 miles! It is therefore practicable to drive to the start, in the knowledge that there will be a comparatively easy and affordable journey back to the car from the finish, even though it does undeniably detract from one's sense of achievement on reaching the end to realise that the start can be returned to by motorised transport in less time than it takes to oven-cook a Bernard Matthews turkey roast.

St Dogmaels to Dinas Head

The route begins at the northern end of St Dogmaels on the banks of the river Teifi, a river noted for its salmon and sea trout, known locally as 'sewin'. Travellers by public transport who have been decanted at Cardigan will have an easy walk to St Dogmaels via the B4546. St Dogmaels is worth a few minutes' exploration; it boasts a number of elegant Victorian cottages, a ruined abbey that was founded in the twelfth century, and a nineteenth-century church containing an early Christian stone monument inscribed in both Latin and also Ogham, which was a script used by ancient British and Irish scholars. Thus was it possible to translate the previously baffling Ogham alphabet in 1848. The start of the route is clearly marked with bilingual signposts bearing the words 'Llwybr Arfordir/Coast Path', and these signposts are provided liberally all the way to Amroth.

The first two miles of the journey, heading north-westwards, are extremely easy, the route following the B4546 to Poppit Sands and then a narrow metalled lane uphill to the hamlet of Allt-y-goed. Here, the reassuring tarmac ends and you continue north-westwards, joining a path which offers excellent views to the mouth of the Teifi and Cardigan Bay across slopes clad thickly with bracken. Straight ahead is Cemaes Head, and here the route swings sharply south-westwards, a direction it will maintain for much of the way to St David's Head, which is over 50 miles away. The contrast between this magnificent clifftop scenery and the homely, gentle surroundings of the riverside communities of Cardigan and St Dogmaels is remarkable. Almost at once you reach Pen yr Afr; at nearly 600ft above the sea this is the highest point of the national trail which is barely three miles old. The sheer cliff faces and the folds in the rocks, legacies of geological activity 400 million years ago, are remarkable.

The next highlights are the waterfalls at Gernos and the nearby cove of Pwllygranant, where there is some stiff up-and-down walking to do; beyond Pwllygranant is Ceibwr Bay, owned by the National Trust and noted for its fulmar colony. The rock folds were made 450 million years ago by Great Caledonian earth movements. No amenities exist here, and indeed there is nothing on offer until you reach Newport. Just beyond Ceibwr Bay is the scenic highlight of the stretch between St Dogmaels and Newport, namely Pwll y Wrach or the Witches Cauldron. It is in fact a collapsed cave, where the sea has gnawed away at soft rocks along a fault. The path descends steeply and crosses a natural bridge over a huge chasm between two faces of steep rock; once you have regained the height lost, the 'bridge' looks almost tightrope-like in narrowness.

There is indeed some very tough climbing beyond Pwll y Wrach as the coast path rises to 500ft again. Towards Morfa Head there are some frightening moments as the path snakes round a small inlet with a strip of grass less than a yard wide separating you from a straight drop of some 300ft. Large areas of bracken on the upper slopes of the cliffs give way to monstrous shale faces that sweep to the water's edge. At Morfa Head, you get your first view of the superb sands of Newport Bay, and also visible are a range of inland hills with a distinctly moorland feel. These hills, which dominate north Pembrokeshire, are called the Preselis; you may wish to store this piece of information for your next pub quiz night or family Christmas gathering in the hope that those competing against you will hazard that Preselis are a type of breakfast cereal or an inferior Channel 4 soap opera of the late 1980s.

The descent from Morfa Head is not easy; the path is very steep, and there are a number of awkward scrambles through outcrops of rock. It is necessary to drop right down to sea level and follow a path which runs beside Newport Sands (at low tide, if you wished to avoid Newport you could cut straight across the sands to the eastern end of Parrog, fording the Nevern estuary en route), and after crossing a stream, reaches a metalled road. The route turns right on to the road, immediately crossing the Nevern estuary and then straight away turning right to follow a path which continues towards Parrog, this time following the south edge of Newport Sands. At length it turns right on to a metalled lane that passes through Parrog.

By staying on the road you have used to cross the Nevern estuary, you will reach Newport (15.5), for centuries a thriving port, but now set back from the sea. It is a useful stopping-place, with a wide range of amenities; it boasts many attractive eighteenth and nineteenth-century cottages of various colours, Norman castle ruins, and a thirteenth-century church with many memorials to seamen in its churchyard, while the lane running down to the old harbour is overlooked by ancient limekilns.

The coast path continues westwards through Parrog and there follows a splendid walk to Cwm-yr-Eglwys, with superb views back to Newport Bay and the Preselis. The two finest features on this section are the coves of Aberrhigian and Aberfforest, and although both coves entail steep descents and ascents, your efforts are amply rewarded. Shortly beyond Aberfforest the route meets a metalled road and drops to Cwm-yr-Eglwys. This is a small but bustling place, its most notable feature being the Sailor's Chapel of St Brynach, almost completely destroyed by a storm in 1859.

At Cwm-yr-Eglwys you have a choice; you may follow a woodland valley walk to Pwllgwaelod, heading roughly westwards and avoiding Dinas Island (not actually an island; it ceased to be one 8,000 years ago, and is now a rugged peninsula), or you may continue on the coastline round Dinas Island via Dinas Head, using the coast path. If you are pushed for time, you may want to opt for the woodland route, which in summer is notable for its variety of butterflies. However the walk round Dinas Head is to be greatly preferred, given the right conditions. The views from Pen y Fan, the headland summit, are breathtaking; Pen yr Afr, now many miles back, is clearly visible, as is the whole of Fishguard Bay and the crests of the Preselis. There have been suggestions that the Wicklow mountains in southern Ireland can be seen from here, but even with a hundred per cent clarity and binoculars, I was unable to pinpoint them when I visited the headland.

Few things are more frustrating for the walker than to be promised a view of a notable landmark from some colossal distance away, without actually getting that view at all. It is particularly irksome to arrive at a viewpoint promised by guidebook writers to offer 'unparalleled views on a clear day, when the coastline and possibly even the spire of St Ethelburga's Church can be observed' only to find a sullen mist or haze hangs obstinately over the coastline, and the aforementioned church, whilst evidently leaping out of the landscape at the more than amply blessed guidebook writer, is about as likely to appear on the horizon as a procession of camels dressed in the club colours of the Plymouth Argyle football team.

Dinas Head to Carregwastad

Slight anticlimax sets in as you descend from Pen y Fan to Pwllgwaelod, and begin the long walk round Fishguard Bay. There is more up-and-down work, following which the coast path negotiates the splendid little sheltered inlet at Hescwm, then climbs back up to follow the clifftops. Thereafter the going is more straightforward, the route keeping to field edges and passing a caravan park. Beyond this, however, there is more magnificent coastal scenery, culminating in the ruins of the late eighteenth-century Fishguard Fort on Castle Point. Three cannons still remain, as if warning off future invaders of these shores. At Castle Point the coast path turns sharply southwards to reach Lower Town, the old fishing port at the mouth of the Gwaun valley.

Once a busy industrial port, it is now a haven for pleasure boats; the car park in the village is known to be given over for boats in the summer. You turn right on to the A487 and follow it briefly for a steep climb up into Fishguard (25.5), one of the largest settlements on the Pembrokeshire Coast Path with all the amenities you are likely to need. The route actually turns right off the main road shortly before the town centre and uses a footpath which snakes round the edge of the town to reach Saddle Point, high above the mini estuary created by the river Gwaun as it flows into Fishguard Bay. The views across the bay to Dinas Head are stunning, and there is the more immediate prospect of Castle Point, extending its face across the water like some giant sea creature.

Beyond Saddle Point the coast path turns resolutely away from Castle Point, heading just south of west and dropping down to the A40. Turning right on to the A40, you proceed beside it as far as a roundabout, then take the second exit off it to cross the railway on a minor road and enter Goodwick (28). The town of Goodwick, which offers refreshment and accommodation, grew as a result of the advent of the railway (Fishguard railway station is in fact at Goodwick) and the port of Fishguard. A breakwater and lighthouse further round the bay, mark the extent of what is known as Fishguard harbour, and it is the quay at Goodwick which serves as the Fishguard ferry terminal and boasts the smart new Stena Line buildings. I clearly recall enjoying a well-earned portion of chicken and chips on the quay on a Saturday night, with Goodwick's principal 'night life' appearing to consist of the assembly, from 9 p.m., of cars and lorries beginning their patient wait for the 3.15 a.m. Rosslare ferry.

The route continues by leaving the minor road very soon after crossing the railway and bearing right (north-eastwards) on to a lane that heads uphill on to the cliffs again, via Harbour Village. Once the village has been left behind and the coast path is regained, you can look forward to many miles of totally unspoilt walking on a well-marked coast path, uninterrupted by towns or busy roads.

The next objective of note is Strumble Head, one of the most prominent headlands on the map of West Wales, and an important stage on the route; once beyond Strumble Head, virtually all of the walking is in a southerly direction. To reach Strumble Head from Harbour Village, however, it is necessary to head northwards to round Crincoed Point, and then north-westwards, turning away from Fishguard Bay at last. Most of the walking is straightforward without any severe descents or climbs. The first of two outstanding features of this section is the delectable wooded valley of Cwm Felin, where you momentarily forget you are on a coast path as you enjoy the brief sensation of sheltered woodland and rushing stream, a most refreshing experience on a hot day.

Emerging from that, you come almost immediately to Carreg Goffa monument above Carregwastad Point, the landing place for the last military force to invade Britain, in February 1797. The plan was for 1,400 ex-convicts from France, under the leadership of Colonel Tate, an American, to land either near Bristol or in Cardigan Bay and raise a peasants' revolt which would divert attention from the main aim: an invasion of Ireland by 15,000 regular soldiers. The landing at Carregwastad was a mistake, and within two days the force capitulated nearby – not helped, one suspects, by the fact that many of the invaders had got themselves drunk on a cargo of wine from a ship that had been wrecked on the coast shortly before.

Carregwastad to Trefin
The walking is uneventful until you reach Strumble Head where you will swing south-west, and indeed for the next thirty miles or so, south-west will be the predominant direction of travel. A coastguard station and a lighthouse, situated on the island of Ynys Meicel, serve to mark Strumble Head, although there are no amenities available. This significant headland, which offers views that stretch as far as the Lleyn Peninsula in north-west Wales, is a

favoured spot for birdwatchers, and basking sharks and Risso's dolphins have been observed in the waters close by. The going thus far from Goodwick has been very easy, but it slows down considerably now as you embark on a stretch of coast where every headland is a volcanic intrusion, beginning with a succession of small hills of volcanic rock. The coast path ceases to be a reassuring strip of green or brown and loses all definition for a while as the route weaves its way through, or round, the outcrops of rock, negotiating streams, ponds, moorland and hillocks as it goes.

Soon after rounding the astonishing cove of Porth Maenmelyn and passing the imposing promontory fort of Dinas Mawr, you have to make a steep climb to Pwll Deri, where you will find what is surely one of the most spectacularly-sited youth hostels in the country. Viewed from further south, it is hard to see what stops it falling into the sea. There is a respite for a few moments as the route turns right on to the hostel approach road, then turns right off it and sets off again along a ridge path. This leads to the wonderful viewpoint of Carn Ogof, providing spectacular vistas of the cliffs that you have recently negotiated.

Between Carn Ogof and Abercastle you will venture through some of the wildest coastal terrain in the British Isles, with hardly a house or even a road in view. If the wind is howling, the sense of isolation and ruggedness is accentuated even more. Soon comes the heather-clad mini headland of Penbwchdy, where the negotiation of craggy outcrops brings your activity more into the realms of scrambling than walking. Things get slightly easier beyond Penbwchdy, the coast path curling round the spectacular sandy cove at Pwllcrochan, guarded on all sides by formidable rocks.

You then drop to the twin beaches of Aber Bach and Aber Mawr, passing a promontory fort at Carreg Golchfa just before Aber Bach; beyond Aber Mawr there is another climb and then faster walking along field edges with just one big fall and rise at Pwllstrodur. Though the walking is more straightforward, the scenery remains fascinating, with the summit of Mynydd Morfa, marked by a triangulation point, to the left, and the little headlands of Penmorfa (where there is a hill fort) and Trwyn Llwynog to your right.

Like so much of this coastline, it is a paradise for geologists. Indeed some walkers may recall having visited the area in their school or college days in the context of field trips, where the interest consisted not so much in the rock formations which were ostensibly the chief purpose of the visit, as the availability of a second helping of baked beans at breakfast, the flavour of the crisps chosen for the day's packed lunch, or the chances of getting off with Amanda in Form 5B.

Shortly beyond Pwllstrodur you reach Abercastle, the first settlement since Goodwick. Although it has no amenities to speak of, it is a picturesque place, and its cosy harbour, guarded by the spectacular island of black rock known as Ynys y Castell, is a delight. Just beyond Abercastle, a detour inland takes you shortly to Carreg Sampson, a cromlech, or burial chamber, built by the Neoliths, who were amongst the first settlers in this area. From Abercastle to Trevine the walking is straightforward with no real up-and-down work, but there are numerous twists and turns as you make your way round a profusion of small inlets and headlands, of which Pen Castell-coch is the most fascinating. Coastal erosion has produced a particularly grotesque range of rock formations hereabouts, as well as small 'islands' of rock, and those who choose to end their day's march at nearby Trefin will enjoy a fine conclusion to their walk.

Trefin, or Trevine (45.5), lies barely two miles from Abercastle by road, but can be reached by a most convenient path which leaves the coast route immediately before the headland of Trwyn Llwyd. Once the site of an Episcopal palace, Trefin offers the best range of amenities since leaving Goodwick; when I visited it recently, it boasted bed and breakfast accommodation, a bus link to St David's (a 6-mile, 15-minute ride; the coast walk is 18 miles long), a caravan site, shop and pub. My visit to the pub, on a Sunday evening in March, demonstrated that respect for the Sabbath still exists in this corner of Wales; I was advised that bar food would not be available until 7.30 p.m. to allow the cook time to get back from church.

Trefin to St David's

If you left the route using the path from Trwyn Llwyd you can
choose to either retrace your steps, or use a metalled road heading
west out of the village to pick up the route again at the inlet of
Aber Draw. Soon afterwards, having passed the small headland of
Trwyn Elen, the coast path descends again to reach the fascinating
village of Porthgain. Its harbour provides strong evidence of the
area's industrial past, and the remains of the old brickworks, last
used in 1931, can still be seen. The harbour is lined with banks of
crushers, bins and shoots where stone quarried from nearby cliffs
was broken, graded and deposited into the waiting ships. On
climbing back on to the clifftops beyond the village, you will see
numerous traces of the old quarries, the most notable of which is
the old tramway cutting.

There follows some splendid cliff scenery, with grandstand views
to the fine beach of Traeth Llyfn, and then a descent to the little
village of Abereiddi, where slate was once quarried. Its bay and
sandy beach, popular with fossil hunters, are guarded by the rocks
of Trwyncastell. After this succession of villages, civilisation is left
behind as you embark on the march to St David's Head, a stunning
journey through completely unspoilt cliff scenery. Soon after
Abereiddi you pass the sites of some ancient forts, then proceed
through the beautiful valley of Pwll-caerog before making the
strenuous ascent to the summit of Penberry.

Beyond Penberry the terrain takes on a distinctly moorland
appearance, with granite boulders protruding from the great carpets
of heather, and after the drop down from Penberry there is a
succession of climbs through relentless thrusts of igneous rock.
The walking has an incredibly remote feel, although you will not
truly be on your own, as wild ponies can be seen gambolling
contentedly among the tufts of heather. There is a marvellous
profusion of wild flowers including sea pinks and oxeye daisies,
and if you feel brave enough to venture to the cliff edge you may
observe grey seals, which thrive in the unspoilt surroundings. There
is a definite sense of building up to something, until at last you
reach St David's Head, the largest igneous thrust of all. It is not
quite the most westerly point in Wales – that will be reached in

just a few miles – but it is a key place on the route. The reward for reaching, and rounding, the headland is a superb view to the nearby cove of Porthmelgan and Whitesands Bay beyond.

Porthmelgan stands in the shadow of 595ft Carn Llidi, an inland hill of mountainous appearance that towers over St David's and its surrounding countryside. Passing Coetan Arthur, another important Neolithic burial chamber, the descent to Porthmelgan is straightforward, as is the rise and drop to Whitesands Bay. This part of the walk is a popular tourist path and steps have had to be taken to curb the resulting erosion. Whitesands Bay, where I obtained refreshment from a useful café, has one of the best sandy beaches on the route, and offers a quick easy road link to St David's on the B4583. However, you may wish to cover a bit more ground before succumbing to its charms, as it will be easily accessible at various times over the next five or six miles.

The walk from Whitesands Bay to St Justinian's, just under two miles, is straightforward; the coast path follows a level course along the cliffs at a modest height above the sea, with the seductive sands of the bay immediately below and the might of Carn Llidi towering up behind. St Justinian's itself is more impressive for its fine setting than its buildings, which include a lifeboat station and a small roofless chapel. Immediately to your right across the water, as St Justinian's is reached, is Ramsey Island, the home of St Justinian himself, and supposedly the resting place of 20,000 saints. Legend has it that St Justinian, having had his head cut off by murderers on the island, walked across the Sound with his head in his arms!

Accessible to visitors by ferry only at certain times of year, the island is a privately owned and farmed nature reserve, and is a nesting and breeding place for more than 30 species of bird including guillemots and razorbills. The strip of water separating the island from the mainland is Ramsey Sound, where fearsome rocks named the Bitches lie in wait to claim careless navigators, while an equally dangerous collection of reefs, known as Bishops and Clerks, lies a little further off the island. The Bitches, according to legend, were all that was left after St Justinian prayed for the destruction of the bridge linking Ramsey with the mainland because he was getting too many visitors.

Once past St Justinian's the walking, round the small bay of Porthstinian and beyond, gets considerably tougher. However, the cliff scenery is magnificent. At Pen Dal-aderyn an important moment is reached; this is the most westerly point on the Welsh mainland, and having rounded the headland, you will find yourself making significant progress eastwards for the first time on the walk. With Ramsey Island behind you and the prevailing wind on your back, you now have St Brides Bay for company, and will continue to do so for most of the next 30 miles. The coast path follows the bay in its entirety, from Pen Dal-aderyn at its north-westerly extreme to Wooltack Point at its south-west tip. The walking is magnificent almost throughout, beginning at once with the National Trust-owned cliffs of Treginnis and the splendidly named cave Ogof Mrs Morgan.

There are exquisite views hereabouts to the rocky islands of Carreg yr Esgob and Carreg Fran, each of which guards the beautiful Porthlysgi Bay. The little hillocks of volcanic rock round Porth Henllys provide ideal platforms not only for views to the bay but also for views back to the hills at the southern end of Ramsey Island. Less than a mile beyond Porthlysgi Bay is Porth Clais (63), a harbour that serves St David's, and though it has seen some industry, it now principally caters for the tourist trade. It is a superbly attractive harbour, with a thin stretch of water protected on each side by lines of tall cliffs. The route must turn inland and drop steeply to cross the water before rising again and returning to the cliffs overlooking the bay.

About half a mile beyond Porth Clais is St Non's Chapel; though built comparatively recently, it was by St Non's Bay, on to which the chapel looks out, that St David, the patron saint of Wales, was supposedly born in the middle of the fifth century. A convenient road link runs from the chapel into St David's, just half a mile away. St David's, the smallest city in Great Britain, is not on the route, but it virtually demands a detour for a short visit at least, if not an overnight stay. The cathedral, which turns what would otherwise be regarded as a village into a city, dates from the end of the twelfth century, and was almost certainly built on the site of a monastery founded by St David in the sixth century. Situated in a leafy valley, the cathedral's most notable features include a decorated sixteenth-century roof and fourteenth-century carved choir screen. In the same valley as the cathedral stand the wonderfully romantic ruins of the fourteenth-century Bishop's Palace.

The status of St David's as a major tourist attraction ensures there is no shortage of shops, tearooms, pubs and other amenities, and it was something of a culture shock for me, having hardly seen a soul on the 18-mile march from Trefin through a landscape that has not significantly changed for millions of years, to sit in a crowded hotel bar watching Liverpool put four goals past Newcastle United on the Sky Sports channel.

St David's to Broad Haven

Between St Non's Chapel and the next major settlement at Solva, there are no real difficulties, and you can make reasonably quick progress eastwards round the top end of St Brides Bay. Interest is provided by a succession of fine small headlands, namely Pen y Cyfrwy, Penpleidiau with an impressive fort, Carreg y Barcud and Ystafelloedd. Stone from cliffs at Caerfai Bay, sitting snugly between the first two of these headlands, was used in the building of St David's Cathedral. Solva itself lies at the end of a narrow hooked harbour; it is actually a drowned river valley which submerged when the sea rose at the end of the last Ice Age. The approach to the village is wonderful, with fine views to the headland on the far side of the harbour. This headland, known as St Elvis Rock, does not point out to sea but curls inwards to provide the narrowest possible entrance to the harbour, which more than one observer has likened to Boscastle Harbour in Cornwall.

Solva (69), a busy port in the early nineteenth century with a brisk trade in cloth, corn, timber and coal, is a cheerful jumble of houses around the harbour, with ample facilities for rest and refreshment, particularly in summer. The route continues in dramatic style beyond Solva, with an ascent, a sharp drop and then a climb round the neck of the St Elvis headland.

Very soon after this comes the promontory of Dinas Fawr, which although a cul-de-sac and not on the coast path itself, is well signposted and easily accessible. It is a detour well worth making;

the walk to the tip of the promontory is along a huge whaleback ridge of rock, and the views throughout are magnificent. Returning to the main path, Newgale looks temptingly close on the map for those who have spurned refreshment opportunities in Solva, and there are good views to the village and its sands once Dinas Fawr has been left behind, but the march to reach it provides some of the toughest walking on the route. There are two big valleys to negotiate, each involving a knee-jarring drop and then a lung-testing climb almost immediately afterwards. The reward – apart from the traverse of a crystal-clear stream which may provide life-saving refreshment on a hot day – is an uninterrupted view of Newgale Sands, one of the finest stretches of sand on the coast of Great Britain.

A brisk descent brings the coast path down to the A487 and right on to this road into Newgale (74). This little settlement, at the head of its 2-mile carpet of golden sand, not only marks the north-eastern extremity of St Brides Bay and an important 'corner' for you to have turned, but the nearby Brandy Brook Stream is said to divide the Welsh-speaking north of Pembrokeshire from the English-speaking south. A glance at the map shows that the place-names from now on are virtually all Anglicised, and if you are unaccustomed to the vagaries of Welsh pronunciation and have to ask for directions, you need not now fear being regarded with a stare normally reserved for those with the intellectual calibre of a bucket of cold potato peelings.

Beyond Newgale, with the route now heading resolutely southwards, the cliffs temporarily cease. The A487 soon heads off inland, and you must choose between the sands, the shingle bank or a metalled minor road as you proceed towards Nolton Haven. As the road veers slightly away from the coast, the route joins a footpath, running parallel to the sands, and then when the sands end the path swings round some old mine workings, and passes a huge towering mound of rock known as Rickets Head. It stays on the clifftop then swings inland to reach the pretty cove and village of Nolton Haven. The village once had a quay where coasters loaded anthracite from a nearby colliery, but only did so in the summer months as the ship insurers, Lloyds, refused to insure vessels for use during the wild winter months. The next in a veritable line of havens is Druidston Haven, with another fine sandy beach; some more tough up-and-down work is required here, the route heading slightly inland to join a metalled road which you follow round Druidston Villa.

On leaving the road, however, and rejoining the coast path, the walking becomes straightforward, with an easy clifftop march towards the sprawling settlement of Broad Haven. Though the sight of its buildings is hardly aesthetically pleasing, the great sweep of golden sand immediately in front of them is more so, and the prospect of a wide range of amenities in the village will encourage you to descend briskly southwards to reach its centre.

Broad Haven (80) became a fashionable resort in the nineteenth century and there is still a Victorian atmosphere about the place, especially on Trafalgar Terrace and Webbs Hill, where a neat chapel built in 1841 stands beside a stream. At the time of my visit the village boasted an excellent shop and post office where I recall parcelling up five days' worth of dirty clothes to send back home in an effort to lighten my rucksack. Whilst it certainly made life more comfortable for me as I continued on the walk, it is not a practice I would commend to you if you wish to return from your adventure to a partner who is still on speaking terms with you.

Broad Haven to Dale

Just a stone's throw from Broad Haven is Little Haven, through which the coast path passes as it begins the march on Wooltack Point at the end of St Brides Bay. The walk from one Haven to the other can be accomplished by walking across the sand at low tide, or by means of a steep lane at other times. Little Haven is a pretty place which, like Nolton Haven, also has a history of exporting coal; it has a limited range of amenities nowadays, but there will be nothing more immediately on offer until Dale, 20 miles away, so you should leave the Havens suitably prepared.

You turn another corner of St Brides Bay as you make the stiff climb out of Little Haven on to the clifftops. As far as Borough Head you are separated from the sea by a strip of woodland, then from Borough Head to the hamlet of St Brides, the route sticks to the coast path which stays on sheer clifftops at between 200ft and 300ft. Beyond Borough Head come the somewhat alcoholic inlets of Brandy Bay and Dutch Gin; the highlight of this easy and straightforward section, however, is a waterfall down a virtually sheer cliff face fed by an innocuous stream that is crossed by means of a simple wooden plank. The route drops to the beach at St Brides (no amenities), then climbs back on to the cliffs to round Nab Head – a Stone Age site for the manufacture of flint tools – and proceeds almost due south, then south-westwards, round Musselwick Sands. Beyond these sands the coast path swings more decisively westwards for the final assault on Wooltack Point and the farewell to St Brides Bay.

As you approach the headland, you pass the picturesque little inlet of Martin's Haven, guarded to its west by Haven Point. You may take a short cut across the neck of the headland, aiming due south from Martin's Haven, but few walkers will wish to spurn the opportunity to follow the headland – known as the Deer Park – right round. The Deer Park is the site of important Iron Age defensive embankments but there is not a deer to be seen. However, not only should the extra walking provide unbeatable views to the bay, and its magnificent coastline that has now been safely accomplished, but there are also views to Skomer Island immediately to the west. Further out to sea, a little to the south-east of Skomer, is the island of Skokholm. Both islands are amazingly rich havens of wildlife, including puffins, petrels and Manx shearwaters, and boat trips are available in season if you have the time and inclination to take a closer look. The rounding of the Deer Park is a crucial moment on the walk; not only does it complete the walk round St Brides Bay but it is roughly the halfway mark of the journey.

The good news for more timid souls is that the second half is gentler, less rugged and less remote than the first, although there is still some fantastic scenery to come. Now heading south-east towards St Ann's Head and continuing on the clifftops, you pass the ominously named Deadman's Bay and Albion Sands, beyond which stands Gateholm Island. The island is accessible at low tide and well worth visiting if you have time; there are some unusual cliff formations here known as the Three Chimneys, where horizontal beds of rock dating back 450 million years have been virtually up-ended into chimneys of eroded stone.

Beyond Gateholm Island, there is then a quite magnificent walk above Marloes Sands, the golden carpet punctuated by outcrops of rock. Although this is quite a popular spot for holidaymakers, those walkers who are about to be introduced to the joys of parenthood may, even at its busiest time, reflect that this would be the ideal place to take their offspring for a beach holiday, particularly if of the opinion that their introduction to the joys of the surging surf will not be fatally harmed by the absence of end-to-end candyfloss stalls, bucket-and-spade emporia, vulgar postcards, and scrawled blackboard signs proclaiming the availability of 'fish n chip's'.

The walking remains highly enjoyable and straightforward beyond Marloes Sands. Once round Hooper's Point, you pass a disused airfield to your left, now owned by the National Trust, and continue on past the sands of Westdale Bay. Nearby is the Cobblers Hole, a classic example of rock-folding in old red sandstone, and a place marked on the map as The Hookses, which sounds like something from the pages of A. A. Milne's poems about Christopher Robin. The village of Dale is a short walk away across the neck of the peninsula, but if you wish to get a few more miles under your belt you will press on to St Ann's Head without difficulty, passing the mini headlands of Long Point and Little Castle Point, and two bays, namely Welshman's Bay and Frenchman's Bay.

St Ann's Head, with its lighthouse that was built on the site of St Ann's Chapel, is another important stage on the route, marking the start of the walk alongside the channel known as Milford Haven, away from the coast. Just across Milford Haven from St Ann's Head you will see Rat Island on the south side of West Angle Bay, where the true coastal walking resumes, but to reach that point, tantalisingly close as the crow flies, requires at least two full days of hard tramping. The route continues north-eastwards now along the water's edge round Mill Bay, with its fine cliffs of old red sandstone; it was at Mill Bay that Henry Tudor (later Henry VII) landed in August 1485 before capturing the English throne at

Bosworth Field. You round two more bays, Watwick and Castlebeach, on the way into Dale, and encounter a particularly delightful wooded valley near Castlebeach Bay.

The tip of the headland beyond this bay is Dale Point, and on the headland is Dale Fort. Constructed in the eighteenth century as a defence against the French, it has been converted into a field study centre. You will pass other defensive forts around the mouth of Milford Haven as the walk progresses, and will thus appreciate the importance that was attached to the deep anchorage of the Haven and the naval installations to which it gave rise. The route joins the approach road to the fort and turns left on to it, dropping down to reach the picturesque village of Dale (101), its shingle beach providing fine views across Milford Haven.

The village is an extremely popular sailing centre, with safe moorings available in Dale Roads off the shingle shore; it really only comes to life when the sailing season begins, although the village pub has catered for the needs of walkers all the year round. When I visited the village, I was struck by the somewhat modest opening hours of the village store, namely 9 a.m. to 12 noon Monday to Saturday, although in fairness this was in early March and longer opening hours may well have applied later in the year.

Shopping in what can be somewhat sparsely stocked village stores may be a rather less rewarding experience for walkers than their weekly trolley dash round the supermarket at home; indeed the fastidious hiker may not relish the thought of the long weary miles ahead with the only sustenance in the rucksack consisting of cooked ham with no obvious means of access through its tight plastic wrapping, a chocolate bar with an unpronounceable name and an even more unpronounceable manufacturer, and an apple, apparently the last one 'until fresh deliveries arrive tomorrow,' which by its discoloured skin would appear to have been pressed into regular service for indoor cricket matches.

Dale to Pembroke Dock
The walk round Milford Haven from Dale to Angle is the least exciting or rewarding section of the route, and some walkers may wish to miss it out altogether. If you have decided to stay with it,

you will have your resolve tested almost immediately as you leave Dale, when you reach a tidal creek known as the Gann which can only be passed at low tide. If the creek is negotiable, it is then a straightforward walk round the edge of the sands and then south-eastwards to the pleasant but unspectacular Musselwick Point. Otherwise a tedious detour is needed to the nearest bridge crossing, following the B4327 Haverfordwest road northwards and over the creek, then as the road swings north-eastwards, soon branching off right on to a minor road heading for the hamlet of Mullock. You then turn right again and use footpaths to proceed southwards to rejoin the coast path just short of Musselwick Point. There is then an improvement as you reach Monks Haven with its wooded valley, lake, impressive castellated walls, and good views across to West Angle Bay.

The walking as far as Sandy Haven, where you reach another obstacle, presents a curious contrast. Though you are not proceeding alongside the open sea, the cliff faces are still impressively rugged; the headlands of Watch House Point, Great Castle Head and Little Castle Head, complete with prehistoric promontory fort, are all delightful and give good views to the shoreline on the south side of the Haven and the charming Thorn Island lying just off West Angle Bay. The beach at Lindsway Bay, just before Great Castle Head, is also very attractive and unspoilt. However, you are now within sight of the oil refineries which, although fascinating in their way, do tend to detract from the beauty of the surroundings.

Beyond Little Castle Head, you walk northwards to Sandy Haven, briefly joining a lane which takes you down to Sandyhaven Pill. This is another tidal creek that is bordered on both sides by pleasant stretches of sand, and again you must hope that the tide will be low enough for you to use the stepping stones and avoid another tiresome detour. The detour itself, if you are unfortunate enough to have to make it, consists of a walk up the road running parallel to and then across the creek; bearing right immediately after crossing over it, you follow the road down to the village of Herbrandston, at the south end of which you join a road that leads westwards back to the east bank of the Sandyhaven Pill to pick up the route. It certainly adds a few unwelcome miles to the walk, and may provoke amongst some hikers the obvious but no less painful quip that it is a bitter Pill to swallow.

Once across the Pill, whichever method is used to negotiate it, you soon proceed south-eastwards into oil country. In the late 1950s, when oil companies were looking for a suitable location to receive and refine crude oil from the Middle East, the broad deep estuarine waters of Milford Haven proved an ideal choice, since the deep-water channel was able to admit oil tankers of over 250,000 tons. During the next decade and a half, a number of different companies adopted Milford Haven in this way, and although some companies have withdrawn, many refineries were still operational towards the end of the twentieth century and in any case considerable paraphernalia has been left by the companies that have gone. The result is a landscape which for the next few miles is dominated by massive chimneys, cylindrical storage tanks and jetties.

The route, though staying close to the estuary and rounding South Hook Point to proceed eastwards, passes right beside the workings of the former Esso refinery, actually passing *underneath* an old jetty. Just beyond this jetty you leave the National Park, dropping down to the uninteresting Gelliswick Bay and briefly picking up a road which follows the bay round. As the road swings to the left, the route leaves it, turning right alongside a school playing field and then along roads heading north-eastwards through the village of Hakin, the route marked with acorn signs on the pavements.

Eventually you drop down to the Victoria Bridge, at the head of the docks, and use the bridge crossing to enter the town of Milford Haven (112). The land on which the town stands was owned by Sir William Hamilton whose wife Emma became Lord Nelson's mistress. It was Hamilton's nephew Charles Greville who in 1800 planned and founded the port, and indeed the planned aspect is obvious from the neat gridiron of streets in the heart of the town. Following the collapse of the town's whaling and Admiralty shipbuilding trades, and the decline of its fishing industry, oil has become the town's saviour, although as has been seen, some refineries – including Esso in 1983 – have closed down in the past two decades.

Having passed through the town, which offers the best range of amenities since St David's, the route leaves the centre by way of Hamilton Terrace, heading towards and then up the left side of Castle Pill. This is yet another tidal creek, on the shores of which various boatyards and an armaments depot have been built. Soon, you reach the B4325 and turn right on to it to cross Castle Pill by means of Black Bridge, from which you have a steep twisty climb, still on the B4325. The climb seems endless, but at last the crest is gained and the route turns right on to a footpath which heads south-east towards the estuary and round the edge of the vast Gulf Refinery. The pipelines connecting the jetty and refinery are crossed by means of an extraordinary bridge where not only on either side, but above you, have been erected iron bars, mesh and barbed wire, so that you get the sensation of walking in a cage.

In due course the path, passing above Wear Point, drops down to a metalled road which heads slightly north of east through the pleasant villages of Hazelbeach and Llandstadwell to rejoin the B4325 round the little town of Neyland (117). As you reach the town, you will rejoice at the sight, immediately ahead, of the Cleddau Bridge, which marks the furthest point of the journey up Milford Haven and the start of the long walk back to the lovely coastline that you have left behind. The bridge was built as recently as 1975 and replaced a ferry. It takes only a glance at the map to spot that walkers wishing to complete the Pembrokeshire Coast Path in its early years without stooping to the indignity of man-made transport for part of the journey would require a detour along either a number of unlovely major roads including the A40 trunk road, or a succession of sinuous and extremely hilly minor roads. If walkers were unwise enough to try and stick to the water's edge, they would encounter a landscape which more often than not was pathless and virtually impossible to negotiate without offending the local landowners. This, of course, pre-supposed the elimination of a fourth option, namely depositing one's rucksack with the ferryman and swimming across, taking care to avoid any maverick oil tankers that might have happened to be passing.

Neyland is not a wildly interesting town; it is notable now only for its picturesque marina, although it was once a terminal for a packet service to Ireland and was actually known as Milford Haven before Greville's town adopted this name. Brunel was aware of the anchorage potential of Neyland for ocean-going ships, and established a special mooring here for the largest of his three steamships, the *Great Eastern*. The national trail leaves the town by passing into a strip of woodland at its north-east end, proceeding northwards through the wood above the marina to reach the A477. You turn right on to this road, which immediately crosses a creek, then half a mile or so later cross the estuary by means of the Cleddau Bridge. The bridge crossing is enjoyable, with good views not only to the estuary but to the waters of the Daugleddau which flow into the estuary, the settlements of Pembroke Dock, Neyland and Milford Haven, and of course the ubiquitous chimneys and storage tanks of the refineries.

However, what follows is anticlimactical in the extreme; it is necessary to remain on the A477 as far as a busy roundabout where the route turns right on to another major road, proceeding into the suburb of Llanion on the outskirts of Pembroke Dock, and then into Pembroke Dock itself (121), heading slightly north of west. While it is good to be heading back towards the coast again, the suburban landscape, with its concentrated housing and out-of-town retail warehouses, is hardly inspiring. At length, having negotiated further busy roads, the route emerges on to the waterfront and a walkway from which there are good views to the Cleddau Bridge.

Pembroke Dock to Pwllcrochan

Pembroke Dock, though certainly not the highlight of the walk, has a colourful past; after the Admiralty moved its operations here from Milford Haven town for economic reasons during the Napoleonic Wars, a new dockyard was built and remained operational until 1926. It was used during the Second World War as a base for boats protecting the Atlantic convoys, and as a result was bombed heavily by the Germans. You can still see the martello tower that was part of the dockyard's defensive system.

Just before the tower the route turns left and proceeds south-westwards, very briefly south-eastwards, and then south-westwards again along metalled roads to leave Pembroke Dock and head towards the Pembroke River. The river presents an impenetrable obstacle to straightforward progress westwards beside Milford Haven. As a result, it is necessary to head south-eastwards – *away* from the coast again – to the nearest available river crossing which is situated in the old town of Pembroke.

After leaving the tarmac at the eastern end of the suburb of Pennar, the route proceeds pleasantly but unremarkably south-eastwards through fields and woodland on the north side of the river, arriving at the A4139 and turning right on to it to cross the bridge. A glance at the map will indicate that since the roundabout on the south side of the Cleddau Bridge, you have done three sides of a big rectangle and could simply have stuck to the A4139 from the roundabout onwards, saving yourself considerable time and effort. The purist will of course respond that Pembroke River's pleasant scenery and Pembroke Dock's colourful maritime history repay exploration for their own sake, and as for the retail warehouses, who knows when one might be visiting the area in future and will be only too grateful, if the need arises, to know how easily one can lay one's hands on a five-kilo bag of cement mix or a sackful of potting compost?

The old town of Pembroke (123.5) is an undeniably attractive place, and is the highlight of the walk from the Cleddau Bridge back to the sea. Its main street contains many old houses, but its chief attraction is its castle with a spectacular riverside setting. With a keep almost 80ft high and walls 20ft thick, it was the birthplace of Henry Tudor in 1457, but parts of it date back nearly 300 years before that. You may either turn right immediately after crossing the bridge and walk round the castle walls to arrive at a road fork, or you may continue from the bridge to a T-junction, turning right to arrive soon at the same spot. The national trail takes the right fork, this being the B4320, and follows it through the suburban village of Monkton, heading just south of west.

At a sharp bend in the road, at the southern foot of a marshy inlet, the route turns right on to a narrower road and shortly right again on to a footpath which proceeds through open country, describing a crude semicircle round the village of Hundleton and reaching a narrow road just west of the village. Walkers pushed for time can simply follow the road through the village and out the other side.

Continuing roughly westwards towards Goldborough, you soon reach a very charming wooded valley, turning right on to a path that emerges from the woods and proceeds north-westwards past the tip of Goldborough Pill, rising gently with good views of Pembroke River. This is pleasant enough walking, as is the mild descent to another attractive wooded valley at Lambeeth, and the climb up the other side to Lambeeth Farm. The route continues along a path heading north-westwards, passing through an area of woodland and then alongside an approach road to Pembroke power station which now monopolises the scene to the east.

The route leaves the approach road, turning right on to a footpath then left on to a lane which leads to the tiny hamlet of Pwllcrochan. Though its pretty church boasts a proud spire, pointing in determined fashion towards heaven, it is dwarfed completely by the towering chimneys of the massive Texaco oil refinery immediately behind. You may recall the lovely cove of Pwllcrochan between Strumble Head and Abercastle many miles back and wistfully compare the magnificent prospect afforded there with the rather less appealing surroundings you face now. The feelings will be similar to those of the avid cinema-goer who goes along to watch *Singin' in the Rain* at his local multiplex, nostalgically recalling the time he saw and adored the Gene Kelly classic, only to find himself watching a rather feeble film about a party of buskers on a day trip to Manchester.

Pwllcrochan to Freshwater West

The route turns right at Pwllcrochan on to another metalled road which leads down towards the south bank of Milford Haven, with the oil refinery immediately to your left. The road peters out but the way forward is obvious as the route now re-enters the National Park and proceeds beside the Haven. It drops down to Bulwell Bay, with the town of Milford Haven visible straight across the water, then cuts round the neck of two mini headlands, Popton Point and Sawdern Point. Fort Popton was built on Popton Point in the last century to defend the Haven and was subsequently incorporated into an oil terminal.

Once past Sawdern Point, you reach Angle Bay. For much of the walk round the bay, famous for its cockles, there is no path and you will have to pick your way through rocks, seaweed and often soggy sand to make progress. Moreover, the scene to your left for the early part of the walk on the foreshore is dominated by the refinery installations. Things do pick up; the refinery is left behind, and soon after joining a lane you arrive at the village of Angle (135), a useful stopping-place and the last spot for many miles with a reasonable level of amenities.

Continuing on round the bay, still following a lane, you pass the Old Point House Inn which contains a fire that supposedly has not gone out in 300 years, then you round Angle Point, and continue past a lifeboat station away from Angle Bay. Excitement now wells up, as the long trek round the Haven is nearly over and the open sea is just a short way away. Heading slightly north of west, the route continues along the modest clifftops past Chapel Bay, then at West Pill swings south-westwards to West Angle Bay. Thorn Island, on which stands an island fort that was built in 1854 and was later converted into a hotel, can be seen just a short way into the Haven, and across the Haven you will see out towards St Ann's Head. The inland section is over and true coastal walking resumes.

The next five miles to Freshwater West provide walking that is truly breathtaking; Rat Island, Sheep Island with its traces of an Iron Age settlement, Guttle Hole and the bays of East and West Pickard, all bring scenes of rugged splendour, the benign green-coated upper slopes giving way to sheer sandstone faces that in turn plunge to the boiling frothing waters. I recall walking this section in a dense fog that blotted out all the views. With no other walkers about, all having the sense to stay indoors and wait for a clearer day, there was an eerie silence which was broken only by the raucous tones of the foghorn at regular intervals. In my exasperation at not getting the views to St Ann's Head to which I had so looked forward during the weary trudge round Milford

Haven, each blast of the foghorn seemed like a redoubled mockery of my efforts, and as wretchedly impotent in helping to improve the prevailing conditions as a lunchtime forecast from Michael Fish.

Freshwater West to Bosherston

Freshwater West is one of Pembrokeshire's finest beaches, the covering of the grey shingle on the foreshore resembling a huge shadow across the golden sands. On the southern edge of Freshwater West is a preserved seaweed collector's hut where edible seaweed was gathered to be made into laverbread. Laverbread, incidentally, is still a popular delicacy in parts of South Wales; the seaweed is boiled and reduced to a black mush, then may be dipped in oatmeal and fried.

Behind the foreshore of Freshwater West stands a long line of grass-topped dunes, known as the Broomhill Burrows. These are diminutive in comparison with the monstrous sandstone piles nearby, but tower nobly above the beach like a miniature mountain range. You may, if you wish, follow the sands, but at high tide it will be necessary to resort to the Burrows, eventually turning right on to the B4319, temporarily leaving the sea behind. The reason is that the coastline from here to Elegug Stacks is owned by the Army and accessible only on special guided tours. Indeed, the whole of the coastline between here and Bosherston, and the areas immediately inland from it, is used for Army activity and it is vital to plan ahead to ensure that the spectacular coastal section eastwards from Elegug Stacks is open and available on the day you are walking this section. (Tourist information offices will advise.)

The route stays on the road as far as Castlemartin (145); it is tedious and anticlimactical stuff, but made bearable by the excitement of what awaits. Either by continuing along the B4319, or turning left on to a minor road at Castlemartin and right on to another road at the village of Warren, the route continues east of Castlemartin to a crossroads, where turning on to a metalled road heading south-westwards takes you down to the sea just west of Elegug Stacks. (If you are unfortunate enough to have chosen a day when this part of the route is closed, it will be necessary to continue on the B4319 through Merrion, turning right at the hamlet of Sampson on to a minor road that leads down to Bosherston. The route from here back to the coast is described below.)

On reaching the sea, the route turns left along the top of limestone cliffs for what is one of the finest parts on the whole national trail. The section commences in spectacular fashion with two fine natural features just out to sea: firstly the Green Bridge of Wales, a wide and dramatic rock arch that rises majestically from the surging waters, and secondly Elegug Stacks, which are two huge limestone teeth shooting upwards out of the sea, and perfect nesting places for seabirds such as guillemots, kittiwakes and razorbills.

The scenery is no less splendid as you continue south-eastwards via Flimston Bay, Bullslaughter Bay, Mewsford Point and the Castle, passing a number of Iron Age forts. There are caves, arches, grotesquely-shaped gaps in the rock known as blowholes because of the spray blown up through the gaps by the swell of the sea, and a succession of terrifyingly tall and steep limestone faces, with the narrowest channels of seawater darting through the gaps at the bottom. Care does need to be taken near to the blowholes, which may be quite alarming to vertigo sufferers in the party. The steepness of the rock faces is attributable to huge earth movements known as the Armorican Orogeny that took place a small matter of 250 million years ago, and which upended the limestone bedding planes on the sea floor. It is the faulting in the rock, and accompanying marine erosion, that has led to the amazing cliffscapes on this section. The most famous fault of all on this section is Huntsman's Leap, a narrow slit in the rock 200 yards long and over 100ft deep but in places only a few feet wide. It got its name from a huntsman who is said to have successfully cleared it on his horse, only to die of fright when he realised what he had done!

As if this natural beauty were not enough, shortly beyond Huntsman's Leap comes one of the most famous landmarks of the whole route, namely St Govan's Chapel. Dating back to the thirteenth century – although the original chapel is thought to date back to the sixth century – this tiny stone structure neatly fills a cleft in the cliff that is so small it seems inconceivable that anyone could build on it. Indeed, the only way to enter it is by leaving the coast path and taking a steep flight of steps that drop directly into its austere interior. By exiting from the west of the chapel it is possible to descend to the beach. At the point where the flight of steps leaves the coast path to reach the chapel, a road comes down from Bosherston; this may be useful to walkers who have had to travel to Bosherston from Castlemartin by the inland route because of firing activity, although this road is also closed at certain times.

From the chapel it is a short walk along the coast path to St Govan's Head, the most southerly point on the national trail, and offering superb views to Stackpole Head a short way to the north-east. Having got round the headland, you proceed north-eastwards past the little creek of New Quay to the lovely sands of Broad Haven – not to be confused with its namesake on St Brides Bay. This Broad Haven is definitely more interesting, not only for its sublime surroundings but also its lagoon, set back from the beach with a carpet of heather along one edge and banks of limestone at its inland end. Separating Broad Haven from Bosherston are a series of lily pools, created by the Earl of Cawdor in the eighteenth century for his Stackpole Estate. Surrounded by woodland, the pools provide a pleasant contrast to the awesome ruggedness of the nearby cliffs, with the lilies at their best in June. Paths on either side of the pools allow a short circular walk via Bosherston, and it is one of the pool-side paths that the eastbound walker will use to get to Broad Haven if Army activity has kept him away from the coast all the way from Castlemartin.

Bosherston to Tenby

Bosherston is a pretty place with whitewashed cottages and a thirteenth-century church, and you may be fortunate enough to obtain refreshments in season. Proceeding from Broad Haven, and rounding the modest Saddle Point, the next objective is Stackpole Head, another fascinating study in limestone, and on rounding this headland, you have a lovely view of the golden sands of Barafundle Bay. Proceeding round the bay, the coast path continues to Stackpole Quay, believed to be the smallest quay in Wales, and once used as a base for the export of limestone. In fact it is at this point that limestone gives way for the time being to old red sandstone, and as the coast path continues via Greenala Point – site of an Iron Age camp – and Trewent Point, the cliffscapes provide a pleasing contrast of lush green and rich brown.

Rounding Trewent Point, the route drops down to Freshwater East (155.5), a bay with a village of the same name on the hillside above it. It certainly lacks the charisma of Freshwater West although accommodation should be found here if needed. I endured one of my least agreeable nights on the national trail at Freshwater East; my host at my bed and breakfast had forgotten he had promised to provide me with an evening meal, there being no pub for miles, and although he did deign to cook for me, the food was simple and expensively priced. There was no bath, the shower spewed out only ice-cold water, and although the absence of a TV was no hardship, there was no lounge to relax in either. I slept so badly that I was reduced to sitting up in bed between 2.40 a.m. and 4.30 a.m. solemnly reading from cover to cover the entire stock of the previous year's brochures and tourist newspapers that were gathering dust on the windowsill and failing to kindle any desire in me to sample the delights of the local glass-blowing works, woollen mill, or nearest preserved steam railway.

From Freshwater East to Giltar Point the walking is truly magnificent. Proceeding round the bay, you pass another Iron Age camp and continue on to West Moor Cliff, on which is a trig. point at a height of just under 300ft. Between the cliffs of West Moor and East Moor is the lovely Swanlake Bay, and beyond East Moor is Manorbier Bay giving easy access to the nearby village of Manorbier. The village is best known for being the birthplace, in about 1145, of Giraldus Cambrensis, or Gerald the Welshman, the author of a vivid account of life in medieval Wales. He was born in Manorbier Castle, a splendid Norman fortification which stands at the south-west edge of the village.

Nearby is a fine twelfth-century church that boasts an impressive tower and a brass memorial to the SS *Satrap*, lost off the nearby coast in 1915. East of Manorbier the cliff scenery is quite outstanding, a firm path following the cliff edge past a succession of narrow chasms in the sandstone. There is a slight inland detour to avoid the old military installations on Old Castle Head but there follows a quite delectable stretch of coastline past Skrinkle Head and Lydstep Point.

Skrinkle Haven consists of three tiny coves, the largest of which is blessed with a beautiful sandy beach and huge limestone cliffs with twin caves cut into the cliff face on the east side. The most easterly of the three coves contains Church Doors, a remarkably tall and thin natural arch of limestone. Lydstep Point, a few minutes beyond, is bypassed by the official route, but a detour is almost mandatory to view the incredible cliff formations – further legacies of the Armorican Orogeny – with huge vertical thrusts of carboniferous limestone interspersed with caves and arches, all constantly vulnerable to the raging seas. There are good views to Caldey Island, where a religious community founded in the sixth century is today maintained by Cistercian monks who sell perfumes and toiletries they make from wild flowers found on the island. Boat trips run to the island in season.

Anticlimax follows as the way drops to the beach at Lydstep Haven with its intrusive holiday park, and there is a stiff climb back on to the cliffs. However the walking soon improves as the route proceeds to Giltar Point past the viewpoint of Proud Giltar, near to which is the splendidly-named hamlet of Bubbleton and Valleyfield Top. (Access to Giltar Point may, again, be restricted by Army activity, in which case you will be diverted by Penally to South Beach, north of Giltar Point.)

After rounding Giltar Point, from which there are fine views to Tenby and Caldey Island, there is another drop and a lovely walk along the firm sands of South Beach to arrive at Tenby (169). This is a justifiably popular resort, with a beautiful harbour, excellent sandy beaches, a commendable restraint on tacky concessions to the tourist trade, and fine views over the sea – more specifically, Carmarthen Bay – to Caldey Island, Giltar Point and the lovely coastline towards Saundersfoot. Arguably the town's most impressive feature is its now ruined castle, built in the twelfth century on a rocky headland, but there is so much else to see, including fine fourteenth-century town walls, quaint narrow streets, rows of Georgian and Regency houses, the part-thirteenth-century church of St Mary (possibly Wales' largest parish church) the fifteenth-century Tudor Merchant's House, and, across the beach, St Catherine's Island, dominated by a nineteenth-century fortress.

Again, the walker will contrast the remote ruggedness of the cliff scenery a few miles back with the carefree holiday atmosphere that pervades the town, and should not be surprised if, upon asking one of the town's shop assistants for literature about the Armorican Orogeny, the assistant either leads the enquirer vaguely in the direction of a shelf full of books on ancient flower-arranging techniques or points discreetly towards a half-hidden assembly of sex manuals.

Tenby to Amroth
Whether you choose to stay within sight of the sea, effectively avoiding the centre of Tenby, or prefer to cut through the town centre, you will exit from it beside North Beach, following Waterwynch Lane just east of north, and enjoying a grandstand view back to the town. The lane peters out just before the tiny hamlet of Waterwynch and there is some tough walking along the coast path towards Saundersfoot, including a particularly steep climb out of the thickly wooded Lodge Valley. The fact that this coastline faces eastwards, and is thus sheltered from the prevailing winds, has made it easier for woodland to thrive here.

Once you have regained the clifftops, there are fine views to Monkstone Beach – another glorious stretch of sand – and the nearby wooded headland of Monkstone Point, which you arrive at shortly. There is an optional but highly recommended detour to the Point itself, from where Amroth, the end of the walk, is visible. There is then a very straightforward walk, most of it through woodland, down to Saundersfoot along the coast path, although the sands can be followed all the way from Monkstone Point to Saundersfoot, and indeed on to Amroth just three miles beyond Saundersfoot, if the tide is right. Another type of rock, known as coal measures, can be found hereabouts, and a tight fold in that rock has produced a remarkable cave just south of Saundersfoot Harbour.

Saundersfoot (173) was in fact established in the nineteenth century as a port for exporting good anthracite coal mined from nearby pits, and mining stopped as recently as the outbreak of the Second World War. It has now become a popular yachting centre and holiday resort, although with none of the charisma or charm of Tenby; my impression of it, I have to say, was of a rather garish place, dominated by tourist amenities of the most unsubtle kind. The last little section of route begins in an unusual fashion, as Coppet Hall Point is negotiated not by means of a traditional coast path but through a number of tunnels built for narrow-gauge railway lines that conveyed coal-bearing trains to Saundersfoot. You remain on the old railway lines, but this time above ground and by the sea, to Wiseman's Bridge. The coal measures can be unstable and you should be aware of the possibility of diversions caused by rock falls.

At Wiseman's Bridge the route turns right on to a metalled road and follows it uphill out of the village, then turns right again on to a path that descends to Amroth (176.5), another village with mining connections. The sands here were used for a full rehearsal for the D-Day landings, witnessed by Churchill, Montgomery and Eisenhower. If you arrive at low tide, it is worth venturing on to the sands where you may be able to observe tree stumps and roots that are the remains of an ancient forest noted by Giraldus Cambrensis in 1183.

On arriving at Amroth, it is an easy road walk past the castle, a comparatively modern structure, to the plaque on a block of stone in the shingle, marking the official ending of the walk, both in English and in Welsh. It is most satisfying to see on the plaque, above the recognition of the opening of the route by Wynford Vaughan Thomas in 1970, the words 'Poppit Sands 180 Miles' (though if the most direct route, avoiding detours, has been taken, it will have worked out a few miles less!). Having experienced the feelings of satisfaction, you must then work out how to get home. It is a long and anticlimactical walk to Kilgetty, the nearest railway station; moreover, trains back to civilisation from there are slow and infrequent, and walkers relying on public transport will have to grin and bear the frustration of a journey of possibly several hours to be reunited with their loved ones, however anxious their nearest and dearest are to be regaled with the heroic exploits of Proud Giltar or thrilled by an intense session of Armorican Orogeny.

SUMMARY OF PLACES OF INTEREST

Pen yr Afr, Witches Cauldron★, Dinas Head, Strumble Head★, Pwll Deri, Porthgain, St David's Head★, Whitesand Bay, St David's, Solva, Dinas Fawr, Newgale Sands, Deer Park, Marloes Sands, Pembroke, Green Bridge of Wales★, Elegug Stacks★, Huntsman's Leap, St Govan's Chapel★, Broad Haven (nr. Bosherston), Barafundle Bay, Manorbier Castle, Skrinkle Haven★, Lydstep Point, Tenby★.

AMENITIES ON OR NEAR THE ROUTE

St Dogmaels (L), Poppit Sands (L), Newport, Fishguard★, Goodwick, Trefin (L), St David's, Solva, Newgale (L), Broad Haven, Little Haven (L), Dale, Hakin, Milford Haven★, Neyland, Pembroke Dock, Pembroke★, Angle (L), Bosherston (L), Freshwater East (L), Manorbier (L), Penally (L), Tenby★, Saundersfoot.

The West Highland Way

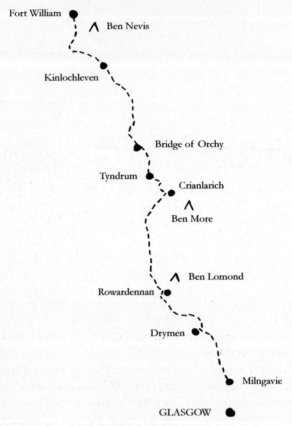

Length: 93 miles.
Start: Milngavie, on the outskirts of Glasgow.
Finish: Fort William, below Ben Nevis.
Nature: A walk through fine Scottish Highland scenery using well-signposted and well-defined paths and tracks.
Difficulty rating: Moderate, strenuous in places.
Average time
of completion: 7–8 days.

The West Highland Way

The West Highland Way provides a splendid snapshot of the Scottish Highlands and an excellent introduction to the particular joys and challenges of walking in Scotland. It was created under the Countryside (Scotland) Act 1967, and was opened in 1980 with the aim of providing a safe and uncomplicated route through the glorious West Highland countryside. This has been achieved using a number of historic routes including drovers' roads, old railway lines, and military roads that were masterminded in the eighteenth century by General Wade and Major Caulfield. There is no particular historic significance in the chosen start and finish points of the route. The start of the journey, on the fringes of the Glaswegian suburbs, is Scottish walking at its most benign and as much suited to Sunday strollers as to long-distance walkers. By the end however, the foot-traveller will be within easy reach of some of the most challenging walks that the country has to offer.

The Way is not especially technically difficult, as the route is so well waymarked and the tracks are usually very obvious, even in bad weather. It is therefore not surprising that thousands of walkers attempt it each year, tempted no doubt by the plethora of guidebooks promising a well-marked passage through the wonderfully romantic Scottish Highland scenery. The surroundings certainly are magnificent. No walker can fail to be seduced by the wildness and remoteness of the heather moorlands, the peace and mystery of the lochs, the hills with panoramic views from their summits, and, of course, the high mountains. With this scenery comes a huge variety of wildlife, from wildcats and otters to ptarmigans and golden eagles.

Yet not all of those who start off from Milngavie full of optimism and enthusiasm will complete the journey. The reasons for failure will vary. Some walkers will have underestimated the degree of patience needed to negotiate the walk beside Loch Lomond. Some will be surprised by the lack of amenities on certain parts of the journey. Some will have quite inappropriate footwear for the negotiation of muddy or flooded sections of the route, or the long hours of pounding the old stony military roads and drovers' tracks. Some will simply be beaten back by the most fickle adversary of all – the weather. A lengthy downpour can transform what would be a painless and exhilarating day's march into a thoroughly demoralising and unhappy experience, prompting the hardiest adventurers to think twice before proceeding any further.

Advance planning, proper equipment and awareness of the facilities that exist – or do not, as the case may be – are all essential, even though they may not seem so to the walker travelling on his suburban train to Milngavie among locals whose feet are encased in high-heeled wedge sandals or fashion boots and whose cranial protection from the elements is confined to their newly-purchased copy of the *Daily Record*.

Milngavie to Balmaha

Milngavie (it may assist walkers attempting to purchase train or bus tickets to the town to know that it is pronounced 'Mull-guy') makes a pleasant start to the Way. A wall-plaque in the town square announces the official start of the route. The Way turns off the square to leave the town in a direction slightly west of north, along the course of an old railway. It then proceeds beside a stream, Allander Water, before turning right into Allander Park and joining a well-defined track which proceeds north-westwards through Mugdock Wood. Mugdock was gifted to the people of Glasgow in 1980 by Sir Hugh Fraser and is now one of some 40 country parks in Scotland.

Continuing along an excellent track, you reach Craigallian Bridge and cross a road, then proceeding close to Allander Water, you carry on in a north-westerly direction to reach Craigallian Loch. The loch is very pleasantly situated amongst trees with the fine backdrop of Craigallian House. The route swings gently north-eastwards as it passes to the left of the loch, then goes forward to pass just to the right of Carbeth Loch. There are good views ahead to the imposing tops of the Campsie Hills, of which Dumgoyne, at around 1,500ft, is the most impressive, whilst the Kilpatrick Hills lie to the west. Having passed Carbeth Loch you continue to the B821. A right turn here would take you to the village of Strathblane, but the Way goes left along the road before soon turning right.

Now the character of the walk changes, turning from a gentle woodland and loch-side ramble to a more exciting march through wilder and more open countryside, as excellent views open out across the farmland of Strath Blane to the mountains around Loch Lomond. You proceed along a good path heading just east of north to pass the buildings of Arlehaven, then swing north-westwards to pass just to the west of the huge wooded hill of Dumgoyach and nearby standing stones which date back to the New Stone Age. You arrive at Dumgoyach Farm where you join a farm road that heads north-eastwards, descending to Dumgoyach Bridge.

Here the character of the route changes again, as it turns left (north-westwards) and for the next four or five miles follows the course of an old railway – the so-called Blane valley line. To the right are splendid views to the summit of Dumgoyne, but much nearer at hand, and one suspects more pleasing to the visitor, is the Glengoyne Distillery, reached by a short detour to the right less than a mile beyond Dumgoyach Bridge. When the connoisseur of fine liquor learns that Glengoyne has been producing malt whisky since 1833 and its shop offers supplies of it all the year round, he may decide to terminate the walk there and then on the basis that the remaining 84 miles would only be an anticlimax.

Stronger-willed West Highland Wayfarers will continue along the old railway line, crossing the A81 at Dumgoyne village and continuing virtually parallel to it as far as a crossing of the B834. The walking can be muddy and becomes uninspiring for a while – a sewage works has to be passed just beyond Dumgoyne village, and the surrounding trees and nearby houses tend to blot out the wider views – but better things lie ahead. After crossing the B834 the route, continuing to follow the old railway line, stays to the right of the A81 but then crosses it and continues north-westwards to reach a minor road. You turn left on to it, leaving the old railway, and soon arrive at the hamlet of Gartness where there is a fast-flowing river, the Endrick, and some modest but charming waterfalls. The Endrick is a fine salmon stream and herons are commonly seen in its waters. Having crossed the river, you follow the road for two miles or so, heading confidently towards Drymen. However soon after a sharp left-hand bend, with Drymen straight ahead, the route turns right on to a path which leads to the A811.

Many walkers will wish to detour to Drymen (12), either continuing along the minor road or turning left at the A811. The half-mile detour alongside this busy road can be trying, but Drymen (pronounced 'Drimmen' and meaning 'little ridge') contains a pretty village green and many attractive buildings of red sandstone, and offers a good range of amenities. There will be precious few of those now for the next thirty miles. The route, having reached the A811, turns right on to it and proceeds beside it as far as the hamlet of Blarnavaid, then turns left. A steady climb takes you into the extensive woodland of Garadhban Forest. Through the woods there are excellent views not only of the Campsie Fells and the low-lying terrain that has been crossed since Milngavie, but also of Loch Lomond, which will become the dominant feature of the walk for many miles.

The forest, dominated by larch and spruce, is home to many woodland birds including finches and crossbills. The Way follows an excellent track through the forest, heading north-westwards. With the western fringe of the woodland in sight, two possible routes are signposted. The main route heads right, continuing north-westwards through the forest. For a month in spring, during the lambing season, you must turn left (south-westwards), initially through the forest and then into open country along a track leading to Milton of Buchanan, then turn right for a rather tedious road walk to Balmaha, where at the car park you meet the main route. Meanwhile the main route emerges from the wood, and strikes out westwards across the bracken-clad moor, with panoramic views to the southern end of Loch Lomond.

After crossing the Burn of Mar there is a big climb up to Conic Hill, which means 'hill above the bog' and is on the line of a great geological fault covering Scotland. This is the first serious test of the lungs of the West Highland Way pilgrim; the ascent is not especially steep but it is long and tiring. It actually goes round the edge of the summit and a detour is needed to reach the very top, at comfortably over 1,000ft. Even if the detour is not made, the surrounding views are magnificent.

Anticlimax then follows with a very steep descent south-westwards on a slippery cobbled surface towards Balmaha on the eastern shore of Loch Lomond. You then proceed on a rather easier track through woodland known as the Balmaha Plantation, the gradient easing as you make further progress, and soon you arrive at the huge car park at Balmaha (19). The village lacks Drymen's charm, and although its setting is delightful, its amenities are limited. Hoping for a pleasant loch-side café to welcome me after the long trek from Drymen, I had to make do with a polystyrene beaker of tea and a greasy ring doughnut, consumed at a sodden table provided on the patio outside.

Balmaha to Ardleish

From Balmaha onwards, the Way follows the eastern shores of Loch Lomond, up to its northern tip. It is an extremely tough walk, immediately beginning with a stiff climb to Craigie Fort which sets the scene for the next 20 miles or so. The next mile, round Arrochymore Point, is innocuous enough as you proceed through pleasant woodland on a good path, and then briefly join a road. The road goes all the way to Rowardennan, which lies on the route, and you might feel tempted to stick to it if pushed for time. The route, however, soon leaves it for a rather circuitous wander through the forest to the left of it, rejoins it near Cashell Farm, forsakes it again for a forest walk to the right, briefly returns to it and then leaves by turning left into the forest again.

The Way stays close to the shore of the loch for a while, but then cuts off the headland of Ross Point to proceed more directly north-westwards, eventually reaching the road once more but immediately leaving it to continue near the loch edge as far as Rowardennan (26). Here the road option ends. Rowardennan offers modest amenities but its setting is splendid, with views across the loch and also to the summit of Ben Lomond. This is the most southerly of the Munros (Scottish mountains over 3,000ft high). Leaving Rowardennan, heading north-westwards on a clear track, the going is deceptively simple.

At Ptarmigan Lodge you have the choice of turning left up a rougher path, giving closer views to the loch and the chance to visit a crag known as Rob Roy's Prison. This area has close connections with Rob Roy. Born in 1671, he became a protection racketeer following the collapse of his cattle-droving business. He gained the reputation of the Robin Hood of Scotland following a feud with the Duke of Montrose, and it is believed that it may have been in this rocky den on the shores of Loch Lomond where he held Montrose's men to ransom.

The main route proceeds along the obvious forest track and progress is fast for the next three miles. Then, however, the firm track gives way to a much more challenging path through the woods. Although the line of the path is clear, there are numerous small obstructions in the form of tree roots and rocks, as well as subtle undulations on often muddy surfaces which make the going exceedingly awkward. It is up to you to decide how best to negotiate the obstructions, but you must take care because a single slip could mean a nasty fall and the end of the West Highland Way adventure. There are numerous crossings of streams, some of which take you over bridges, but others require some energetic fording. After rain, which comes frequently to the loch, the path can be extremely boggy. There is one brief respite from the woodland walking as you pass the charming house at Cailness, but forestry remains the primary theme as you struggle on to Inversnaid (33).

The reward for reaching this oasis is a very impressive waterfall and a hotel offering welcome refreshment. Inversnaid is not without historic interest either; a garrison was established here in 1713 in an attempt to control the MacGregor clan. Beyond Inversnaid, the going – still alongside the eastern shore of the loch – is deceptively easy for a while, but beyond the boathouse the gentle wide track narrows to provide several miles' more awkward walking through the woods.

The trickiest section is around Rob Roy's Cave. The cave is somewhat less dramatic than it sounds, being merely a crack in the rock. Walkers may waste valuable time and energy in the middle of a tiring day trying to trace something grander, although the view at the almost sheer outcrops of rock in the midst of the thick woodland is impressive. Whilst you may feel slightly nonplussed that such features as Rob Roy's Prison and Cave are so difficult to locate, you might do well to consider the unpalatable alternative: wide access roads, capacious car parks and shops selling everything from Rob Roy sew-on rucksack badges to Rob Roy assorted caramel fudge.

The walk continues through the woods up the eastern side of the loch, the going marginally easier than it was south of Inversnaid, but still slow and awkward at times. Ironically, cars can be seen heading effortlessly along the A82 on the western shore of the loch. Now you can appreciate the contrast between the two ends of the loch: at its southern end, a wide lake set in gentle rolling countryside, and at the northern end, a much narrower and deeper trench of water with a more formidable background of mountains and hills, formed by earlier glacial activity. At its deepest point the loch is 630ft and at its widest it is five miles. It contains 30 islands, some of which were populated by Irish missionaries from the fifth century who hoped that the island setting would protect their monasteries and convents from marauders.

The loch, and the woodland on its banks, is home to a stunning array of bird life. Peregrines, merlins, red harriers, willow warblers, tree pipits, tufted ducks, green wagtails, chaffinches, jays, woodpeckers, redstarts, pine martens, nesting pied flycatchers and dippers can all be seen on this section of the Way. Foxes and deer are not uncommon and if you are very fortunate you may see a wildcat or an otter; otters have often been seen on the burns and rivers that feed the loch.

Continuing from Inversnaid towards the northern end of the loch, you will pass one of the loveliest of the islands, named Island I Vow which contains a sixteenth-century castle ruin. In the spring the island is awash with daffodils. Half a mile after leaving I Vow behind, the path turns slightly away from the loch to give an easier walk, before passing the hamlet of Doune and descending back to the lochside. Across the loch is the village of Ardlui, reachable at certain times by means of a ferry. At the ferry 'terminal,' the route turns away from the loch, heading still north-westwards past the buildings of Ardleish. Here you reach the head of the loch and can sigh with relief, knowing that the most difficult section of the route is behind you.

Ardleish to Bridge of Orchy

The Way, now heading north, climbs up to a superb vantage point just to the east of the modest summit of Cnap Mor, and from here the view down Loch Lomond is staggering. Looking at the way in which the wooded east bank slopes so steeply, it is quite impossible to see how a path could have been forged through it! A good path initially across moorland, past the tiny Dubh Lochan, and then downhill through woodland brings you to the hamlet of Beinglas and its unusual assembly of wooden wigwams, which at the time of writing were offering accommodation. There is a fine waterfall just to the east of the route, as Ben Glas Burn tumbles down to meet the river Falloch. Nearby is the slightly larger settlement of Inverarnan (39), reached by a walk across a field, over a footbridge across Glen Falloch, and alongside the busy A82.

The Drovers at Inverarnan offered one of the more bizarre night's stays that I experienced on my walk up the Way, its more memorable characteristics being a prodigious array of stuffed animals, and a TV only offering access to an obscure satellite channel. Thus it was that I spent a curious evening listening to the incessant rain pouring down outside whilst watching a clearly disturbed young man attempting to cross the River Thames by tightrope.

With Loch Lomond left behind, the Way now proceeds initially northwards and then north-eastwards, along the east bank of the River Falloch, which flows into the loch. The A82 is now a much closer companion, immediately beyond the west bank of the river, and beyond the A82 is the railway. This is the famous West Highland Railway linking Glasgow with Oban, Fort William and Mallaig. Opened in 1894, it is a remarkable feat of engineering and one of the most scenic lines in Great Britain. For a few miles the path, river, road and railway proceed together up Glen Falloch, all four thoroughfares sandwiched between massive inhospitable mountain wildernesses. The going is clear and excellent, and also exciting, contrasting happily with the closed claustrophobic walking in the woodlands by Loch Lomond.

Two miles or so beyond Beinglas are the Falls of Falloch. These are at their best after heavy rains, when they become a quite breathtaking spectacle. There are numerous sets of falls, with vast volumes of white water being hurled through the narrowest and rockiest of gorges, all with the fine backcloth of the hills and mountains beyond Glen Falloch. The river becomes more subdued beyond the falls, but here heavy rainfall can be a distinct disadvantage, for the path hereabouts is liable to flood and even the provision of planks may not prevent boots, socks and feet taking an unscheduled soaking.

At the pretty farm of Derrydaroch, you cross the Falloch and proceed immediately adjacent to it; at one point a massive waterfall careers down to hit the ground barely a yard from the course of the path. Shortly afterwards you cross both the road and railway in close succession, and continue along an old military road, climbing steadily away from Glen Falloch although still proceeding north-eastwards. In just about a mile, however, the route abruptly changes direction, swinging north-westwards into an extensive area of woodland.

By continuing north-eastwards you may detour to visit Crianlarich. This village contains the best range of amenities since

Drymen, and also has a railway station on the West Highland Railway, although trains are infrequent. Alfred Wainwright, the famous fellwalker, relates how, having planned to catch the 8.30 a.m. train from Crianlarich to Fort William, he set off from his hotel to the station and, to his horror, saw his train leaving, having been timed to depart at 8 o'clock, with no more trains to Fort William until the evening. Even great men can make mistakes . . .

The Way proceeds north-westwards through the forest. Unlike the Loch Lomond walk, the path here is much wider and clearer, and there are frequent views to the valley of Strath Fillan to the right, as well as the huge 3,843ft summit of Ben More. There are numerous other Munros nearby, including Ben Lui, Ben Oss, Beinn Dubhchraig and Ben Challum. Wainwright says he has a soft spot for Ben More, it being one of the few Scottish mountains with a name he can pronounce with confidence! Deer are common hereabouts, and you should look out for buzzards and even eagles.

Always well-marked, the route snakes its way north-westwards; it is the best sort of walking, being comfortable and easily navigable but in surroundings that are quite magnificent. Having gained some height since the crossing of the A82 beyond Derrydaroch, the Way now drops down into Strath Fillan to cross both the railway and the A82 again. You turn left to proceed alongside the A82 then turn right to cross the wide River Fillan. Just like Glen Falloch, Strath Fillan nestles cosily between formidable mountains, and manages to accommodate road, river, railway and West Highland Way. The Way remains in Strath Fillan as far as Tyndrum. After crossing the river, it heads briefly north-eastwards on an obvious track, soon passing the remains of St Fillan's Priory. St Fillan was an Irish monk who brought Christianity to many Highlanders twelve centuries ago.

Near Kirton Farm the Way swings north-westwards on a metalled track, gaining a little height, then at Auchtertyre swings south-westwards to return to and cross over the A82 at Tomna Croiche. Here there are excellent views to Ben Lui and Beinn Dubhchraig. The route proceeds in a roughly westerly direction alongside the river through a moorland landscape, crossing a narrower tributary stream and entering an area of woodland on a

wide track. Shortly however, the Way leaves this track, turning right
to head north-westwards on a path through the woods. This path
can get very muddy and in wet weather you may be forgiven for
wishing you had stuck to the A82 which proceeds more directly to
Tyndrum (51).

The Way reaches a metalled minor road by Tyndrum (Lower)
Station, and turns right to reach the A82 and the village centre.
Just the other side of the A82 is Tyndrum (Upper) Station, giving
Tyndrum arguably more railway stations per head of the population
than any other village in Great Britain and possibly much of Europe.
The village enjoys a good range of amenities including, at the time
of writing, a self-service restaurant that is a favoured stopping-place
for A82 drivers. The wet and weary walker approaching the village
in search of refreshment can only pray that his visit is not
immediately preceded by that of a coach party which quickly forms
a queue that snakes halfway round the room, leaving him to tag
miserably on the end and shuffle wretchedly food-hatchwards for
the next 20 minutes whilst octogenarians ahead of him debate
earnestly with the serving staff the relative merits of mushroom-
filled jacket potatoes or beef and onion hotpot, and fiddle in the
recesses of their pockets and purses for the requisite cash.

The next six miles to Bridge of Orchy must rank as one of the
fastest and easiest sections on the whole route. Since it follows an
old military road for much of the way, the surface is firm and the
track so wide that only a genius could get lost. Moreover, after an
initial climb there is a steady descent and then comparatively level
walking all the way. Initially the route squeezes neatly between
A82 and railway climbing steadily northwards; this is the branch
heading for Fort William and Mallaig, the Oban branch having
parted company with it at Crianlarich. While the A82 strikes out in
a more north-westerly direction, the Way continues northwards,
dropping down gradually and proceeding beside a river named Allt
Coire Chailein, with the railway maintaining a somewhat higher
elevation to the right.

As you approach the valley bottom, you have the quite
magnificent spectacle of the 3,530ft Beinn Dorain straight ahead
of you, the starkness of its summit perhaps underlined by the

flatness of the river valley immediately to hand. At length you arrive on the valley bottom and, having crossed the river of Allt Kinglass, swing north-westwards on a wide track that heads unerringly on to Bridge of Orchy, with no gain or loss in height. Progress is extremely easy and the walking remains both interesting and enjoyable; the broad flat valley gives fine views to some of the most dramatic Highland scenery, with bleak craggy slopes and thickly forested hills. On reaching the village (57), you cross the railway – this is the last you will see of the West Highland Railway until Fort William – and join a metalled road that goes forward to reach the A82.

Bridge of Orchy has for a long time served walkers' needs well, the station providing trains to Glasgow and the hotel offering both luxury and budget accommodation. Its bar is a popular meeting place for West Highland Way walkers, who are now far enough up the route to compare copious notes about their experiences. I will not easily forget the man in his late twenties who, never having done any long-distance walking before, decided to accomplish the route in style, travelling from London to Glasgow by air and setting forth in a pair of brand new Chris Brasher boots that he had never worn before, let alone broken in. They were giving him so much pain that he was now virtually immobile and was making plans to fly home the next day!

Bridge of Orchy to Kinlochleven
After crossing straight over the A82 and the River Orchy on a bridge that dates back to 1750, the route resumes innocuously enough along a metalled road, but as this bends to the right the Way goes straight ahead, following a track north-westwards through an area of forest and climbing steeply. Emerging from the forest the track continues to climb round the edge of the mini summit of Mam Carraigh. There are fine views from here, most notably ahead to Loch Tulla, its shores bedecked with mature Scots pine. Then, almost at once, you descend in a westerly direction to reach a metalled road by the Inveroran Hotel (60). You turn left on to the road, and make easy progress briefly south-west, then north, along the tarmac. As you go, you cross the Victoria Bridge over the river

known as Abhainn Shira which flows into Loch Tulla, clearly visible to the right.

Beyond Victoria Bridge you go forward to Forest Lodge. This is a crucial moment on the journey, for here the metalled road gives way to the track that will take you over Rannoch Moor. For the next six miles, until civilisation is reached in the form of the next A82 crossing, the Way proceeds northwards over the immense wilderness of the moor; Wainwright describes it as 'a desolation fashioned by Nature and right well has she succeeded. It is [. . .] a labyrinth of bogs, pools, lochans and lochs, stagnant watercourses unable to decide which way to go, and squelching morasses [. . .]. It is the stuff of which nightmares are made.' The good news as far as you are concerned is that the track, a drovers' road, is well-defined and firm, proceeding confidently over the moor with no difficulties of navigation or negotiation even in bad weather, although after heavy rain there can be some flooding on the path itself. Despite its firm surface, the track remains but a slender lifeline amidst surroundings that are terrifying in their bleakness. There are acres upon acres of peat and long, reedy grass, concealing expanses of water and bog that would engulf the walker in an instant; desultory patches of pine forest; streams that curl round the accumulations of peat and broaden into lochs or lochans; and frowning down on the scene are the summits of Meall Beag, Beinn Chaorach and their neighbours, forming a natural barrier to what lies beyond the moor and adding to the sense of total isolation.

There are a few isolated patches of forest which serve as useful landmarks for the walker. Near to one of these, just north-west of Meall Beag, is Ba Bridge, underneath which flows the Ba, one of the many watercourses on Rannoch Moor. On a fine day it is the perfect place to stop and take in the surroundings, but on a wet day it presents a hostile and unwelcoming spot. A mile or so beyond Ba Bridge the track climbs slightly, and the A82 comes into view. As the A82 is approached, the track becomes rougher and you must pick your way carefully along the boulder-strewn path to reach the path that leads to the White Corries ski lift.

You go forward to cross the A82 and join a well-surfaced track on the opposite side. Half a mile down this track, proceeding north-westwards, you reach the Kingshouse Hotel (69.5), surely one of the most isolated hotels in Britain. It gets its name from the fact that the building was used after the Battle of Culloden as barracks for the King's troops. I arrived here shortly after midday, having fought my own battle against rain and wind all the way from Bridge of Orchy over the past three and a quarter hours. Seeking refuge in the Climbers' Bar I met two walkers tucking into a hearty meal, but when I asked them how much walking they had done that day to gain an appetite for their wholesome repast, they reported that they had not even *started* their day's walk yet!

From Kingshouse Hotel the West Highland Way joins a metalled road heading north and then west, and shortly before the road reaches the A82 it branches off and heads along a track heading north-west. The track is in fact an old military road that is as well-defined as the drovers' road across Rannoch Moor, but follows a somewhat erratic course north-westwards, never far from the A82. In due course you return to the A82 and proceed right alongside it, finally joining it at Altnafeadh. On a fine day, the walk from Kingshouse to Altnafeadh is magnificent, with views to the nearby Buachaille Etive Mor whose very distinctive and imposing peak resembles a massive pyramid. It is an extremely difficult mountain to climb; Wainwright says that it is a mountain he can look at for hours without any thought of trying to climb it, being content to 'let it remain one of my Scottish virgins!' It is known as the gateway to Glencoe, and indeed that remarkable glen, full of romantic and historical significance, is just a few minutes' drive away.

At Altnafeadh the route turns right away from the A82, following a track which passes through a patch of woodland and then into an open and much more exciting rugged landscape. A testing climb now ensues. This ascent to the saddle between the peaks of Stob Mhic Mhartuin and Beinn Bheag is known as the Devil's Staircase, and the summit of the pass, at 1,800ft, is the highest point of the route. The Devil's Staircase, though long and lung-testing, is not actually as bad as it sounds, with no difficulties of navigation even in bad weather as the path is so clear. The view from the top certainly gives ample reward for the hard work, with magnificent mountain vistas back to Buachaille Etive Mor and forward towards Ben Nevis.

As the long descent begins, you will catch your first tantalising glimpse of Kinlochleven, the first settlement of any size on the Way since Drymen. However, this is still six miles away and you may wish to pause before continuing in order to gird up your loins for the descent. You can also enjoy the magnificent scenery around you – there is nothing quite as good as this to come – and perhaps amuse yourself by looking at the astonishing names given to streams and mountains nearby. As you proceed, you will need to ford the streams of Allt a Choire Odhair-bhig and Allt a Choire Odhair-mhoir, and to the left are the hills of Sron a Choire Odhair-bhig and Meall Ruigh a Bhricleathaid. One can only marvel at how these wondrously unpronounceable names came to be attached to these places. However the necessary consensus was reached, it is clear that those responsible gave precious little thought to the sensibilities of those who might have to say them out loud, still less those of their listeners who if asking them for directions might be well-advised to carry with them either an umbrella or sufficient shampoo to remove from their hair the plenteous quantities of phlegm that must inevitably rain down upon them.

The descent to Kinlochleven is long and sometimes arduous, and may take a lot longer than you perhaps think it should. However, the route, although initially rough underfoot, is clearly defined; the obvious path follows an old military road which winds its way north-westwards, widens to negotiate a zigzag section that passes a dam and a reservoir, and then continues downhill at a more gentle gradient. The more height is lost, the less barren and more wooded the surroundings become, and the buildings of Kinlochleven, both residential and industrial, become more dominant, although there are good views to the Mamore hills beyond.

In due course you arrive in the valley of the river Leven, passing round the edge of the aluminium works that dominate the village. There is no doubt that the works, powered by the Blackwater Reservoir and connected to it by a huge pipeline coming off the hills, are something of an eyesore, but they are an integral part of the local economy. The route actually runs alongside the pipeline as it nears the works. Then, just before the aluminium works, you swing to the right to cross the pipeline and then the Leven, swing left to join a metalled road past some suburban housing, then go left again along a riverside path which arrives at a road. The route turns right on to the road, although most of the amenities of the village (78.5) can be found by turning left.

After the wilderness of Rannoch Moor and the noble grandeur of Buachaille Etive Mor, it seems somewhat incongruous that just a few hours later you should be marching through a sprawling industrial village, which, it has to be said, is rather lacking in charm. The setting, however, is magnificent, with delightful views across Loch Leven, on the eastern shores of which the village is situated. Before the ferry across Loch Leven was replaced by a bridge at North Ballachulish, this road through Kinlochleven was the only through road link between Fort William and Glencoe. Walkers can, however, be grateful for the amenities which this formerly important road link, as well as the A82, have spawned; it is in fact the last point on the Way before Fort William that supplies are available. A significant variety of sources, from path-side information signboards to satellite TV in the hotels and bed and breakfasts, can inform the walker that the weather tomorrow is going to be just as bad as it has been for the last six days.

Kinlochleven to Fort William

The route, having turned right on to the road, follows it round a sharp bend then heads westwards, still along the road. Shortly it bears right and leaves the road, heading north-westwards along a path. There follows a long uphill slog, but the views provide more than ample reward for your efforts, particularly those across Loch Leven to Sgorr na Ciche, a mountain better known as the Pap of Glencoe. Ahead are the Mamore hills, with numerous Munros all around, each having romantic and mysterious names – Stob Coire na h-Eirghe, Sgorr an Fhuarain, Stob Ban and Sgurr a Mhaim. As with the peaks around the Devil's Staircase, they seem to be a challenge to pronounce, let alone climb! The West Highland Way avoids these lofty summits but even so you certainly need a pause for breath as the path levels out and Kinlochleven and its industrial paraphernalia disappear from view.

An extraordinary section of the route follows, as you take a steady level course westwards through a giant mountain pass, using the lower slopes of Stob Coire na h-Eirghe. Views are restricted to the barren rocky summits on either side, although in fine weather the surroundings will not seem intimidating, and you can enjoy a straightforward walk, keeping your eyes out for short-eared owls, kestrels and ravens. There is the same sort of feeling that Rannoch Moor will have provided – a good firm path in the midst of a remote wilderness offering little or no shelter or sign of habitation. Two ruined farmhouses are testimony to the harsh reality of the surroundings. Eventually, the path swings from west to north-west and, dropping fairly gently, heads towards an area of forest. Indeed, forest walking is to dominate the remainder of the walk.

Proceeding on a good path, an easy but nondescript march northwards through the woods brings you to Blar a'Chaorainn with nothing of note except a metalled road and a signboard giving the heartening news that Fort William is just six and a half miles away. In bad weather you could simply follow the metalled road to Fort William. However, the official route, eschewing tarmac, swings in a more decisive north-easterly direction, emerging from the forest, and the summit of Ben Nevis is now clearly visible as you embark on a pleasant section of more open walking. Soon the Way enters woodland again, emerges briefly and then plunges into the trees once more, following a narrower and more undulating track.

The track, heading north-eastwards through Nevis Forest, is easy enough to follow, and there is some dramatic scenery; at one point the path drops steeply to cross a magnificent rocky gorge before rising again. The conifers are tightly packed and there is an almost surreal blackness and stillness amongst them, with the track itself passing narrowly between them and inducing understandable feelings of claustrophobia. As the path rises, you can make a detour to the right to visit the Iron Age hill fort of Dun Deardail, in a magnificent open setting away from the forest.

Soon after Dun Deardail you reach a clearing that gives the first really good view to Glen Nevis and the outskirts of Fort William. The end is now truly in sight. Nonetheless, the descent is lengthy and tiring, like the drop to Kinlochleven. You meet a forest track and turn left on to it, making fast progress northwards, although the pounding on the hard surface provides more punishment for the feet which, at this late stage in the walk, may have been protesting for some time. It will be of little consolation to the exhausted walker, as the route eventually turns right off the forest track, to see from the map that two cemeteries are situated close by, one marked ominously on some maps as 'Grave Yard.'

Having turned right off the track, you follow a narrower path quite steeply down to a metalled road, passing the aforementioned graveyard. The metalled road in fact links Glen Nevis Youth Hostel, a significant landmark for reasons as stated below, and Fort William. The route turns left on to the road and simply follows it for roughly a mile and a half until Nevis Bridge (93) on the outskirts of Fort William. Here, as the A82 is reached again, you will be welcomed by a prominent 'End of West Highland Way' sign erected by the nearby Ben Nevis Woollen Mill store, which I understand offers souvenirs for those who successfully complete the path. It is certainly reassuring to have it confirmed that the walk has ended and that you can, with a perfectly clear conscience, secure more comfortable transport to take you into the centre of Fort William, reached by turning left along the A82.

Fort William is the largest settlement you will have seen since you left Milngavie; it derives its name from a fort that, having been built of earth and wattle in 1655 by General Monk, was rebuilt in stone in 1690 by order of William III. The Jacobites failed to capture it both in 1715 and 1745 and it continued to be garrisoned until 1855 when it was demolished. Nowadays it is a very busy tourist centre, the principal shopping centre in the west of Scotland north of Glasgow, and a useful base for exploring the areas of Lochaber and the Great Glen, providing some of the loveliest and most spectacular scenery in Great Britain. Having taken perhaps eight days to walk here, you can now hop on a coach and be back in Glasgow, where you started, in just three hours. If the Scottish weather has lived up to its popular reputation during the previous week, you might wonder whether you would have been better off doing the outward leg by coach as well.

Ben Nevis

Climbing Ben Nevis following your arrival at Fort William can avert anticlimax. Unless the weather is very bad there are no difficulties in making the climb. Although there are many ways up the Ben, as it is known, the most straightforward path begins at Glen Nevis Youth Hostel – easily reachable by bus from Fort William. It is this path which is taken by thousands of walkers each year, every one of them anxious to climb the highest mountain in the British Isles; unless conditions are unspeakable or too dangerous, you will not make the climb without meeting many others en route to the summit.

Having taken the bus to Glen Nevis, you should turn left away from the road, heading north-eastwards on a well-marked path. A brisk ascent on a cobbled surface brings you to a T-junction of paths where you turn right and follow a steady but not over-demanding ascent, the path often zigzagging to gain height more comfortably. The path momentarily levels out as it passes the landmark of Lochan Meall an t-Suidhe, and an opportunity can be taken to pause and enjoy the surroundings to the full, perhaps training the binoculars for ptarmigans, ravens and golden eagles that can all be seen on the slopes of the Ben. However, the graft soon begins again as the path swings sharply right. Then, not long after crossing Red Burn and its fine waterfall, reckoned to be the halfway mark from Glen Nevis, the path embarks on a succession of giant zigzags.

All around are large areas of scree, and it is interesting to contrast the rocky, boulder-strewn landscape here with the lusher, greener surroundings that prevailed during the earlier part of the ascent. As the ground rises, first past the 3,000ft and then the 4,000ft mark, it is significant that the route, though seemingly unmistakable in fine weather, should need to be cairned; the fact remains that even modest cloud cover can render navigation extraordinarily difficult at times.

It is a magnificent moment when, after several hours' hard graft (I took just under three hours from Glen Nevis in the most benign conditions imaginable) you finally reach the summit. At 4,406ft above sea level, it is the roof of Great Britain and is marked by a ruined observatory, the Peace Cairn – a tribute to the dead of the Second World War – and a triangulation point where all walkers who have made the summit will wish to be photographed. The views are, naturally, astonishing; it is exhilarating and not a little frightening to look immediately down at the precipitous gullies on the north face of the mountain. Care is needed at all times, but on days of good visibility – of which there are precious few on the Ben – the panorama of peaks and lochs surpasses any other. If you confine your travels to the British Isles you can rest assured that you will literally never get this close to heaven again.

Because so many inexperienced walkers and holidaymakers want to climb the Ben, and the so-called tourist route is so well-trodden, the ascent and conquest of Ben Nevis can be belittled by serious Munro-baggers. Nonetheless, there is no feeling quite like that of knowing that you are higher above the sea than on any other piece of ground in the British Isles, having got there under your own steam. Especially if the weather is bad, a trouble-free descent following successful conquest of the Ben will be cause for celebration and perhaps the odd whisky or two in Fort William that night, the immensity of the achievement not to be dulled by Wainwright's rather deflating comment that Ben Nevis 'is a friendly giant, accepting geriatrics and infants with open arms.' Then again, how can one really trust the word of one who doesn't even know the time of the first morning train out of Crianlarich?

SUMMARY OF PLACES OF INTEREST

Craigallian, Dumgoyach, Conic Hill, Loch Lomond*, Rob Roy's Cave, Falls of Falloch, St Fillan's Priory, Beinn Dorain, Rannoch Moor, Ba Bridge, Buachaille Etive Mor, Devil's Staircase, Kinlochleven, Dun Deardail, Ben Nevis*.

AMENITIES ON OR NEAR THE ROUTE

Milngavie, Drymen, Balmaha, Rowardennan (L), Inversnaid (L), Inverarnan (L), Crianlarich, Tyndrum, Bridge of Orchy (L), Kinlochleven, Fort William*.

The Southern Upland Way

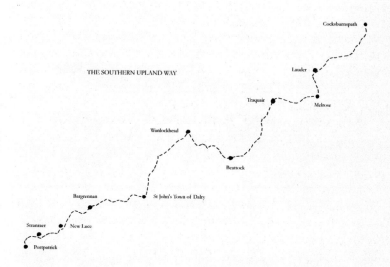

Length: 212 miles.
Start: Portpatrick, near Stranraer.
Finish: Cockburnspath, near Dunbar.
Nature: A coast to coast walk across high-level and often remote terrain of Southern Scotland.
Difficulty rating: Strenuous, severe in places.
Average time of completion: Between 2 and 3 weeks.

The Southern Upland Way

The Southern Upland Way, opened in 1984, is the only official waymarked coast to coast walk described in this book, running from Portpatrick on Scotland's west coast to Cockburnspath on its east coast. While at 212 miles it may not be the longest of the paths in this book, it is certainly one of the toughest, proceeding through the uncompromising and often exceedingly remote terrain of southern Scotland, with villages and towns few and far between. There are mountains, huge forests and long stretches of desolate moorland to negotiate, as well as a great deal of hill-climbing and, at the start and finish, some rugged coastal walking.

Unlike Offa's Dyke Path or the Ridgeway Path, the route has not been designed to follow a particular historic construction or track; the satisfaction lies in marching from the Irish Sea to the North Sea through some of the most unspoilt and underrated scenery in Britain. Logistically it calls for careful planning. Even if you decide to camp you need to ensure you have sufficient supplies to carry you through the long amenity-less stretches, and if you are relying on a 'proper' bed for the night you must be prepared for some very long days indeed.

The journey to Portpatrick, where the walk starts, is not straightforward; I used the overnight coach from London to Stranraer – used chiefly by those travelling on the Stranraer–Larne ferry – and found myself being decanted from the vehicle at 4.15 a.m. Deciding to walk to Portpatrick via the Southern Upland Way itself, and then catch a bus back to Stranraer, I began tramping through the streets of the town, the deathly silence around me suddenly being broken on a street corner by the sounds of an all-night party that even at 4.40 a.m. was still in full swing!

Portpatrick to Stranraer

Portpatrick, reachable by bus from Stranraer, is a lovely place to begin the walk. At one time it was the terminus of the main ferry route between Scotland and Northern Ireland, although this has since been transferred to Stranraer. It is now a peaceful holiday centre with attractive stone houses and cottages, while half a mile south are the ruins of the sixteenth-century Dunskey Castle. In the heart of the village are the preserved ruins of a seventeenth-century parish church in which runaway marriages – often between couples eloping from Ireland – were performed at a fee of £10 for the officiating minister, before the ceremonies were stopped by the Church in 1826. It is with some reluctance that you will set off from this pretty place and begin the long walk across Scotland.

As with Wainwright's Coast to Coast Walk, the journey begins with a coastal walk slightly west of north, effectively taking you further away from your ultimate objective. It is a splendid walk, firstly rounding the tiny coves of Port Mora and Port Kale, and then climbing steeply to pass the little headlands of Catebraid and Stronie, continuing on to the bigger headland of Black Head and Killantringan lighthouse. You turn right on to the lighthouse road and follow it away from the coast, as far as the B738; you turn left along this road then right up a narrow metalled road past the intriguingly-named settlement of Knock and Maize.

At a T-junction of roads you bear right, then shortly right again on to a lane which peters out after a turning to High Auchenree, and you continue just north of east across Broad Moor. The route, which can be quite juicy underfoot, is very indistinct on the ground and you should follow the waymarks carefully. However, this is an attractive section, with the Knockquhassen reservoir immediately to your left and, beyond that, views to Stranraer, Loch Ryan and the distinctive summit of Ailsa Craig. You reach a metalled road, turning right to follow it and navigation is very easy for a while, as the Way makes use of a succession of metalled roads, with just one small intervening stretch of path, to head south-eastwards past Ochtrelure and arrive at the A77.

Ochtrelure is as near as the route gets to Stranraer, which is not only a ferry terminal but a pleasant town with good facilities for walkers and holidaymakers. Its sixteenth-century Castle of St John became the town jail and in the late seventeenth century held Covenanters (about which more below) during campaigns of religious persecution by Graham of Claverhouse. Nowadays the town is probably most likely to spring to national prominence in the context of Scottish league football, and it would be a forgetful walker who did not recall ITV's *News at Ten* with Alistair Burnet managing to make room, amongst stories of earthquakes, typhoons, droughts and civil wars, for news of Stranraer's 1–0 home defeat to Gala Fairydean in a Scottish Cup first round replay.

Stranraer to Laggangarn

The next section is very easy going, with little indication of the rigours ahead. You follow another succession of lanes north-eastwards across land lying just a few feet above sea level; this is the 'neck' of the so-called Rhins, a thin peninsula that stretches right down to the Mull of Galloway. Having passed under the railway bridge, you turn right through a strip of woodland running parallel with the railway to reach Castle Kennedy, a pleasant village with a mixture of modern housing and some cottages dating back to 1860. You arrive at the A75 Stranraer–Newton Stewart road, and cross to head north-eastwards through the grounds of the original Castle Kennedy. Built around 1600 for John Kennedy, fifth earl of Cassilis, it was gutted by fire in 1716 and is now roofless. However, a new mansion house, Lochinch, was built in the grounds between 1864 and 1868, and the two buildings – the ruined original and Lochinch – stand at either end of an isthmus created by two large lochs in the ground, Black Loch and White Loch. The gardens are particularly noteworthy for their outstanding display of plants.

The Way does not take in much of the grounds but soon returns to the Castle Kennedy–New Luce road, turning left to follow it to Chlenry, where you turn right and follow a path quite steeply uphill north-eastwards, through a mixture of woods and open land. You keep the road quite close to your left, and shortly return to it, enjoying magnificent views to the surrounding hills and moors. Having turned right to follow it again, you soon forsake it once more, turning right on to a track that plunges south-eastwards into a forest, and embarking on the first of many long forest marches on this route. You swing eastwards and just keep going past the seemingly endless rows of trees, along a path which can be very squelchy, and it is a relief when the forest relents a little to provide excellent views southwards to Luce Bay.

Now you swing north-eastwards, and proceed downhill by way of Craig Fell, the going steep and boggy in places, to a crossing of the Glasgow–Stranraer railway. A glance at the map will show that from Girvan to Stranraer the line is forced by the nature of the terrain to take an extremely circuitous course. I well remember taking the overnight train from Crewe to Stranraer nearly two decades ago; it was full of ferry passengers for the Larne crossing, and there was something almost surreal about a train passing through miles of totally remote uninhabited countryside, each coach packed with noisily irritable travellers, beer cans and cigarette ends lying at their feet, and mothers trying everything possible to pacify their restless children, from promises of lavish sweet allocations on arrival home, to the application of a shoe or boot in the spot where it was likely to do most good.

Having crossed the railway by means of a footbridge, you drop down south-eastwards to the delightful Water of Luce, then swing north-east to hit the Glenluce–New Luce road. Although you could follow this road northwards to New Luce, where food and accommodation are available, you may wish to get a few more miles under your belt, as New Luce is easily reachable again a little further on. The Way, having arrived at the road, turns left on to it then shortly bears right to proceed north-eastwards along a track towards

Kilhern, gently gaining height. After the easy miles of lowland road bashing, it is quite a contrast to be proceeding across a remote, albeit comparatively low-lying stretch of moorland, with a sense that civilisation is now left behind and the real work has begun. The track, though well-defined on the map, can be exceedingly boggy and progress may be especially slow in bad weather. At the ruined buildings of Kilhern, quite a sad but at the same time dramatic sight in the formidable surroundings, you swing left and head north-westwards, passing just to the left of the Caves of Kilhern, a ruin of a chambered cairn dating back to the third millennium BC. You pass along the right-hand edge of a patch of woodland and gently drop to a metalled road (23).

By detouring left you will soon reach New Luce, an attractive village with some eighteenth-century buildings, although much of the village, including its church and bridges, is nineteenth-century. The Southern Upland Way however turns right on to the metalled road, away from New Luce, soon passing a waterfall and keeping the Cross Water of Luce to the left. Where a road fork is reached, you turn left and proceed uphill north-eastwards, keeping to the lane, climbing steadily past the settlement of Balmurrie. Beyond Balmurrie the lane swings north-westwards towards Kilmacfadzean, but before reaching this house you turn right off the lane and strike out north-eastwards across the moors, keeping Closs Hill to your left and Balmurrie Fell to your right.

More immediately to the right is Cairn-na-Gath, a long cairn which again is of the third millennium BC. The path is somewhat unclear on the ground; in good visibility you will be guided by the excellent marker posts but in bad weather you may need a compass to steer you safely across the moors and into the forest. You then proceed north-eastwards along a wide path through the thick woodland, although in wet weather this can seem like a treadmill. A clearing in the forest heralds the remarkable standing stones of Laggangarn; the sandstone slabs, each bearing a cross with arms broadening outwards, were probably erected during the second millennium BC. It is a quite remarkable thing to find in such a remote spot, but walkers who question the sanity of those who transported the stones to these wild surroundings might equally well be asked what had motivated *them* to leave the comfort of their twenty-first-century cars, beds and full Scottish breakfasts to go out and inspect them.

Laggangarn to Black Water of Dee

The Way continues north-eastwards through the forest, along the lower slopes of Craig Airie Fell. At certain times tree felling may be in progress, so care is needed to follow temporary signposting. Shortly after passing just to the right of the fell summit, marked by a triangulation point well over 1,000ft above sea level, you arrive at a clearly defined forest track. Route-finding difficulties cease for the moment, as you turn right on to the track which eventually turns into a metalled road, and you keep on it for some four miles, heading just south of east, passing the little settlements of Derry, Polbael and Waterside. Although the forest relents a little as you pass to the south of Loch Derry, it soon returns and dominates the walk on to the B7027 Barrhill–Newton Stewart road.

In wet weather it is at least good to have a firm surface underfoot, and the surrounding scenery, though hardly hospitable, is an impressive mixture of forest and moorland. A shelter is available for walkers at Waterside; doing this section in drenching rain, I well remember stopping for lunch here, and having to set off after a few minutes because I was so cold. You turn right on to the B7027 and soon arrive at the little village of Knowe (an appropriate name because in answer to any question about amenities, the answer is likely to be negative) where you turn left and head north-eastwards through an extremely juicy area of forest, emerging at a metalled road by Glenruther Lodge. You turn left on to the metalled road, still going north-eastwards, climbing steadily. If the weather is bad, you could simply remain on this road as far as the house at Garchew, but the Way opts for a more direct route across country to reach that point.

Turning right as the road bends slightly left, you take a path that climbs to the triangulation point at the Hill of Ochiltree, then head north-eastwards over Glenvernoch Fell, descending through a small clump of woodland to reach Garchew. It is imperative to follow the marker posts as the path here is unclear, but there is always the escape route provided by the road to the left. The views are awesome; the prospect to the north is a massive area of coniferous forest, and trees – lots of them – are visible in every direction.

Just to the east of Garchew you bear left off the metalled road and head north-eastwards across open moorland, dropping gently to reach the A714 at Bargrennan (40.5). There is little of historic interest here save for a pretty nineteenth-century church, built as a chapel of ease, but the main significance of this village is that it is the last settlement of any consequence for 25 miles and thus an almost obligatory staging post for the walker. There is hotel accommodation here at the House o' Hill.

Though this hotel is used to catering for footsloggers, many hotels are not; a fact that becomes obvious if a rain-soaked walker finds himself in such an establishment. Having hauled himself and his saturated equipment into the immaculate reception area, his discomfiture will redouble when he has to take his place in the queue behind guests sporting the latest designer wear and without a hair out of place. When his turn comes, the proprietor may endeavour to reduce his unease with such hideous understatements as, 'Bit damp out there today' or encouraging remarks like, 'Forecast's even worse for tomorrow' before leading his new guest up four flights of stairs and preventing him from getting out of his sodden clothes by an interminable exposition of the hotel's meal arrangements, the multiplicity of different settings of the shower unit, and the intricacies of the satellite television system.

Immediately after leaving Bargrennan, and having crossed the A714, you plunge into Glentrool Forest, proceeding generally in an easterly direction. Again, this can be very unpleasant underfoot during or after wet weather. However, better things lie in store; you soon cross a metalled road and arrive at a river called the Water of Minnoch, and it is then a quite delightful walk along the right bank of the river. When the Water of Minnoch meets the Water of Trool, you simply continue alongside the latter river, proceeding just north of east. This is lovely walking on a clear path.

There is a temporary and somewhat unwelcome brush with civilisation as you find yourself passing through the Glen Trool caravan park, but after leaving this behind you can enjoy a superb walk along the southern shore of Loch Trool, still heading just north of east. Dominating the scene across the loch is the Fell of Eschoncan, comfortably over 1,000ft high, and a bit further to the north-east is Buchan Hill, more than 1,600ft high. Though the going is undulating, the path is clearly defined and nothing like as hard as the tramp up the side of Loch Lomond which West Highland Way walkers will recall. Having reached the east end of the loch, you swing south-eastwards past Glenhead and climb through the woods to join a forest track, turning left on to this track to begin eight miles of forest track walking. At first you climb, then having obtained your first view of Loch Dee, keep this to your left as you continue south-eastwards to Black Laggan, swinging north-eastwards towards the River Dee, also known as Black Water of Dee. To your right, beyond the forest, there are views to the 1,800ft summit of Cairngarroch.

As the track swings eastwards there is a left-hand turn that you miss at your peril; a moment's inattention might result in your carrying on literally miles out of your way, and the surroundings are so remote that there is slim likelihood of meeting anybody who can put you right. It may indeed be that your only inkling that something is wrong is when you find yourself at the A712 just west of a wild goat park which is so far from the correct route that you may be forced to obtain transport to get you back to somewhere near it. You could, of course, console yourself that had you kept to the route, you would have missed out on a pint or three in Newton Stewart as well as a close encounter with a cluster of playful nanny-goats.

Black Water of Dee to St John's Town of Dalry

Having made the necessary left turn on to another track, you cross the Dee and soon reach a T-junction of tracks, turning right. Off you go again, heading just south of east. The surroundings are so thickly forested that the going is uninteresting, but at least it is fast, with no route-finding problems. At length you reach Clatteringshaws Loch, a welcome oasis amidst so much woodland, and boasting a wildlife centre on its eastern side. You proceed along the north side of the loch, but then the track swings north-eastwards, away from the waterside, and soon after crossing Pulcagrie Burn, reaches a narrow metalled road and the end of the long forest track walk. By turning right on to the metalled road you can get to the A712 which proceeds down to the wildlife centre (it *is* a long way) but your route bears left on to the metalled road, following it briefly.

You then bear right and begin to climb, swinging just east of north, along a path which seems quite rough after the firm forest tracks. The landscape is again primarily woodland, but at length you emerge at the summit of Shield Rig. Though little more than 950ft up, and dwarfed by the Rig of Clenrie and Meikle Millyea to the west, this is an excellent viewpoint in the heart of the Galloway Hills, with superb views to the surrounding moorland, mountains and hills, and a real sense of isolation. You continue north-eastwards but begin descending, picking up a stony track at Clenrie and going forward to a small car park, then swinging south-eastwards along the track which turns into a metalled road.

Heading in a generally easterly direction, you then keep walking along the road, eventually being joined by Garroch Burn which runs parallel with it. There is the feeling of returning to civilisation, with a number of houses and farms dotted about the surrounding rolling landscape. It seems quite a long tramp along tarmac, but as the road moves more decisively south-eastwards again, you turn left on to a path that crosses the burn and climbs eastwards up on to Waterside Hill. Walkers who have come all the way from Bargrennan in one day may resent this last stiff climb, but the reward is a fine view down to the Water of Ken and the welcome sight of the village of St John's Town of Dalry. There is a sharp descent to the A762 and then, after crossing this road, there is a curious end to the day's work, consisting of a peaceful walk over the meadows and across the Water of Ken into St John's Town of Dalry, usually shortened to Dalry (66).

A stop here is virtually obligatory, as there are no more amenities for the next 26 miles – and they are very tough miles. The most interesting historical feature in the village is an ancient block of stone in the rough shape of a chair, and known as St John's Chair which, according to local legend, John the Baptist rested on during his supposed travels through Britain. St John was the patron saint of the medieval religious order known as the Knights Hospitallers who once owned the land on which the village lies. This is how the village got its rather lengthy full name. Dalry boasts attractive cottages and an early nineteenth-century church, the churchyard of which has a Covenanter's Stone marking the grave of two murdered Covenanters (see below).

On a more prosaic note, it has some useful shops and accommodation, and a welcome bar in the Lochinvar Hotel, its name doubtless inspired by Lochinvar, a small loch three miles to the north-east with the ruins of an island castle that is said to have been home to the eponymous hero of a romantic ballad by Sir Walter Scott. My night's stay in the village was not a happy one. Given a tiny room with no furnishings save the bed, no other facilities except the bathroom, and no access to a lounge, I had a perfectly wretched night's sleep, made no easier by the regular peals from the nearby clock tower, through all of which I remained awake except those proclaiming the hours of 5 and 6 a.m.

St John's Town of Dalry to Allan's Cairn

The next section, on to Sanquhar, is one of the most challenging on any route described in this book. There are sections elsewhere that are more technically demanding, but they can be shortened. On this section of 26 miles however, you will see but a handful of buildings, no accommodation except a single bothy, and no places of refreshment (nor any easy detours to find them), and although there are roads, no public transport serves them. Furthermore the terrain, although posing no particular terrors, is rough, and careful navigation is essential.

Having proceeded along Dalry village street along the A702 you turn left to head just east of north – your direction of travel for the first three miles or so – and proceed up an obvious track. This peters out and you proceed across undulating open grass moorland, going by the house at Ardoch and passing to the east of Ardoch Hill, approaching an area of forest. You keep to the west of this woodland, enjoying a pleasant walk beside Earlstoun Burn but taking great care to follow the marker posts. Having followed quite close to the edge of the woodland, which is bordered by Lochinvar to its east, you then swing left to head northwards and reach a metalled road. You join it, proceeding in the same direction, swinging marginally east of north and crossing Black Water at Butterhole Bridge. Already, Dalry seems a very long way away.

After crossing the bridge, the road swings more clearly north-eastwards, and as it does so, you leave the comforting tarmac and climb steadily northwards on to Culmark Hill, dropping down to the house at Culmark. The path is by no means obvious on the ground but if you lose the route you can simply aim for the house – possibly with the help of a compass if visibility is poor – and there pick up a track that proceeds north-westwards to the B729.

On your approach to the B729 you cross the Stroanfreggan Burn, a tributary of the Water of Ken, while nearby is a prehistoric burial mound named Stroanfreggan Cairn, and a hillside named Stroanfreggan Craig. Walkers who have not yet suffered a sense of humour failure by tramping the remote and publess moors and forests of Galloway might see the potential for the name Stroanfreggan, particularly if delivered with a certain virulence, to be employed as a peculiarly Scottish expletive, and may perhaps be moved to remark, as the B729 was reached, that it would be nice to find thereon a roadside inn, complete with roaring fire, where they could dry off after two stroanfreggan hours' struggling through the stroanfreggan rain.

The Way turns right on to the B729, then just short of the tiny hamlet of Stroanpatrick, turns left to begin the most gruelling part of this long section, consisting of a climb north-eastwards to Benbrack. Following a path, you head across an area of moorland, and into a large forest plantation. There is not the claustrophobic feel of some of the forest walking elsewhere on the route; the trees are well spaced and it is a lovely open walk on to Manquhill Hill, just under 1,400ft high. The extremely well-defined path skirts the summit, and looking back there are tremendous views to some of the wildest scenery in southern Scotland.

It is now good fast walking downhill on an excellent path, before an uncompromisingly steep climb to the summit of Benbrack, the highest point yet reached on the Way at just over 1,900ft. As you pause every so often to catch your breath and stop at the triangulation point on the summit, it is essential to look back and enjoy the increasingly spectacular views. Rough peaty walking follows as you proceed northwards across open moorland between two large areas of forestry to reach Cairn Hill, then turn eastwards on to Black Hill.

Now things get easier. Swinging northwards you begin to descend, skirting the western edge of the forest then turning north-eastwards into it as far as Allan's Cairn. This pillar of red sandstone commemorates two Covenanters (Scottish Presbyterians subscribing to various bonds or covenants for the security and advancement of their cause). One of the most celebrated covenants was that directed against the Laudian Prayer Book imposed by Charles I, while in 1643 a further covenant pledged the Scots to preserve Presbyterianism in Scotland and extend it to England and Ireland. Covenants were declared unlawful in 1662 and Covenanters were brutally persecuted for the next 25 years by troops of the Episcopalian government of the Stuart king Charles II. The Covenanters put up a brave resistance; in 1666 they actually mounted an uprising in Dalry, but many who were involved were subsequently tortured and hanged.

Allan's Cairn to Wanlockhead

The Way swings north-westwards at Allan's Cairn and soon turns left, briefly heads south-westwards on to a forest track, then shortly bears right on to another forest path that heads downhill. It makes a wide loop, briefly swinging south-westwards again to reach the Chalk Memorial Bothy. This is the only chance of shelter between Dalry and Sanquhar; although facilities are basic, in extreme weather it may be a virtual life-saver, and if you are carrying any surplus food, it may be a nice gesture to leave some for any benighted walkers coming along after you.

That said, one should perhaps check the best before date on the packet; a party of bedraggled hikers, collapsing into the bothy after battling over Benbrack in a blizzard, may be less than grateful for your offering of three stale unwrapped Happy Shopper custard creams and four paper-wrapped slices of wafer-thin ham that are no longer simply on the turn but are now locked in mortal combat with each other to see which can get out of the door first.

Soon after passing the bothy, you reach a junction of tracks where you turn right and proceed just north of east. Having passed the settlement of Polskeoch, the track turns into a metalled road which you follow as far as Polgown, about two miles further on, where you turn left on to a path that climbs again, heading north-eastwards. This is a tough climb, not only because it comes towards the end of a long day, but also because the going underfoot is rough and often very muddy. Again, it is essential to follow the marker posts. There are tremendous views to the surrounding moors and hills, but the most satisfying moment comes when, having hauled yourself to the hill crest just to the north-west of Welltrees Hill at well over 1,500ft high, you see Nithsdale and the town of Sanquhar below you, with nothing to separate you from the town but a steady downhill march. The spirits rise as you proceed confidently north-eastwards down an excellent path, your objective now gloriously clear. However it will almost certainly take you longer than you think, with several stiles guarded by electric fences to negotiate as you drop down.

At length you pick up a track running north-eastwards from Euchan Cottage and follow it to Ulzieside, where, having reached the valley bottom, you turn left on to a metalled road and follow this north-westwards past a golf course to a T-junction. At the junction you turn right to cross the river Nith by means of Blackaddie Bridge, then immediately right again along a path to head south-eastwards round the back of Sanquhar and pass by its castle, most of which dates back to the sixteenth century, although there is some earlier work. Just beyond the castle you arrive at the A76, on to which you turn left to enter the town (92). You have just completed the hardest part of the Way.

Sanquhar has all the amenities a tired, hungry walker could wish for, as well as a station with rail links to Dumfries and Glasgow, and is an interesting little town in its own right. As well as the castle there is a granite monument marking the spot where Covenanters formulated declarations in 1680 and 1685 in their fight to defend Presbyterianism against the Stuarts. The town also has a post office that has been in business since 1738.

The next settlement of any size, Wanlockhead, is just eight miles away, giving weary walkers the opportunity of a lighter day, although this section, proceeding into the Lowther Hills, is no pushover. Turning right off the A76, you leave Sanquhar by a path that heads north-eastwards, gently uphill. A lane is briefly joined and then forsaken for another path which strikes out across pleasant open countryside with one short wooded interlude, soon after which you cross a burn, and just beyond that you join the lane leading to Brandleys. Before reaching Brandleys Cottage, however, you bear left, and still heading north-eastwards, you begin a climb which increases in severity the further you get from the lane. The views are spectacular, particularly as you traverse the shoulder of Coupland Knowe and look left to the equally impressive Conrig Hill.

It is a pity to have to descend steeply to Cogshead, keeping an area of forest to your left, but having reached the foot of the hill you bear right and ascend again, on to Highmill Knowe, from where the views are magnificent. It is then a steep but clearly defined descent to a wide track where you turn right. (During the shooting season, it is necessary to follow an alternative route to this point from Cogshead, following a winding track northwards through frankly rather uninspiring areas of forest, eventually emerging and heading south-eastwards alongside Wanlock Water along the wide track at which the main route arrives after descending from Highmill Knowe.)

You then proceed south-eastwards along the wide track into the village of Wanlockhead (100), an attractive place, with many cottages of bright colours, some dating back to the middle of the eighteenth century. What may surprise some visitors is that, standing 1,380ft above sea level, it is the highest village in Scotland; one might have expected that honour to go to a village in the Highlands. The most interesting aspect of the village, however, is that it is effectively a vast museum of lead-mining, its principal industry until 1934 and again briefly in 1957–58. Many of the mine-shafts, smelters and wagonways can be seen in and around the village, while also on show is a nineteenth-century beam engine, a water-wheel pit and ruined miners' cottages. Gold and silver have also been mined in the area, and gold from near the village was used in the Crown of Scotland.

As the visitor looks at the old smelting works, tramway, beam pump, adits and other paraphernalia of the mining industry, he cannot fail to be reminded of the extraordinarily tough life of a miner in these remote uplands of southern Scotland. Such thoughts may put into perspective the irritations the present-day walker has to face in the village, whether it is the long uphill walk from his bed and breakfast to the pub, or a choice of only three types of pastry in the visitor centre tearoom.

Wanlockhead to Beattock

The start of the next section is impressive indeed. Having passed through the village, you cross over the B797 and follow a track past the pub, joining a path that climbs dramatically, heading south-eastwards. In due course you reach a metalled road and, still proceeding south-eastwards, alternate between road and path to climb to the summit of Lowther Hill, marked by what looks like a giant golf ball, but which is actually part of a civil aviation radar system. At just under 2,400ft, it is the highest point on the route and the views are absolutely magnificent – ample reward not only for the climb but for the long miles of forest walking earlier in the journey. If you have good weather, the walk from here to the A702 – south-eastwards via Cold Moss and Comb Head as far as Laght Hill, then swinging just north of east – is the most exciting and rewarding on the whole route.

It is a great rollercoaster of a walk, involving some unbelievably steep descents and climbs, but with a tremendous sense of space and openness, glorious views and a well-defined path with no route-finding problems. I was fortunate to see a mountain hare on this section, jumping up a hillside with remarkable agility.

From Laght Hill it is a steady descent to the A702, where slight anticlimax sets in; you turn left along the road, then right on to a path which first crosses then runs beside Potrenick Burn, before crossing Portrail Water. Swinging south-eastwards, you enter an area of forest and shortly pick up a forest track that heads firstly south-eastwards then in a more easterly direction, emerging into more open countryside before diving back into the forest again.

You arrive at a metalled road and turn left on to it, dropping down to Daer Water. You cross over the water then leave the road, bearing right on to a track, then left on to a path which skirts the edge of Daer Reservoir and its associated works, heading initially north-eastwards then south-eastwards. You sense that it is only a matter of time before you begin climbing, and indeed, having passed the end of the strip of woodland separating the works from the path, you turn left and begin climbing very steeply away from the reservoir on to Sweetshaw Brae, just north of east. The going, on rough grass moorland, can be squelchy underfoot.

Beyond the summit of Sweetshaw Brae, just under 1,500ft, the gradient relaxes and it is easier going, still just north of east, on to Hods Hill, just over 1,850ft. The views are quite stupendous; the Lowther Hill golf ball is an obvious landmark, but further away you can see Solway Firth and the Lakeland fells. Walkers who have spent holidays in the Lake District, perhaps as part of their apprenticeship for hill-walking, may reflect smugly that on Hods Hill they have a view which is every bit as good as that from those fells at which they now stare, but without the company of at least a dozen other hikers and without having had to pay £1.50 for the privilege of parking the car at the bottom.

From the top of Hods Hill you swing south-eastwards and then, turning just west of south, descend dramatically before rising again to the summit of Beld Knowe. You have reached the edge of another large area of conifer forest which, as you climb to Beld Knowe, you keep close to your left. Then, swinging south-eastwards again, you plunge into the forest and embark on a long march south-eastwards through the middle of it, beginning with a long descent, then a climb to Craig Hill, then another drop. The walking is not too claustrophobic; the Way follows a wide avenue through the trees, and there are breaks, including one very pleasant open interlude during which you cross over Garpol Water. It is fast, easy walking on clear paths, and it is only near the end that your way appreciably narrows.

Eventually you emerge at a metalled road, turning left and following it initially uphill through woodland and then out into more open country, before descending into Annandale. You cross over the London–Glasgow railway and swing from south-eastwards to north-eastwards to reach a T-junction at the long, straggly village of Beattock (120), spread out along the road you have just reached. The Way is left, over Evan Water (a tributary of the river Annan), and then almost immediately right.

Beattock is the first habitation of any size since Wanlockhead, and offers some amenities, but the town of Moffat is only a mile and a half away to the north-east via the A701, and has the full range of creature comforts. The statue of a ram in Moffat's wide high street emphasizes that this is an important sheep-farming area, while its popularity as a holiday resort grew from the discovery, in the middle of the seventeenth century, that the water from the wells of the town had medicinal qualities. Robert Burns was one of those who came to take the waters and was inspired to compose the drinking song 'O Willie brew'd a peck of Maut.' Beattock is reckoned to be just past the halfway point on the Southern Upland Way, although it is not certain how much a comfort that would be to the walker who, after glancing at his map and realising that a line drawn due south from the village would still pass well to the west of the Irish Sea-facing towns of Morecambe and Blackpool, might well feel his peck of Maut turning more than a little sour in his throat.

Beattock to Blackhouse

Having turned right off the metalled road running through Beattock, you pass underneath the A701 and A74(M). This is a very busy road and the traffic noise stays with you for some time; it can seem very intrusive after the quiet unspoilt walking you have enjoyed. Immediately beyond the motorway you join a metalled road, heading eastwards to a T-junction and just before this junction you pass over the river Annan. At the T-junction you cross straight over on to a path, climbing steeply then dropping just as quickly to reach another road. You turn left on to this, but shortly you reach a junction and here turn right across Moffat Water then immediately left to head north-eastwards, following a delightful path that passes through woodland and then beside the river. It is a surprising but charming interlude amidst so much rugged scenery; the meadows and hedgerows are a delight, and you can refresh yourself with wild raspberries in summer. Shortly after crossing a metalled road, the spell is broken as you leave the riverbank and turn right to head initially south-eastwards, proceeding uphill. The Way, now an obvious track, swings to the left to head just north of east and continue uphill into another large area of forest. It is quite a slog, but before you get into the forest there are magnificent views not only back to Moffat but also to the golf ball on Lowther Hill.

Once in the forest you continue to gain height and the walking becomes rather more mechanical, but it is important to concentrate on keeping to the right path through the trees. Patience is, however, rewarded. The Way, as if bored with the long tramp through the endless conifers, suddenly darts off left, heading north-eastwards, and, following alongside a lovely stream, climbs spectacularly to the crags of Craigmichen Scar, with the summit of Loch Fell to the right and Croft Head to the left, both over 2,000ft high. You emerge from the forest and suddenly find yourself faced with a stunning panorama of big fells, steep gullies, streams, forestry and moorland; I walked this section under cloudless blue skies, and considered it the highlight of the whole route.

Still climbing, you continue north-east across the watershed which, like the watershed crossings experienced on the Coast to Coast and on the Pennine Way, is a boggy wilderness, and the sense of isolation is quite palpable. This is the closest you get to the great Eskdalemuir Forest, a short way to the south-east. You might ask yourself why the name Eskdalemuir rings a bell, then recall that it sends weather reports to the news agencies and is frequently recorded in the papers as having been the wettest place in Britain on the previous day. Of course, in times of freak weather, the papers may seize on Eskdalemuir as an example of climatic norms turned upside down ('Och aye, the Phew! Eskdalemuir hotter than Luxor!'), but when it is your turn to walk that section you can be sure the papers will conveniently forget to report that it is still 40 degrees in Luxor but chucking it down in Eskdalemuir.

Beyond the watershed you reach Ettrick Head, a crucial landmark in the walk. Not only is this the source of Ettrick Water, a tributary of the Tweed which flows into the North Sea (your ultimate objective), but generally speaking the walking from now on, whilst still challenging, lacks the formidable qualities and logistical headaches of the western half of the route. At Ettrick Head the Way picks up a clear track which drops down north-eastwards through forest and then more open country to the houses of Over Phawhope and Potburn. Beyond Potburn, still heading north-eastwards, the track turns into a narrow metalled road which you follow for five miles, beside Ettrick Water, past a number of isolated settlements.

This area is associated with James Hogg, the so-called Ettrick Shepherd who became a prolific poet; he was particularly well known for his composition of romantic ballads in the early nineteenth century. The road walk is not unpleasant, and though tarmac crunching is not the best sort of walking, the surroundings are delightful and it is very fast going.

Finally, at Scabcleuch you leave the tarmac (the birthplace monument of James Hogg at Ettrickhill lies a mile or so further along it) and turn left to head first just west, then just east of north, uphill on a path that at over 1,600ft contours the hillside of Peniestone Knowe and goes forward to Pikestone Rig. This is glorious ridge walking on springy turf with wonderful views across lofty green hills and neat patches of forest, and the enticing prospect of Loch of the Lowes to the north-west. It is important not to be sidetracked on to the path that drops down to this loch; you do indeed drop down, but north-eastwards, keeping the loch well to your left.

Descending steeply past Riskinhope Hope you cross the delightfully refreshing Crosscleuch Burn, then gird up the loins and climb again, passing along the west fringe of another area of forest and just to the east of the summit of Earl's Hill. The path arrives at a clear track, and the Way turns left on to this track to head north-westwards and descend to St Mary's Loch (141). It is a long, long descent, but the views to the loch are magnificent and the walker who has tramped here from Moffat – there being no amenities at all en route – will feel a real sense of achievement. Accommodation and food are available at the Tibbie Shiels Inn by the lochside. Tibbie was the wife of a mole-catcher and, having opened the inn when her husband died in 1824, continued to run it until her death in 1878 at the age of 96!

Turning right at the loch, you enjoy a lovely loch-side walk north-eastwards along a good path, which widens into a track, then just beyond the loch you turn right on to a path which swings north-westwards to meet the A708 Moffat–Selkirk road. Crossing straight over, you continue in the same direction, climbing somewhat laboriously to Dryhope Tower. At a T-junction of paths you turn right and head north-eastwards again – your direction of travel virtually all the way to Traquair.

There follows a lovely moorland walk along a fine path which initially passes to the west of the 1,380ft Ward Law and the east of South Hawkshaw Rig, the ground thereabouts rising well over 1,600ft. The Way then descends to the attractive little hamlet of Blackhouse, in a quite idyllic setting, nestling as it does in the valley of Douglas Burn with a beautiful woodland backcloth. The Way briefly picks up a track to pass by Blackhouse and its tower, then enters the wood immediately behind and ascends once more, on a lovely grassy path which is kind to aching feet. In hot weather this woodland walking is delightfully refreshing and it lacks the hemmed-in feel of some other forest sections on the route, with a marvellous view back to St Mary's Loch as you gain height.

Blackhouse to Galashiels

Emerging from the woodland you find yourself on open moorland just east of Deuchar Law, and keeping a steady elevation of around 1,500ft as you proceed past Blake Muir, you can enjoy a glorious ridge-top promenade with views across miles of wonderful scenery including mountains, heather-clad hills, forests and the welcoming sight of the town of Innerleithen. All good things must sadly come to an end, and there follows a rather slow anticlimactical descent into the Tweed valley.

Eventually you arrive at the B709 and turn left on to it, following it for a mile to reach Traquair (153). With its neat cottages and gardens, and eighteenth-century church, it is a pleasant place to linger, but walkers who have reached the village in good time and have a couple of hours to spare should continue beyond the village centre (virtually no amenities) to visit Traquair House, one of Scotland's oldest inhabited mansions.

Built in the tenth century, and virtually unaltered in the last 300 years, it has been visited by 27 Scottish and English monarchs and has many interesting features, including embroidery by Mary, Queen of Scots, an eighteenth-century library, and a Brew House which is equipped as it was two centuries ago and is licensed to sell its own beer. A mile to the south-west of the village there is a knoll which is the site of St Bryde's Church, believed to have existed since before the twelfth century.

The Way turns right off the B709 in Traquair, but by continuing along it you can reach Innerleithen, which contains an excellent range of amenities. I passed a very pleasant afternoon here, then returned to a quiet bed and breakfast – or so I thought – some way from the town centre, only to have my night's sleep curtailed by the sound of a cockerel which began its vocal exercises at five-thirty in the morning.

Beyond the B709 at Traquair, and as far as the magnificent viewpoint known as the Three Brethren, the Way follows a course slightly south of east. You begin by following a track, which proceeds clearly but quite steeply uphill, and indeed in less than three miles you will rise from 500ft to well over 1,600ft. You enter an area of forest and proceed along a clear path through the woods on to Pipers Knowe. A path leading off to the right hereabouts provides an uphill detour to the spectacular viewpoint of Minch Moor, well over 1,850ft above sea level and offering a fine panorama. The Way itself steers a steady high-level course along a small strip of open land between the thickly-planted conifers, before emerging into open country.

It is an exhilarating march along an old drove road, crossing over Brown Knowe and skirting Broomy Law before climbing to one of the undoubted highlights of the whole route, the Three Brethren. The Brethren are in fact tall neat cairns, and from this vantage point you will enjoy another tremendous view in all directions, encompassing heather-clad moorland, rolling green hills and large patches of forest. The eye is drawn particularly to the Eildon Hills, the very distinct volcanic hills behind Melrose, which, rising to 1,476ft, will be a feature of the landscape for many more miles.

The Way turns sharply right here and drops steeply, but rather than continuing uphill to Peat Law, turns abruptly left, enters woodland and proceeds in a north-easterly direction that will be maintained virtually all the way to Galashiels. It will have been noted that several hills close to or on the route are given the name Law; the walker with a penchant for playing on words might decide that Common Law would be a good name for a hill walked by unmarried cohabitees, Parkinson's Law a suitable name for a hill which the walker who is ahead of schedule walks up very slowly, and Sod's Law the ideal description of a hill which is totally shrouded in mist whilst the land beneath it is completely cloudless.

The descent through the woodland is undoubtedly anticlimactical, and indeed the walking now assumes a less remote feel which persists all the way to Lauder, some 16 miles further on. Having descended, you continue along a woodland track to the hamlet of Yair, turning right along a lane that leads to the A707, meeting it at the attractive triple-arched Yair Bridge across the Tweed. You go over the bridge, turning left at the T-junction and then immediately right on to a track. It is galling, after losing so much height since the Three Brethren, to have to haul yourself up again, but you must proceed over Hog Hill and forward on a path which is not wonderfully clear.

The reward for your efforts is a good view to Galashiels, now immediately ahead of you, and of course the Eildons. Having dropped to just 350ft or so at Yair Bridge, and climbed back to nearly 1,000ft, you drop down again to pick up a path that snakes round the edge of Galashiels (166). One would have thought a more logical route would be over the wooded summit of Gala Hill, around which the route describes a large semi-circle, but it is nonetheless good to have a largish town close to the Way, with the best range of on-path creature comforts since Sanquhar. It has derived much prosperity from tweed, and its Scottish College of

Textiles is the headquarters of the Scottish tweed manufacturing industry. The town's motto 'Sour Plums', which can be seen on the municipal buildings, refers to a Border foray in the fourteenth century when a party of English raiders were slain whilst they picked wild plums.

Galashiels to Lauder

From Galashiels the Way swings south-eastwards past the eastern fringe of Gala Hill, climbing and then dropping down to meet a track, turning left and following it to meet the A7. You cross this busy road and continue downhill to be reunited with the river Tweed, turning left to follow alongside it, now heading north-east. There is quite a contrast hereabouts; across the river is the serenely beautiful Abbotsford House, the home of Walter Scott, but ahead is a rather dreary combination of industrial estate, modern housing and busy road. Having passed underneath the road bridge over the Tweed, you join a road which takes you past a sewage works, then turn right on to the course of an old railway (now a footpath) and proceed south-eastwards. This is tame stuff after what has gone before, but soon you bear left off the old track and having crossed a metalled road, follow a pleasant path south-eastwards along the south bank of the Tweed.

Tweeddale is noted for its great variety of wildlife, including otters, herons and kingfishers, and you may be fortunate enough to observe some of these creatures as you pass along the bank and through the meadows to reach Melrose. The highlight of this attractive town, sheltered by the Eildon Hills and the resting place of the heart of Robert the Bruce, is the ruin of Melrose Abbey, a Cistercian abbey founded by David I in 1136, partially destroyed two centuries later, and wrecked in 1545. Commemorated in verse by Walter Scott, it has elaborately carved stonework and fine traceried windows, and contains the tombs of Alexander II and the wizard Michael Scot, who legend says caused the Eildon Hills to split into three.

Like Galashiels, the town has plenty of amenities including several excellent eating places and a couple of takeaways. The fish and chip shop was shut on the night I stayed there, so I resorted to a Chinese takeaway meal and sat by the abbey to eat it, just at the moment that a coach drew up and deposited a huge crowd of Eastern European tourists. To this day I am not sure whether their abiding memory of Melrose would have been its noble ecclesiastical remains, encapsulating many notable milestones in Scottish history and heritage, or of a weatherbeaten and weary walker on a town bench grappling with a piece of chicken in an extremely sticky lemon sauce.

The Way crosses the Tweed by means of a footbridge just to the north of the town centre, then turns left and doubles back on itself, following the north riverbank westwards to reach the B6360 just west of Gattonside. There is then a right turn and for a while the Way heads north then just east of north, initially on a path, then a lane, then another stretch of path. Gradually you gain height, from just over 330ft in the valley to over 800ft and, swinging west of north, you continue on a path that widens into a lane. This is very fast, easy walking, and it is really enjoyable as well, with extensive views across a most attractive rolling landscape.

You reach a crossroads of lanes and go straight over, heading initially just east of north along a metalled road, but then turn left and join a path heading north-westwards across a stretch of grassy open land. You cross a metalled road and suddenly the surroundings become dramatic, as you quickly lose height, then swing north-eastwards, keeping a deep grassy gorge to your left. On your right is a golf course and ahead are the Lammermuir Hills, your last real challenge on the Way. Before that though, you drop down into the little town of Lauder (179). The Way skirts the edge of the town, meeting the A697 at the town's south-east end, but most walkers will want to detour into the centre as it is the last place on the route where supplies can be obtained.

It is a very pretty town; its most interesting features are its tollbooth where dues were once extracted from stallholders at street fairs, and a sixteenth-century church with an octagonal spire. The town's name may remind walkers of the singer Harry Lauder, himself a Scotsman although not from these parts. One of his song titles, 'Keep Right On to the End of the Road,' could not be more apt for a hiker who is now less than 35 miles from the end of this long journey, but with the far from hospitable Lammermuirs looming ahead, and the obvious danger of being benighted somewhere amongst them, there may be more than a hint of the prophetic in his composition 'Roamin' in the Gloamin'!'

Lauder to A1 crossing

The Way turns briefly right on to the A697, then left on to a path which enters the grounds of Thirlestane Castle, and uses a footbridge to cross Leader Water before heading north-eastwards through a pleasant area of woodland beside Earnscleugh Water. You turn right at Drummonds-hall on to a track which leads to and crosses another arm of the A697, joining a path that leads to the curiously-named settlement Wanton Walls. Here you branch left to head decisively north-eastwards – your direction of travel almost all of the way to Twin Law, the climax of this section.

You proceed uphill to enter an area of woodland, and in the wood turn right on to a track, soon emerging at the south-eastern tip of the woods, then turning left to proceed uphill along the fringe of the woodland. As the fringe begins to swing from north-east to north-west, you leave the woodland altogether, and there is a dramatic change to the character of the walk as you find yourself pitched from pleasant rolling farmland and woodland into remote moorland terrain. When I walked the route I chose this very moment to go off course; it is extremely important to follow the waymarks or, if bad weather precludes this, to take a compass bearing. The path is very indistinct on the ground as, from the edge of the woods, you strike out north-eastwards across the moors into the heart of the Lammermuir Hills, shortly crossing Shawdon Burn then continuing through an extraordinarily barren, almost eerie landscape. You begin to lose height, and turn right on to a path that drops down to cross Blythe Water at its confluence with Wheel Burn, then climb back up on a far from obvious path to reach the southern tip of a patch of woodland on Scoured Rig.

Now the going is a lot more straightforward. You follow the south-east-facing fringe of the wood, arriving at a clear wide track on to which you turn left, the track soon leaving the wood behind and dropping down to the buildings of Braidshawrig. Ignoring the left turn over Easter Burn, you swing round eastwards to climb uphill, and then follow this trusty track slowly but surely higher and higher into heather moorland which seems to become more formidable and inhospitable with each step. Finally you turn sharply south-eastwards and proceed triumphantly to Twin Law, over 1,360ft above sea level. This is the Lammermuirs' answer to the Three Brethren – two huge and beautifully constructed cairns in a fantastic setting, with wonderfully extensive views including the Eildons and, on a clear day, your first glimpse of the North Sea.

Now heading just north of east, you drop quickly downhill to a track, turning left on to it and then shortly right on to another track which in due course turns into a proper metalled road. You follow this all the way to Longformacus, initially maintaining a north-easterly direction, then swinging south-eastwards to pass the eastern edge of Watch Water Reservoir, before turning north-eastwards through much less formidable woodland scenery and proceeding downhill into the village (194).

Most walkers without camping gear will wish to call it a day here, having tramped 15 weary miles from Lauder, but accommodation and amenities are severely limited and those who have been foolish enough to leave such matters to chance may have to resort to a taxi to Duns, the nearest town and the best part of ten miles away. Walkers who recall the Covenanters from sights seen earlier in the walk may actually be interested to visit Duns Law, a hilltop near the town where the Covenanters camped in 1639. It is also the birthplace of John Duns Scotus, a monk and theologian whose ideas were so ridiculed by the established Church that his followers became known as 'dunces,' from his middle name Duns. As the hapless walkers wait for taxis to get them back to Longformacus the next day, with all the expense this entails, they might well feel this epithet has more than a little application to their situation as well.

The Way turns right on to the main street of Longformacus then shortly left on to a road which heads north-eastwards away from the village. As the road curves a little to the left towards Dye Water, you turn right off the road, climbing initially south-eastwards, then swinging north-eastwards to pass along the edge of Owl Wood and dropping down through Lodge Wood to reach the B6355. You turn left on to it then shortly right, climbing again before descending steeply and picking up a track that proceeds northwards then north-eastwards through woodland. It is lovely woodland walking, never far from the very attractive Whiteadder Water to your left, and culminates in the lovely village of Abbey St Bathans where refreshment may be available.

You cross the water then turn left to follow alongside it before climbing out of the valley and proceeding uphill across fields along rather poor paths, heading northwards to join a track leading to the hilltop hamlet of Whiteburn. You cross a minor road and continue northwards on a track, then turn eastwards on a field path to a road, turning left along it and shortly bearing right to follow a lane that heads north-eastwards past the buildings of Blackburn. The lane becomes a proper metalled road and having swung briefly south-eastwards, turns north-eastwards again and descends to the A1. All this is desperately anticlimactical walking, aggravated by the fact that you will probably be extremely tired by now.

You cross over the A1 then turn left to proceed northwards on a path that is sandwiched between this highway and the London–Edinburgh railway, which you soon cross. The sight of high-speed trains gliding effortlessly beneath you seems all the more galling as you struggle to make it to the end of the route, with the sheer effort of placing one foot in front of the other at this late stage so great that just for a moment you might feel tempted to attempt to flag down a passing train and hop aboard whatever the cost, whether a fine of £350 for trespassing on the railway or a public rendition in the buffet car of Harry Lauder's celebrated ditty 'Stop yer Tickling, Jock.'

A1 crossing to Cockburnspath

Having crossed the railway you continue north-westwards through the attractive Penmanshiel Wood with its pines, gorse, ash, elm and sycamore, initially remaining on the valley floor, then climbing quite steeply. It is a cruel ascent with the end so near, but you are rewarded by your first really impressive view of the North Sea and the coastline as it stretches towards Dunbar. You descend to the A1107 which you cross, then drop very steeply along a path downhill, north-eastwards towards the sea, until after crossing a metalled road, you reach a caravan park. Swinging left, you pass round the caravan park, and climb again on to the clifftops. This is a magnificent moment, for you can now justly claim that you have walked from coast to coast, and the trudge from Abbey St Bathans is quite forgotten as you enjoy a wonderful cliff walk north-westwards.

In just a short piece of coastal marching you negotiate a rugged headland and pass above the lovely Cove Harbour with its twin jetties, then shortly afterwards you turn left and head southwards back to the metalled road you crossed just before gaining the cliffs. You cross back over it, then follow a path westwards, back under the railway and A1, into Cockburnspath (212), reaching the official end of the route at the market cross in the pleasant village centre. At the time of writing, direct buses run from here to Dunbar and Edinburgh; expecting a conventional bus, I was somewhat nonplussed when the 3.50 p.m. Edinburgh service on a July Friday afternoon turned out to be more of a van, which would certainly not have been big enough to accommodate any more than a select few triumphant coast to coast walkers.

As you speed away towards Scotland's capital – assuming there was room for you in the vehicle – you will be bound to reflect back on what has been an astonishing walk, whatever the prevailing conditions. You may have enjoyed it so much, and be so captivated by Britain's coast as a basis for long-distance walking, that you will soon be annoying your family by planning your next pilgrimage; perhaps attempting to form a giant circular walk that, beginning with Cockburnspath, goes along the coast to Robin Hood's Bay, along Wainwright's Coast to Coast Walk to St Bees, and then up the coast to meet the start of the Southern Upland Way at Portpatrick, from whence it is little effort to trot back to Cockburnspath again. Or the whole experience may have been so unpleasant that you will be only too pleased to consign the rucksack to the loft, and confine any more mention of Stranraer to their Scottish Cup battles with Gala Fairydean.

SUMMARY OF PLACES OF INTEREST

Portpatrick, Castle Kennedy, Laggangairn, Loch Trool, Clatteringshaws Loch, Dalry, Manquhill Hill, Benbrack, Allan Cairn, Sanquhar Castle, Wanlockhead, Lowther Hill, Hod's Hill, Ettrick Head, Peniestone Knowe, Blake Muir, Traquair House, Minch Moor, Three Brethren, Melrose Abbey, Twin Law, Abbey St Bathans, Cove Harbour.

AMENITIES ON OR NEAR THE ROUTE

Portpatrick, Stranraer★, New Luce (L), Bargrennan (L), Dalry, Sanquhar, Wanlockhead (L), Beattock (L), Moffat, Innerleithen, Galashiels★, Melrose★, Lauder, Longformacus (L), Cockburnspath (L).

FURTHER READING AND BIBLIOGRAPHY

AA Book of Britain's Countryside (1998, Midsummer Books)

AA Book of British Villages (1980, Drive Publications)

AA Illustrated Guide to Britain (1977, Drive Publications)

Betjeman, John *Collected Poems* (1958, John Murray)

Dillon, Paddy *Trail Walker's Guide to the National Trails of Britain and Ireland* (1994, David and Charles)

Hutchinson Encyclopaedia of Britain (1999, Helicon)

Jenkins, Simon *England's Thousand Best Churches* (1999, Allen Lane)

Marriott, Michael *The Footpaths of Britain* (1981, Queen Anne Press)

Millar, T.G. *Long Distance Paths of England and Wales* (1979, David and Charles)

National Trail and Recreational Path Guides (1989-96, Aurum Press)

Nicolson, Adam *The National Trust Book of Long Walks* (1981, The National Trust)

Pevsner, Nikolaus et al. *Buildings of England series* (1951-74, Penguin)

Pilton, Barry *One Man and his Bog* (1985, Corgi)

Plowright, Alan *Plowright Follows Wainwright* (1995, Michael Joseph)

Wainwright, Alfred *A Coast to Coast Walk* (1992, Michael Joseph)

Wainwright, Alfred *Pennine Way Companion* (1992, Michael Joseph)

Wainwright, Alfred *Wainwright in Scotland* (1988, Mermaid Books with BBC)

John Wassner

espresso with the
HEADHUNTERS
A JOURNEY THROUGH THE JUNGLES OF BORNEO

summersdale *travel*

TOM CUNLIFFE

good vibrations

COAST TO COAST BY HARLEY

'A PITHY THROBBER OF A BOOK' CHRIS STEWART

summersdale *travel*

Donna Carrère

MONKEYS
IN THE RAIN

TRAVELS, TRIALS AND TRIBULATIONS
IN SOUTH EAST ASIA

summersdale *travel*

RAMBLING
ON THE ROAD TO
ROME

Peter Francis Browne

summersdale *travel*

some
like
it
cold

NEVILLE SHULMAN

ARCTIC
AND
ANTARCTIC
ADVENTURES

FOREWORDS BY
SIR RANULPH FIENNES
& DAVID HEMPLEMAN-ADAMS

summersdale *travel*

RAMBLING
ON THE ROAD TO
ROME

Peter Francis Browne

summersdale *travel*

some like it cold

ARCTIC AND ANTARCTIC ADVENTURES

NEVILLE SHULMAN

FOREWORDS BY
SIR RANULPH FIENNES
& DAVID HEMPLEMAN-ADAMS

summersdale *travel*

THE BACKPACKER

JOHN HARRIS

summersdale *travel*

MARK MANN

THE GRINGO TRAIL

summersdale *travel*

the hotel on the roof of the world

five years in Tibet

alec le sueur

summersdale *travel*

THE WORLD COMMUTER
GREAT JOURNEYS BY TRAIN

CHRISTOPHER PORTWAY

summersdale *travel*

two feet,
four paws

walking the dog 4,500 miles

Spud Talbot-Ponsonby

Foreword by Ffyona Campbell

summersdale *travel*

For a current publishing catalogue
and full listing of
Summersdale travel books,
visit our website:

www.summersdale.com